RECLAIMING ACCOUNTABILITY

RECLAIMING ACCOUNTABILITY

Improving Writing Programs through Accreditation and Large-Scale Assessments

Edited by
WENDY SHARER
TRACY ANN MORSE
MICHELLE F. EBLE
WILLIAM P. BANKS

UTAH STATE UNIVERSITY PRESS
Logan

Published by Utah State University Press
An imprint of University Press of Colorado
5589 Arapahoe Avenue, Suite 206C
Boulder, Colorado 80303

 The University Press of Colorado is a proud member of
The Association of American University Presses.

The University Press of Colorado is a cooperative publishing enterprise supported, in part, by Adams State University, Colorado State University, Fort Lewis College, Metropolitan State University of Denver, Regis University, University of Colorado, University of Northern Colorado, Utah State University, and Western State Colorado University.

The paper used in this publication meets the minimum requirements of the American National Standard for Information Sciences—Permanence of Paper for Printed Library Materials. ANSI Z39.48-1992

The University Press of Colorado gratefully acknowledges the generous support of East Carolina University toward the publication of this book.

ISBN: 978-1-60732-434-8 (pbk.)
ISBN: 978-1-60732-435-5 (ebook)

Library of Congress Cataloging-in-Publication Data
Reclaiming accountability : improving writing programs through accreditation and large-scale assessments / edited by Wendy Sharer, Tracy Ann Morse, Michelle F. Eble, Will Banks.
    pages cm
  ISBN 978-1-60732-434-8 (pbk.) — ISBN 978-1-60732-435-5 (ebook)
1. English language—Rhetoric—Study and teaching. 2. Report writing—Study and teaching. I. Sharer, Wendy B., editor. II. Morse, Tracy Ann, editor. III. Eble, Michelle F., 1974– editor. IV. Banks, Will, editor.
PE1404.R379 2015
808'.0420711—dc23
                              2015011299

CONTENTS

RECLAIMING ACCOUNTABILITY

INTRODUCTION
Accreditation and Assessment as Opportunity

Wendy Sharer, Tracy Ann Morse,
Michelle F. Eble, and William P. Banks

In the fall of 2007, the Council of Writing Program Administrators (CWPA) Executive Board called on WPAs and writing instructors to respond to large-scale writing assessment and higher education accreditation. The Board's letter outlines specific actions "to help stakeholders understand" that "only effective, valid, and reliable assessments that are context-specific and discipline-based can be used to improve student learning" (Council of Writing Program Administrators 2007). These actions include learning about accrediting bodies and accreditation procedures and meeting with the Director(s) of Assessment at members' institutions. The message throughout the letter is clear: those who teach writing and those who administer writing programs need to be involved in defining the terms and setting the parameters of large-scale writing assessment so that any changes implemented in response to assessment are in keeping with what research and practice have demonstrated to be truly effective in helping student writers.

We see this collection as a resource for writing instructors and WPAs looking to answer the call to action in sustainable, research-driven, practice-tested ways. Contributions to the volume help readers to accomplish three key things:

1. Understand the goals and limits of large-scale writing assessment from both the perspective of the accrediting bodies that require it and the writing instructors and WPAs who design, implement, and, ideally, benefit from it.

2. Consider strengths and weaknesses of assessment structures and assessment-driven improvement initiatives that have been implemented at a variety of types of institutions (included are contributions from writing specialists from schools of differing sizes, student populations,

DOI: 10.7330/9781607324355.c000

geographical locations, and writing program structures). As the CWPA
points out in their letter of fall 2007, "specific stories about successful assessment processes are compelling to a range of audiences." The
examples offered in the chapters that follow thus provide invaluable
support for writing instructors and WPAs as they attempt to persuade
other faculty and upper administrators to implement responsive and
responsible assessment processes. At the same time, contributors to this
collection do not hesitate to identify struggles and setbacks that they
encountered in the processes of conducting large-scale assessment and
responding to assessment results. The examples are useful for the support as well as the cautions that they provide to readers.

3. Use ongoing accreditation and assessment imperatives to cultivate
   productive campus-wide conversations that increase faculty members'
   ability to meet students' writing and learning needs. A benefit of
   large-scale assessment that receives attention in a number of chapters in this collection is the fruitful and revealing discussion about
   what is valued in writing across disciplinary contexts. Institution-wide
   assessment initiatives, then, can be occasions to discover and disrupt
   unstated and incorrect assumptions that "good writing is good writing" regardless of where it occurs in the university. Writing specialists and WPAs are in a unique position to lead the development of
   authentic writing assessment on their campuses and, through their
   efforts, to change campus understandings of and approaches to writing instruction in ways that have not been possible since the birth of
   the Writing Across the Curriculum (WAC) movement.

We recognize that what is true of writing is also true of assessment: context always affects what can be effective in any given situation. In response, we bring together here a series of critical case studies of writing programs from across the country that have planned,
implemented, and assessed the impact of large-scale, accreditation-
supported initiatives. Some of the chapters explore writing program
responses to the Southern Association of Colleges and Schools (SACS)
requirement that member institutions design, implement, and assess a
Quality Enhancement Plan (QEP), a university-wide, five-year program
aimed at improving some aspect of student learning. Other chapters
explore writing-focused institutional responses to the demands of other
higher education accrediting bodies. For example, the North Central
Association of Colleges and Schools' Higher Learning Commission
requires an Academic Quality Improvement Program (AQIP), and the
Western Association of Schools and Colleges, as well as the Middle States
Commission on Higher Education, require institutional reviews that
include programmatic assessments.

This list of accrediting agencies requiring assessment and documented improvement initiatives shows that the impetus for large-scale assessment and public accountability has moved into higher education. Many readers may recognize that we have borrowed part of our title from Chris Gallagher's (2007) book, *Reclaiming Assessment: A Better Alternative to the Accountability Agenda*, which chronicles the grassroots, context-appropriate assessments for local school districts in the state of Nebraska during the beginnings of the high-stakes testing environment of No Child Left Behind. Gallagher argues that engaging in this accountability work and focusing on local contexts is best for students and teachers when it comes to assessment and improving learning. As institutions of higher learning have increasingly been asked to account for student learning and to take action to improve their student learning, accreditation and the large-scale assessment it entails become one driver of this work. At East Carolina University, our home institution, we are witnessing first-hand the kinds of large-scale change that can result from engaging in institution-wide, context-specific assessment and accreditation processes. The work that the four of us have done as part of ECU's accreditation through SACS has substantially benefitted our program, our institution, and our students. Among other things, we have gained

- a major curricular revision in our composition program that moves the second of our required writing classes to the sophomore year and refocuses that course on the transition to writing in disciplinary contexts;
- a new, technology rich University Writing Center space;
- a new, tenure-track position for a Director of our University Writing Center;
- a set of coherent learning outcomes for our WAC program;
- a "Writing Liaisons" program: Writing Liaisons are faculty from across the university who regularly teach writing-intensive courses in their departments and who meet several times during the year with the leadership of our composition and WAC programs to ensure that students get consistent information about writing expectations and writing strategies;
- an electronic portfolio structure in which students compile writing samples and self-analyses of their own writing across their time at the institution; and
- expanded professional development opportunities for faculty.

Getting to this point has not been easy. Details about how WPAs at other institutions have used accreditation and large-scale assessment projects to bring positive change—as well as failure narratives and cautionary tales about working with faculty, upper administration, and

accrediting bodies in such projects—would likely have made our journey much smoother, but such material has not been easy to come by.
Rather, it has been located primarily within institution-specific accreditation documents and assessment reports, which only some schools have
elected to make publicly available on their websites. When we set out
to find the most productive ways of using assessment and accreditation
opportunities at our institution, there were few published accounts of
how these kinds of endeavors had been pursued at other institutions.
This collection helps fill that gap.

The contributors to part one consider how specialists in composition and rhetoric can work most productively with accrediting bodies in
order to design assessments and initiatives that meet requirements while
also helping those agencies to better understand how writing develops
and how it can most effectively be assessed. Angela Crow, Cindy Moore,
and Peggy O'Neill explore the historical connections between accrediting agencies and writing programs, urging readers to draw on lessons
learned from past assessment mandates. The field, Crow, Moore, and
O'Neill make clear, has been and must continue to be vigilant in monitoring and responding productively to assessment mandates so that our
programs and our students are not held accountable to standards that
do not reflect what our research has shown us about writing pedagogy
and the processes of learning to write. With growing calls from the public and politicians for stronger regulation of and greater comparability
across higher education curricula, our attention to accreditation processes is critical if we wish to maintain the kinds of "context-informed
assessments" that we know to be most valid and useful.

One way to advocate for what we know to be good practice in assessment, Susan Miller-Cochran and Rochelle Rodrigo suggest in chapter two, is to work with and for accrediting agencies. More specifically, Miller-Cochran and Rodrigo explore the role of the "QEP Lead
Evaluator," a member of the SACS team that visits institutions undergoing reaccreditation. If writing is the focus of a school's QEP—and
this is often the case because writing, as we know, is essential to student
learning across the curriculum—the QEP Lead Evaluator selected by
SACS will, in all likelihood, be a composition specialist from another
institution. Through the role of QEP Lead Evaluator, Miller-Cochran
and Rodrigo explain, composition experts can share knowledge and
research about writing pedagogy and writing assessment with faculty and
key administrators at other institutions, thus providing invaluable external validation for and reinforcement of proposed curricular revisions
and programmatic changes.

In the final chapter of part one, Shirley Rose offers an overview of the principles that have historically guided the work of regional accrediting associations and the elements that have traditionally been part of the accreditation process, including cyclical review, institutional self-study, face-to-face interaction with stakeholders, and detailed, individualized institutional reporting of accreditation results. Rose argues that collaborations like those undertaken by Miller-Cochran and Rodrigo are extremely valuable because they position writing program administrators and composition specialists within accrediting organizations that, since their origins in the nineteenth century, have spearheaded the process of determining criteria by which evolving initiatives in higher education will be evaluated. Having writing specialists involved with this work is particularly important because these initiatives, such as the recent growth of dual-credit programs that offer both high school and college credit for the same course, frequently have a direct impact on first-year writing.

The remaining two parts of the collection present case studies of how institutions have used ongoing accreditation and assessment imperatives to better meet student learning needs through programmatic changes and faculty development. Our goal in presenting these case studies is to provide concrete examples of productive curricular (part two) and instructional (part three) changes that can follow from accreditation mandates while, at the same time, highlighting and providing guidance for navigating challenges and pitfalls that WPAs may encounter within shifting, and often volatile, local, regional, and national contexts. We hope that the successes detailed within the chapters of parts two and three can be used by readers to bolster arguments for resource commitment from upper administration. In addition, contributors have included materials within their chapters and appendices that might be revised and repurposed by readers who are planning for and implementing assessment-driven change at their own institutions. At the same time, contributors have consciously included discussions of what has not gone as planned so that readers might be alert to these challenges and better prepared to respond if similar issues arise.

Within part two, chapters are organized according to the relative development of the institution's writing programs prior to assessment-driven change. The section begins with guidance for faculty who are looking to use the accreditation moment to build an institution-wide writing program from the ground up. Jonathan Elmore and Teressa Van Sickle, WPAs at Beaufort Community College, a small two-year institution in coastal North Carolina, used the SACS QEP mandate to establish a WAC program, a writing center, and an online writing lab. As Elmore and Van Sickle explain, large-scale assessment demands can provide the spark needed to start a writing program where one had not existed before.

The next two chapters provide insight into how large-scale assessment can drive significant change to existing programs that have resisted change. Jessica Parker and Jane Chapman Vigil discuss how a reaccreditation visit from the Higher Learning Commission (HLC) to Metropolitan State University of Denver, Colorado spurred change to the university's general education program, a program that had remained fairly static at this urban school of over 22,000 students for 20 or more years. The chapter recounts the composition program's journey from square one—with no stated learning outcomes, no method of collecting materials for assessment, and no system in place for conducting assessment of any kind—to robust process of assessment and, as indicated by the assessment, curricular revision and implementation of co-curricular support. Drawing from the struggles they encountered along the way, Parker and Vigil provide "pointers" for other writing instructors and WPAs embarking on an assessment journey. These tips include strategies for constructing rubrics, calibrating readers and aligning different perspectives on what "good" writing means, fostering instructor buy-in for the assessment process, and ensuring that what is learned through assessment is clearly applied through changes in curriculum, curricular resources, or faculty support.

In a similar vein, David Weed, Tulora Roeckers, and Melanie Burdick provide an in-depth exploration of curricular streamlining within the composition program at Washburn University, a public, open-admissions institution of roughly 7,000 students in Topeka, Kansas. Concerns at Washburn about institutional reaccreditation through the Higher Learning Commission led to a university-wide mandate that "all general education courses be redesigned to incorporate common assessments worth 30% of the course grade" (112). The composition program at Washburn did not have a history of standardization across sections of composition, but this mandate necessitated some level of it. Weed, Roeckers, and Burdick explain how they met the challenge of establishing a common structure for the composition program while also maintaining a good deal of autonomy for sometimes resistant instructors who were used to operating independently. The chapter details the collaborative processes the authors used to identify common course objectives and to transform those objectives into an assessment rubric. Interviews, focus groups, and artifacts collection from several pilot sections that used the new objectives and assessment rubric highlighted for Weed, Roeckers, and Burdick the importance of involving faculty in the process of establishing shared outcomes that are broad enough to allow individual instructors some control over their pedagogy yet narrow enough to ensure that instructors and students recognize that they are participating in a larger, coherent program.

Accreditation concerns similarly propelled the development of an identifiable writing program at Onandaga Community College. It took pressure from the Middle States Commission on Higher Education, Malkiel Choseed explains, to lead to the creation of a WPA position, Writing Program Coordinator, in 2003. From this beginning, the teaching of writing at OCC evolved from a curriculum based on "lore" and the literary training of most faculty to one based on composition theory and writing research. Furthermore, Choseed highlights how large-scale, accreditation-driven assessment can lead to meaningful collaboration between WPAs, writing instructors, and stakeholders beyond the institution. More specifically, the alignment of writing-related learning outcomes across courses in a program, across programs in an institution, and across institutions in an educational system, such as the State University of New York system of which OCC is a part, can bring momentum and power for change to both individual institutions and to the institutional networks of which they are a part. In the case of OCC, connections Choseed made with other professionals during the processes of large-scale assessment and reaccreditation provided a foundation for additional curricular (and financial) development in the form of a multi-institutional collaboration, with funding from the US Department of Labor, aimed at preparing working adults for career changes.

Accreditation and assessment demands can also be channeled into innovation for programs that have been actively engaged with current, research-based curricular practices. For example, Karen Nulton and Rebecca Ingalls recount how they have used the Middle States Commission on Higher Education's accreditation process at Drexel University in Philadelphia to improve their composition program, a program that already embraced rhetorical awareness and a writing-about-writing approach. Nulton and Ingalls parlayed the Middle States process into an occasion to engage faculty, both within and beyond the composition program, in productive conversations about what they really value in student writing and to establish procedures for assessing the contributions that the composition program makes to students' progress toward those outcomes. In discussing their program revisions, Nulton and Ingalls introduce a theme that runs through the rest of the collection: the fact that large-scale assessment of writing across the university can spur extensive discussion about differences and similarities in what writing is and does in different disciplinary contexts and can enable the creation of a shared vocabulary about writing and a mechanism—in this case, a reflective analysis—for assessing student achievement across writing contexts.

The final chapters in part two provide insight into additional innovations that large-scale assessment and accreditation processes can bring to schools with established writing programs. Jim Henry used accreditation pressure from the Western Association of Colleges and Schools (WASC) to establish a program that embeds writing tutors, known as writing mentors, in composition courses at the University of Hawai'i, Mānoa. In addition to more individualized instruction that benefits student writers, this new program enabled faculty in the composition program to "advance financial resources for the program, advance research agendas for faculty and graduate students, and advance the program's institutional reputation and visibility" (163). Henry recounts the moves through which he and his colleagues navigated the assessment and accreditation process while also garnering financial support locally and nationally; involving graduate students in research, presentations, and publications drawn from the writing mentors initiative; and raising the institutional visibility of the composition program online, within the university's Assessment Office, and at institution-wide conferences and workshops. These moves, Henry suggests, can be adapted to other institutional contexts for similar benefits in the wake of accreditation.

Ryan Hoover and Mary Rist round out part two with details about the implementation of electronic assessment portfolios as part of accreditation-related activities in the composition program at St. Edward's University, a four-year school in Austin, Texas, that has offered an undergraduate major in Writing and Rhetoric since 1987. Not only has this program been in place for over two decades, it is currently the sixth largest major on campus, yet even this well-established program seized the moment of accreditation to make productive changes. Portfolios not only made assessment easier for the program by "tracking evaluation scores and calculating historical trends," but also brought additional benefits for students and faculty within the program and across the university (187). Through ePortfolios, multi-modal composing became a serious topic of discussion and instruction across disciplines, students' investment in reflecting on their work as represented in the ePortfolio grew, and ePortfolios were adapted with good results for faculty involved with program assessment and for students in majors across the university as they planned for careers after the university.

Part three builds on part two by exploring examples of a common benefit fostered through large-scale assessment and accreditation processes: professional development programs that foster campus-wide commitment to writing and that focus on teaching writing in different disciplinary contexts. In chapter 11, Polina Chemishanova and Cynthia Miecznikowski present a QEP that brings together curricular change and professional development. The SACS requirement enabled the creation of a WAC program within a context of productive, cross-curricular conversations about what good writing means. Chemishanova and Miecznikowski's experience with establishing a WAC program at the University of North Carolina at Pembroke, a four-year, MA-granting institution of approximately 6,000 students in rural southeastern NC, illustrates how a seemingly top-down requirement, imposed from outside of the institution, can be used to facilitate, rather than impede, faculty-driven change. Linda Adler-Kassner and Lorna Gonzalez then detail the accreditation-inspired processes through which they, in collaboration with faculty from across the University of California at Santa Barbara, developed writing assessment instruments that respond to diverse disciplinary expectations for writing. These collaborations led participating faculty to reevaluate their approaches to teaching writing as they became more aware of the variations in writing that students encounter as they take courses across disciplines and even as they take courses within the same discipline. Such revelations have, Adler-Kassner and Gonzalez explain, led faculty to request additional professional development opportunities related to writing and the teaching of writing.

In a similar vein, Maggie Debelius explores how Georgetown University's reaccreditation through the Middle States Commission on Higher Education became an occasion to engage faculty from diverse disciplinary backgrounds in discussions of what they value in writing. As part of their accreditation plan, Debelius and her colleagues worked with faculty to identify "threshold concepts" or "specific core ideas" within a discipline that are fundamental to success in that discipline. Debelius explains how this exploration of threshold concepts shifted faculty's perceptions of writing from something that can be used to test students' achievements to something that disciplinary members actively use to accomplish shared goals. The process of accreditation, then, enabled a significant change in how faculty understand writing and the teaching of writing: the perception of writing in disciplinary contexts moved from a view of writing as a static entity that students should be taught how to replicate to a view of writing as a dynamic process that students should be taught how to participate in. This shift brought about a change in how faculty across the university viewed responsibility for writing instruction and writing assessment, with faculty in individual departments taking ownership of writing-related curricula and establishing writing assessment procedures within their own disciplinary areas.

Joyce Neff and Remica Bingham-Risher provide further insight into the potential impact of accreditation-related professional development. Two central initiatives of Old Dominion University's QEP involve faculty development: a series of workshops designed to help faculty discover strategies for using writing-to-learn and for teaching writing in disciplinary contexts, and an internal grant program that supports faculty innovation in the teaching of writing. Recognizing that changing faculty perceptions and practices is often essential to the kinds of broad institutional change called for by reaccreditation processes, Neff and Bingham-Risher suggest that other schools consider developing "Faculty Learning Outcomes" (FLOs) to supplement and complement the Student Learning Outcomes (SLOs) that are often required as part of reaccreditation processes. To help other institutions with the development and assessment of FLOs, Neff and Bingham-Risher provide a draft of their university's FLOs and detail the procedure that they implemented to measure the impact of professional development workshops on faculty members' construction, revision, and implementation of writing assignments in courses across the disciplines.

To conclude part three and the collection, Angela Green, Iris Saltiel, and Kyle Christiansen write from the perspective of having finished their accreditation cycle. With their five-year impact report on their writing-focused QEP approved by the SACS, Green, Saltiel, and Christiansen reflect on the long-term, substantial impact that their accreditation-related assessment work has accomplished at Columbus State University in Georgia. Most notably, they describe and document how this work has led to "a fundamental shift in faculty attitudes about the role that writing can play in classrooms across the university" (306). Despite the fact that participation in the CSU QEP was voluntary, institutional priority given to the accreditation work, along with the careful planning and timing of implementation, enabled QEP leadership to effect the kinds of changes that a number of other institutions discussed in this collection are working toward: "Writing moved from being the responsibility of the English department to being viewed as the responsibility of all, as well as a significant mode of teaching and learning in any subject" (306).

While ultimately successful, the accreditation-driven changes at CSU did not occur without challenges. These challenges, the authors explain, are likely to be faced by others endeavoring to make similar changes at their institutions. To help others meet similar challenges, Green, Saltiel, and Christiansen provide examples of successful initiatives and assessment structures and discuss how they were able to overcome obstacles such as administrative/personnel turnover during the accreditation cycle and the inevitable and unpredictable budgetary restrictions faced by state schools in tough economic times.

References

Council of Writing Program Administrators. 2007. "Executive Board Letter re Writing Assessment and Higher Education Accreditation." Accessed January 5, 2015. http://wpacouncil.org/node/887.

Gallagher, Chris. 2007. *Reclaiming Assessment: A Better Alternative to the Accountability Agenda*. Portsmouth, NH: Heinemann.

PART ONE

Laying the Foundations
Educating and Learning from Accrediting Bodies

The chapters in part one address the first objective of this collection: to help readers better understand the potential advantages and drawbacks of large-scale writing assessment from both the perspective of the accrediting bodies that require this assessment and the writing instructors and WPAs who, ideally, design, implement, and benefit from it. Compositionists have long recognized that assessment, if it is to be valid and meaningful, cannot operate at a distance from local contexts. As early as 1996, Brian Huot outlined a "New Theory of Writing Assessment" based upon assessment "procedures [that] recognize the importance of context, rhetoric, and other characteristics integral to a specific purpose and institution. The procedures are site-based, practical, and have been developed and controlled locally" (Huot 1996, 552).

Just as local contexts—local concerns, local student populations, local faculty attributes and attitudes, local budgets, local communities—need to be studied for assessment to be meaningful and for resulting initiatives to be effective, larger contexts in which the demand for assessment is shaped and through which local assessments are coordinated should be considered. Together, contributors to this first section provide a broad historical account of the longstanding, sometimes-cooperative and sometimes-conflicted, relationship between writing programs and accrediting agencies. Cindy Moore, Peggy O'Neill, and Angela Crow explore how compositionists have responded to assessment mandates dating back to the middle of the last century. Often, these responses have served to undermine the validity of writing assessments based on testing scenarios and to promote process-oriented approaches such as portfolio assessment. Shirley Rose provides additional historical context through her account of the evolving purposes and goals of regional accrediting agencies and how those purposes and goals intersect with the institutional location and mission of first-year writing. These intersections, she explains, mean that accrediting agencies can be valuable "partners with writing program faculty and administrators in providing a social good by making the work of higher education both visible and legible to those it serves" (52–53).

In keeping with the belief that there are benefits to be gained through involvement in the accreditation process, each of the three chapters in part one include suggestions for what compositionists can take to further the tradition of working with and through accrediting bodies. The writers of each of the three chapters in this section emphasize that members of the field should become more aware of and involved in the regional and national mechanisms that establish the terms of assessment data collection and analysis. Susan Miller-Cochran and Rochelle Rodrigo provide a specific example of how to do this, using their work with the Southern Association of Colleges and Schools (SACS) to illustrate how writing specialists can exert influence outward by educating accrediting agencies and campus administrators about what we know about teaching writing, learning to write, and measuring writing abilities. Collaborating with these agencies, Miller-Cochran and Rodrigo point out, can do more than just protect writing programs from ineffective assessment mandates: it can create excellent opportunities for the field as a whole to gain a better understanding of how different writing programs are structured and how they function within and across diverse institutional contexts. This accreditation-driven insight can then inform policies and actions taken by the field's own regional and national organizations.

References

Huot, Brian. 1996. "Toward a New Theory of Writing Assessment." *College Composition and Communication* 47 (4): 549–66. http://dx.doi.org/10.2307/358601.

1
ASSESSING FOR LEARNING IN AN AGE OF COMPARABILITY
Remembering the Importance of Context

Cindy Moore, Peggy O'Neill, and Angela Crow

As compositionists attempt to navigate the ever-changing landscape of contemporary higher education accreditation, we can draw on our rich history of using external assessment mandates to our advantage. Given recent calls for more standardized assessment methods, and developments in processing, sharing, and analyzing big data sets based on those standardized methods, it is imperative that we work with accreditors, employing our expertise, as we have in the past, to develop approaches to assessing students and teachers that improve learning and are consistent with our disciplinary theories about writing, teaching, and assessment. Below, we review compositionists' responses to earlier assessment mandates and illustrate how a knowledge of such work can help current program administrators and faculty negotiate an accreditation context increasingly influenced by public calls for higher ed accountability and the new technologies that offer a means to achieve it.

LEARNING FROM THE PAST: WRITING ASSESSMENT AND ACCOUNTABILITY IN CONTEXT

Because of the consequences of assessment for both teaching and learning, writing administrators and faculty have, for decades, seen externally inspired writing assessment initiatives as opportunities to document student achievement, gather information about program strengths and challenges, and use that information to improve curriculum and instruction. The literature in our field is replete with articles and books that illustrate our willingness—and ability—to make assessment mandates serve our more specific interests while also satisfying requirements imposed by state legislators and accreditors.

DOI: 10.7330/9781607324355.c001

During the mid- to late-twentieth century as the college-bound student population diversified, calls for writing placement and proficiency tests increased, and composition faculty became more involved in writing assessment. Understanding "the sociopolitical implications of these tests for students and teachers" (Greenberg 1982, 743), many compositionists worked throughout the 1970s and 1980s to ensure that externally imposed writing assessments were informed by current theory and research and served the needs of their particular students (Cooper and Odell 1977; Gere 1980; Greenberg 1982; White 1984). For example, one study investigated "the effect of different kinds of testing upon the distribution of scores for racial minorities" (White and Thomas 1981, 276), examining the consequences of a standardized multiple-choice test of usage and a local exam designed by California State University faculty in conjunction with testing experts. The study showed that scores for white students were similar for the standardized exam and the essay portion of the CSU exam, but the results for black and Latino students were quite different: the standardized multiple-choice exam "rendered a much more negative judgment of these students' use of English than did the evaluators of their writing" (1981, 281). White and Thomas argued that the results cast "some real question upon the validity of usage testing as an indicator of writing ability" (1981, 280).

Through research such as this, writing scholars realized the power of assessments to influence teaching and learning and wanted to minimize the chances that "writing teachers [would] find themselves administering writing proficiency tests that [bore] little relationship to their perception of college-level writing ability" and that administrators would use "the results of a test they consider inadequate or inappropriate" for placement or promotion" (Greenberg 1982, 367). While such efforts were not directly linked to accreditation demands, they highlighted the importance of balancing the needs of a particular local context with outside interests, for example, university administrators or policymakers (Greenberg 1982).

In the 1980s, one of the most influential responses to an external assessment mandate was the portfolio assessment system developed by Pat Belanoff and Peter Elbow to replace a university mandated proficiency exam. Belanoff and Elbow (1986) argued that the portfolio assessment, which involved teachers working in groups for norming during the semester and then at the end for the formal portfolio evaluation, promoted better teaching and more learning because, in part, the teachers developed shared evaluation criteria and the group discussions informed their work with students in their classrooms. The portfolio program Belanoff and Elbow designed kick-started the portfolio movement in college composition, a movement that shaped writing assessment, teaching, and research. Though Belanoff and Elbow did not frame the portfolio assessment in terms of accreditation, it was part of a university assessment mandate that undoubtedly would have been reported to accreditors.

While many compositionists focused on research and development of individual placement and proficiency tests, some compositionists created more comprehensive writing programs in response to university assessment mandates. The best-known example of this type of work was done by Richard Haswell (2001) and his colleagues at Washington State University. Haswell led the effort to build a multi-tiered, integrated writing assessment program in response to a university general education program that mandated assessment of the composition program. Their "adventure into writing assessment" resulted in a program that encompassed placement testing upon entrance, portfolio exit assessments for first-year composition, a WAC requirement, and a rising junior portfolio that combined an impromptu essay, a reflective piece, and a collection of papers produced for courses across the curriculum. At all levels writing teachers were involved in the assessments, and a comprehensive writing center provided support for students, including required small-group sessions for those who did not pass the junior portfolio (Haswell 2001).

The WSU writing program, which received a commendation from its accrediting agency in 1999, illustrates some of the basic principles of writing assessment documented in the composition scholarship: (1) assessing and teaching writing are closely linked, and (2) the goal of writing assessment is to facilitate students' development as writers and improve students' writing. Such principles not only influenced how compositionists responded to earlier assessment mandates, but they offered theoretically grounded guidance for negotiating an accreditation landscape that became informed by similar principles. Since the mid-1990s, accreditation agencies have been focusing more on how university resources, including those dedicated to instruction and assessment, are being used to promote student learning. Though this shift from a concern with "inputs" (such as faculty expertise and per-student expenditure) to the "outcomes" of such investments reflected educational theory and research, it was also a response to growing public pressure to ensure that students were acquiring the knowledge and skills promised by higher ed institutions. Because the only way to really show that learning has occurred is through work completed by students, accreditors began asking schools to demonstrate that students had met learning outcomes with direct assessment evidence. Writing, as compositionists have long understood, is one of the best, most direct methods for making student learning visible. Thus, as accrediting agencies turned their attention to what and how much students were learning, results from writing assessments began to figure more prominently in accreditation processes.

As they did when faced with earlier placement and proficiency mandates, writing specialists have used changing accreditation requirements to their advantage, documenting student learning and program effectiveness for their own purposes while also helping their institutions meet accreditation standards (Carter 2003; Walvoord 2004). One of the best examples of such work has been documented by John Bean and his colleagues at Seattle University who developed discourse-based assessments to respond in part "to pressures from the Northwest Association of Schools and Colleges" (Bean, Carrithers, and Earenfight 2005, 6). Bean used his expertise in WAC to work with disciplinary faculty across the campus to (1) identify the knowledge and skills that graduating students in their fields should have developed, (2) develop an embedded assignment to collect direct evidence of the students' performance of particular skills or knowledge, and (3) use this information to improve teaching and learning, so students would meet the desired learning outcomes. While Bean's work was a direct outgrowth of an accreditation visit, other recent work has reflected a more proactive approach to accreditation concerns (Carter 2003; Broad et al. 2009; Adler-Kassner and O'Neill 2010).

Composition, then, had a history of using assessment to improve student learning before it was emphasized so much by accreditors. Likewise, we understood the link between learning assessment and teaching improvement before accreditors made the connection explicit. For example, White (1985) noted 30 years ago that "the assessment of writing and the teaching of writing were intimately related" (xv). Advocates of using teachers to score student writing samples argued that "it brings together English teachers to talk about the goals of writing instruction" and that the teachers "take away from the experience much that is valuable to their teaching" (White 1984, 408). With the proliferation of portfolio evaluation in the 1980s and 1990s, the link between student assessment and faculty development—and, to some extent, faculty evaluation—became even more prominent (Hamp-Lyons and Condon 2000, xv). Therefore, when accreditors began in the 1990s to formalize the link between learning and teaching by adding faculty-performance criteria focused on student outcomes and recommending faculty-development workshops as a way to use data about learning to "close the loop" of assessment, compositionists were ready. For example, in the early 2000s Bean began offering discipline-specific workshops that helped faculty examine their courses, identify learning outcomes, develop effective teaching practices, and design course-embedded assessments in response to the accreditors' expectations (Carrithers, Ling, and Bean 2008). And while accreditors have tended not to enforce standards that emphasize the importance of aligning instruction with "the learning goals of academic programs" and ensuring that faculty evaluation results in "reliable" data that are "used to improve instruction" (Western Association of Schools and Colleges 2011, 5.16 and 5.18), when they begin to do so, we have an impressive history to draw upon. Our field has long embraced, for example, the multiple-method faculty evaluation approaches endorsed by a growing number of accreditors concerned with validity and reliability of faculty assessment. We have argued for years that "teachers should never be evaluated only by student perceptions," nor by a single "class visit" (White 1989, 168), and that the teaching portfolio—or collections of materials akin to it—is the best method for both evaluating instruction and inspiring real improvement (Anson 1994; Minter and Goodburn 2002).

One reason compositionists have been able to see the relationship with accreditation productively is that our discipline has always prioritized student learning. Further, as accreditors shifted their attention to documentation of student learning, their principles and criteria began to match with our disciplinary values. For example, our approach to student-learning assessment as "context-sensitive," "rhetorically based," "accessible," and "theoretically consistent" (O'Neill, Moore, and Huot 2009, 56), closely aligns with accreditation directives to engage in "ongoing systematic collection and analysis of meaningful, assessable, and verifiable data" (NWCCU), collected through "multiple direct and indirect measures" (HLC). Like our accrediting agencies, we see assessment as a means to "fulfill" our school's "mission" and "improve instruction" on our campuses (NEASC). In addition, at least since the 1990s our understanding of important assessment constructs such as validity and reliability has mirrored those of our accreditors. Consistent with writing assessment theories (Smith 1993; Huot 2002; Broad 2003; Conference on College Composition and Communication 2009), accrediting agencies agree that establishing validity of assessment results requires collecting evidence about content, process, consequences, and local and disciplinary contexts. Likewise, agencies view reliability as not simply a matter of consistency and correlations, but rather the result of an argument that requires, among other things, attention to purpose, context, and ultimate use, a view consistent with that of writing assessment experts (O'Neill 2011).

However, there is evidence to suggest that our ability to work productively with accreditors is changing. Though regional accrediting agencies have traditionally positioned themselves as peer collaborators whose priority is to help institutions articulate the quality of their programs, they are feeling pressure to respond to a public that has grown cynical not only about what we teach and why but about the basic value of a college degree. What these developments mean for accreditors is that they should be prepared for Congress to "further regulate accreditation and . . . assert further oversight" (CHEA 2012) in a way that satisfies a public desire for some degree of standardization across higher ed institutions. Pulled between responsibility to schools and responsiveness to an increasingly hostile public, accreditors are starting to say and do things that appear at odds with their stated commitment to honor individual institutional histories and missions. Within this context, it is reasonable for compositionists to wonder what our local assessments will mean, how the results of those assessments will be used, and whether we can maintain our focus on what the students in our classrooms need so they can learn and thrive.

FROM ACCOUNTABILITY TO COMPARABILITY: THE THREAT TO CONTEXT-BASED ASSESSMENT

Historically, public criticisms of education and calls for accountability tended to be directed toward K–12 educators with little attention to higher education. Since the mid-1980s, though, such criticisms have expanded to include post-secondary educators, as reflected in debates over the periodic reauthorizations of the Higher Education Act, which have articulated goals for student access to college and responsible stewardship of the tuition and taxpayer dollars being spent to meet those goals. This more general sentiment that colleges and universities should be held publicly accountable gained significant traction in 2006, with the release of A Test of Leadership, a report compiled by a special commission appointed by then US Secretary of Education, Margaret Spellings (Miller et al. 2006). Known as the Spellings Report, the document questioned not only the soaring costs of education but the quality provided to students and taxpayers who, "despite increased attention to student learning" by schools and accreditors, have no way of knowing "how much students learn in colleges or whether they learn more at one college or another" (Miller et al. 2006, 13). Among the commission's recommendations were the introduction of "innovative means to control costs" and "creation of a consumer-friendly information database with reliable information," including college costs, admissions, completion and graduate rates, and "eventually" student achievement of learning outcomes as measured by standardized achievement assessments like the Collegiate Learning Assessment (CLA) (26-37).

More recently, this drive for accountability through collection and publication of comparable data was captured by President Obama's State of the Union address, in which he criticized colleges and universities for not providing "our citizens with the skills they need to work harder, learn more, and reach higher" and remarked on the "soaring cost of higher education," which "taxpayers cannot continue to subsidize" (Obama 2013). In order to help schools "do their part to keep costs down," he explained, the Department of Education had designed "a new 'College Scorecard,'" to allow families to compare the costs, graduation rates, loan default rates, median borrowing, and employment rates of colleges and universities, so they can determine which schools offer "the most bang for [their] educational buck" (Obama 2013).

Calls for higher education to be more "accountable," more "transparent," and more "affordable" are not new; we have heard them for decades. In fact, accreditors' shift toward a concern with learning outcomes was, in large part, a response to public critiques of higher education in the 1980s. Links with business interests, reflected in lamentations about lack of appropriate job skills, are also not new, especially in times of economic challenge. What is new is the emphasis on comparability across institutions with different histories, missions, and student populations, and concrete efforts by people outside of the higher ed community (e.g., within government and private industry) to become more involved in the business of determining comparable goals for higher ed and proposing how those goals might be achieved and assessed. Such an emphasis, facilitated now in ways impossible to imagine before the advent of the Internet (and interoperability of various platforms for data collection), raises many questions about the relationship between assessment and learning.

Two recent efforts that reflect the expressed desires of both government and industry are the Voluntary System of Accountability (VSA) and the Degree Quality Profile (DQP). Whereas the VSA acts as more of a clearinghouse for higher ed assessment information (as well as data on costs and student demographics), the DQP, developed with funding from the Lumina Foundation, serves as a guide for assuring program quality through recommended college "competencies" and assessment methods. In many ways, these efforts, the result of collaborations between higher ed administrators and business leaders who were inspired by governmental reports and policy initiatives, are intended to produce the data that government and industry thought the accreditors should have collected. Both the VSA and the DQP are attractive to accreditors who value the local needs of particular schools and students but are under extreme pressure to show how higher education, in general, is preparing students for life after college, as well as which schools are doing a better job of it, for the money. Both of these initiatives also emphasize comparability across institutions, which, again, had not been emphasized in earlier accreditation (and other) assessment mandates. As Linda Adler-Kassner notes, the accreditors have been criticized for "allowing institutions to set their own learning standards and develop their own assessments" and for a "lack of comparable data" on learning (Adler-Kassner 2012, 123). The allure of a document like the DQP is perhaps best illustrated by a recent WASC (Western Association of Schools and Colleges) 2013 accreditation re-design informed by stated DQP principles and specified "areas of learning" as well as an initiative to encourage its member schools to voluntarily pilot the DQP "to assess its usefulness as a framework for assisting institutions to assess the quality of degrees or portions of degree programs" (Draft 2013 Handbook, Standard 3; Western Association of Schools and Colleges 2012). While many WASC-accredited schools have signed on to the DQP pilot initiative, the relationship between the accreditation agency and a suspected big-business interest has raised concerns among some educators. Faculty within the University of California system, for example, expressed worry that adoption of the DQP (and accreditation standards informed by it) would "weaken faculty control over the curriculum" and "shift" the nature of program evaluation "away from peer review toward external review via a formulaic process" undertaken by people who may not be subject-area experts (University of California Academic Senate 2012).

While neither the VSA nor the DQP target writing programs directly, they do include written communication in their frameworks and, therefore, will potentially impact writing programs, including instruction and student-learning assessment. For example, the VSA asks for information about "expected learning gains of students in critical thinking and written communication" and endorses the Collegiate Learning Assessment, which requires essay writing. The DQP includes communication fluency as one of its competencies, with writing embedded in other competencies, such as "Use of Information Resources," which specifies at the bachelor level that students "incorporate multiple information resources," using appropriate citation conventions in "projects, papers or performance" (Lumina Foundation for Education 2011, 15). As accreditors like WASC attempt to link with the DQP and other similar initiatives, writing teachers and administrators hear too many echoes from the past, when standardization was considered sufficient for claims of reliability, which was considered sufficient enough to make claims for validity. Such attempts also inspire concern that K–12 accountability efforts, such as the Common Core and its forthcoming exams, will be extended to include higher education, that is, that we'll end up with national standardized college curriculum and exams of some type, as recommended by the Spellings Report. In fact, higher ed leaders, business executives, and academic scholars have joined members of the Spellings Commission in celebrating the positive potential of the CLA, a standardized exam meant to assess the development of critical thinking and analytical writing abilities among college students. Most educators do not necessarily know that development of this test was funded by such groups as Lumina (the developer of the DQP) and is being promoted as an exemplary "value added assessment" for the (now more than 300) public schools willing to voluntarily submit data to the VSA as well as the private-school VSA counterpart, the Council of Independent Colleges.

In the past, accreditation has required writing faculty and administrators to negotiate some degree of pressure for standardization *within* our institutions (e.g., by way of standardized student placement and proficiency exams and standardized faculty evaluation methods), but the current desire for more comparability of results across college campuses creates a new challenge for us. So far, as a field, we have not been successful at designing assessments that satisfy the disciplinary criteria for best practices yet produce results that are comparable across institutions. In terms of student-learning assessment, for instance, the inter-institutional study published by Pagano et al. (2008) demonstrates some of the challenges involved in trying to design a writing assessment that can account for the local situation while also establishing "effectiveness relative to national norms, or if not in terms of norms, at least with results contextualized beyond the local institution" (287). After working on creating a common embedded assignment and rubric for use across different institutions, the authors concluded, "Composition programs have commitments to certain kinds of writing and writing pedagogies, so it was not easy, or even possible, to standardize a writing task and administer it at all participating sites" (Pagano et al. 2008, 310). Acknowledging "serious threats to reliability," Pagano et al. explained that they "sacrificed reliability (controls) for validity (respecting local practices and philosophies)" (2008, 311).

A similar kind of tension between the context-informed assessments that compositionists value and the standardized "tests" that typically devalue context can be felt in national conversations surrounding assessment of teaching. Though attention to various contextual issues that may influence the faculty-evaluation process is an important validity concern (Ory and Ryan 2001), the desire for a traditional kind of reliability, based on decontextualized comparisons among and across faculty, is keen. Many institutions have adopted nationally normed faculty-evaluation surveys, in recognition of the theoretical and legal liabilities associated with "homegrown" course evaluations that "have not generally undergone the rigorous psychometric and statistical procedures required" to support claims about their appropriateness (Arreola 2007, 100, 110). Though these standardized forms appear more theoretically sound and do an admirable job of reflecting the complexity of teaching, their inability to capture idiosyncrasies of the local teaching context is cause for concern, especially among writing instructors who face ever-changing student bodies and curricular expectations. While non-profit organizations like ETS and IDEA have offered "systematically validated" alternatives to locally developed course surveys, even they acknowledge validity problems by outlining sources of error and stressing that validity is enhanced when results are used with "additional evaluation tools" that capture "other dimensions of teaching" (IDEA Center n.d.).

Though accreditors have not been asking universities for evidence of teaching effectiveness as a way to document program quality, this may be changing. Revisions of accreditation agency standards over the past decade seem to more fully articulate the relationship between instruction and learning outcomes. Perhaps the best example of this is the SACS recommendation, first made in the early 2000s, that potential for effective teaching among faculty job applicants be judged, in part, on the ability to meet student learning outcomes (Southern Association of Colleges and Schools 2011). Revised editions of popular institutional assessment guides also highlight the role that instruction plays in student achievement of learning outcomes. In *Assessing Student Learning*, for example, Linda Suskie, a former Middle States accreditor, argues that instructors may need to "take a hard look" at curriculum, including the "content and requirements" of individual courses and "reconsider [their] teaching methods" if learning-assessment results appear "disappointing" (Suskie 2009, 303–5).

The concern is not that this common-sense connection is being made more explicit but how it is being made by some accreditors within a national accountability context. The connections between the WASC re-design and Lumina's DQP do not end with curriculum or "competencies," or even student-learning assessment, but extend to faculty evaluation. The competencies are discussed as "a point of departure for agreement on more detailed and specific expectations regarding the development of programs, *courses, assignments and assessments*" (Lumina Foundation for Education 2011, 2; italics added). Given the role instructors play in development of courses, assignments, and assessments, and given the growing public skepticism about what faculty do, it is not hard to imagine that "agreement" on how faculty should be *assessed* across member schools would soon be on the agenda of the Council for Aid to Education, Lumina, and other organizations now in the business of "saving" higher education. The VSA College Portrait, for instance, is supported by ETS, a corporation not only in the business of standardized student exams, such as the SAT, but also the SIR II, a standardized national faculty evaluation offering "comparative data from nearly eight million students in more than 107,000 two-year and more than 117,000 four-year college courses nationwide" (ETS). Up to this point, these companies have been careful to design faculty surveys that do not assume a particular curriculum or set of outcomes. In fact, their designers have tried hard to accommodate various teaching methods and goals that may or may not be directly aligned with program or accreditation outcomes. However, the connections between educational-assessment companies like ETS and educational-outcomes advocates like the Lumina Foundation (by way of the DQP) raises the specter of a common assessment of faculty based on common educational outcomes—a standardized faculty assessment designed along the lines of the CLA.

STANDARDIZATION ON STEROIDS: THE PROMISE AND PERILS OF BIG DATA

The business community's interest in the future of higher education is not just about value-per-tax-dollar and matching learning objectives with job requirements; it's about profit. Many corporations have responded to public calls for transparency and comparability by, for example, developing and promoting new or "improved" standardized assessment products, and these ventures have proven highly lucrative. With advancements in digital technology that allow for integration of teaching and learning with evaluation as well as collection of "big data" pools that can be readily aggregated and shared, standardized assessments create new challenges for writing programs. Beyond compromising the locally controlled, context-sensitive, theoretically informed approach to assessment that we have always valued, mass-marketed assessments can undermine learning and threaten the privacy of students and teachers.

Educational publishing companies like Bedford/St. Martin's and Pearson have been involved in designing and marketing online courseware that facilitate writing-program assessment. Pearson enjoys a larger share of this market with a significant number of writing programs and individual teachers opting into MyCompLab. Bedford offers re:writing and, most recently, the Bedford ePortfolio.[1] While the platforms are marketed as tools to support teaching, at least with Pearson, permissions can be set (with individual faculty approval) that allow an administrator to pull students' writing into a larger pool of samples for assessment purposes. Local administrators may choose an online program because it serves particular needs, but they may not be able to predict how publishing houses will mine the data generated by students and teachers using their courseware now and in the future. Thus, a company like Pearson can opt to place composition papers into its own data stream, creating an ever-growing pool of students' documents that can be shared and compared beyond individual programs. While the implications of these programs for learning and teaching are not yet clear, they do raise alarms about potential challenges to faculty control over curricula and student control over their writing.

While standardized writing tests are an automatic source of data for companies, two trends contribute to the possibility of amassing and using actual writing samples from students' coursework. First, many of the smaller publishing imprints have been bought up by two companies at the same time that courseware companies have agreed to standards for interoperability (the ability to share data); and second, shifting FERPA regulations have facilitated an increased emphasis on data collection that can be shared among companies. Pearson (American Association of Publishers) and the Holzbrinck company (Georg Holtzbrinck) dominate composition imprints. Bedford/St. Martin's shifted, in 2012, to include the MacMillan moniker (also associated with McGraw Hill), both of which are owned by Holzbrinck, a German company which has, similarly to Pearson, bought up smaller imprints. Pearson and Holzbrinck both increasingly emphasize online resources and the ability to share data among their individual companies, allowing for the possibility of gathering larger sets of data. Smaller e-portfolio companies (e.g., Desire2learn's e-portfolio, Chalk and Wire, or LiveText, Canvas by Instructure) emphasize interoperability as a selling feature with their courseware and/or ePortfolios (Pearson interoperability and Schools Interoperability Framework). For example, most of these courseware or ePortfolios allow for the integration (through interoperability) of Turnitin, a company that is all too aware of the kind of data it has collected and how it might be useful to other organizations. With information gathered about each student's essay submission and the capability to analyze and compare writing across institutions, Turnitin often highlights important discoveries from its data ("Turnitin Releases Analysis" 2013).

The focus on interoperability has been accompanied by FERPA policies that have altered the way data can be shared by institutions and publishing companies. In 2012, FERPA regulations went into effect that facilitated a range of data sharing possibilities between state educational agencies (SEA), companies that contract with SEAs, and other government agencies. For companies such as Pearson, who already enjoy large contracts with state educational agencies, the potential exists for a range of data tracking options that involve an assessment of both students and faculty. The changes in FERPA regulations allow entrepreneurs to participate in the data sharing/analysis and fall in line with the climate of greater accountability, an accountability that also affords profitability for companies focused on education and assessment.

The shift in FERPA regulations, coupled with increased interoperability, facilitates some large industry data collection projects and allows for increased data analysis within large data sets. For example, Paul Fain's article, "Big Data's Arrival," reported on a study that examined a "database that measures 33 variables for the online coursework of 640,000 students—a whopping 3 million course-level records" and from those records suggested policy implications. The data "seem[ed] to suggest . . . that for students who seem to have a high propensity of dropping out of an online course-based program, the fewer courses they take initially, the better-off they are" (Fain 2012). While Fain's example explores online students' success, the focus on large data pools could easily be shifted toward data analysis of student essays, with teacher influence as one of the possible variables. While it may well be that the big data pools will move universities in positive directions, the negative effects could also be significant. What happens if faculty are assessed outside the local context, and based on values determined by assessment companies like Pearson, with little or no input from experts in field? While we have yet to see significant studies emerging from data mining of a vast pool of students' essays, small signs are on the horizon.

Turnitin, for example, released information on the top sources students access for papers, demonstrating the potential for student writing to be assessed outside the institutional context, based on educational publishing companies' decisions about data analysis. With the increasing demands for comparability of data among universities, made possible by standardized methods such as the CLA that are produced by companies such as ETS and Pearson, we can anticipate that student writing, produced for courses and local program assessments, may soon be used to compare programs and universities. Given the interoperability of data pools, we may see faculty teaching portfolios linked into the data analysis as well. What this may mean for instructors in terms of control over their teaching materials, evaluation processes, and academic freedom is unknown as of yet although there are some indications of its potential. For example, Joseph Moxley (2013) writes about how the online course platform they developed at the University of South Florida allows administrators to not only monitor composition instructors' evaluation of student writing, but also to intervene if they determine it is needed during the semester. If such platforms are used for submission of teachers' dossiers, instructors' autonomy and privacy could be compromised even more, especially if material is collected and analyzed beyond the local level. Importantly, the shift to big data not only allows for such comparisons, but it changes what counts as knowledge, as danah boyd and Kate Crawford argue. It also can change who decides what counts. Part of this shift happens because big data requires a "'data cleaning' process." Someone with the skills to understand databases makes "decisions about what attributes and variables will be counted, and which will be ignored. This process is inherently subjective" (boyd and Crawford, 2012).

CONCLUSION: WHAT CAN WE DO GIVEN THE CHANGING CONTEXT OF ACCREDITATION?

While in the past our field has used externally mandated assessment initiatives as an opportunity to document the effectiveness of writing programs, balancing the needs of the local context with disciplinary values and public demands, the current emphasis on comparability threatens to change our relationship with assessment and accreditation. Historically, our field has worked to improve writing instruction, attending to student learning within local programs and addressing validity concerns through "processes and methodologies to assess student learning reflect good practice, including the substantial participation of faculty and other instructional staff members" (Higher Learning

Commission 2014 4.B.4). We need to draw on that tradition as we continue to respond to accreditation expectations and negotiate with education companies whose bottom line is impacted by the assessment choices we make. To use this tradition, we must know it, and, like early assessment practitioners, we must understand the rapidly changing contexts in which we work and the challenges they create.

As a large community of scholars who share relationships with companies like Pearson and Bedford/St. Martin's, we need to understand the implications that our decisions about ePortfolios and other instructional software matters can have (more thoroughly, of course, than we can address in this chapter). We need, as a field, to create guidelines for working with these companies and others who participate in the collection of student data. While big data should be approached with an awareness of the potential challenges, big data may also help to address student learning in ways that are consistent with our theory and research. For the most part, analysis of that kind of data is left to the education companies who shape the research questions. We need to negotiate for disciplinary access to the data and hire our own data cleaners, our own people for analysis of that data, so that we are contributing to the conversation in a way that reflects our disciplinary values. Like the faculty within the University of California system, our field needs to raise concerns regarding faculty control over curriculum and call attention to the ways validity can be compromised through the standardized review processes promoted by educational companies, who remain unregulated. They currently wield enormous power in the public discourse about education, including which kinds of assessment and assessment results will matter.

Likewise, we need to extend our relationships with accreditors and become active participants, not passive recipients, in establishing guidelines appropriate for instruction and assessment that will also satisfy the needs of the accreditation agencies. Accreditors, despite increased scrutiny, aim to serve faculty and students (after all, accreditors are themselves educators), so we will need to try to find ways to partner with accreditors to show that we can have high standards without standardization. We do share a common goal with accreditors: the desire to promote best practices in teaching and assessment as a way to improve learning. This kind of work can also provide opportunities, as we have seen in the past, to create new theories and practices, to make knowledge that contributes to our discipline.

Many writing practitioners are already doing this kind of work. Bean's research illustrates the way a WAC program can be re-imagined to improve teaching and learning while accommodating accreditor's assessment demands (Bean, Carrithers, and Earenfight 2005). The University of South Florida's development of in-house courseware for both the teaching and assessment of student writing, which was specifically designed to meet the SACS requirements, showcases the potential implications of standardization in a digital environment that allows for big data analyses (Moxley 2013). Pagano et al.'s (2008) research, while not necessarily directly linked to accreditation, contributes to the larger discussion about cross-institutional comparability. Perhaps, though, we could follow Chris Gallagher's (2010) proposal to develop a heuristic for creating validation arguments of writing assessments. The heuristic, he argues, should be grounded in the local program as well as the basic principles of writing assessment articulated by scholars and professional organizations such as the CCCC, CWPA, and NCTE. One might even imagine a way for writing program administrators to load the types of local assessment plans promoted by these scholars into a national database, shaping the selection criteria by size of school, student population statistics, types of composition courses taught, etc. If we were able to map where these pools of data were being collected, collaborate on the ability to share these data pools, and offer ways for individual colleges to contribute to them, we could both use this big-data capability to improve our own assessments and to negotiate alliances with organizations like Pearson, who rely on data from our students, in ways that work for teaching and learning.

Of course, it is not always easy to keep up with important assessment-related developments, let alone consider how to take advantage of them on our campuses. Time and resources are as limited as ever and, despite decades of productive field-wide engagement with accreditation, many faculty still resist the idea that responsible education is responsive— not just to the needs of students but the questions and concerns of the broader communities in which we work. If anything about the future of assessment is clear, it is that ignoring the changing contexts of higher education—including the increasing demand for comparability and the creation and uses of big data—will not serve our programs and will not lead to improved teaching and learning. All one has to do is look at what is happening in K–12 education to realize what is at stake.

Note

1. These types of commercial programs offer platforms for writing courses that integrate and store student writing, peer review, teacher feedback and evaluation, and other aspects of a writing course.

References

Adler-Kassner, Linda. 2012. "The Companies We Keep or the Companies We Would Like to Try to Keep: Strategies and Tactics in Challenging Times." *WPA: Writing Program Administration* 36 (1): 119–40.

Adler-Kassner, Linda, and Peggy O'Neill. 2010. *Reframing Writing Assessment to Improve Teaching and Learning*. Logan: Utah State University Press.

Anson, Chris M. 1994. "Portfolios for Teachers: Writing Our Way to Reflective Practice." In *New Directions in Portfolio Assessment: Reflective Practice, Critical Theory, and Large-Scale Scoring*, ed. Laurel Black, Donald A. Daiker, Jeffrey Sommers, and Gail Stygall, 185–200. Portsmouth, NH: Boynton/Cook.

Arreola, Raoul A. 2007. *Developing a Comprehensive Faculty Evaluation System: A Guide to Designing, Building, and Operating Large-Scale Faculty Evaluation Systems*. 3rd ed. San Francisco: Anker.

Bean, John C., David Carrithers, and Theresa Earenfight. 2005. "Transforming WAC through a Discourse-Based Approach to University Outcomes Assessment." *WAC Journal* 16:5–21.

Belanoff, Pat, and Peter Elbow. 1986. "Using Portfolios to Increase Collaboration and Community in a Writing Program." *WPA: Writing Program Administration* 9 (Spring): 27–40.

boyd, danah, and Kate Crawford. 2012. "Critical Questions for Big Data: Provocations for a Cultural, Technological, and Scholarly Phenomenon." *Information Communication and Society* 15 (5): 662–79. http://dx.doi.org/10.1080/1369118X.2012.678878.

Broad, Bob. 2003. *What We Really Value: Beyond Rubrics in Teaching and Assessing Writing*. Logan: Utah State University.

Broad, Bob, Linda Adler-Kassner, Barry Alford, and Jane Detweiler. 2009. *Organic Writing Assessment: Dynamic Criteria Mapping in Action*. Logan: Utah State University Press.

Carrithers, David, Teresa Ling, and John C. Bean. 2008. "Messy Problems and Lay Audiences: Teaching Critical Thinking within the Finance Curriculum." *Business Communication Quarterly* 71 (2): 152–70. http://dx.doi.org/10.1177/1080569908318202.

Carter, Michael. 2003. "A Process for Establishing Outcomes-Based Assessment Plans for Writing and Speaking in the Disciplines." *Language and Learning Across the Disciplines* 6 (1): 4–29.

Conference on College Composition and Communication. 2009. *Writing Assessment: A Position Statement*. Rev. ed. National Council of Teachers of English. http://www.ncte.org/cccc/resources/positions/writingassessment.

Cooper, Charles R., and Lee Odell, eds. 1977. *Evaluating Writing: Describing, Measuring, Judging*. Urbana, IL: National Council of Teachers of English.

Council of Higher Education Accreditors. 2012. *CHEA Initiative Final Report*, 1–12. Washington, DC.

Educational Testing Service. n.d. "About the SIR II Instructional Report." Accessed May 13, 2013. http://www.ets.org/sir_ii/about/.

Fain, Paul. 2012. "Big Data's Arrival." *Inside Higher Ed*, Feb 1. http://www.insidehighered.com/news/2012/02/01/using-big-data-predict-online-student-success.

Gallagher, Chris W. 2010. "Assess Locally, Validate Globally: Heuristics for Validating Local Writing Assessment." *WPA: Writing Program Administration* 34 (1): 10–32.

Gere, Anne Ruggles. 1980. "Written Composition: Toward a Theory of Evaluation." *College English* 42 (1): 44–8, 53–8. http://dx.doi.org/10.2307/376032.

Greenberg, Karen L. 1982. "Competency Testing: What Role Should Teachers of Composition Play?" *College Composition and Communication* 33 (4): 366–76. http://dx.doi.org/10.2307/357949.

Hamp-Lyons, Liz, and William Condon. 2000. *Assessing the Portfolio: Principles for Practice, Theory, and Research*. Cresskill, NJ: Hampton Press.

Haswell, Richard H., ed. 2001. *Beyond Outcomes: Assessment and Instruction within a University Writing Program*. Westport, CT: Ablex.

Higher Learning Commission. 2014. "Criteria for Accreditation." http://policy.hlcommission.org/Policies/criteria-for-accreditation.html.

Higher Learning Commission of the North Central Association of Colleges and Schools. 2012. "Criteria for Accreditation." https://www.hlcommission.org/.

Huot, Brian. 2002. *(Re)Articulating Writing Assessment for Teaching and Learning*. Logan: Utah State University Press.

IDEA Center. n.d. "Research and Papers: Value and Limitations of Student Ratings." http://www.theideacenter.org.

Lumina Foundation for Education. 2011. *The Degree Qualifications Profile*.

Miller, Charles, James B. Hunt Jr., Richard Stephens, Nicholas Donofrio, Arturo Madrid, Louis W. Sullivan, James J. Duderstadt, Robert Mendenhall, Sara Martinez Tucker, Gerri Elliott, et al. 2006. "A Test of Leadership: Charting the Future of U.S. Higher Education: A Report of the Commission Appointed by Secretary of Education Margaret Spellings." US Department of Education. http://www2.ed.gov/about/bdscomm/list/hiedfuture/reports/final-report.pdf.

Minter, Deborah, and Amy Goodburn. 2002. "Introduction: Why Document Postsecondary Teaching?" In *Composition Pedagogy and the Scholarship of Teaching*, ed. Deborah Minter and Amy Goodburn, xv–xix. Portsmouth, NH: Heinemann, Boynton/Cook.

Moxley, Joseph. 2013. "Big Data, Learning Analytics, and Social Assessment." *Journal of Writing Assessment*. http://www.journalofwritingassessment.org/article.php?article=68.

New England Association of Schools and Colleges. 2011. *Standards for Accreditation*. Commission on Institutions of Higher Education. http://cihe.neasc.org/standards_policies/standards/standards_html_version.

Northwest Commission on Colleges and Universities. "Standards and Policies." www.nwccu.org.

Obama, Barack. 2013. "Transcript of Obama's State of the Union Address." Accessed March 3, 2013. http://abcnews.go.com/Politics/OTUS/transcript-president-barack-obamas-2013-state-union-address/story?id=18480069.

O'Neill, Peggy. 2011. "Reframing Reliability for Writing Assessment." *Journal of Writing Assessment* 4. http://journalofwritingassessment.org/article.php?article=54.

O'Neill, Peggy, Cindy Moore, and Brian Huot. 2009. *A Guide to College Writing Assessment*. Logan: Utah State University Press.

Ory, John C., and Katherine Ryan. 2001. "How Do Student Ratings Measure Up to a New Validity Framework?" San Francisco: Jossey Bass. *New Directions for Institutional Research* 2001 (109): 27–44. http://dx.doi.org/10.1002/ir.2.

Pagano, Neil, Stephen Bernhardt, Dudley Reynolds, Mark Williams, and Matthew Killian McCurrie. 2008. "An Interinstitutional Model for College Writing Assessment." *College Composition and Communication* 60:285–320.

Smith, William. L. 1993. "Assessing the Reliability and Adequacy of Using Holistic Scoring of Essays as a College Composition Placement Technique." In *Validating Holistic Scoring: Theoretical and Empirical Foundations*, ed. Michael M. Williamson and Brian Huot, 142–205. Cresskill, NJ: Hampton Press.

Southern Association of Colleges and Schools. 2011. *The Principles of Accreditation: Foundations for Quality Enhancement*. http://sacscoc.org.

Suskie, Linda. 2009. *Assessing Student Learning: A Common Sense Guide*. 2nd ed. San Francisco: Jossey-Bass.

"Turnitin Releases Analysis of Internet Sources Used in Student Writing that Reveals Potential Plagiarism and Unoriginal Content." 2013. http://turnitin.com/en_us/about-us/news-releases/analysis-of-internet-sources-used-in-student-writing.

University of California Academic Senate. 2012. "WASC Revisions Postponed in Response to UCEP, Senate Concerns." *The Senate Source.* Accessed May 14, 2013. www.senate .universityofcalifornia.edu/WASC.march2012.html.

Walvoord, Barbara F. 2004. *Assessment Clear and Simple: A Practical Guide for Institutions, Departments, and General Education.* San Francisco, CA: Jossey-Bass.

Western Association of Schools and Colleges. 2011. *Handbook of Accreditation.* http://www .wascsenior.org.

Western Association of Schools and Colleges. 2012. "Degree Qualifications Profile." http://www.wascsenior.org/redesign/dqp

White, Edward M. 1984. "Holisticism." *College Composition and Communication* 35 (4): 400–9. http://dx.doi.org/10.2307/357792.

White, Edward M. 1985. *Teaching and Assessing Writing.* San Francisco: Jossey-Bass.

White, Edward M. 1989. *Developing Successful College Writing Programs.* San Francisco: Jossey-Bass.

White, Edward M., and Leon L. Thomas. 1981. "Racial Minorities and Writing Skills Assessment in the California State University and Colleges." *College English* 43 (3): 276–83. http://dx.doi.org/10.2307/377241.

2

QEP EVALUATION AS OPPORTUNITY
Teaching and Learning through the Accreditation Process

Susan Miller-Cochran and Rochelle Rodrigo

The growing number of writing-focused professional development projects developed within the process of reaffirmation of accreditation, such as Quality Enhancement Plans (QEPs) in the Southern Association of Colleges and Schools (SACS) Commission on Colleges (SACSCOC) region, have placed a new emphasis on writing at many college and university campuses across the country. At the same time, such reaccreditation projects have placed many writing scholars in a new assessment role, that of QEP Lead Evaluator, a member of a SACSCOC On-Site Review Committee whose primary role is to review and assess the QEP. While administrative work is nothing new in rhetoric and composition, the unique role of the QEP Lead Evaluator puts writing scholars in a generally unfamiliar rhetorical situation where the language, processes, roles, and conventions are typically more familiar to other members of the committee. Yet the QEP Lead Evaluator is invited as "expert" to inform the On-Site Review Committee about the pedagogical, administrative, and assessment choices that align most closely with effective writing instruction. Negotiating these waters can be intimidating, but they also provide a valuable opportunity for both professional growth and administrative outreach. In this chapter we explicate the SACSCOC criteria for the QEP from the perspective of the Lead Evaluator, explain the on-site review process from the perspective of the committee, and complicate the complex subject position of the QEP Lead Evaluator within the process.

THE QUALITY ENHANCEMENT PLAN: A FLEXIBLE FRAMEWORK FOR LEARNING

The QEP Lead Evaluator's role on the On-Site Review Committee is to focus exclusively on the proposed QEP and evaluate it according to the

DOI: 10.7330/9781607324355.c002

criteria established by SACSCOC. There are two accreditation standards associated with the QEP, and those two standards govern the review process and focus the attention of the On-Site Review Committee:

> CR 2.12: The institution has developed an acceptable Quality Enhancement Plan (QEP) that includes an institutional process for identifying key issues emerging from institutional assessment and focuses on learning outcomes and/or the environment supporting student learning and accomplishing the mission of the institution. (Quality Enhancement Plan) (SACSCOC 2012b, 21)

> CS 3.3.2: The institution has developed a Quality Enhancement Plan that (1) demonstrates institutional capability for the initiation, implementation, and completion of the QEP; (2) includes broad-based involvement of institutional constituencies in the development and proposed implementation of the QEP; and (3) identifies goals and a plan to assess their achievement. (Quality Enhancement Plan) (SACSCOC 2012b, 27)

The two standards are often broken down into five indicators for an acceptable QEP, each divided into two related parts. These indicators generally serve as the criteria by which an On-Site Review Committee judges the effectiveness and acceptability of the QEP:

1. A. An institutional process
    B. Key issues identified that emerge from institutional *assessment*

2. A. Focus on learning *outcomes* and accomplishing the mission of the institution
    B. Focus on the *environment* supporting student learning and accomplishing the mission of the institution

3. A. Capability to *initiate* the plan
    B. Capability to *implement* and *complete* the plan

4. A. Broad-based involvement of institutional constituencies in the *development* of the plan
    B. Broad-based involvement [of] institutional constituencies in the *implementation* of the plan

5. A. Identified goals for the quality enhancement plan
    B. A plan to assess the achievement of the goals of the quality enhancement plan (SACSCOC 2012a)

Within the parameters of these 10 criteria, QEP Lead Evaluators focus their response to a plan in conversations with both the individuals at the institution being reviewed as well as members of the review committee. At the same time, QEP Lead Evaluators also have the opportunity to learn during the review process from seeing how these criteria are met within an institutional context that is different from their own and by hearing the perspectives and opinions of experienced administrators on the On-Site Review Committee in response to the proposed plan.

An Institutional Process that Identifies Key Issues from Assessment

In the first indicator, the key phrases include "institutional process" and "key issues from assessment." The On-Site Review Committee is specifically looking for indications that the QEP did not solely develop out of the wants and needs of a specific group or individual at the institution; instead, the topic should develop through carefully crafted institutional planning and assessment that is ongoing. If the QEP is focused on outcomes related to writing, the institution should already have institution-wide plans, usually associated with strategic planning documents or other institution-level planning and assessment efforts, which demonstrate a need for the proposed project. Often these institution-level plans may not be explicitly connected to writing; instead, they might include identified goals such as preparing students for participating in professional work environments or twenty-first-century literacies. In such a case, a QEP Lead Evaluator might rely on various position statements from organizations such as the Council of Writing Program Administrators (CWPA), the Conference on College Composition and Communication (CCCC), and the National Council of Teachers of English (NCTE) to help flesh out a dialogue about the connections between writing, work, and twenty-first-century literacies. Ultimately, these broader categories should be connected to writing through a more explicit, institution-wide assessment process that draws connections between a focus on improving and/or transforming writing instruction and meeting the goals of the strategic plan.

A QEP Lead Evaluator with a background in rhetoric, composition, and writing studies would look carefully at the assessment process already in place, learning from it, as well as discussing ways it might revised, especially through the QEP assessment process. The fields of rhetoric, composition, and writing studies have a rich scholarly history of writing assessment that writing-focused QEP Lead Evaluators can draw on (and sometimes recommend). For example, a QEP Lead Evaluator might share with people at the institution who are designing, developing, implementing, and/or evaluating a writing-focused QEP such resources as NCTE's (2013a) position statements related to assessment and testing as well as some key introductory resources like John

Bean's (2011) *Engaging Ideas,* or some of the Bedford/St. Martin's professional development guides, such as Edward White's (2007) *Assigning, Responding, Evaluating* and Brian Huot and Peggy O'Neill's *Assessing Writing* (Huot and O'Neill 2009). This list, of course, only scratches the surface, and many resources about writing assessment are context-specific. Depending on the particular focus of an institution's QEP, the institutional context and mission, and the student population it serves, some resources might be more useful and relevant to share.

Focus on Student Learning Outcomes and Institutional Mission

While the first criterion for the QEP focuses on the development of the QEP, the second indicator emphasizes the heart and soul of the project: student-learning outcomes based on the institutional mission. As mentioned in reference to strategic planning documents above, the institutional mission may not explicitly mention writing, but it might emphasize goals such as preparing students for work or developing twenty-first-century literacies. Although QEP Lead Evaluators might see immediate connections between the writing-focused QEP and the institutional mission, this criterion provides a chance for the QEP Lead Evaluator to listen to and learn from both the institution under review as well as the other administrators on the on-site review committee.

A key challenge to meeting this criterion is that many QEPs must include an element of faculty development to successfully implement changes in writing or writing instruction. Although any teacher or administrator would likely agree that one of the primary methods for impacting student learning is to work with faculty on developing effective pedagogical approaches, the QEP should maintain a primary focus on students and student learning and not just on faculty or faculty development. While faculty development can comprise an element of the plan, the balance of the resources and effort in the QEP should be directly focused on students. One of the primary ways the QEP demonstrates this focus on student learning is through specifically identified goals and measurable student learning outcomes, which are the primary focus of the fifth indicator.

Discussions about student learning outcomes related to writing benefit as well from grounding in scholarship and position statements that help articulate specific outcomes for writing identified within the writing studies community (CWPA 2008; CWPA, NCTE, and NWP 2011), as well as philosophies and theories of teaching and learning writing, specifically scholarship related to the specific context and focus of the QEP. Position statements from institutional organizations and annotated bibliographies available on CompPile (http://comppile.org/) and through the Writing Across the Curriculum (WAC) Clearinghouse (http://wac.colo state.edu/) can provide a very useful starting point for finding relevant research and theoretical grounding for the development of a QEP. Just as QEP committees on campus might need to be reminded to maintain an emphasis on student learning, they might also need to be reminded that writing is a complex, recursive set of strategies that are difficult to learn. While a QEP Lead Evaluator who is well-grounded in writing research and active in disciplinary conversations about writing can assume some common theoretical assumptions when talking to others in the same field, foundational concepts about writing and writing instruction are not necessarily a given when talking to an audience who hasn't been reading the same scholarship and participating in those same scholarly discussions. On the other hand, a QEP Lead Evaluator also needs to remain open to learning and reading about scholarship that could be related to writing and writing instruction that he or she might not necessarily place within the sometimes insular conversations that take place within the disciplinary field. Likewise, the QEP Lead Evaluator must balance knowledge of the most recent research in the field with an understanding of the institutional context in which the QEP is designed and implemented. One of the rewards of serving as a QEP Lead Evaluator is gaining the perspective of other faculty and administrators who are passionately interested in writing and writing instruction but are tackling writing-focused questions from different disciplinary and institutional perspectives.

Capability to Initiate, Implement, and Complete Plan

With the keywords *initiate, implement,* and *complete,* the third indicator focuses on the logistics of the QEP. Questions to help review this aspect of the QEP include:

- Initiate: How will you bring faculty, students, and necessary personnel together to initiate the plan? Who needs to be on board?
- Initiate: What institutional structures are in place that might prevent the plan from getting underway?
- Implement: Are the key people in place already?
- Implement: Do you have the resources to get it off the ground? What resources are needed to get the plan started?
- Complete: Can you sustain and carry this through to completion?
- Complete: Are there realizable, achievable goals (within a 5-year period)?

This particular indicator introduces the concepts of feasibility and sustainability, and it places a spotlight on the institution's allocation of resources for the project. While QEPs need only be sustainable for a five-year period (the point at which the institution under review must submit a report to SACSCOC), widespread implementation of changes in writing instruction on campus for even a five-year period require a great deal of support. When responding to this indicator, QEP Lead Evaluators have the opportunity to advocate for the kinds of material working conditions that will make writing programs sustainable and effective in the long-term.

Assessing this particular indicator also gives the QEP Lead Evaluator a wonderful opportunity to listen and learn from all the other experienced administrators on the On-Site Review Committee. These individuals can discuss how the various logistics need to fit into a larger institutional framework. A QEP Lead Evaluator also has significant scholarship from the field to draw upon, including Myers Zawacki and Rogers's (2012) *Writing Across the Curriculum* and its many core essays about WAC and Writing in the Disciplines (WID) programs or Condon and Rutz's (2012) recent article "A Taxonomy of Writing Across the Curriculum Programs: Evolving to Serve Broader Agendas." Hopefully, however, QEP Lead Evaluators will also learn from others at the institution under review or on the On-Site Review Committee about resources they have used and relied upon for designing, developing, and delivering institution-wide programs.

Broad-Based Involvement in Development and Implementation

A successful QEP must demonstrate and track involvement of faculty, staff, students, alumni, community, and other relevant audiences in *both* the development *and* implementation of the plan. Since writing studies is a field that relies heavily on temporary, non-tenure-track faculty and/ or graduate students who often struggle for fair and equitable working conditions and a voice in curricular and institutional matters, QEP Lead Evaluators with expertise in writing studies often must emphasize the need for the QEP to involve the people who will be implementing the plan as an integral part of the planning and discussion process. QEP Lead Evaluators might specifically ask to talk to these groups to see if they have been brought to the table and empowered to contribute to discussions about the design and implementation of the QEP. The experienced administrators on the On-Site Review Committee will most likely also have a variety of experiences from which to draw from about how to incorporate and support a variety of constituencies in an institution-wide project. In these contexts, the QEP Lead Evaluator can help facilitate productive dialogue by listening, learning, and asking questions.

QEP Lead Evaluators will most likely recognize that many of the different constituencies, both in the institution under review as well as on the On-Site Review Committee, will probably define and understand "writing" in a variety of—often competing—ways. This disparity alone could be a good way to initiate dialogue that bridges to other topics and concerns related to the design and implementation of the project.

Clear Goals and a Plan to Assess

Articulating clear goals associated with learning objectives and then designing an assessment plan to evaluate whether or not the plan works is often where writing-focused QEPs run into trouble. Writing is difficult to assess, and writing assessment doesn't always follow easy to define rules of validity and reliability.

First, the goals and the assessment plan need to be aligned. Does the QEP start with clear, measurable outcomes, and is there an assessment plan in place that matches those outcomes? As many writing scholars and administrators are aware, stakeholders outside of writing studies often have firmly held beliefs about writing assessment that may or may not align with either a scholarly understanding of writing studies or the specific goals of the QEP. The QEP Lead Evaluator might be in the position, for example, to defend an assessment plan that might not follow a standard experimental research design but that clearly follows a sound plan for outcomes-based assessment through writing portfolios. Likewise, the QEP Lead Evaluator might need to suggest revisions to an assessment plan that uses standardized test results or machine-scored essays to assess complex rhetorical writing outcomes. The QEP Lead Evaluator can draw upon both scholarship about the assessment of writing and the experience of other members of the On-Site Review Committee to respond to such challenging assessment questions.

Second, QEP Lead Evaluators will also want to ask detailed questions about who will collect the data and how it will be stored, as well as how the data will be analyzed and interpreted. Since writing programs at many institutions of higher education are already institution-wide programs, QEP Lead Evaluators might look into plans for how the QEP assessment data will be used, especially in relation to management and funding of the writing program.

The indicators outlined in this section are the primary evaluation criteria used for the QEP; however, SACSCOC provides lists of other helpful evaluative prompts and questions in various support documents. For example, in the *Handbook for Review Committees* (SACSCOC 2005), SACSCOC lists helpful evaluation questions that are "guidelines only" and are not to be considered exhaustive (35–36).

Many of our suggestions reference specific scholarship in the field of writing studies and may imply that the QEP Lead Evaluator will be performing a scholarly review that explicitly references work in the field during the on-site review, as well as in the report. The on-site review is too fast and furious, and the report is too streamlined for this to be the case, however. Instead, it is more common that the QEP Lead Evaluator will know and draw upon this disciplinary knowledge, remaining ready to reference it as needed, while also being open to the context of the institution under review as well as the knowledge and experience of the other members of the On-Site Review Committee.

THE ON-SITE REVIEW PROCESS: FAST, FURIOUS, AND FASCINATING

Many aspects of the review process are hidden from view, and they might go unnoticed by most faculty members at an institution undergoing reaccreditation by SACSCOC. For example, even faculty members who are at an institution undergoing the reaccreditation process do not always realize that there is an off-site reaccreditation review prior to the on-site review unless they are intimately involved in the reaccreditation effort at their school. The institution applying for reaccreditation submits an extensive report, centered on standards and criteria established by SACSCOC, that an Off-Site Review Committee reads and responds to. The Off-Site Review Committee is comprised of different members than the On-Site Review Committee, and the QEP is not part of the off-site review process. Once the institution receives the response of the Off-Site Review Committee, it submits a revised report addressing the items found not to be in compliance with accreditation standards by the Off-Site Review Committee. Historically, the purpose of the on-site review was for a team to follow-up on any standards that the Off-Site Review Committee found to be non-compliant. With the introduction of the QEP into the reaccreditation process (SACSCOC 2001), a new element was added to the on-site review. Now the on-site visit is both about verifying standards originally judged non-compliant by the Off-Site Review Committee *and* evaluating the QEP, which is not read or reviewed prior to the on-site visit.

Just as many faculty members do not realize that there is an off-site review prior to the on-site review, many do not realize that a great deal of the work involved in the on-site review occurs prior to the actual campus visit. On-site reviews can be broken down into three major periods: before, during, and after the campus visit.

Before the Campus Visit

About six to eight weeks prior to the campus visit, all of the On-Site Review Committee members receive a packet of information from SACSCOC that provides information about SACSCOC, the reaffirmation of accreditation process, as well as logistical paperwork for the campus visit. All of the committee members are expected to read the materials. Depending on the QEP Lead Evaluator's prior experience with a reaccreditation process, this stage of the process can be very enlightening and potentially overwhelming. While QEP Lead Evaluators are not expected to respond to compliance items during the on-site review, having institutional context can help with understanding the QEP itself and the reaccreditation process as a whole. QEP Lead Evaluators who are new to the process can ask questions and clarify their roles at this point with the chair of the On-Site Review Committee and/or the SACSCOC representative.

Approximately six weeks in advance of the campus visit, the On-Site Review Committee receives copies of the institution's original Compliance Certification (a packet of materials demonstrating how the institution meets the criteria for reaccreditation), the QEP, the off-site committee's findings in the form of the draft of the Report of the Reaffirmation Committee (Reaffirmation Report), and any Focused Reports that the institution may have submitted based on the results of the off-site review.[1] QEP Lead Evaluators should plan to read the QEP closely, multiple times, as well as skim the other materials for institutional context.

Once the committee has the materials from the institution, committee members will begin communicating with each other under the direction of the chair, probably with at least one conference call and frequently via email. The chair of the On-Site Review Committee assigns committee members specific portions of the Reaffirmation Report to write based on experience and expertise. Likewise, the chair will divide up the reading and commenting responsibilities for the QEP according to the five indicators outlined above, and he or she will assign each section to appropriate committee members based on their expertise (e.g., Chief Financial Officers will likely assess the indicator dealing with appropriate resources for implementation). The QEP Lead Evaluator, on the other hand, will be responsible for the entire QEP, including all five indicators. Committee members will write responses to the QEP, including any questions and/or concerns. The chair will compile all the responses and send out a revised draft of the Reaffirmation Report to the committee. This period of synchronous and asynchronous dialogue is one of the first opportunities the QEP Lead Evaluator has to share his or her expertise while also carefully listening to the experienced perspectives of the other committee members.

Just prior to the on-site visit, committee members are responsible for reading the revised draft of the Reaffirmation Report and making a new round of comments, questions, and/or concerns. At that time, committee members also compile requests to meet with specific groups of individuals while on the campus visit.

During the Campus Visit

The campus visit is an extremely fast and overwhelmingly busy event for the On-Site Review Committee. In approximately 48 hours, the members of the committee meet with a variety of different groups who provide more details about different aspects of the Reaffirmation Report, especially about the QEP since that is the only "new" information added to the reaccreditation process. When not meeting with individuals from the campus, the committee members continue to revise the report. Often only 2–3 committee members attend an interview with a given group of institutional representatives, and multiple interviews might occur at the same time. The nature of the process requires the committee members to share information with each other to complete the revisions to the report and the response to the QEP, and to gain consensus within the committee on the response.

The campus visit ends with the committee finalizing the draft of the report and preparing to meet with key members from the campus during the exit conference. There are two major components of the exit conference: reporting the results of the on-site review and briefly answering any questions. The QEP Lead Evaluator carries a major responsibility during the exit conference: summarizing the review committee's understanding of the QEP, summarizing the committee's response, and outlining any suggestions for revision.

After the Campus Visit

The vast majority of the work is completed during the campus visit. The On-Site Committee Chair and the SACSCOC representative make one or two more passes through the Reaffirmation Report and then send it out one last time to the rest of the committee. At this point, the report is in the equivalent of page proofs. The report will then be officially submitted to SACSCOC.

At this point, the Reaffirmation Report is still in draft form. It is not officially accepted until the SACSCOC Compliance and Reports Committee as well as the Executive Council and the full Commission approve the report and reaffirmation.

THE QEP LEAD EVALUATOR: A COMPLEX SUBJECT POSITION

Although it might appear that a "Lead Evaluator" would have a great deal of authority through the process of evaluating such an important aspect of the institution's effort toward reaccreditation, individuals in the QEP Lead Evaluator role often find themselves in a position where authority can be in constant flux. While there should be no question about the Lead Evaluator's expertise in the topic of the QEP, the Lead Evaluator's age and professional experience, in comparison with other members of an On-Site Review Committee, provides an additional layer of complexity in establishing credibility. QEP On-Site Review Committees are generally made up of presidents and provosts, Chief Academic Officers (CAOs) and VPs of Instruction, Chief Financial Officers (CFOs) and VPs of Business Affairs, as well as other VPs and deans. In short, members of the On-Site Review Committee are usually individuals who have been working in higher education for many years and have a great deal of authority on their own campuses. Part of the reason they are members of the On-Site Review Committee is because of their experience; these individuals can compare, contrast, and extrapolate what they see with what works in various institutional contexts. They also serve on On-Site Review Committees to become familiar with the most recent revisions in the accreditation process so their own campuses will be prepared for their next review. These review committee members help assess the overall reaccreditation criteria; however, they also bring this broader experience to the evaluation of the QEP itself. CFOs help evaluate whether the QEP has allocated enough resources to be successful. Presidents and CAOs contribute to discussions about campus-wide adoption and assessment. As "experienced" administrators, the members of the On-Site Review Committee have the experience and perspective to critically assess the viability and sustainability of the QEP—whether or not the project will generally survive and ideally thrive in the institution as a whole.

A QEP Lead Evaluator must negotiate his or her subject position within the context of his or her upper-level administrative team members. For example, a QEP Lead Evaluator who has an official title as a Writing Program Administrator (WPA) might have experience to draw upon in evaluating the appropriate deployment of resources and assessment plans. Even officially titled WPAs, however, do not always manage their own budgets, have authority in personnel matters, or design and implement their own reviews and assessments. Professional experience is also often an indicator of longevity in a profession, and some QEP Lead Evaluators, as was the case for both authors of this chapter, might find themselves to be the members of the On-Site Review Committee with the least experience in higher education. While age is certainly not a marker of expertise on its own, the QEP Lead Evaluator can find herself in a complex position of feeling the need to demonstrate expertise and/or earn respect on the committee. The broader institutional perspective that comes from upper-level administrative experience is something a QEP Lead Evaluator might also have to cultivate during an on-site visit, often through sitting back and listening to the kinds of concerns and questions that other members of the committee ask.

Within this complex subject position lays a tremendous opportunity, though, for the QEP Lead Evaluator who navigates those complexities effectively. Through the lens of the QEP Evaluative Criteria and through the process of evaluation, the QEP Lead Evaluator has an opportunity to discuss writing, writing instruction, and the effective administration of writing programs with both administrators at the institution being accredited and the administrators serving on the On-Site Evaluation Team. During the evaluation process the QEP Lead Evaluator has the opportunity to raise awareness about best practices in the teaching, learning, and assessment of writing by drawing upon the research in the field. Rich discussions can result in such an evaluative context about issues such as institutional resources needed to develop effective writing programs and ways to align student learning outcomes and curricular goals with sound pedagogical and assessment methods. A QEP Lead Evaluator might share a variety of resources and professional position statements with the On-Site Review Committee, depending on the nature of the QEP, such as:

- The Council of Writing Program Administrators' Outcomes Statement for First-Year Composition (CWPA 2008)

- The Framework for Success in Post-Secondary Writing (CWPA, NCTE, and NWP 2011)
- Both the Conference on College Composition and Communication's (CCCC 1982) as well as the Two-Year College English Association's (TYCA 2004) position statements on the preparation of teachers of writing
- Various position statements from the CCCC and the National Council of Teachers of English (NCTE 2013b)
- Criteria used for selection for the Writing Program Certificate of Excellence, awarded annually by the CCCC (2013)

The QEP Lead Evaluator might also be in the position to advocate for the institution designing the QEP. The evaluator can help ensure that the QEP has the support it will need to make it successful, which might involve sharing the same guiding principles with upper administration at the institution undergoing accreditation that are shared with the other members of the On-Site Review Committee. During the interviews conducted for an on-site visit, a QEP Lead Evaluator might ask to meet with the teachers or staff who would be affected by the changes in the QEP and expected to implement the changes in their classes, to get a sense of what they need for support. He or she might even ask, "What should I be paying attention to in order to make sure you have the support you need to make this plan a success?"

QEP Lead Evaluators also have the opportunity to learn a great deal about the complex relationships between individual curricular programs and larger university structures through their willingness to listen to and learn from the perspectives of other members of the On-Site Review Committee. The process of participating in a SACSCOC reaccreditation on-site review provides the QEP Lead Evaluator with the chance to learn about institutional policies and processes in a unique environment while listening to experienced administrators dialogue about the potential challenges and solutions that institutions of higher education face. QEP Lead Evaluators have the opportunity to learn a great deal about how institutions of higher education "work," but they also have the chance to hear the perspectives of administrators on the committee about their specific experiences with writing programs.

Because of the tremendous amount of responsibility placed upon the QEP Lead Evaluator, and because of the importance of the success of the QEP for the overall reaccreditation effort, institutions select QEP Lead Evaluators very carefully. The QEP Lead Evaluator is recommended by the institution undergoing accreditation and must be knowledgeable in the content area targeted by the QEP and, ideally, familiar with the context of the type of institution being accredited. For example, a community college would generally want a QEP Lead Evaluator who also brings community college experience and contextual knowledge. For a writing-based QEP, this presents a unique opportunity for the institution to bring someone to campus who can fairly evaluate the QEP because the person understands the goals and theoretical foundation supporting the plan. Institutions generally consider three things when recommending people to SACSCOC as lead evaluators for their institutions:

- Someone with expertise in the specific areas addressed by the QEP
- Someone who understands the institutional context
- Conflict of interest (The QEP Lead Evaluator can't be in same state as the institution being considered for reaccreditation and shouldn't have co-authoring or other close working relationships with faculty members at the institution.)

Of course, an institution is also served well by selecting a QEP Lead Evaluator who has knowledge of, and perhaps even experience with, the SACSCOC accreditation process. A carefully chosen QEP Lead Evaluator can present a wonderful opportunity for both the evaluator and the institution under review.

SERVING AS THE QEP LEAD EVALUATOR: A CONCLUSION

After serving on an On-Site Review Committee, one of the authors was asked by a committee member to provide some tips about being a QEP Lead Evaluator. Because the nature of QEPs means that many faculty who would not otherwise be asked to serve on SACSCOC On-Site Review Committees might find themselves in a Lead Evaluator position, we wanted to end with these suggestions:

- Feel free to focus just on the QEP related information. Don't ignore other materials, but know that it is acceptable and expected that you focus your energies on the QEP itself.
- Read through all the materials that SACSCOC sends; it's helpful to get into the mindset of the On-Site Review Committee. Consider rereading and/or heavily annotating the SACSCOC materials explicitly discussing QEPs.
- As soon as you receive materials from the institution, read through the QEP and draft your initial responses to the five indicators. Then put it aside for a couple of days or a week. Reread, re-respond, and then send your thoughts to the chair. Do *not* send your thoughts to the whole committee first. Others on the committee will be assigned as primary writers for each of the five indicators. Let them develop

their own responses first; you will learn from them and gain new insights. The chair will then share all the responses with the whole team before the actual visit.

- Feel free to request to meet with specific individuals/teams while on the campus visit.

- Before the visit, reread the QEP and all of the text the team wrote related to the QEP. Also reread all of the SACSCOC materials explicitly related to the QEP. Based on everything you read from SACSCOC, the school, your own notes, and your on-site committee members, start drafting suggestions for revising the QEP.

- Develop questions you want to ask (both about making sure the QEP meets the criteria as well as questions that prompt them to improve their QEP). Be sure to organize your questions in relation to the five indicators the QEP is being evaluated upon. This step will help you keep your notes organized so that you can easily incorporate them into the Reaffirmation Report, a revision task that must take place within the 48-hour period of the on-site visit.

- Once you are on-site, quickly take ownership over revising the content about the QEP at the *end* of the Reaffirmation Report. There is very specific language that goes into the numbered areas in the middle of the report. Do not worry about those sections as you will get the language from your SACSCOC representative. Start revising ASAP and keep it up throughout the visit (feel free to carry around a laptop).

Finally, and perhaps most importantly, listen, learn, and enjoy the experience. Serving on an On-Site Review Committee is an honor that few faculty members in higher education get to experience, and the insight and perspective gained are worth the tremendous amount of effort.

Note

1.   The SACSCOC (2005) *Handbook for Review Committees* explicitly outlines the process of both the Off-Site and On-Site Review Committees. It also explicitly lists what materials the committee members will receive at what time.

References

Bean, John C. 2011. *Engaging Ideas: The Professor's Guide to Integrating Writing, Critical Thinking, and Active Learning in the Classroom.* San Francisco, CA: Jossey-Bass.

Condon, William, and Carol Rutz. 2012. "A Taxonomy of Writing Across the Curriculum Programs: Evolving to Serve Broader Agendas." *College Composition and Communication* 64 (2): 357–82. http://www.ncte.org/library/NCTEFiles/Resources/Journals /CCC/0642-dec2012/CCC0642Taxonomy.pdf.

Conference on College Composition and Communication (CCCC). 1982. "CCCC Position Statement on the Preparation and Professional Development of Teachers of Writing." http://www.ncte.org/cccc/resources/positions/statementonprep.

Conference on College Composition and Communication (CCCC). 2013. "CCCC Writing Program Certificate of Excellence." http://www.ncte.org/cccc/awards /writingprogramcert.

Council of Writing Program Administrators (CWPA). 2008. "WPA Outcomes Statement for First Year Composition." http://wpacouncil.org/positions/outcomes.html.

Council of Writing Program Administrators, National Council of Teachers of English, and National Writing Project (CWPA, NCTE, and NWP). 2011. "Framework for Success in Postsecondary Writing." http://wpacouncil.org/files/framework-for -success-postsecondary-writing.pdf.

Huot, Brian, and Peggy O'Neill. 2009. *Assessing Writing: A Critical Sourcebook*. Boston, MA: Bedford/St. Martin's.

Myers Zawacki, Terry, and Paul M. Rogers. 2012. *Writing Across the Curriculum: A Critical Sourcebook*. Boston, MA: Bedford/St. Martin's.

National Council of Teachers of English (NCTE). 2013a. "NCTE's Position Statements on Assessment and Testing." http://www.ncte.org/positions/assessment.

National Council of Teachers of English (NCTE). 2013b. "NCTE's Position Statements on Key Issues." http://www.ncte.org/positions.

Southern Association of Colleges and Schools Commission on Colleges (SACSCOC). 2001. *Principles of Accreditation: Foundations for Quality Enhancement*. Decatur, GA: Southern Association of Colleges and Schools Commission on Colleges. http://www .sacscoc.org/pdf/PrinciplesOfAccreditation.PDF.

Southern Association of Colleges and Schools Commission on Colleges (SACSCOC). 2005. *Handbook for Review Committees*. 2nd ed. Decatur, GA: Southern Association of Colleges and Schools Commission on Colleges. http://www.sacscoc.org/pdf/hand books/Exhibit%2018.HandbookForReviewCommittees.pdf.

Southern Association of Colleges and Schools Commission on Colleges (SACSCOC). 2012a. *Quality Enhancement Plan Guidelines: Indicators of an Acceptable Quality Enhancement Plan*. Decatur, GA: Southern Association of Colleges and Schools Commission on Colleges. http://www.sacscoc.org/pdf/Quality%20Enhancement%20 Plan%20Guidelines.pdf.

Southern Association of Colleges and Schools Commission on Colleges (SACSCOC). 2012b. *The Principles of Accreditation: Foundations for Quality Enhancement*. Decatur, GA: Southern Association of Colleges and Schools Commission on Colleges. http://www .sacscoc.org/pdf/2012PrinciplesOfAcreditation.pdf.

Two-Year College English Association (TYCA). 2004. "Guidelines for the Academic Preparation of English Faculty at Two-Year Colleges." *National Council of Teachers of English*. http://www.ncte.org/library/NCTEFiles/Groups/TYCA/TYCAGuidelines .pdf.

White, Edward. 2007. *Assigning, Responding, Evaluating: A Writing Teacher's Guide*. 4th ed. Boston, MA: Bedford/St. Martin's.

3

UNDERSTANDING ACCREDITATION'S HISTORY AND ROLE IN HIGHER EDUCATION

How It Matters to College Writing Programs

Shirley K. Rose

In this chapter, I write from my perspective as both a writing program director and a program evaluator to provide some context explaining the evolving role of higher education accreditation in the United States and its interest in issues related to college writing instruction. I am a Writing Program Administrator (WPA) with decades of experience directing university writing programs; I have served as a peer reviewer for the Higher Learning Commission of the North Central Association of Schools and Colleges, the largest regional accreditor in the United States, for over a decade; I have been an external academic program reviewer for several university English Departments; and I am the current Director of the Consultant-Evaluator Service of the Council of Writing Program Administrators. This work has given me a variety of opportunities to develop my understanding of a variety of purposes and practices of program review in higher education. These practices and purposes range from program-wide assessment of student learning outcomes as a means of evaluating a new curriculum for a college writing course to system portfolio reviews for higher education institutions seeking reaccreditation from their regional accrediting associations.

In what follows, I offer readers a lens for "zooming out" to look at the role accrediting bodies have played and are playing in the evolution of higher education in order to contextualize accrediting bodies' interest in writing programs. I also seek to encourage readers to become involved in the work of their regional accrediting associations in order to help set the future direction and development of these groups. I hope to persuade readers to view higher education accreditors, particularly regional accrediting associations, as partners with writing program

DOI: 10.7330/9781607324355.c003

faculty and administrators in providing a social good by making the work of higher education both visible and legible to those it serves.

In 1983, Kenneth Young et al. defined accreditation as "a process by which an institution of postsecondary education evaluates its educational activities, in whole or in part, and seeks an independent judgment to confirm that it is substantially achieving its objectives and is generally equal in quality to comparable institutions or specialized units" (Young et al. 1983, xi). I've chosen this definition, rather than one that might have been articulated at the origins of American higher education accreditation in the late nineteenth century when associations of higher education institutions that would become accrediting organizations were first developing, and rather than a definition that might be crafted now, in the second decade of the twenty-first century, in order to call attention to some basic principles that have grounded the accreditation enterprise in American higher education for nearly 130 years, specifically self-study and peer review. Note that in the definition above it is the institutions themselves that conduct the processes of evaluating their activities—that is, self-study is a foundational practice. To seek independent judgment of whether they are achieving their purposes, however, requires external evaluators; and determining whether the institution is equal in quality to comparable institutions requires that these reviewers be peers.

These two basic principles ground accreditation practices because they began as voluntary, nongovernment processes. To understand self-evaluation and self-improvement as central to accreditation is to understand accreditation's role in the informal system of self-regulation that has characterized American higher education from the start. However, it could be argued that the accreditation process has become less "voluntary" over time as federal and state government involvement in accreditation has expanded. Understanding this aspect of the history of the evolution of higher education accreditation can help writing program faculty and administrators to recognize and choose opportunities for their own involvement in accreditation associations' work for the future. Awareness of other factors contributing to the history of higher education accreditation in the US, including the histories of the various regional accreditors, can also help readers to recognize and understand significant differences in their practices and processes, particularly in the degrees to which they seem to be prescriptive and their respective emphases on either compliance or improvement. Knowing that the accrediting associations, which worked largely independently for most of their existence, have only recently sought to work collaboratively can help WPAs around the country understand how and why one another's experiences with accreditation processes have varied.

Writing program administrators might have occasions to interact with any of these four types of accrediting organizations in the United States, though to a varying degree: (1) programmatic accreditors, who accredit professional schools and programs such as medical schools, law schools, and engineering programs; (2) national career-related accreditors that accredit career-based institutions such as trade schools that are typically for-profit institutions; (3) national faith-based accreditors who work with primarily non-profit degree-granting religiously-affiliated or doctrinally-based schools and colleges; and (4) regional accreditors, which accredit both public and private, two-year and four-year, primarily degree-granting non-profit institutions. Most college and university writing programs are located in institutions that are accredited by regional accreditation associations, although there are writing programs associated with some of these other types of institutions. WPAs may have been asked to evaluate credits from writing courses in schools or programs that are accredited by one of these other types of organizations; if their institutions have engineering schools, they may have been asked to provide sample syllabi for required first-year composition or upper division technical writing courses when their school is going through periodic review by the Accrediting Board for Engineering and Technology (ABET). Some universities in other countries have sought and/or maintained recognition from American regional associations, as is the case with the American University of Beirut, which is accredited by the Middle States Commission on Higher Education, and international campuses of US-based universities, such as Michigan State University's branch campus in Dubai.[1] However, outside the United States the responsibility for quality assurance in higher education typically belongs primarily to government agencies that employ quite different evaluation practices, such as inspection.

Judith S. Eaton's (2012) *An Overview of U.S. Accreditation* is a useful resource for WPAs who need an orientation to the topic. Eaton provides explanations and descriptions of accrediting associations' work, summarizing by characterizing accreditation as a "trust-based, standards-based, evidence-based, judgment-based, peer-based process" (5). Although some things have changed for accreditation associations even in just the past two or three years, Eaton's list of values and beliefs of accreditation suggests the extent to which the ways they define their major responsibilities have not changed since their origins, underscoring principles of self-regulation, centrality of institutional mission, institutional autonomy, academic freedom, decentralization, and diversity:

1. Higher education institutions have primary responsibility for academic quality; colleges and universities are the leaders and the key sources of authority in academic matters;

2. Institutional mission is central to judgments of academic quality;

3. Institutional autonomy is essential to sustaining and enhancing academic quality;

4. Academic freedom flourishes in an environment of academic leadership of institutions;

5. The higher education enterprises and our society thrive on decentralization and diversity of institutional purpose and mission. (3)

Eaton also identifies four elements of accreditation in the US that are shared across all accrediting organizations, elements that will be familiar and perhaps even seem self-evident to writing program faculty and administrators who have been involved in their own institution's processes for maintaining accreditation, but must not be taken for granted.

The first of these elements is that member organizations undergo review processes that are regular and ongoing—*periodic* (every 10 years, for example), cyclical, or continuous. That is, institutions don't simply earn their accredited status once but must maintain it. Second, institutions prepare their own self-studies in which they offer a coherent and comprehensive discussion of how the information they present constitutes evidence that they have met the accrediting association's standards. Third, the review process includes a campus visit by a review team during which they are able to meet face-to-face with groups of faculty, students, staff, and other stakeholders in the institution. Fourth, every institution that is a member of the association undergoes the review process and a specific and explicit decision is made about the accreditation status of every institution that is a member of the accrediting association (Eaton 2012, 5).

I rehearse and elaborate on the four elements of accreditation Eaton identified in order to point to opportunities WPAs and other writing faculty in colleges and universities have to participate in and potentially improve and strengthen accreditation processes: first, nearly every higher education institution will go through an accreditation cycle at least once every 10 years, and many will be involved in a program that requires a review every five years, such as the Academic Quality Improvement Program of the Higher Learning Commission of the North Central Association of Schools and Colleges, a program typically chosen by two-year colleges in the membership of the association. Most WPAs will have a chance to participate in their institution's review activities at some point in their professional lives. Second, to be effective, all self-study processes, though varied and evolving, require systematic and thorough collection and analysis of information followed by honest introspection and reflection in order to develop useful and effective ways of making arguments about the quality of programs. Most WPAs are skilled at marshalling a variety of types of evidence to support arguments, and these skills will be needed when institutions in the North Central Association, for example, develop their Assurance Arguments to explain how they interpret data about their performance and how they will use it to make choices about where to focus efforts and resources.

Though the regional accreditors share the basic principles and practices I've discussed above, their specific processes and procedures for employing them differ. For example, an explanation of ways a WPA in a university that is a member of the Southern Association of Colleges and Schools (SACS) has participated in a Quality Enhancement Project (QEP) focused on developing a design for assessing student learning outcomes for developing writing abilities can be puzzling for WPAs at schools that are members of the North Central Association of Schools and Colleges, who have participated in AQIP (Academic Quality Improvement Program) Action Projects designed to develop a process and choose measures for periodic review of their institutions' general education curriculum.[2] However, both of these WPAs have been involved in processes that reflect a critically important aspect of the way the regional accreditation associations have operated: the quality improvement projects have been chosen by faculty and administrators themselves because they are consistent with their institution's central mission and contribute to achieving their strategic goals.

In the paragraph above, I have used some language that will be familiar for readers who have been engaged in higher education accreditation work in the last few decades, during which continuous quality improvement principles have guided the regional accreditors' practices and procedures. However, the language of "strategic plans" and "measures" and other terms taken from continuous quality improvement can be alienating for writing faculty and administrators who have not encountered it before, but it is important for them to recognize the ways it reflects a focus on process that has allowed institutions to maintain control of the kinds of data that are collected and how it is analyzed and interpreted. As more and more institutions use shared measures (such as those identified for the Voluntary System of Accountability) and common instruments for collecting related data (such as the CLA) in order to determine how their performance has changed over time and how it compares to institutions they identify as their peers, the critical aspects of reflective self-study and peer review may be eroded if faculty do not actively participate in the work of crafting arguments about how to interpret and use the data to make choices about where to make changes. At the same time, because CQI approaches have dominated the regional accreditation practices for long enough to have become so familiar as to seem self-evident, it might be useful for writing faculty and administrators to consider alternative approaches to evaluating the work of higher education institutions. Ourania Filippakou (2011), writing from the perspective of the United Kingdom where quality assurance in higher education is a responsibility of the government, has suggested that "the idea of quality in higher education is ideologically constructed and conducted . . . the ideological character of the idea of quality in higher education is evident in the discourses—themselves an interlink in networks. These discourses and networks are backed up by power and this helps to sustain their ideological character" (15).

Work by Blanco-Ramírez and Berger (2014) can also provide a helpful perspective on alternatives to current practices. They argue for an approach to understanding quality as "an organizationally-embedded phenomenon that is part of a larger agenda in the development and growth of higher education as an increasingly important contributor to individual, national and international development" (95), describing the current approaches to quality as predominantly techno-rational[3] and advocating greater awareness of the bureaucratic, political, symbolic, systemic, and collegial aspects. Blanco-Ramírez and Berger (2014) explain that each of these other dimensions implies a question that can inform decision making: the bureaucratic dimension asks, "what are the formal structures and regulations that guide the pursuit of quality in higher education?"; the political dimension asks, "what interests are served by varying approaches to and definitions of quality and what power bases are being used to further which agendas?"; the symbolic dimension implies the question, "what meanings and values are associated with different approaches to quality and how are those transmitted through symbolic norms and representations?"; the systemic dimension implies the question, "what broader forces beyond higher education institutions influence the construction, delivery and assessment of quality?"; and the collegial dimension asks, "who is involved and what voices are invited to engage in the important peer-review processes used in determining quality at the ground level of higher education delivery?" (97). For WPAs and other faculty, these questions can serve as a heuristic for identifying and potentially creating opportunities to approach accreditation processes from a more critical perspective somewhere between unquestioning compliance and unproductive resistance.

Staci Provezis (2010) makes a similar point about faculty involvement in accreditation when she offers five recommendations for advancing learning outcomes assessment as an objective of engagement in the accreditation process. Provezis's occasional paper, "Regional Accreditation and Student Learning Outcomes: Mapping the Territory," reports on the outcomes of a study she conducted with representatives from the regional accreditation associations. After discussing her findings regarding similarities and differences in the ways each of the regional accreditors supports assessment of student learning outcomes, and noting the kinds of assistance with assessment materials and designs as well as guidance for how to use results of assessment practices for institutional improvement efforts, Provezis closes her study by recommending better communication with the public about assessment of student learning outcomes, greater involvement of faculty through collaborative work with disciplinary and professional organizations, greater transparency about the accreditation process, increased willingness for institutions to take the initiative in deciding how outcomes assessment will be used, and more sharing of resources and training efforts among accrediting bodies and the institutions in their memberships.

Understanding some of the history of higher education accreditation in the US may help WPAs understand the ways it is likely to evolve in the future and how that evolution will involve writing programs. As Ryan Skinnell's (2014) recent *Rhetoric Review* essay documents, first-year composition programs have been implicated in American higher education from the start. Skinnell's study focuses on the role of Harvard in efforts to develop college admissions criteria that eventually led to the establishment of the New England Association of Schools and Colleges in 1885. In *The Standardization of American Schooling: Linking Secondary and Higher Education, 1870–1910*, VanOverbeke (2008) gives a thorough account and explanation of the origins of higher education accreditation in the need to distinguish secondary education institutions from post-secondary institutions in the late nineteenth century, a time of rapid growth in the number of colleges and schools across the United States. VanOverbeke focuses a chapter on the role of the University of Michigan in establishing what was to become the North Central Association of Schools and Colleges, now the largest regional accrediting association in the United States. Efforts by James B. Angell, president of the University of Michigan from 1871 to 1909, to develop a system for inspecting and accrediting the high schools from which the university drew applicants quickly expanded across the Midwest and, along with parallel projects in New England and the South, eventually evolved into our current system of regional accrediting associations which are now a primary agent of quality assurance for higher education in the United States. VanOverbeke points out that at the time, no state- or federal-level government agency had the authority to create a system that could clarify the differences between schools and colleges, identify which institutions qualified as which, and create an efficient way for them to work with one another to assure that students who were admitted to college were prepared to do college-level work. These reforms ultimately led to the establishment of associations of schools and colleges that developed systems of mutual accountability for meeting educational standards they collectively articulated and adopted. As VanOverbeke (2008) explains, "Reformers highlighted the importance of national standards and uniformity at a time when lay boards of education predominantly shaped the direction of secondary schools in line with local expectations, and many Americans regretted what was being lost. Although these reformers hoped to balance local needs with national norms and expectations, they ultimately promoted a system that tilted toward uniformity and standardization" (3). Maintaining that balance has been an enduring challenge that has helped to set direction as higher education accreditation purposes and practices have evolved.

VanOverbeke's summary explanation of the role Angell's program at Michigan played makes clear for WPAs how and why college-level writing has been an interest of accrediting organizations from the start:

> Angell had started the transition from an admissions system based on exams to a credential, and the spread of the inspection program solidified this approach throughout the Midwest and other regions of the country. . . . As more universities embraced the program, they began to cooperate in accepting students from schools on the accredited lists of other universities. This cooperation led to a de facto standardization in entrance requirements, much to the benefit of secondary schools. These schools now found it easier to prepare students for a number of different colleges, since most institutions of higher education in a region came to accept students from any accredited school without demanding separate standards. (VanOverbeke 2008, 59)

Young et al. (1983) also sketched a history of accreditation in American higher education from the late nineteenth century to the 1980s in *Understanding Accreditation*. Writing in 1983, they described the shift in accreditation from 1905 to the 1980s as a change "from a quantitative approach (expressed in specific requirements) to a qualitative approach (based on more general standards); from an emphasis on making institutions more alike to recognizing and encouraging institutional individuality; from a system heavily dependent on external review to a system based more on self-evaluation and self-regulation; from an initial focus on judging (and accepting or rejecting) an institution to a primary goal of encouraging and assisting an institution to improve its educational quality" (9). Reading their summary now from the perspective of 2015, as we wait for more details about the report of the National Advisory Committee on Institutional Quality and Integrity (NACIQI), and as we observe the widening adoption of tests such as the Collegiate Learning Assessment (CLA) and others discussed by O'Neill et al. in this collection, it may seem that future developments of the accreditation system will reverse the direction of the shifts Young and his co-authors identified.

Barbara Brittingham (2009), then President and Director of the Commission on Institutions of Higher Education of the New England Association of Schools and Colleges, offered an account of conditions and events contributing to the development of higher education accreditation that addressed a number of criticisms higher education critics and others had directed at the system over the previous decade or so. Brittingham charts[4] the development of American higher education history in relation to developments in accreditation, beginning with the establishment of Harvard Colleges by vote of the Great and General Court of Massachusetts Bay Colony in 1636, and highlighting other important events such as the adoption of the US Bill of Rights which reserved powers not mentioned in the Constitution to the states or the people in 1791, the *Dartmouth College* decision by the US Supreme Court preserving the right to operate chartered private colleges without state takeover in 1819, the establishment of the first of the regional associations, the New England Association of Schools and Colleges in 1885, and the establishment of the last of the regional associations, the Western Association of Schools and Colleges (WASC) in 1922. Brittingham explains that it was not until the Veterans Readjustment Act, which was passed in 1952, tied financial aid to institutional accreditation that the federal government had any involvement in higher education accreditation, and even then it was indirect. After the Higher Education Act was first passed in 1965, which expanded financial aid, membership in an accrediting association became involuntary for all intents and purposes for any schools that wanted to participate in these financial aid programs. A few years later, a formal process for federal recognition of accreditors was established.

Understanding the chronology of these events and others can help writing teachers and administrators understand why higher education accreditation is organized and operates in relation to federal and state governments in the way it does today.

Similarly, Paul Gaston (2014) points to changes in accreditation practices in the past decade made in response to criticisms that were articulated in the Spellings Commission's report. Some of the developments, such as increased disclosure of findings, are a response to calls for increased transparency; changes designed to clarify how demonstrating accountability related to state or federal standards differs from strengthening institutions in areas that are not addressed by these standards—for example, faculty governance, students' opportunities to learn through extracurricular activities, and engagement with communities—reflect a desire to clarify their role for their member institutions as well as the broader public. Other changes, such as more flexible protocols for review and more robust training for peer reviewers, reflect a desire to make the review process more useful to participating institutions; and still others, such as more automated reporting, reflect developments in technology that make collecting, storing, accessing, and presenting information more consistent over time and less labor intensive.

Writing instruction, particularly first-year composition courses and programs, has continued to be a focus of American higher education accreditation because writing courses have been implicated in nearly every development in the evolution of accreditation since its origins in the late nineteenth century because they are universally required, because they involve huge numbers of students, and because they operate at the entry point to college-level work. Our writing programs will most likely be implicated in future developments as well. Gaston (2014) identifies several changes he sees ahead for American higher education accreditations, including increasing interest in competency-based education, more collaboration among regional associations, more attention to affordability and student debt, and creation of different levels of review that support both newer and more established institutions. Each of these developments will have an impact on writing programs. If competency-based education as an alternative to credit-based education gains adherents, writing abilities will not be certified by earning credit for writing courses but by demonstrating that specific learning outcomes have been met. For some readers, that possibility can sound uncomfortably familiar and far too close to giving credit for high CLEP scores or AP Exam scores for comfort. Because I know how important writing is to learning and to demonstrating learning,

I would argue, however, that a move away from learning defined in terms of courses taken and credits completed and toward defining learning in terms of what students demonstrate that they can do is a move that could radically change for the better the way writing instruction is valued. Writing specialists have an opportunity to contribute to the conversations among higher education accrediting associations as these organization work to develop ways of supporting this shift and evaluating its effectiveness in their member schools that are beginning to experiment with competency-based learning.

Accreditation associations' recent collaborative work to develop criteria for reviewing dual-enrollment or dual-credit programs is another effort to which writing faculty and administrators can and should contribute, as the number of these programs that offer dual credit—that is, high school English credit and first-year college composition credit for the same course—rapidly increases and affects not only our college composition enrollments but also our curricula for our writing courses beyond first-year composition. College writing programs are also implicated in the increases in college student loan debt and college completion rates. Required courses like first-year composition and any of the courses that might be made prerequisite to FYC for some students will get special scrutiny if there is a possibility that placement decisions are not being made carefully and accurately because they could be contributing to unnecessary tuition costs, prolonging students' time in courses, and delaying their completion of their degrees. This too presents an opportunity for writing faculty and administrators to influence accreditation review processes by arguing for writing placement instruments that are fair, valid, and reliable.

Throughout this chapter I have emphasized what college and university writing faculty and administrators can do to influence accreditation processes through participation at the local institutional level and as peer reviewers for their regional accrediting associations. They can also work collaboratively and collectively with their peers at other institutions to develop means of demonstrating student learning outcomes and the effectiveness of areas of support that contribute to student learning such as faculty qualifications and professional development as well as faculty involvement in curriculum development and review. This work takes time and patience, and it is a kind of work college faculty are typically not trained to do or rewarded for doing. We must work for change of those circumstances as well.

Notes

1. The Dubai campus closed in 2011.
2. Paul L. Gaston's 2014 book, *Higher Education Accreditation: How It's Changing, Why It Must*, discusses many of these differences among practices of the regional accreditors at some length and suggests ways of unifying them that could lead to greater efficiency and effectiveness for the review process.
3. See Blanco-Ramírez (2013), "Studying quality Beyond Technical Rationality: Political and Symbolic Perspectives," for a discussion of the techno-rational approached to quality.
4. See Brittingham (2009, 8), "Table 1.1 A Chronology of Higher Education and Accreditation in the United States."

References

Blanco-Ramírez, Geraldo. 2013. "Studying Quality beyond Technical Rationality: Political and Symbolic Perspectives." *Quality in Higher Education* 19 (2): 126–41. http://dx.doi .org/10.1080/13538322.2013.774804.

Blanco-Ramírez, Geraldo, and Joseph B. Berger. 2014. "Rankings, Accreditation, and the International Quests for Quality: Organizing an Approach to Value in Higher Education." *Quality Assurance in Education* 22 (1): 88–104. http://dx.doi.org/10.1108 /QAE-07-2013-0031.

Brittingham, Barbara. 2009. "Accreditation in the United States: How Did We Get to Where We Are?" *New Directions for Higher Education* 2009 (145): 7–27. http://dx.doi .org/10.1002/he.331.

Eaton, Judith S. 2012. *An Overview of U.S. Accreditation*. Washington, DC: Council for Higher Education Accreditation; http://chea.org/pdf/Overview%20of%20US%20 Accreditation%2003.2011.pdf, Accessed September 14, 2014.

Filippakou, Ourania. 2011. "The Idea of Quality in Higher Education: A Conceptual Approach." *Discourse (Abingdon)* 32 (1): 15–28. http://dx.doi.org/10.1080/01596306 .2011.537068.

Gaston, Paul L. 2014. *Higher Education Accreditation: How It's Changing, Why It Must*. Sterling, VA: Stylus.

Provezis, Staci. 2010. "Regional Accreditation and Student learning Outcomes: Mapping the Territory." Occasional Paper No. 6. National Institute for Learning Outcomes Assessment.

Skinnell, Ryan. 2014. "Harvard, Again: Considering Articulation and Accreditation in Rhetoric and Composition's History." *Rhetoric Review* 33 (2): 95–112. http://dx.doi .org/10.1080/07350198.2014.884406.

VanOverbeke, Marc A. 2008. *The Standardization of American Schooling: Linking Secondary and Higher Education, 1870–1910*. New York: Palgrave. http://dx.doi.org/10.1057 /9780230612594.

Young, Kenneth E., and Charles M. Chambers, H. R. Kells, and Associates. 1983. *Understanding Accreditation*. San Francisco, CA: Jossey-Bass.

PART TWO

Curriculum and Program Development through Assessment and Accreditation

If accreditation and assessment processes uncover a need for support beyond what a school is currently providing for student writers, writing faculty and WPAs need to be able to enhance curricula and add programmatic support in a feasible (resource-effective) way. Part two provides a toolkit of methods for responding to such needs. Because not every approach is suitable for every program, we include several options for addressing gaps that may be revealed through assessment. As mentioned in the introduction to this collection, the examples provided here can be used to garner resources needed to meet students' needs. For better or worse, administrators and colleagues often find the argument that "they did something similar at University Y with great success" to be more convincing than an argument that draws on "what research in the field shows." The case studies that follow draw on research, but they have the added persuasive power of application: they show not only what research suggests but what actions based on that research can accomplish.

A theme that runs through the chapters that follow is that assessment results that suggest a need for curricular and programmatic change need not lead to the top-down imposition of restrictions or rigid plans. Rather, such results can mark the beginning of a new or reinvigorated writing program. Taken together, chapters in this section demonstrate how demographically diverse institutions (including, among others, a large, private, urban university in the Northeast; a small, rural community college in the Southeast; a mid-sized state university in the Midwest; and the flagship campus of the University of Hawaii), with varying levels of preexisting writing support and writing program infrastructure, have parlayed large-scale assessment and accreditation reviews into kairotic moments for program development. Program developments and curricular changes explored in part two range from building a WAC program from the ground up, to replacing a decades-old, lore-driven curriculum with a curriculum grounded in current scholarship, to expanding the curriculum of a long-standing, research-driven writing program to include electronic portfolios and an emphasis on multimodal composition.

Chapters in this section also provide valuable insight into how assessment and program development can bolster faculty's investment in teaching writing. Many faculty at the schools and programs detailed in this section became, as Karen Nulton and Rebecca Ingalls explain of faculty at Drexel University, "intensively engaged in creating pragmatic assessment models to foster faculty dialogue and support" (145). "Through this complex process," they continue, "we have come to understand that participating in accreditation-driven assessment can actually foster relationships and help colleagues uncover shared values and goals" (145). To be sure, creating new, shared course outcomes and designing new curricula to support those outcomes is a long, difficult process that can garner resistance from some faculty, but, as illustrated in the chapters that follow, the process can be productive and engaging if faculty are carefully and consistently involved in determining outcomes, designing curricular options, measuring the impact of curricular changes on student learning, and discussing strategies for improving student learning where assessment demonstrates a need.

4
GOING ALL IN
Creating a Community College Writing Program through the QEP and Reaccreditation Process

Jonathan Elmore and Teressa Van Sickle

We write this piece in and for a time of great change. The era of big data and accountability confronts those working in any field of higher education with significant challenges, but this era also offers opportunities heretofore unimaginable. Even at our small, rural community college, we have seen firsthand the incredible possibilities the current climate opens for writing programs. This chapter, then, serves two purposes. It is a case study of what we have done in creating and developing our own writing program, which consists of a writing center (WC), a writing across the curriculum program (WAC), and an online writing lab (OWL), that we hope can serve as a guide for other Writing Program Administrators (WPAs), especially at other small community colleges. This chapter is also an argument for thinking big at small schools. The climate and time is here for institutions of all sizes to achieve fully formed writing programs—programs that not only serve students but are also central to their institutions' curricula, internal and external assessments, and funding.

The convergent fields of writing center, writing program, and writing assessment scholarship have responded to this new environment with their customary zeal and insightfulness, offering numerous perspectives and approaches to harnessing the current culture of higher education to empower and improve writing programs both for ourselves and for the students we serve. While we are not going into a full review of this literature, largely because this work has already been done (Bell and Frost 2012), we highlight a few trends in the recent scholarship that speak directly to what we have seen and what we hope to offer WPAs striving to create, develop, and maintain a WC, WAC, and OWL.

DOI: 10.7330/9781607324355.c004

As the field has acknowledged and even called for, one of the changes in this new era will be our very identities and self images. At the turn of the century, Muriel Harris's (2002) "Preparing to Sit at the Head Table: Maintaining Writing Center Viability in the Twenty-First Century" looked forward and forecast exactly what was coming: the need "to recognize our role in helping students use—or learn to use—technology as part of their writing processes"; the fact "that distance learning is clearly here to stay" and that writing centers must meet their students increasingly online; "the fact that we face growing commercial competition" and that "as we recognize potential problems with commercial online tutoring, we need to articulate them" to the decision makers; that we must be "more precise than we have been about answering" questions about writing center effectiveness (16–19). While she hit the mark with all of her assertions, perhaps the most important contribution is in the governing metaphor of her title: meeting these challenges "will not only make us viable and ensure us a place at the institutional table, it may very likely earn us a place-setting at the head of the table where the speaker's podium awaits" (Harris 2002, 19). This ascension to the head of the table will not only require convincing others of the writing program's place there but also convincing ourselves. As Phillip Gardner and William Ramsey contend just a few years later: "Having lived on the margins for so long, we cannot relinquish the language and paradigm of an oppressed group" (Gardner and Ramsey 2005, 26). They go on to assert that "positioning ourselves in terms of marginality has neared the end of its usefulness" (26).

The same is true for WAC programs. In 1991, David Russell wrote that "without structural changes to integrate writing into the disciplinary fiber of institutions, without a commitment to permanent change in the way academia values writing in pedagogy, WAC programs will always work against the grain" (Russell 1991, 304). We find these points to be particularly salient for community college WPAs. While all writing programs and centers have worked against the grain and dealt with the marginalizing attitudes of the past both from within and from without, community college WPAs also face the same kind of "lesser than" thinking about community colleges in comparison to universities. However, in the current climate, community college writing programs are positioned to achieve far-reaching success and institutional influence. Hence, disavowing others and ourselves of the mindset of marginalization is particularly crucial for writing programs at community colleges.

This era of big data has caught some sectors of higher education a bit flat-footed, but it comes as a boon to WPAs who have longed for ways "to prove" the importance of their programs to administrators. Until very recently, WPAs have almost exclusively employed our writing centers to prove our program's necessity on campus, citing "use counts and satisfaction surveys" as our primary, and often only, numerical justification for resources and attention (Thompson 2006, 14). While these practices are worthwhile, they alone are simply not compelling enough to vault writing programs to positions of greater influence or to garner significantly increased resources. However, in the current climate, WPAs find many more tools at their disposal. As Myers Zawacki and Gentemann (2009) write, "No institution can ignore the need to focus on effective methods for assessing and improving writing among its students" (50). A result of this change in institutional cultures is that WPAs can now draw data from their entire writing programs to justify their necessity. Over the last decade, numerous case studies, articles, books, and conference talks articulate how WPAs can assess their programs and then tie the gathered data to broad institutional goals and obligations: student learning outcomes, program reviews, and reaccreditation needs (Bell 2000; Bean, Carrithers, and Earenfight 2005; Condon and Rutz 2012; Welch and Revels-Parker 2012). In addition, as Lerner (2003), Bell and Frost (2012), and others have noted, WPAs now have the means to correlate the impact of writing programs to retention, persistence, and completion rates, and this work is underway at institutions across the country, including our own college.

While the means to show the positive impact of writing programs on retention, persistence, and completion is an opportunity for WPAs at all types of institutions (from high schools to research universities), this trend is particularly crucial for community colleges where, in several states (e.g., Washington, Ohio, Indiana, and Tennessee), funding is becoming increasingly tied to student completion (Altstadt 2012). In our own state, the North Carolina "Completion By Design" initiative aims to attach state funding not to student enrollment but to student completion. Certainly there are many implications of such funding models, and we do not think that these trends are entirely positive. However, they are probably irreversible in most locales. The silver lining is that these changes offer opportunities for WPAs to design writing programs that serve students *and* help fund institutions. In a funding model that ties state dollars to student retention, persistence, and completion, WPAs that can correlate even a small increase in student completion to their writing program can literally tie that percentage of institutional income to their work. This type of direct splash on the bottom line could inaugurate an era wherein WPAs can make the case for their programs based not only on the positive impact for students and faculty but on the fundamental financial well-being of the institution. While such a goal is still in progress at our college, and at institutions across the country, this is the kind of opportunity that we, as WPAs, must seize. Doing so requires thorough planning. Paul Eschholz, former director of the Vermont Writing Program, reminds us, "The biggest mistake . . . in implementing a writing program is not planning far enough ahead. It is a three-to five-year venture" (qtd. in Nagin 2006, 92).

In our case, that planning took the form of writing our institution's Quality Enhancement Plan (QEP). A core requirement for reaccreditation mandated by the Southern Association of Colleges and Schools (SACS), the QEP is intended to be a five-year project completed by institutions every 10 years. As SACS explains,

> The Quality Enhancement Plan (QEP) [. . .] is a document developed by the institution that (1) includes a process identifying key issues emerging from institutional assessment, (2) focuses on learning outcomes and/ or the environment supporting student learning and accomplishing the mission of the institution, (3) demonstrates institutional capability for the initiation, implementation, and completion of the QEP, (4) includes broad-based involvement of institutional constituencies in the development and proposed implementation of the QEP, and (5) identifies goals and a plan to assess their achievement. (Southern Association of Colleges and Schools Commission on Colleges 2012b, 7)

The QEP itself is not writing program specific, but as the projects written about in this collection demonstrate, it can often be leveraged to create or expand writing programs. When "writing" is the goal, the actual composition of the QEP requires authors intimately familiar with the inner workings and language of writing centers and writing programs, as well as institutional assessment. The task of composing such documents tends to be arduous, but it is also an opportunity for WPAs to set the table for a writing program.

COMPOSING AN AMBITIOUS QEP DOCUMENT

Ostensibly, the QEP is an externally mandated component of reaccreditation; however, it can also be a powerful tool for advancing and improving writing programs and instruction. The first challenge faced by those harnessing the QEP process for furthering a writing program is to keep this dual identity of the QEP in mind as it is planned and composed. This duality changes how the five-year length of the QEP functions both conceptually and in practice. The QEP offers writing program administrators five years of greatly increased institutional influence and support. Hence, the duration of the QEP should be simultaneously viewed as the deadline for the impact report that goes to the accrediting agency and the deadline for getting the writing program fully integrated into institutional culture. Once the QEP's energy and sense of urgency dissipates, a writing program that relies on that energy for its existence is vulnerable and possibly not sustainable.

Five years is a relatively short period within which to make a writing program fully sustainable, and it is crucial to use the QEP to establish the full breadth of the writing program up front. In our case, prior to the start of the QEP five-year cycle, we had no writing center and no writing across the curriculum program. Consequently, our Dean of Arts and Sciences established the foundation for a writing program by composing a QEP document that stated a campus writing center, a writing across the curriculum program, and an online writing lab (including virtual tutoring) would be created in the first year of the QEP's five-year cycle. Our writing program was then conceived, and exists, as an amalgamation of the writing center, WAC program, and OWL, with the writing center functioning as the hub of data collection, analysis, and response for all three components—the hub of writing program assessment. Whatever the particular goals for an institution's writing program, it is essential that all of them are written into the actual document of the QEP to be set in motion as early as possible in the five-year process. Along the same line, we have found it essential to compose the QEP so that as many departments and programs are involved in the writing program as possible. Because the QEP document has tremendous weight in guiding the project over its five years, it is also important to include language that clearly identifies ways in which the writing program will assist other programs and the institution as a whole in achieving reaccreditation goals. Without that articulation, the QEP is vulnerable to troubling revisions to the original intent as the project moves forward.

While there is substantial overlap between what makes a QEP successful for reaccreditation and what makes it successful for furthering a writing program, we have found that there are five elements of implementation to consider during the composition of the QEP to give the writing program the best chance to thrive. When drafting the QEP, we have found it beneficial to build in language that supports these five elements of writing program implementation:

1. Staff the writing program fully for flexibility, availability, and sustainability.

2. Establish mutually dependent writing services to create unity in the writing program.

3. Build collaborative partnerships to grow a writing-focused community culture based on a critical model.

4. Designate the writing center as the hub of writing program assessment, and integrate writing program assessment into broader institutional goals.

5. Tie the writing program to retention, persistence, and completion rates.

Having these five elements explicitly written into the QEP document, and therefore directly tied to reaccreditation, provides a solid foundation and garners the necessary support to implement a healthy and sustainable writing program. During the QEP cycle, while the energy is high and the institutional focus is on writing, each element of the QEP document must be implemented fully to increase sustainability of the writing program as it was intended to function and to serve students beyond the five-year cycle. The QEP document provides accountability for administrators and stakeholders to remain committed to supporting complete implementation; once fully implemented, the interdependency of the writing program and other institutional programs will help ensure the writing program's longevity. The ultimate test of sustainability, though, is the writing program's ability to show a positive correlation of data between writing program and student retention, persistence, and completion. The more specific the elements contained within the QEP document and the further along in the implementation process the program is when the impact report goes out, the higher the likelihood of sustainability becomes. The urgent nature of a reaccreditation-imposed timeframe helps avoid common delays in progress: approval of funding, administrative turnover, allocation of physical and digital space, access to professional development, lack of buy-in among faculty, and other potential obstacles.

Before going into our implementation narrative, we want to acknowledge the risks of what we suggest. As we and others argue, the current era of higher education offers significant opportunities for writing programs, and the stakes are very high. We see the risks associated with our model as coalescing around four concerns: it is extremely labor intensive; it requires a significant degree of autonomy; it is dependent on friendly administration (at least initially); and it is tied to enrollment (intentionally). Our model requires a significant up-front and continuing investment in labor dollars. In addition the personnel hired with this investment must possess the diverse skill sets and ambition necessary to fulfill the specific positions we will outline below. Our model requires a writing program that is autonomous in its scheduling of services, in its professional development activities, data gathering and reporting procedures, and in its training of staff and tutors. Though our model could work in a Learning Commons environment, where various student services such as the library, TRiO, Academic Skills Center, and Early Alert are physically cohesive, it would require a great deal of administrative/ procedural autonomy. Even though the QEP process and larger accreditation and funding concerns offer writing programs leverage in negotiations with administration for resources, and even though models like ours add to that leverage, to get such a program going requires significant administrative buy-in early on. While we argue for the power of tying the work of writing programs to enrollment, retention, and persistence, there are obvious risks associated with doing so. Once a writing program ties itself to enrollment, then it is *tied to enrollment*, and while this may empower the program, if enrollment decreases, then the program can become vulnerable.

We articulate these risks prior to the narrative of our model, not as arguments against such a model, but rather as framing devices for thinking through writing programs. Our narrative is a very positive one, an empowered, passionate model for seizing opportunities and realizing possibilities. However, we acknowledge that our model puts WPAs "all in" right from the start, necessitating that the risks of such a move be well-balanced with the rewards and that institutional context and commitment be considered carefully before embarking on such a writing program.

IMPLEMENTING THE QEP
Staff the writing program fully for flexibility, availability, and sustainability

Implementation of an ambitious writing program-focused QEP requires more than one full-time position dedicated to administration of the writing program. We suggest two full-time WPA positions, each with no more than a two-course teaching load per semester. In our model, one WPA's focus is on the writing *center* and the other WPA's focus is on the writing *curriculum*, while both WPAs supervise development and management of the OWL. A consistent presence of one WPA in the writing center is optimal, and having two full-time WPAs allows for that presence as well as the availability of one WPA who can devote a large portion of time to outreach efforts—fostering and maintaining collaborative partnerships, designing professional development for faculty and training for tutors, and attending to curricular needs and changes. These duties require frequent visits to classrooms, flexible availability to instructors and other program administrators across campus, and off-campus visits with WPAs at other schools, local employers, and curriculum superintendents in the local high schools. The two WPAs should share appointments on committees that are central to the work of the writing program, such as the WAC committee, the accreditation committee (SACS committee in our case), the curriculum committee, and the Distance Education committee. Of course the roles and duties of the two WPAs can be blended or divided in a number of ways to meet the needs of the individual institution and the availability of human capital; the key is to have two full-time WPA positions because one cannot effectively maintain a consistent presence in the writing center and manage the outreach work that is vital to the success of a writing program such as the one we describe here.

In addition to the two WPA positions, our writing program employs two mid-level positions as well as professional tutors and peer tutors. The two mid-level positions in our writing program—the OWL manager and lead tutor—represent rich spaces for sustainable development. With the right people in these positions, the two WPAs can (and we argue, *should*) foster development of the individual skill sets of the OWL manager and lead tutor. By doing so, not only are the WPAs practicing sound managerial methods, but they are also increasing the likelihood of sustainability for the writing program. Supporting and encouraging the mid-level positions to develop their skills benefits both the individual employee and the writing program as a whole. It increases employee satisfaction and creates continuity within the writing program.

With two WPAs and two mid-level positions in place, the final area of staffing that needs to be addressed is part-time employees, including a data processor and tutors. Although not many hours per week are needed for data processing, it is a crucial part of organizing a writing program that is tied to the QEP and institutional assessment. Consistency is helpful in this position, and the data processor should have dedicated, uninterrupted time for data entry and data management. We recommend a mixture of professional and student tutors with student tutors shouldering a substantial portion of the tutoring load (International Writing Centers Association 2007). Student tutors are recommended to WPAs by English instructors. Our professional tutors are adjunct English instructors. We conduct weekly training sessions and require professional and peer tutors to attend, which often requires multiple training sessions each week to accommodate all participants' course schedules. This need for flexible scheduling of training is one of the many benefits of having two WPAs.

Establish mutually dependent writing services to create a unified writing program

Central to our model is a unified writing *program* rather than three separate writing-focused *services*. Though the term "codependency" sometimes carries a negative connotation, we view the mutual dependency of writing services as a positive attribute because it is a vital component of program unity, strengthening the sustainability of what could otherwise be viewed as separate, and easily expendable, services. As WPAs, we encourage and facilitate a recursive flow of information among the WC, WAC, and OWL, which then extends exponentially into digital spaces and physical spaces across campus, the local community, and the larger professional community.

A primary example of the interconnected nature of the WC, WAC, and OWL at our institution is the way we repurpose most items created for use in one area of the writing program for use in other areas of the writing program. For example, in addition to participating in face-to-face training sessions, writing center tutors can access training documents at any time on the OWL. Instructors of writing intensive courses can engage in critical inquiry with other instructors through professional development modules on the OWL as a means of extending this community of practice (CoP) beyond the physical professional development sessions held in the writing center and inviting a larger number of faculty (even those who do not teach writing intensive courses) to contribute to discussions of writing pedagogy. WAC resources for students and instructors are available in the writing center and on the OWL, which contains a set of sub-pages devoted to WAC. When a WPA visits a classroom to teach a writing mini-lesson, we capture it on video and post it as a resource for distance learners who use the OWL. Not only does this mutual dependency between the WC, WAC, and OWL help our program grow rapidly, but it also fortifies otherwise discrete and potentially vulnerable writing services by braiding them into a unified writing program, a program large enough and embedded enough in the institutional structure to be a hallmark of institutional effectiveness. Likewise, this triad of writing services (WC, WAC, and OWL) allows the writing program to claim its own identity distinct from other programs on campus. The WC is not viewed as part of the student services or remediation programs. WAC is not considered simply an extension of the English department. The OWL is not tucked under the expanding umbrella of the Distance Education program.

Programatizing writing through the use of the QEP and reaccreditation can afford WPAs an empowered voice and agency, both of which are necessary to achieve the goals of a thriving WC, WAC, and OWL. The writing program can then participate on an equal playing field among the other institutional programs. This equality opens the door for successful collaboration. A delicate balance of empowered voices is a strong factor in collaborative work, and that balance is more likely to tilt unfavorably against individual pieces of the writing program if they are acting as separate services rather than as one united program.

Build collaborative partnerships to grow a writing-focused community culture based on a critical model

A symbiotic relationship is not only important among the parts of the writing program but also between the writing program and other programs. WPAs need to involve their writing programs in both inter-campus and intra-campus (physical and virtual) partnerships. Creating partnerships with individuals and groups not only on the physical campus but also on the virtual campus and beyond the college's physical and virtual campus to other campuses (including universities, other community colleges, the local K–12 schools, and local businesses who are potential employers of our graduates) is beneficial in multiple ways. By continually broadening our scope of relationship building, we have not only reached a wider audience with our services but have also gained new insights on how to better meet our audience's needs and how to do so more efficiently and effectively.

As WPAs of our institution's writing program, we built and continue to maintain intra-campus relationships with the Dean of Student Services, TRiO Student Support Services program (TRIO-SSS), the Early College High School (ECHS), the Learning Resources Center (LRC) and the Distance Learning (DL) program. TRIO-SSS and the ECHS are free programs available to students at our institution and many other community colleges in the nation: "The Federal TRiO Programs (TRIO) are Federal outreach and student services programs designed to identify and provide services for individuals from disadvantaged backgrounds . . . to serve and assist low-income individuals, first-generation college students, and individuals with disabilities to progress through the academic pipeline from middle school to postbaccalaureate programs" (Office of Postsecondary Education 2013). An Early College

High School is physically located on our community college campus and is "designed so that low-income youth, first-generation college goers, English language learners, students of color, and other young people underrepresented in higher education can simultaneously earn a high school diploma and an Associate's degree or up to two years of credit toward a Bachelor's degree—tuition free" (Early College High School Initiative 2013). The Learning Resources Center (LRC) coordinates audio-visual, library, and online resources and maintains the college's content-sharing platform (LibGuides). Our institution's Distance Learning (DL) program uses the Blackboard learning system platform and coordinates all online, hybrid, and web-enhanced course management as well as classes serving students in our most remote service areas via the North Carolina Information Highway using video conferencing.

WPAs work with individual instructors as well as the Dean of Student Services, TRIO-SSS coordinator, and the Special Populations coordinator. Through this triad of collaboration (writing program, TRIO-SSS, and program of study), we keep the student at the center of discussions as we develop informed, targeted strategies to meet the student's needs. We also work closely with the TRIO-SSS coordinator to develop and conduct resume workshops specifically geared to students served by the TRIO-SSS program. We participate in a collaborative partnership among the ECHS on our campus, the English department, and the writing program to vertically align the curriculum and discuss best practices for introducing ECHS students to writing center services and for tutoring ECHS students in writing for their specific courses. The Distance Learning coordinator sets up a special Blackboard course for the WPAs, English lead instructor, and ECHS director to use as a collaborative space.

By far the most fruitful collaborative partnership, in terms of widespread impact, has been the partnership the writing program has with the Distance Learning program and Learning Resource Center (library/media services) because it helps us manage and link our resources, through the use of our OWL, with other campus resources, programs, and services which are all hosted on the LibGuides platform used by our institution. For instance, after discussing with our Special Populations coordinator the needs of visually-impaired students, we were then able to work with the LRC staff to provide transcripts to supplement our video files on the OWL, making them accessible to visually-impaired students who have laptops equipped with text-to-voice software. The collaborative partnership between the writing program and the LRC and DL program has increased the efficiency and impact of all programs involved, allowing each program to reach more students and making resource acquisition easier and more streamlined for students.

In addition, our collaboration with the LRC and DL program helps us reach instructors and create a writing-focused community climate that is based on a critical model in which instructors engage in critical reflection on the ways they use writing in their individual courses. Our OWL contains a self-paced professional development module, space for professional learning communities, assistance in designing writing assignments, advice for instructors who are responding to student writing online, archives of writing assignments and assessment rubrics, and a writing guide that is a resource instructors can share with their online students who need help with specific elements of writing. When instructors invite a WPA to visit their classes to introduce the services offered by the writing center and the OWL or to provide a tailor-made mini-lesson for their class, further relationship building occurs. With the help of the LRC and DL, when a WPA visits classrooms to work with students, those visits are live-streamed through the North Carolina Information Highway to students in off-site locations, and they are digitally recorded and uploaded to the OWL for long-term access.

The OWL also helps us bridge lingering communication gaps between the writing program and some faculty members who have not previously used other writing program services. Instructors who are fairly new to online teaching find themselves in an unfamiliar spot when responding to student writing in an online environment and are more willing seek resources in this scenario than when they feel very confident in a seated classroom. They often turn to the OWL for support, which gives us an "in" to establish relationships and build trust with individual instructors.

We value all opportunities to work with individual instructors for many reasons, one of which is because we support the theory of "writing in the course." WPAs frequently work with individual instructors to discuss how they use writing in their courses, what their goals are for writing assignments, how to design assignments that meet those goals and how to assess the students' writing in a manner that matches well with the goals of the assignment and the objectives of the course. Our work reflects what Christopher Thaiss (2011) asserts is true of most WAC programs: "Even when workshops are conducted within single departments or among smaller units, the preponderance of workshop materials and topics has centered on the individual course, irrespective of discipline" (317). Yet another benefit of the collaborative efforts of the Writing Program, the LRC, and the DL program is that, together, we can archive individual writing courses (including all low-stakes and high-stakes writing assignments and rubrics used in the courses) that are taught online and, with permission of the instructor, use them in part or as a whole for training and professional development sessions.

In addition to helping foster relationships on our own campus, the OWL collaboration with the LRC and DL program has given the writing program a voice that is heard beyond our campus. As WPAs at other schools have seen our OWL, they have contacted us to arrange on-site visits of our writing center or to hold phone and virtual conferences to gather ideas and advice. As such, the OWL serves as an icebreaker of sorts to initiate new inter-campus partnerships. A section of the OWL devoted to the Early College High School students is easily adaptable to meet the needs of other K–12 schools. Through the process of contacting universities to ask permission to link some of their OWL resources to our own OWL, we have made even broader connections.

Any writing program, but especially a community college writing program, also must ensure its collaborative efforts and critical reflection include the voice of the non-academic community: the workplace. Our writing program has plans in place to create data-capturing polls and questionnaires on the OWL to help us determine the types of writing skills and concerns local employers have in regards to the graduates of our college who are their potential future employees. In this and other ways previously mentioned, the OWL acts much like a "passive income" source, building relationships and collecting data for us while we are working on other connections, such as engaging in professional organizations and meeting with representatives of the local university and the National Writing Project; therefore, the collaboration between the writing program, the LRC, and the DL program to create, maintain, and grow the OWL is the writing program's most significant collaborative partnership to date.

In our case, the QEP sets the table for a writing program based not on a missionary model, where the WPAs are on a mission to construct the writing standards, objectives, and assessments for the institution, but on a critical model like Donna LeCourt (1996) supports: a writing program that initiates "both pedagogical and theoretical change [because] if change is not included as part of [our] work, we effectively silence ourselves as much as the missionary model silences our colleagues" (403). One benefit of a critical model is that it increases buy-in. Faculty, administrative, and community buy-in takes time and is important, but it alone will not ensure sustainability. In the efforts to achieve sustainability, anecdotal evidence from faculty members who have witnessed the growth of their students' writing abilities is powerful, yet qualitative *and* quantitative proof of the writing program's effectiveness are necessary. Quantitative data must come not from the writing center alone but also from writing intensive (WI) courses, the OWL, English courses, and various programs with which the writing program has collaborated. To capture that type of data, the writing program needs not only support and goodwill but also collaborative contributions of fellow professionals and programs within and outside the college. For this reason, we stress devoting an equal amount of time and human capital in outreach and collaboration prior to and during data collection.

Designate the writing center as the hub of writing program assessment, and integrate writing program assessment into broader institutional goals

Without a doubt the most effective way a writing program can make the case for itself and its future is through clearly demonstrating and articulating its impact on students and the institution. In the current climate that can best be done through what is broadly defined as assessment. In our case, assessment of the writing program was mandated through the QEP process, but sustainability of the writing program can only be achieved through integrating that assessment into as many areas and levels of the institution as possible. To achieve the overall integration of our writing program assessment, we designed an assessment plan that unified what students were doing in the writing center with what students and instructors were doing in the classroom, and the demographic, course of study, and progress toward completion data that the college already maintains for every student.

In order to demonstrate what students are doing in the writing center, we did what writing center directors have been doing for decades: track frequency of student visits, the courses they seek assistance with, their instructor, and so forth. We use *Accutrak* to maintain these records. In order to demonstrate what students and faculty are doing in their courses, WI course instructors and WPAs collectively identified seven writing outcomes for writing-intensive courses: (1) Students will develop their ideas in writing; (2) Students will use paragraphing to organize their writing; (3) Students will develop and use an appropriate voice in their writing; (4) Students will develop and use an effective vocabulary; (5) Students will use and cite research effectively; (6) Students will develop and use effective sentence fluency; (7) Students will demonstrate correct use of conventions. Each of these outcomes is used to assess student writing across the curriculum, but individual instructors retain the flexibility to write course-specific descriptors for each of the outcomes. In consultation with faculty, we developed rubrics assessing the writing outcomes appropriate for particular writing assignments. Every student enrolled in a writing intensive course writes at least one and as many as five writing assignments in that course, and those assignments are assessed using the common writing objectives and the individual objective descriptors to allow for flexibility. The writing center collects scored essays and rubrics throughout each semester and enters the data into a basic spreadsheet organized by an ID number assigned to each student.

We partnered with Institutional Effectiveness to create a dashboard in Excel that enables us to combine the data collected in the writing center and WI courses with the demographic and academic information maintained by the college. For example, we study the correlation between student performance in the first semester of FYC and the second to streamline the vertical alignment of our curriculum; the correlation between student performance in FYC and in later WI courses to see how well our composition courses prepare students for writing in college; and the relationship between particular writing assignments in individual courses and student success in those courses. We also examine the relationship between particular writing outcomes (development, organization, conventions, etc.) and student performance on individual writing assignments and the relationship between writing center visits and student success. Our Excel dashboard allows us to filter these queries by race, age, gender, veteran status, financial aid status, family educational history, instruction platform (i.e., online, hybrid, evening, traditional), instructor, and program of study.

Being a small college, we have yet to accumulate a large enough sample size at the individual course level to draw statistically reliable conclusions; however, trends are emerging that offer encouraging indications of the success of our FYC sequence and the writing center on student performance of college writing tasks more broadly. Moreover, we do have a substantial sample size (over 1700 artifacts of scored student writing) across the entire writing program to begin to establish relationships between certain variables. For example, of our seven writing outcomes, three (development, organization, and conventions) demonstrate a relationship[1] with the final grade on a particular assignment. In other words, development, organization, and conventions are the measures that faculty most heavily use to determine student success with their writing. We have also established a relationship between writing center attendance and student pass rates in writing intensive courses. We are excitedly looking forward to the next 18–24 months when we will have amassed large enough samples to examine these relationships at the level of individual courses.

These results are encouraging and enable us to make a case with administrators for the need for more resources to staff the writing center, to offer professional development sessions for the faculty, and to develop instructional resources. In addition, these results will allow us to make a successful impact report to SACS at the completion of the QEP's five-year cycle. However, we also know that the end of the QEP cycle leaves the writing program vulnerable. In order to solidify the writing program's institutional position, we need to make our data work beyond simply our own program. We seek to render the writing program essential on as many fronts as possible. To that end we have incorporated our writing program assessment into course, program, and institutional assessments. Our goal is to continue enriching student writing beyond the writing center and classroom by leading the college's assessment of student performance, the development of curriculum in regards to writing, and the collaboration among faculty in the instruction of writing based on a critical model. At the same time, we entrench the writing program in the college's culture and workflow.

At the course level, our WAC program consists of writing intensive courses (at least one in every degree program the college offers). Within each WI course we identified at least one and as many as five high-stakes writing assignments. Each of the WI courses already had a writing component in the student learning outcomes; hence, as we collect scored essays and compile data for our WAC program, we simultaneously generate data that we can give back to faculty, lead instructors, and department heads that assists them in assessing student learning outcomes for their courses.

This recursive relationship wherein faculty both generate data for assessment of the writing program and receive data from the writing program to aid them in Student Learning Outcomes (SLO) assessment is crucial beyond just the data generated. This relationship contributes to the ever elusive "faculty buy-in," as we are able to offer faculty a tangible return (in terms of labor) on their WAC efforts. In addition, this recursive relationship between faculty and the WAC program positions the WPAs as campus leaders in the area of assessment, and the critical model keeps WPAs from being "the authority" on "good writing." In our case, the writing center, which houses and manages the WAC data, (in addition to WC data and OWL data), has become a center of institution-wide writing assessment which, as a result of the QEP, is a large part of institutional assessment at our particular college. Most important, once other departments rely on the writing program to provide critical data necessary for assessing their own courses and programs and for meeting their institutional obligations, then the writing program ceases to be merely a service offered to some students and faculty largely on a volunteer basis and becomes an integral part of the faculty's own work.

The writing program has been integrated into Student Services, Distance Learning, and the English curriculum. The writing center was added to three accreditation standards pertaining to Student Services: "Learning Resources and Services," "Continuing Education/Service Programs," and "Academic Support Services." Consequently, the writing center has become embedded in the compliance narrative the college submits for each of these standards. Again, the writing center, and by extension the writing program, ceases to be an appendage and becomes a component of how Student Services demonstrates its compliance with reaccreditation standards.

Our integration into Distance Learning happens largely through our OWL and virtual tutoring services. We have an asynchronous email tutoring element to our writing center which helps DL serve its students and helps them with their reaccreditation requirements. The SACS/COC "Distance and Correspondence Education Policy Statement" (2012b) requires institutions to provide "[a]cademic support services [that] are appropriate and specifically related to distance and correspondence education" (3). In addition, "the institution [must] regularly assess the effectiveness of its provision of library/learning resources and student support services for distance or correspondence education students" (Southern Association on Colleges and Schools Commission on Colleges 2012a, 3). Hence, both in our distance tutoring and in the data we collect on that work, we offer DL a component of their compliance report.

Through our close partnership with the English department, we integrated the assessment of all composition courses with the assessment of the writing program. This confluence has had many positive and strengthening ramifications for both the writing program and the English department: the writing program becomes increasingly identified campus-wide as the center for writing assessment; we provide a valuable service for the English department which also grants us a significant voice in their writing curriculum and assessment practices; and, since composition is the largest curriculum on campus, conflating the assessment data with that of the writing program puts us in direct contact with institutional effectiveness and broader campus assessment obligations.

At the institutional level, we have integrated the writing program with both the externally mandated program review and the review of general educational competencies.[2] For both standards, course level data is required in order to demonstrate compliance. The office of Institutional Effectiveness draws from the dashboard that they created for us to pull course level data from our WI courses for use in the college's compliance report. This integration is incredibly important as the broad instructional compliance standards represent perhaps the most challenging component of reaccreditation. Having our work become part of the college's largest assessment further solidifies our place as not simply a service but a crucial institutional program.

Tie the writing program to retention and completion rates

We looked ahead to the coming funding model based on student completion and worked with Institutional Effectiveness to study the effects of the writing program on student retention, persistence, and completion. The IE office established criteria for student retention, persistence, and completion by examining a variety of contributing factors: financial aid status, demographics, educational background, program of study, and so forth. Once the IE study was complete, we would be able to analyze student use of the writing center and OWL and success in WI courses within the demographic context of our students, allowing us to focus on various at-risk and underserved groups. It is a relatively simple matter (given the dashboard we have in place) to compare students who have been using the writing center and who have taken WI courses with the general population of students. Initial data comparing students who use the writing center head-to-head with students who do not showed that students who use the center are 12 percent more likely to complete the course for which they visited. We did not simply compare students who pass the course with those who fail; our comparison examined students who receive passing grades with those who fail, withdraw, or are dropped. Hence, our writing center not only increased student success but also persistence. When we filtered these results by WI courses, the rate increased to 14 percent. When we filtered the results by students who have visited the center three or more times, the rate jumped again to 19 percent. While these results affirmed the work our writing center and program have done, they also speak directly to the future of writing programs in general.

CONCLUSION

Since this chapter/book project began, our lives have moved in different directions, taking us both away from the community college QEP project we have reported on here. Though we did not see the final leg of our critical model come to fruition at that particular institution, we believe in the model, continue to work to see it embraced at other colleges, and hope to inspire readers who have the desire, the means, and a supportive institutional philosophy to employ the "all-in" critical model as they establish their own writing programs. What we continue to take away from the experience of implementing such a large-scale assessment is how important it is to develop sustainable, highly networked projects, especially where writing assessment is concerned. The five key points above each articulate why a networked approach, one which engages various stakeholders across multiple nodes of connection, establishes a project that can survive one of the ultimate realities of college life: the somewhat constant turnover among individual WPAs, writing center directors, and other types of administrators. At a moment when our accrediting agencies have mandated long-term, large-scale assessment projects, writing studies has the opportunity to develop such sustainable projects. We are eager to see how projects, like the one we reported on and the others explored in this collection, may transform and strengthen writing programs in higher education.

Notes

1. Here we use a Pearson Correlation Coefficient wherein 0.5 and higher indicates a relationship.
2. We are referring to SACS standards 3.3.1.1. and 3.5.1, but other accreditation agencies have similar broad instructional standards.

References

Altstadt, David, ed. 2012. "Tying Funding to Community College Outcomes: Models, Tools, and Recommendations for States." *Jobs for the Future.* Accessed February 12, 2013.

Bean, John, David Carrithers, and Theresa Earenfight. 2005. "Transforming WAC through a Discourse-Based Approach to University Outcomes Assessment." *WAC Journal* 16:5–21.

Bell, Diana Calhoun, and Alanna Frost. 2012. "Critical Inquiry and Writing Centers: A Methodology of Assessment." *Learning Assistance Review* 17 (1): 15–26.

Bell, James. 2000. "When Hard Questions are Asked: Evaluating Writing Centers." *Writing Center Journal* 21 (1): 7–28.

Condon, William, and Carol Rutz. 2012. "A Taxonomy of Writing across the Curriculum Programs: Evolving to Serve Broader Agendas." *College Composition and Communication* 64 (2): 7–28.

Early College High School Initiative. 2013. Accessed August 8, 2013. http://www.early colleges.org/overview.html.

Gardner, Phillip J., and William Ramsey. 2005. "The Polyvalent Mission of Writing Centers." *Writing Center Journal* 25 (1): 43–60.

Harris, Muriel. 2002. "Preparing to Sit at the Head Table: Maintaining Writing Center Viability in the Twenty-First Century." *Writing Center Journal* 20 (2): 13–21.

International Writing Centers Association. 2007. "Position Statement on Two Year College Writing Centers." Accessed August 19, 2013. http://writingcenters.org/wp -content/uploads/2008/06/twoyearpositionstatement1.pdf.

LeCourt, Donna. 1996. "WAC as Critical Pedagogy: The Third Stage?" *Journal of Advanced Composition* 16:389–405.

Lerner, Neal. 2003. "Writing Center Assessment: Searching for the 'Proof' of Our Effectiveness." In *The Center Will Hold: Critical Perspectives on Writing Center Scholarship*, ed. Michael A. Pemberton and Joyce Kinkead, 58–73. Logan: Utah State University Press.

Nagin, Carl, and the The National Writing Project. 2006. *Because Writing Matters*. San Francisco: Jossey-Bass.

Office of Postsecondary Education. 2013. Accessed August 8, 2013. http://www2.ed.gov /about/offices/list/ope/trio/index.html.

Russell, David. 1991. *Writing in the Academic Disciplines, 1870–1990: A Curricular History*. Carbondale: Southern Illinois U.P.

Southern Association of Colleges and Schools Commission on Colleges. "Distance and Correspondence Education: Policy Statement." 2012a. Accessed Feb 3, 2012.

Southern Association of Colleges and Schools Commission on Colleges. 2012b. "Principles of Accreditation." Accessed Jan 1, 2012.

Thaiss, Christopher. 2011. "Theory in WAC: Where Have We Been, Where Are We Going?" In *WAC for the New Millennium: Strategies for Continuing Writing Across the Curriculum Programs*, ed. Susan H. McLeod, Eric Miraglia, Margot Soven, and Christopher Thaiss, 299–325. Urbana, IL: National Council of Teachers of English.

Thompson, Isabella. 2006. "Writing Center Assessment: Why and a Little How." *Writing Center Journal* 26 (1): 33–57.

Welch, Kristen, and Susan Revels-Parker. 2012. ""Writing Center Assessment: An Argument for Change." *Praxis*." *Writing Center Journal* 10 (1). Accessed March 24, 2013.

Zawacki, Terry Myers, and Karen M. Gentemann. 2009. "Merging a Culture of Writing with a Culture of Assessment: Embedded, Discipline-Based Writing Assessment." In *Assessment in Writing*, ed. Marie C. Paretti and Katrina Powell, 49–64. Tallahassee: Association of Institutional Research.

5
MOVING FORWARD
What General Studies Assessment Taught Us about
Writing, Instruction, and Student Learning

Jessica Parker and Jane Chapman Vigil

What follows is our journey into assessment at Metropolitan State University of Denver. When our assessment project began, Jane served as the Director of the First Year Writing Program and Jessica was a lecturer in the department. Now Jessica coordinates the writing program and is in her third year of a tenure track position. Jane spent two years as English Department assistant chair and Senior Faculty Associate for Program Assessment at the university and then served as Interim Director for the Center for Faculty Development at MSU-Denver. Our stories are separate yet intertwined as we came from different perspectives and different backgrounds. In the end, our stories blend and our projects merge to strengthen and unify our First-Year Writing program.

GETTING STARTED WITH WRITING ASSESSMENT

Keeling, Underhile, Wall, and Dungy (2008) in *Assessment Reconsidered* write, "[a]ssessment in higher education primarily responds to two forces: external demands for accountability and internal commitments to improvement" (1). While Jessica and I would like to think that our work at Metropolitan State University of Denver[1] revolves around that internal commitment—the idea that what we do is for the betterment of our students—sometimes it is that external demand that pushes us in the right direction, getting us started on a strong and purposeful look at student learning. For two decades our institution circumvented significant revision to our general studies program, including meaningful assessment. However, following a 2007 Higher Learning Commission (HLC) reaccreditation visit, the institution pushed forward and created a new general studies program with student learning outcomes (SLO) and a partial assessment plan.

DOI: 10.7330/9781607324355.c005

Many academics are wary of assessment, and who can blame them in the educational culture where high-stakes testing is tied to teacher performance and monies. But we see assessment as a good thing—a way to make our writing program better, more competitive with the other state schools, more recognized for the hard work we do on our own campus. Of course, writing assessment can easily be morphed into something cumbersome and threatening, so it is important that those in charge look at the purpose and intent of assessment and not just respond to the demands of administration or outside accreditation.

In July 2008, the department chair called Jane to her office to inform her that the department had "volunteered for assessment." The chair had attended a meeting with program directors and chairs from various general studies program and the newly hired director of Assessment, Dr. Sheila Thompson (a totally new position for the institution), where a call for volunteers to do some assessment met with such a resounding silence in the room that it made the English department chair anxious and she volunteered when no one else stepped up. The timing, though, was ideal to initiate some subtle and some not so subtle changes to our two-semester freshman writing sequence. We embraced the opportunity. In Jane's first year as the writing program administrator (WPA), she quickly discovered that there were things that needed to be changed: curriculum, classroom practices, and student placement, to name a few. Through conversations with instructors, visits to classes, and student complaints she realized there was an inequality in the education students were receiving and there was a frustration on the part of instructors about what they should be teaching. However, there were not numbers or evidence or anything concrete, just a gut feeling.

Jane met with the assessment director within the next week, taking notes and putting on a serious "I know what you're talking about" face and nodding at all the right times as the two explored past assessment practices (none), current needs, and future hopes. The assessment director presented different approaches and options to get the writing program started and involved with program assessment. It was more than overwhelming at first. We didn't know what outcomes or direct measures or sample size meant, but we trusted that this could potentially make learning better for our students. From initial conversations and some quick reading, Jane took the ideas to the composition committee and presented four basic principles about how to approach assessment and improve student learning in a university writing program:

1. Create measurable student learning outcomes reflective of our program and goals.

2. Provide authentic learning opportunities for students to demonstrate abilities.

3. Collect artifacts from students and assess them on a regular basis using consistent tools.

4. Look at the results to inform decisions about curriculum, learning outcomes, and the assessment process. Curriculum decisions should be, in part, based on what we learn from students and not just creating a course that we think would be great to teach.

While the university may have neglected general studies for two decades, it was probably closer to three decades since our writing curriculum had undergone any significant revision and tackled the sticky problems related to required courses, advancements in the field, and a changing student body. Linda Suskie (2009), in her common sense guide *Assessing Student Learning,* points out that "Assessment brings neglected issues to the forefront . . . [O]utdated general education curricula . . . a fragmented and incoherent curriculum, or outmoded pedagogies. Launching an assessment effort often requires addressing issues that probably should have been tackled long ago. Some people find that assessment processes are even more useful than their products: these initial conversations and work yield greater benefits than the eventual assessment results" (59–60). That's what we discovered—ENG 1010 (Composition I) and ENG 1020 (Composition II) courses that were interchangeable, student behavioral learning objectives that were obsolete, teachers struggling to figure out what they were supposed to teach and why they were teaching it, and students struggling to understand why they had to take two courses and what they were really supposed to be learning. After the first few months of inquiry, the purpose of the assessment became clear: "to improve curricula and pedagogies to bring about even greater learning" (Suskie 2009, 59). It's all about the students—not the Higher Learning Commission, not the Provost or the Board of Trustees, and not even the department chair. From the beginning we have stressed to faculty and students that this is about student learning on a program level.

Mary J. Allen (2006), in *Assessing General Education Programs,* agrees that as educational pedagogies and methodologies shift from a teaching focus to a learning focus, a stronger need for assessment arises. She states, "[t]his change naturally leads to the question: did students learn what we wanted them to learn? Assessment helps us identify what is working well and what needs attention, and we make adjustments when we are disappointed with results" (1–2). What were our students learning? Anything? The right stuff? Different stuff? We both admit that we started second-guessing our own teaching and wondered if we had helped or harmed writing students for the past decade plus. In our own classes we focused attention on what we were teaching and how students responded. It didn't take long to see the gaps in our own instructional practices.

Our initial goal, after meeting with the composition committee, was to determine whether students, upon completing ENG 1010 and ENG 1020, learned the basic skills the syllabus said we would teach and what we were telling the university we were teaching. For example, in 2008, the following were the Student Behavior Learning Objectives for ENG 1010 and ENG 1020. They are basic and straight forward and probably mirror many other writing program outcomes. However, just because the outcomes were listed on an official paper doesn't mean they went anywhere nor does it mean instructors knew what to do with them. Maybe things were fine, but all we had were course grades and anecdotal evidence to show us about learning, and neither was very helpful.

DATA COLLECTION METHODOLOGY

As we gathered information and ideas for the assessment, we relied heavily on Suskie's (2009) four characteristics of useful assessments, or the "must haves":

- We needed honest data—even if that data wasn't sparkling and pretty—so that we could use the results with "confidence to make plans and decisions" (Suskie 2009, 37). We did not want instructors to fix papers or hide flaws in an attempt to make them look better or students smarter. We weren't looking at individual instructors or individual students. We needed actual writing.
- We needed an action plan for the results—no point in letting the numbers sit lost and forgotten in the back file room.
- We made connections with the faculty, including part-time instructors, lecturers, and tenure-track and tenured members of the department, and let everyone know what was happening—no surprises. This included the emphasis on program-level assessment and the need for honest data.
- We gathered information important to the students and to the institution and did not spend time gathering unneeded data (Suskie 2009, 37). In other words, the rubric we created reflected what members of the composition committee felt were significant for student learning at this level.

Table 5.1. Composition SLOs

English 1010	English 1020
1. Use the writing process to compose formal, academic essays by working through pre-writing, drafting, revision, and final editing.	1. Use an academic library and electronic research methods to find a variety of credible sources.
2. Generate writing in a variety of forms.	2. Evaluate the reliability of sources in light of scholarly and disciplinary expectations.
3. Use writing as a tool for acquiring knowledge across the curriculum.	3. Identify different types of primary and secondary research sources.
4. Recognize the critical relationship between a text's purpose and its intended audience.	4. Recognize and analyze argumentative methods in sources and use these methods in their own writing.
5. Recognize, analyze, and clarify the thesis in various texts.	5. Synthesize sources and their own analysis into a coherent and well organized argumentative essay.
6. Support and develop thesis statements through strong supporting detail.	6. Use statistics, judgments, primary research, or authoritative inferences to support reasoning.
7. Critically read, summarize, engage, evaluate, and analyze academic texts.	7. Write a disciplined-based argumentative paper addressed to an intelligent general reader.
8. Produce prose characterized by clear sentence structure, clear diction, and control of mechanics in appropriate Standard English.	8. Meticulously quote, paraphrase, summarize, and document sources to avoid plagiarism.
	9. Correctly use MLA and APA in-text and bibliographic citation styles.

For the initial assessment procedure, the director of Assessment randomly selected 20 sections to participate in the assessment, giving us an adequate sample size for our enrollment. The sections were selected to make sure all populations of students were assessed—online, evening, and traditional daytime classes. The sample size, based on a 95 percent confidence rate, also allowed for our 35 percent attrition rate in face-to-face classes and our 49 percent attrition rate in online classes and gave us a bit of wiggle room in meeting our n. In addition, we felt it important for the director of Assessment to randomly select the 20 sections in order to avoid any appearance of showing negative favoritism. At the end of the term, students submitted two copies of their final researched essay to their instructor. The second copy was given to the Assessment Office where names, sections numbers, and students ID's were deleted. Duplicate copies were made and returned to the English office. In 2012, the University started using Blackboard Outcomes to collect data. At that time the English department had all sections participate with students uploading their own artifacts, and a random sampling is now drawn from the overall student population.

During the first assessment semester, several English faculty from the composition committee met and worked on a scoring rubric for assessment purposes based on our syllabus expectations and some loosely defined general studies learning outcomes. Raters participated in an intense norming session for four hours and worked closely with their partner reader throughout the scoring process. We asked that partners check with each other after every 10 papers and recalibrate when necessary. If scores differed by more than a one point value or if one rater had a score from the top half and the other rater had a score from the bottom half, a third reader read the paper. With this rigorous norming approach, issues such as standard deviations didn't appear. Since the rubric is a four-point scale, we looked at scores of one and two as bottom half and three and four as top half. In the assessments run by the department, we matched English faculty with faculty outside the department, and we received financial support from administration to pay readers. Each artifact had two raters, one from the program and one from outside the program. Raters would be trained and paid.

When the data came back at the end of the semester, we were not surprised by the numbers. We have been teaching composition at MSU-Denver since 1996, and we are aware where our students struggle most. Based on a four-point rubric, student averages were:

Table 5.2. Eng 1020 Results

ENG 1020 Assessment Rubric Element	May 2009 Average
Thesis	2.56
Support	2.48
Sources and Quotes	2.41
Audience Awareness	2.53

The following year we duplicated the process using ENG 1010, and the averages were:

Table 5.3. Eng 1010 Results

ENG 1010 Assessment Rubric Element	May 2010 Average
Thesis/Focus	3.01
Organization	2.84
Support and Reasoning	2.68
Audience Awareness	2.70
Style/Mechanics	2.87

Overall, the numbers meant little, but they gave us a base-line, or a starting point, to measure learning. We recognized the limitations of the data, specifically that we had no trend data and that there were inherent problems with the rubric through the first cycle. The two of us did not see the results as overly disappointing or negative or that our students had unsatisfactory writing skills. However, this was not true of the department as a whole. When the data chart shown earlier was presented at a department meeting, there was significant anger. In fact, one rater from the English department said in the meeting that if he had known the numbers were to be divided by top half and bottom half, he would have given more top half numbers. Whereas we looked at the data for ways to improve the program, other faculty looked at the numbers as a reflection of failure on their parts. Some members of the department were shocked and wanted to keep the numbers quiet because they did not show strong averages. Unfortunately, this is a side effect of poorly understood assessment.

Despite the negative reaction from full-time faculty, we moved forward. What we saw was a befuddled curriculum where report writing trumped argument writing, research skills were haphazardly strewn through two semesters, and narrative was emphasized at the cost of other important writing strategies and skills. As Linda Suskie (2009) said, our program needed some serious conversations to look at our curriculum, the support we gave instructors, and the expectations we had for our students at the end of 15 weeks.

REVISION BASED ON WHAT WE LEARNED: MAYHEM AND THINGS THAT MATTER MOST

The most important thing we learned in our initial assessment attempt is that the rubric matters, and we did not get it right the first time. As we designed the initial rubric, we really felt it effectively covered what we wanted students to have learned by the end of the class. But when those who helped create the rubric actually used it as readers, it was evident there were problems. For example, the categories we established did not always work. We had "being able to cite properly in MLA or APA style" and "being able to integrate sources well" as a single category, but students often have one skill and lack the other, which made assigning a score in the area difficult. If we view assessment as simply something required by the Higher Learning Commission (HLC) or the university administration, this might not seem that important since it still produces data. However, since our project was to find practical ways to apply what we had learned from the assessment to improve our program, this data wasn't nearly enough. In our first attempt we learned as much about the rubric and assessment as we did about our students' skills. Because we learned we needed to revise the rubric, we got a second chance to look at the program as well. Were our program goals clear? Were they actually things we could measure or items we really wanted to measure? As teachers, were we teaching the skills we asked students to demonstrate in the assessment artifact (the unfortunate answer to that was we weren't always)? We had to question ourselves: were we teaching or assigning? Could more class time be spent with guided practice? The rubric (see appendix 5.A) itself provided a way for us to talk to our colleagues about what we valued and to clarify what the program should be and do. In fact, an initial conversation, greatly welcomed by our part-time faculty who teach 90 percent of our writing courses, focused on how much time is spent teaching documentation versus source integration.

Through our initial assessment, we also learned how strongly different readers value different things. We certainly were aware of this in a vague sort of way before the assessment project, but the norming and assessment scoring with a partner highlighted how rarely professors have discussions about what constitutes good writing with colleagues inside their department and, even more rarely, with colleagues from other departments on campus. In the norming sessions, the emphasis some professors placed on stylistic and usage concerns became exceedingly clear. Differences in prescriptive and rhetorical approaches to grammar were highlighted. While some had good experiences with the partners they were paired with (one English faculty and one Chemistry faculty worked well together several times), it was quickly clear that what we saw as good often differed from what the other partner valued. We set this up so partners could discuss areas of disagreement and usually come to some kind of negotiated agreement, but in the reader trainings it was clear that those differences in opinions and values were real and potentially problematic.

These differences then had to become the basis for conversations about what "good" writing means so we could come to some agreement about what we were actually seeking (e.g., does a thesis have to be in the first paragraph?). Sometimes these areas of disagreement were about values we hadn't clearly articulated before, even to ourselves. This heightened awareness of differing values was a great basis for ongoing conversations with our instructors in the department and with colleagues from the university as a whole. It informed our participation in the creation of university-wide rubrics for our General Studies program adopted in the 2013–2014 academic year. We have no writing across the curriculum (WAC) program on campus, but writing is required in eight of the nine general studies categories. It also helps us examine whether our choices (both personal and at the program level)—in the syllabus, in the classroom, in our assignments—have the pedagogical implications we want them to have. In our view, and as alluded to earlier, these conversations and the changes and new ideas that they can generate, are more important than any assessment numbers themselves.

FACULTY BUY-IN TO CHANGES SPARKED BY ASSESSMENT AND COLLABORATION

For some faculty, assessment is scary. They may assume assessment will be used to judge their teaching or their students rather than the program itself. Others are skeptical of the value large-scale assessment will have for teachers, students, or the program as a whole. Still others see it as a vehicle for the imposition of top-down decrees that will inhibit their own academic freedom or pedagogical choices and style. For faculty to buy-in to the changes wrought by assessment and to collaborate in making the assessments and the program better, these fears have to be acknowledged and effectively addressed. For Jessica, that meant starting by acknowledging her own positions on assessment. This is where, at first, there was a clear-cut difference in the purpose and value of assessment. Jessica entered into the first assessment as an assessment skeptic. She was not afraid that assessment was a plot to get rid of people, but she was skeptical that much of anything would come of the assessment project. She had been in higher education long enough to know that ideas, especially those that require resources to be effectively implemented, can come and go quite rapidly. She also wasn't sure that anything would happen after the assessment was done. Despite her skepticism, she volunteered to be on the committee that would design the rubric and also to be a reader during the assessment itself. And why she volunteered showed another side: self-interest. She genuinely wanted our program to be the best it could be, but she volunteered so that if changes were to be made to the classes based on assessment results, she wanted a seat at the table since at that point she taught a lot of composition classes—three per term. If the changes that she doubted would happen did materialize, she wanted to have a hand in shaping those changes.

And so her educational journey in assessment and her conversion to being a supporter of assessment began. Ultimately, she bought into assessment because she learned to be a better teacher. Even if nothing had happened at the program level beyond our initial assessment, she had seen ways that her own classes could be improved. The issues that she saw while grading her own students' papers were the issues she also saw in the papers from other sections that she assessed. There was something about seeing those issues (for instance, inability to integrate sources effectively; dangling, strange, or out of context quotations; weak arguments) in papers that she had no connection to that made her re-think how she taught those skills in her own classes. The distance truly gave her perspective. If she wanted students to integrate sources more effectively, she had to devote more time and energy to that skill in class and in homework assignments. If she wanted her students to be able to summarize instead of quote where it would be more effective, she had to not only teach how to write a summary but *why* summarized evidence is useful. Assessment helped her identify what needed to change in her own teaching and gave her real reason to implement those changes.

For her, the instructional changes started in her own classroom. She rearranged course content to more strongly and frequently empha-size argument. She created some new assignments that focused on the analysis of arguments in what the students read and how they could apply those lessons in their own writing. She started explicitly teaching why we might want to quote or paraphrase or summarize and how to connect sources to each other and to students' own ideas. She adapted her research report assignments to give students opportunities to prac-tice these skills and get feedback long before they were trying to draft the essay itself. And she saw encouraging results. Her students started to use summary and paraphrase more often; they used fewer quotes, espe-cially long ones. When they did quote, it was more effective.

But in a large program like ours (150–160 composition sections taught each semester by roughly 60 part-time faculty, five lecturer posi-tions, and five to ten tenure-track faculty), not everyone can be involved in assessment and have these experiences for themselves. So how can we get those faculty members who will not be directly involved in the assessment through designing rubrics or assessing artifacts to believe in the value of the assessments, to not fear what might happen? In a large program, the writing program administrator (WPA) acts as a bridge between the assessment process and the data it produces and the faculty who actually teach the courses.

The WPA's role in getting buy-in from faculty relies on seeing support of the faculty in applying the results as the central concern. Supporting instructors involves first demystifying assessment: making clear no one gets fired based simply on poor assessment results; making sure faculty understand the assessment is a method of evaluating the program, not teachers or students; explaining how the assessment results will be used and how those results are reported (in our cases, average scores for the rubric categories with no breakdown by instructor). The WPA must provide opportunities for faculty to enhance their own pedagogy and respect the expertise they already have. For instance, one of our general studies SLOs involves appropriate use of technology, an area many of our faculty members are uncomfortable with. Because we will have to assess how our program is addressing this SLO, we have to provide tech support for our faculty as we move forward. Making this support available helps assuage fears about assessment and increases faculty willingness to engage in program changes based on assessment results.

Because support is the central concern, practical applications of what we learn from assessment are the most important (even when the data itself is interesting or when the faculty largely don't find the data interesting). As we make curricular improvements through aligning what we want to happen with things like the master syllabi for our composition classes, explicit support for instructors helps in creating cohesion across sections. Effectively communicating what we want instructors to do based on the assessment results (without removing autonomy— just setting parameters for each composition class) generates buy-in. Ultimately, the vast majority of our faculty want to be better teachers; they want to help our students become the most effective writers they can be. By tying assessment results to practical applications we can effectively support both teachers and students by helping all of us know both what we do well and where we can stand to make some progress.

THE PRACTICAL APPLICATIONS AND LINGERING QUESTIONS

Several concrete changes have grown out of our assessments, even though some are about areas the assessment itself didn't really address:

- Workshops for composition faculty
- Syllabus and assignment audits
- A composition resource page
- Full-day syllabus workshops.

Our workshops for composition faculty address areas the assessments have shown the program could do better. We require our part-time faculty to attend at least one workshop each semester, and the goal of each workshop is to provide a practical take- away, whether that is a class activity faculty can use, a new approach to syllabus design, or a best practice.

For example, because our first assessment had identified source use as one of the weak areas for our students, Jessica took what she had learned from the changes she made in her own classroom and, with a colleague, developed a workshop about quotation integration. In the workshop we had a great conversation with colleagues who attended around the idea of source integration and where to focus class instruction for more guided practice. We shared ideas and frustrations. And we all left with ideas of changes we could make, with different ways to think about some of these issues, and also with knowing we were not alone in struggling to help our students develop these skills. The sense that faculty are in this together—especially in our struggles—is one of the most important ways the workshops help create faculty buy-in. We have both been part-time faculty and know from experience that it can be an isolating experience; many of our part-time faculty teach nights or weekends or at our two satellite campus locations and rarely see other faculty members. Prior to these workshops, our part-time faculty had few opportunities to meet their colleagues and discuss their teaching, and so had few ways of knowing whether what they were doing was similar to or very different from what was happening in their colleagues' classrooms. The workshops help foster a sense of community and of buy-in to the program, its goals and structure, and the usefulness of assessment. Of course, it's important to note that very few full-time faculty attend the workshops.

The department offers these workshops each semester now, usually nine or ten per term. We have each given several and attended most. We always come away with something we can use in class, new questions to think about, and a stronger sense of community. These make us better teachers and make our program a better program. We also now have part-time faculty lead some of the workshops each semester; this provides an opportunity for them to share their experience and expertise and shows how we, personally, and the institution as a whole, value their labor, their skill, and their commitment to our students.

In addition to the professional development workshops, we also instituted syllabus and assignment audits in order to more fully understand what we are doing well in the program and to identify where faculty and the program need more support. These audits also allowed us to see how cohesive the program is and how much curriculum drift has occurred in such a large program. Another useful aspect of our syllabus audits is that they allowed us to gather information from our instructors about how they meet our departmental and General Studies SLOs. In Spring 2011 we gathered syllabi and assignments, along with an SLO matrix, from every affiliate instructor teaching composition. The SLO matrix listed the SLOs and asked instructors to identify class activities they use to help students build those skills and what major assignment(s) they use to assess those skills. This matrix was not only informative for us as the program administrators, but for the instructors as well. It allowed them to truly look at the alignment of what they were already doing in their classes and how that related to department goals and our new General Studies outcomes. It allowed us a way to see their expertise in action and to identify patterns—for instance, a struggle in teaching logical fallacies—that we could use both in interpreting the assessment data we had and in planning new ways to support the faculty. We read them all and learned a lot (far more, in our opinion, than we can learn from the observation of a single class meeting) about what is happening in our composition classrooms. We gathered this information again in Fall 2011 for ENG 1010, our first course in the sequence. Reading syllabi and looking at assignment examples and how instructors see those assignments as meeting SLOs allows us to see where the program as a whole is in alignment with the SLOs and with what we think we are doing. Because of this information, we are able to choose workshop topics to effectively address areas where we are not in alignment. Perhaps most important, the information we gathered through the syllabus workshops informed our revision of the master syllabus for ENG 1010 to reflect the emphasis on argument that we want the course to have. While the sixty-plus affiliate faculty members in the department were not on the revision committee, their work informed it, especially since we found that there were significant areas of agreement in the approaches to teaching the course. These audits also highlighted areas where faculty themselves felt they needed more training to be effective, particularly in the use of technology in the class. Because faculty are able to openly self-identify areas where they are least comfortable or feel least effective, we are able to design workshops that fit their needs, creating a more bottom-up approach to the professional development we do. This takes the application of the assessment beyond "just" the numbers—the courses improve, we can provide appropriate professional development workshops, and we can all work at being better.

The syllabus audit and SLO matrix were sparked by the assessment project, but they also allowed us to see more general areas of concern, like grading and attendance/tardy policies, that we addressed through full-day syllabus workshops and through clarifications about our expectations of the part-time faculty who teach the majority of our composition sections. With a grant from the Dean's office, we were able to pay our part-time faculty to participate in the syllabus workshops. The full-day format allowed us to use a workshop model built on conversations and sharing among the affiliate faculty, reaffirming our commitment to relying on their expertise.

The final concrete change to grow out of our assessment practice was the creation of a composition resource page, which was something our part-time faculty had previously expressed interest in. Prior to the syllabus and assignment audits, the authors had the assignments and activities that we had used over our careers, but we didn't have a larger body of material to put on a resource page. We had been reluctant to create a resource site based only on the assignments we had created; we worried that this would seem too prescriptive. However, the assignment audits gave us examples from the entire composition faculty. When instructors had identified a particular activity or assignment as highly effective, or when we thought it was particularly intriguing in approach or covered an area part-time faculty had asked for help with, we asked the instructor who had created the assignment if they were willing to share the activity or assignment, with the appropriate credit, with their colleagues. This produced a wide range of ready-to-use class activities, homework, and essay assignments. The assignments were created by part-time faculty members and so drew on their deep well of expertise and experience. The resource page allows sharing beyond the workshops and really highlights the contributions our part-time faculty make to the program. This change highlights one of the most important issues with the application of assessment data to changes in programs and practices—the risk of failure. While the resource page was a good idea on paper, and while faculty had expressed interest in having a resource like this, in practice, the resource page was not effective. The institution required that the resource page be password protected rather than open access. It was also located several clicks into the English department website. While Jessica provided the direct URL and the password to faculty, these two requirements were a barrier to easy use and, as a result, faculty did not use the page much. Any change made based on assessment carries this risk—not all changes will work. On the whole, the assessment has helped us create practices that allow the program to be better, even in areas that the assessment did not directly address.

In addition to the concrete changes we have implemented based on the assessment results, there have also been more intangible benefits to the program. These benefits are as important to our program and student success as the more concrete actions. In our view one of the most important benefits to come out of our assessment and the changes we've implemented is a stronger sense of community among the affiliate faculty. As higher education relies more and more on the labor of part-time faculty, many of whom are cobbling together a living by working—often fairly invisibly—at several schools, it becomes more important to make explicit their value to the programs they teach in and to explicitly acknowledge their expertise. Part-time faculty often do not see many of their colleagues and can feel alienated (experience Jessica frequently had through a decade of working as a part-time instructor at several schools). Building a sense of community, a way in which part-time faculty can see their value to the program, see what others are doing, and actually meet others, creates a better program. The various ways in which affiliate faculty members have been involved in our assessment loop shows our clear respect for affiliate faculty expertise; we want them to not just do things our way but rather to help shape the direction of the program.

We've used a part-time faculty member's idea as one of our new technology assignments, which we use as an assessment artifact. Part-time faculty run some of the professional development workshops. In this type of acknowledgment and sharing, all of the faculty—part-time, full-time non-tenure track and tenure track—can get better as we learn from each other in true collaborations. As we get better, so does the program. The program also becomes more cohesive since the assessment results help us to (or perhaps force us to) truly look at what works and what doesn't. In our program, this was particularly visible in the changes part-time faculty made in moving to comply with the removal of research-based writing in our first course in the composition sequence, ENG 1010. As we built community and clarified our expectations through the changes outlined above, in only one year we saw a drop from 77 percent using research in 1010 to over 40 percent requiring it, to just over 30 percent using it, and finally to almost no one requiring it, demonstrating the usefulness of our assessment process.

However, there are some real and important issues remaining. Many faculty still see "low" numbers in the assessment data as reflecting a failure of students, teachers, or both. They want to see higher numbers as proof of success. For us this is further complicated by a change the university made from assessment run in the departments to a centralized General Studies assessment program run by a new General Studies Program Assessment committee. The change to General Studies assessment meant a change in rubric (for General Studies Rubric, see https://www.msudenver.edu/media/content/generalstudies/Writtten.pdf), and because of a change in rubric, the loss of trend data. We have new data, but this data is not truly comparable. Furthermore, while the university plan with our new General Studies program and our first data collection for writing in fall 2013 was to continue the practice of pairing a rater from inside the department with one from outside the department, this was not possible due to not having enough raters from the department itself. The rater training was reduced from four hours to two hours, which meant that less norming occurred. Raters also did not recalibrate as they worked through their assigned artifacts.

While the statistical validity of the assessment remains the same (the General Studies assessment is overseen by a statistician), the change to a centralized assessment process with more outside raters than raters from inside the English department has somewhat curtailed the conversations about the program and "good" writing that our initial assessment process sparked. We still have conversations about the results—the numbers—with all of our colleagues, but these conversations lack the depth of those sparked by norming and calibration and rubric design inside the department.

One additional effect of the move to a university rather than department assessment process has both positive and negative elements—some faculty who were anxious and angry about assessment when we started this journey are now apathetic. This apathy has in some ways meant a smoother process since faculty are less apt to argue the need for assessment (at least to satisfy our reaccreditation requirements). However, it has also meant less interest overall in creating change in individual courses. This suggests an important and lingering question for us (and other programs) to consider: how do we create sustained faculty buy-in? The most useful assessments are long-term and need faculty buy-in to be long-term as well.

JANE AND JESSICA: WHERE DO WE GO FROM HERE?

Our journey has been informative. We are finding new ways to address student learning and make a difference at our institution. As we move forward, gathering more assessment data and refining the changes we've made, we want to continue the collaborative nature of our use of assessment results. In the 2013–2014 academic year, we shifted from our program rubric to one created by faculty across campus that address the Written Communication skills agreed upon for General Studies (see appendix 5.B).[2] While we have to do assessment to fulfill the demands of reaccreditation and the increasing calls for accountability and transparency, we want to do it because it fulfills a more basic (and luckily for us, widespread) desire in our faculty—to better serve our students, to be better teachers. The rubric will shift again, so our trend data will be flawed by looking only at the numbers. Nevertheless, for our purposes, and looking at general curriculum revisions and support for instructors, the numbers can still tell us where those needs are.

However, we recognize the limitations of the data. Despite some faculty's desire to see much higher average numbers, we do not expect that type of increase because of our student population and number of transfer students. In addition, because writing is such a complex skill, and the top score (four) on the rubric indicates mastery, we do not anticipate that most students in a first-year writing program and 16-week semesters can reach that level. We hope that the institution will recognize the importance of ongoing writing instruction within disciplines.

Looking back at the four basic principles Jane started with, we have updated our curriculum with SLOs that reflect our program, we have created (as a community) and shared authentic assignments that help students learn and measure their learning, we have a data-collection cycle that is useful and not overwhelming and, finally, all of our decisions have been informed by the data we've gathered.

We really are in it together—WPA, tenure-track faculty, non-tenure-track full-time faculty, part-time faculty, and students. We must continue to close our assessment loop in ways that allow our part-time faculty to both have input and benefit from the assessment processes. Our students, oblivious to the hours spent on assessment, curriculum development, and best practices, benefit from our work as their whole experience within the first-year writing classroom is better. We must continue to mindfully create community. We must continue to build on the expertise we bring to the table and recognize and use the expertise our faculty members offer. By doing both, and allowing assessment data to inform our teaching rather than just being data we report to HLC or our administration, we can best reach our mission: to better serve our students.

APPENDIX 5.A

Writing Rubric
English 1020
Metropolitan State College of Denver
January 6, 2009
Revised March 10, 2011
(adapted from Barbara Walvoord)

Criteria	1	2	3	4
1. Thesis/Focus SLO 3 SLO 6	Reader cannot determine thesis and purpose OR thesis has no relation to the writing task.	Thesis and purpose are somewhat vague OR only loosely related to the writing task. Thesis relies on logical fallacies.	Thesis and purpose are fairly clear and match the writing task. Thesis points to an argument.	Thesis and purpose are clear to the reader and closely match the writing task. The thesis clearly states an argumentative claim and avoids logical fallacies.
2. Organization SLO 3	Unclear organization OR organizational plan is inappropriate to thesis. No transitions.	Some signs of logical organization. May have abrupt or illogical shifts and ineffective flow of ideas.	Organization supports thesis and purpose. Transitions and sequence are mostly appropriate.	Organization fully supports thesis and purpose. Sequence of ideas is effective. Transitions are effective.
3. Support/Reasoning –ideas –details SLO 3 SLO 6	Offers simplistic, undeveloped, or cryptic support for the ideas. Inappropriate or off-topic generalizations, faulty assumptions, errors of fact.	Offers somewhat obvious support that may be too broad. Details are too general, not interpreted, irrelevant to thesis, based on fallacies, or inappropriately repetitive.	Offers solid reasoning, but ideas stated are not developed. Assumptions are not always recognized or made explicit. Contains some appropriate details or examples.	Substantial, logical (avoiding fallacies), and concrete development of argument. Assumptions are made explicit. Details are germane, original, and convincingly interpreted.

Continued on next page

Criteria	1	2	3	4
4. Documentation and design in APA or MLA SLO 1 SLO 7	Does not accurately use a Works Cited or Reference List nor uses appropriate technical format.	Attempts to accurately use a Works Cited or Reference List and technical format.	May not always conform to required style manual and technical format. Works Cited or Reference List accurately reflects sources used in paper.	Uses required style manual and technical format, accurately reflects sources used on the Works Cited or Reference List with expertise.
5. Quality of Sources SLO 1 SLO 2	Little or no awareness of an effective use of technology to locate sources, evaluate their authenticity, validity, and reliability as applied to a specific purpose.	Attempts to accurately demonstrate an effective use of technology to locate sources, evaluate their authenticity, validity, and reliability as applied to a specific purpose.	May not always demonstrate an effective use of technology to locate sources, evaluate their authenticity, validity, and reliability as applied to a specific purpose.	Demonstrates an effective use of technology to locate sources, evaluate their authenticity, validity, and reliability as applied to a specific purpose.
6. Integration of Source Quotations SLO 3 SLO 7	Overuse of quotations or paraphrase to substitute writer's own ideas. (Possibly uses source material without acknowledgment).	Uses relevant sources but lacks in variety of sources and/or the skillful combination of sources. Quotations and paraphrases may be too long and/or inconsistently referenced.	Uses a variety of sources to support, extend, and inform but not substitute writer's own development of idea. Doesn't overuse quotes. Borrowed material integrated into the writing.	Uses a variety of sources to support, extend and inform but not substitute writer's own development of idea. Synthesizes material from a variety of sources, including personal observation, scientific data, and authoritative testimony. Doesn't overuse quotes. Borrowed material skillfully integrated into the writing.

Continued on next page

Continued from previous page

Criteria	1	2	3	4
7. Audience Awareness SLO 5	Little or no awareness of audience or form's requirements. Egocentric. A written form of speech for one's self.	Stance is that of a novice attempting to write for instructor. Little or no attempt to address counterarguments.	Writer meets reader's needs with some skill, but is not as consistently successful. Anticipates possible objections to the argument.	Writer consistently and skillfully anticipates reader's needs by explaining specialized language and jargon and providing appropriate depth of context for the subject. Anticipates and answer objections to the argument.
8. Style/ Mechanics and Usage SLO 5	Superficial and stereotypical language. Oral rather than written language patterns predominate. Mechanics and usage errors so severe that writer's ideas are lost.	Sentences show little variety, simplistic. Diction relies on clichés. Tone may have some inconsistencies in tense and person. Repeated weaknesses in mechanics and usage. Pattern errors.	Sentences show some variety and complexity. Uneven control. Diction generally appropriate, less advanced. Tone is usually appropriate. Mechanical and usage errors that do not interfere with meaning.	Sentences are varied, complex, and employed for effect. Diction is precise, appropriate, using advanced vocabulary. Tone is consistent, suitable for topic and audience. Evidence of control of diction and mechanics.

APPENDIX 5.B

Metropolitan State University of Denver Course Descriptions for the two-semester sequence addressed in the paper.

ENG 1010 (Composing Arguments) is a course focusing on the process of writing and revising college level texts in three major categories: arguments through personal reflection, arguments through analysis, and arguments through interpretation. The course employs lecture, discussion, workshop, and conference methods. Students learn how to read, summarize, and analyze texts. Students demonstrate their ability to generate, organize, and produce writing for appropriate audiences. Coursework does not include research and documentation of secondary sources. Students must receive a C- or better to earn course credit.

ENG 1020 (Freshman Composition: Analysis, Research, and Documentation) is a course in the process of writing extended essays supported by research. The course includes an introduction to library use, research techniques, and the conventions of MLA and APA styles of documentation as well as practice in critical reading, thinking, and writing across the disciplines. Students can expect to do a series of shorter writing and research assignments leading to the longer, documented paper. ENG 1020 includes hands-on instruction on the use of computers in research and writing in a computer lab. Because of continual development in research technology and techniques, credits 10 years or older, from any institution, will not transfer. ENG 1020 requires a grade of C- or better to fulfill the General Studies requirement.

Notes

1. Founded in 1965, Metropolitan State University of Denver is a comprehensive university offering bachelor's and master's degrees from its campus in downtown Denver, Colorado. Nearly 24,000 students are enrolled at MSU Denver, and the First-Year Writing program serves 7,500 of those students each year in our two-semester writing sequence.

2. For information regarding Metropolitan State University of Denver's General Studies program, please visit: https://www.msudenver.edu/generalstudies/.

References

Allen, Mary J. 2006. *Assessing General Education Programs.* San Francisco: Jossey-Bass.
Keeling, Richard, Ric Underhile, Andrew F. Wall, and Gwendolyn J. Dungy. 2008. *Assessment Reconsidered: Institutional Effectiveness for Student Success.* Washington, DC: NASPA.
Suskie, Linda. 2009. *Assessing Student Learning: A Common Sense Guide.* 2nd ed. San Francisco: Jossey-Bass.

6

MAKING PEACE WITH A "REGRETTABLE NECESSITY"

Composition Instructors Negotiate Curricular Standardization

David Weed, Tulora Roeckers, and Melanie Burdick

At its most promising, standardization attempts to create educational experiences that are equal, consistent, and fair. At its worst, standardization reintroduces the destructive "cult of efficiency" that overtook American education in the early twentieth century (Callahan 1962), which reduced schooling to industrial management. While the conversation surrounding standardization today is initiated upon student learning and outcomes, we know that student learning ultimately is connected to teacher performance, and when teachers are given autonomy and support, their classroom practices improve (Hyslop-Margison and Sears 2010). Studies have shown that general teacher autonomy is connected to increases in professionalism, job-satisfaction, and perceived empowerment (Pearson and Moomaw 2005), and this effect appears across grade levels. Therefore, as we think about standardization at the university level, we must consider the way that the process affects instructors' autonomy. Instructors' perceptions of their role(s) in the standardization process will certainly affect their teaching and rapport with students and other faculty. As Ingersoll and Alsalam (1997) stated: "Advocates of increases in faculty influence and increases in teacher autonomy argue that teachers will not only make better informed decisions about educational issues than district or state officials, but that top-down decision making often fails precisely because it lacks the support of those who are responsible for the implementation and success of the decision" (7). The process of standardization must come, as Ingersoll and Alsalam explain, from "those who are responsible for the implementation" and should therefore be created in a more organic and generative space where the main stakeholders, the instructors, create and evaluate the standardization through their own teaching contexts (7). This is the only logical

DOI: 10.7330/9781607324355.c006

place that assessment can be "continually nurtured, evaluated, and refined in order to ensure success" (Banta 1996, 5).

Much of the recent focus on standardization of university programs is based on this need to assess. One assumption about a reliable and valid assessment situation has been that courses must look exactly the same, with the same objectives, activities, instructional materials, assessments, and measures. Assessing writing is complicated to say the least, but there are concepts that most composition scholars and instructors can agree upon: writing assessment should be locally created; writing should be assessed by the teachers who are assigning the writing; whenever possible, assessment should take into consideration the processes used to create the finished piece.[1] These assumptions are a part of the foundational idea that writing (even that which is created in a classroom) is a social act that is affected by context. When assessment is taken out of the teachers' hands and defined by someone who may not fully understand or be fully aware of the learning context, it may appear on the surface to make the assessment more objective and valid. In fact, this practice destroys validity because it ignores the context.

Thus, assessment and standardization as rigid, "top-down" mandates are likely to be more harmful than helpful because they disregard all local needs and considerations. If the model of writing instructors as knowledgeable, independent agents is no longer feasible, then the question becomes whether a solution exists that accounts for both global requirements and local needs. More than 60 years ago, Ralph Tyler (1949) produced the form for curriculum design that remains current today, and his work offers a framework for understanding effective teaching and learning organization. In his book, *Basic Principles of Curriculum and Instruction*, Tyler (1949) explains that educators should ask four central questions:

1. What educational purposes should the school/instructor/program seek to attain?

2. What educational experiences can be provided that will allow students to attain these purposes?

3. How can these experiences be organized?

4. How can we assess whether the purposes were attained? (1)

Standardization, then, is a way to make sure that these questions are answered in a systematic and consistent way across classrooms, contexts, teachers, and students. When each of these questions is answered in strict and detailed ways and then standardized across classrooms, there is very little space for teachers to make professional judgments and adaptations for their educational contexts. However, question number one (the objectives) and question number four (the assessment) can be standardized in a way that leave questions two and three open and flexible. This kind of curricular design allows instructors to determine particular teaching goals and objectives as well as the structure and organization of the "educational experience." Instructors can select and implement the class content and procedures depending upon their understanding of student needs, classroom contexts, and their own expertise.

There is a spectrum of possibilities when it comes to standardization of writing assessment, and because of the hyper-assessment that has invaded American K–12 schools, we can observe a spectrum of results. When standardized assessments become high-stakes and controlled outside the context of the school, they negatively impact teacher and student attitudes toward the act of writing and writing instruction (Mabry 1999). These high-stakes writing assessments narrow curricular goals (Ramirez 1999), and because they are often written on-demand responding to a standardized prompt, they decrease reflective, locally-informed and individualized instruction (Ketter and Pool 2001). Such problems make it questionable as to whether on-demand assessment can accurately reflect higher-level, more complex learning, such as evaluation and synthesis.

As accreditation pressures create new expectations for standardization and assessment in first-year composition, we can learn from the lessons of K–12 classrooms and make choices to take control of the process, "to assess ourselves before assessment is done unto us."[2] As we negotiate ways to standardize and assess ourselves, we should be mindful of the ways that we can continue to keep assessment local, flexible, and open to adaptations that account for classroom context and teacher autonomy. In her article, "Standardizing a First-Year Writing Program: Contested Sites of Influence," Sheila Carter-Tod (2007) speculates about the challenges of creating a standardized and still theoretically sound writing program: "Many programs court a standardizing process that seems to run counter to what the discipline defines as ideal for writing classrooms. At such a time, it may help to consider whether it is possible to standardize first-year writing programs in ways that are based in the theoretical and pedagogical practices of the field and that are cognizant of students' needs" (Sheila Carter-Tod 2007, 76). Due to a university-wide mandate initiated to meet accreditation requirements, faculty in Washburn University's composition program have entered into just "such a time" as we are now grappling with standardization and face Carter-Tod's conflict.

OUR CONTEXT AND OUR DILEMMA

As important as it is to understand the learning context when considering writing assessment strategies, it is also important to understand the context of Washburn University's composition program before discussing our process for standardizing the curriculum. Washburn University is a public, open-admissions university in an urban area of the state capital, Topeka, Kansas. Approximately 7,000 students attend the university, and the composition program is housed within the English department. We are fortunate to be employed in an English department that highly values composition. All English faculty, whether tenured, tenure-track, or full-time lecturers, teach composition as part of their course load. The program itself includes four courses ranging from Developmental Writing to junior-level Advanced Composition.

The culture of instruction in Washburn's composition program has historically been that of pedagogical freedom. There are no standard syllabi, required textbooks, standard assignment sequences, or common assessments. Most of the composition faculty are Ph.D. or M.F.A. holding tenure-track or full-time instructors who have been allowed to construct courses based on their own experiences with and knowledge about teaching composition. The autonomy signified that composition faculty did not need the kind of oversight that standardization necessitates. Pedagogical independence is highly valued and deeply engrained in the professional personae of instructors in the program.

This pedagogical freedom has reflected the English department's philosophy regarding the composition program. Until 2011, there was no director of composition at Washburn. Through 2010, there was a coordinator of Freshman Composition, and a separate faculty member oversaw a placement exam for Intermediate and Advanced Composition, but the retirement of the coordinator and the elimination of the placement exam because of budget cuts left composition without leadership beyond a full-time lecturer who received a course release in order to hold meetings among adjunct composition faculty as a way to keep them connected to the department. In 2011, Melanie Burdick, one of the authors of this article, was hired as director of composition. The first task assigned to Burdick by the department chair was to create better alignment among the various sections of freshman composition on campus and in the high schools (as part of Washburn's Concurrent Enrollment Program). Burdick spent significant time her first two years visiting the CEP high school teachers' classrooms and developing relationships with the composition faculty. The department has funded four composition faculty dinners each year, and attendance has ranged from 19 to 24 faculty members. In her first year at Washburn, Burdick collected and examined syllabi, and she created and distributed a survey in order to gain a better understanding of the faculty's perspectives on the freshman composition curriculum. She then formed a committee of composition faculty members, which used the survey results to create an English 101 teaching framework (see appendix 6.A). The following year the university announced that the department would be required to submit a common syllabus and common assessment for composition courses by January 2013. The preliminary work helped to provide a foundation for the new requirements for a common syllabus and assessment.

In order to address accreditation standards, the university mandated that all general education courses be redesigned to incorporate common assessments worth 30 percent of the course grade. Given the history of instructor autonomy in the composition program, this requirement to standardize curriculum and assessment caused discomfort among the faculty, and the understanding that the requirement would involve some complex "negotiations" prompted this study. In particular, the composition instructors had to negotiate ways to meet the new university requirements while maintaining a sense of ownership of their classes. Some faculty saw the mandate as insulting and disrespectful to their professional expertise. Freshman Composition was the first that was standardized, and through that process faculty volunteered to teach "pilot courses" to gauge the effects of adapting the new standards into their own teaching methods. This study follows the perceptions of these pilot instructors as they respond to the process of learning to teach with a standardized curriculum.

OUR PROCESS FOR CREATING A STANDARDIZED CURRICULUM

As we shaped our standards for Freshman Composition, we were influenced heavily by assessment scholarship that suggested a collaborative standardization process. Matching our program's culture, we worked to create a process that valued all instructors' voices and considered the collective knowledge of their various instructional experiences. We attempted to create what Broad, Adler-Kassner, et al. (2009), described as "dynamic criteria mapping" (DCM) or, more simply, "locally produced writing assessment." We began by collecting syllabi from all composition instructors. From the objectives that we found in the various syllabi, we created a survey and asked faculty to rate the objectives based upon their importance. These surveys were tabulated, and the results were presented at a faculty dinner meeting where, in small groups, faculty evaluated the survey results and tried to determine the common values across our composition program that the data expressed. We then created a smaller committee that applied the survey results to the creation of a list of common objectives for our freshman composition courses.

In summer 2012, this committee met for a week to create an assessment tool and course objectives for Freshman Composition. The committee reviewed other writing programs' assessments and surveyed the research on assessment to try to locate a method that would both meet university requirements and suit the department culture. Knowing that the program valued the learning context of writing as one of process and reflection, the committee considered a portfolio assessment to be the most reliable way to assess these learning objectives. Portfolio assessment might also feel more comfortable to our faculty, who would perhaps balk at the idea of teaching common paper assignments. Thus, the portfolio would allow faculty autonomy and freedom to create assignments as long as those assignments conformed to the standardized objectives. Since the university also required a common assessment for only 30 percent of the course grade, portfolio assessment also appeared to give instructors the freedom to design their own writing assignments as long as they conformed to the common course learning objectives. Finally, the committee turned the learning objectives into a rubric that met the university assessment requirements yet still could be used holistically to review student portfolios.

After creating these documents, we asked faculty to volunteer to pilot the new common objectives and assessments one year before the curriculum would be implemented. In essence, our study aimed to answer the following questions:

1. How do individual composition instructors experience and adapt to pedagogical standardization?

2. How does context (high-school concurrent enrollment versus on-campus college enrollment) affect the understanding and experience of standardization in a composition program?

3. How does standardization of first-year composition curriculum affect instructors' perceptions of their teaching and of student performance?

We believed that these questions could be answered through a process in which we collected various data over the course of the semester.

METHODOLOGY

Participants

Participants were recruited via e-mail from the pool of Washburn composition instructors who were scheduled to teach Freshman Composition
for the spring semester and who had volunteered to pilot the new EN
101 curriculum in their classes. Seven volunteers signed consent forms
to participate, and they were made fully aware of the scope and purpose
of the study before signing. To ensure anonymity, each participant has
been assigned a pseudonym in this article. Our participants had varied
backgrounds, including specialists in creative writing, literary studies,
and composition and rhetoric. The participants also had a wide range
of experience. Two of them, Mary Zimmerman and Jeremy Huber, were
high school teachers who taught composition through our Concurrent
Enrollment Program (CEP). Sophie McManus and Mike Ecklund were
tenure-tracked faculty in the department. The remaining three, Jacob
Carson, Malik Skoda, and Dwight Wagler, were full-time lecturers.

Question Selection

In general, our questions were structured to encourage participants to
provide holistic impressions of the standardization process, as well as
to discuss feelings about specific elements related to the process. We
designed the initial questions, which were sent to the participants by
e-mail, to elicit comments about the way that instructors envisioned
integration of the new course objectives into their individual classroom
practices and to see the kinds of preconceptions about standardization
they held. We posed these questions in order to stimulate conversation
about the benefits and challenges of standardization in general and the
new curriculum in particular:

1. What benefits do you anticipate experiencing because of the new standards and assessment?

2. What challenges do you anticipate?

3. How do you feel about the standardization of objectives and assessment
   in English 101?

4. How do you expect that standardization will affect your course and
   your teaching overall?

Questions e-mailed to participants at midterm were very similar to
those posed before the beginning of the semester. However, we also
wanted to know the participants' feelings about the process in medias

res, while their perspectives were fresh and while issues that may have arisen were still being resolved. In addition, we hoped to glimpse the way that instructors felt the introduction of the standardization criteria affected their students' learning and to understand any other changes made by the instructors in their efforts to integrate these criteria into their teaching:

1. Have you noticed any benefits from the new standards and assessment?

2. What challenges have you encountered?

3. How much would you say that you have had to change your class?

4. Please describe any changes that you have made. How do you perceive students reacting and responding to the new curriculum?

Lastly, we believed that interviewing participants in focus groups would be important to this study because focus groups often motivate richer and more detailed data samples through conversation between participants (Fontana and Frey 2005) and because focus-group data is premised on the understanding that knowledge is socially constructed (Marshall and Rossman 2006). Especially in our context where the standardization was created through collaboration, our data should also partly reflect collaboration and social construction of meaning. For these final in-person interviews, the questions were altered from those asked in the questionnaires in order to capture the participants' impressions of the final portfolio assessment. We also wanted to see whether any of their positive or negative views of standardization persisted throughout the semester, as well as changes in their attitudes toward standardization after the instructors had time to relax and reflect. The questions posed in the focus groups were more detailed in order to foster more thorough responses and to fuel conversation:

1. How would you describe your attitude toward the standardization process before the pilot, and do you believe your attitudes changed at all through the pilot process?

2. Looking back on your experience with the pilot, what implications did it have specifically on your teaching?

3. What implications do you think it had on your students?

4. Can you describe what you have seen in the portfolios and how it might have compared to your students' writing before the standardization?

5. Can you describe a story or an example from your classroom work that could illustrate your experience with the standardization?

Data Collection and Analysis

Given that our belief was that assessment is a process that must occur in context, and since our focus for this study was on the ways that instructors react and adapt to the demands of assessment over the course of a semester, we determined that questionnaires needed to be distributed at key points during the term. Participant interviews were recorded both individually (three participants) and in groups of two (four participants), and lasted approximately 30 to 40 minutes each. The exit interviews also served as debriefing sessions, as our volunteers were again reminded of their rights as participants and told more about out study interests and goals. After transcribing the interviews, we individually reviewed all of the data we collected and identified emerging themes and attitudes. We then shared our findings and created categories based on common threads. These threads were used to go back to the materials we had in order to locate, categorize, and analyze specific examples of the participants' attitudes and experiences.

During the three intervals in which we collected data, our participant response numbers fluctuated somewhat (see Table 6.1).

To gain further insight into the decisions that the participants made as they adjusted to the new standardization requirements, we asked them to submit artifacts from the pilot-program semester. Some instructors were able to adapt materials easily from previous semesters, while others found it necessary to create new assignments to meet the expectations of the portfolio assessment. The artifacts we collected included syllabi, assignments, and activity plans; participants were allowed to choose the number of items to submit for the study. A total of 25 documents were submitted by five of the participants.

Notably, some degree of experimenter bias may have been involved in our study because of the amicable nature of the department. Participants may have held back negative commentary to a degree in light of the fact that one of the experimenters was also directly responsible for implementing the assessment and its success. However, although the participants occasionally seemed hesitant to respond in the interviews, they did not completely stop vocalizing concerns, and the dialogue generated by the study appears to be genuine albeit couched in positive terms about standardization at times. For future study, employing interviewers who are not so clearly attached to the success or failure of the assessment process implemented by the department may be the way to ensure this kind of bias does not occur.

Table 6.1. Participant responses

Participant	Questionnaire		
	1 (pre-term email)	2 (midterm email)	3 (post-term interview)
Mike Ecklund	•	•	•
Jacob Carson	•	•	•
Dwight Wagler	•	•	•
Jeremy Huber	•		•
Mary Zimmerman	•		•
Malik Skoda			•
Sophie McManus			•
Totals	5	3	7

AUTONOMY VERSUS STANDARDIZATION: PROMINENT FINDINGS

Given the amount and degree of initial resistance to standardization among some members of the composition faculty when it was initially mandated by the administration, we were surprised to find the extent to which instructors discovered tangible benefits from standardization as they integrated the new requirements into their courses. In particular, they located ways that standardization would benefit students at Washburn University, but they also commented that a composition program that appeared more cohesive, systematic, and directed would reflect positively on the program itself.

Adjusting to Standardization

Some instructors readily accepted the mandate to standardize the composition program, but several were dubious. As noted above, instructors at Washburn University had traditionally been granted wide latitude in terms of choosing course materials and developing content, so some of them worried that standardization would cripple their autonomy. By the end of the semester-long pilot program, however, even the most resistant instructors agreed that the benefits of standardization made relinquishing some freedom worthwhile. Those instructors felt that they had exchanged some autonomy for a cooperative effort that ultimately benefitted both their students and their teaching. Among the instructors, McManus found the transition into standardization the easiest: she had few problems integrating the new standards into her course: "I thought that the proposed standards fit pretty well with what I did already and therefore didn't see that doing the things for the pilot study was going to be particularly disruptive. I was in favor and wanted to be supportive, and I didn't see any problem with the general goals that had been established as the standard being out of step with the kinds of assignments that I gave."

The high-school teachers with concurrent-enrollment Freshman Composition courses were the most familiar with standardization processes, which made them amenable to a similar kind of process at the university level. For instance, Zimmerman stated, "I had always been involved in standards-based curriculum in public school anyway. That's all I've ever known, so adjusting at this particular level was just par for the course, really. Beforehand, I always thought that having some sort of set clear objectives among a group is good for students and for us because it gives us direction." Similarly, Huber noted that standardization had been part of his experience as a public school "forever." He thought that portfolios in particular allowed a good balance between the individual instructor's teaching style and the needs of the whole program: "I think that portfolios are a wonderful assessment tool, and it's easy to create a plan, as we've done here, that works well for everyone and that allows flexibility for an individual teacher's ideas and teaching approaches, but kind of keeps us all grounded together so that we're working towards the same goals." Zimmerman's comment is important for writing program administrators. Concurrent-enrollment instructors may seem to be on the margins of curricular design because of their locations on the periphery of the campus-based program conversations. We found these instructors to be extremely valuable in our process of creating a more standardized curriculum. Zimmerman and Huber were both longtime public school teachers with advanced degrees. Because of their training in curriculum and teaching and their experiences with standards-based curriculum design and high-stakes standardized testing, they brought insight into the process that other composition instructors lacked. Zimmerman and Huber were the two most positive participants in our study. Following the pilot, their attitudes and expertise have helped other instructors understand and adapt to the new course expectations.

On the other hand, two of the full-time Washburn faculty members, Carson and Skoda, expressed perhaps the most anxiety about standardization, seeing it initially as a challenge to their autonomy. Carson noted, "I had been pretty vocal that I'm skeptical of the standardization process as a model. I have lots of reservations about it, not the least of which is I think that it has a tendency to undercut teachers' ability to do what works best for them in their own classrooms." Skoda noted that he had always appreciated the autonomy that instructors were allowed in the English department at Washburn and had considered it a strength. He reflected upon when he was first hired: "I was encouraged to use my own unique blend of experiences to teach my students. Consequently, when I heard the word standardization being applied to our department, it concerned me because I thought that it would affect the strength of the autonomy that we previously had the freedom to practice." Wagler saw the changes that he made to his course as specific adjustments in order to make it correlate with the new standards. He replaced a graphic novel that he had planned to use as a means of "explor[ing] composition in a non-traditional way" with a more traditional essay that focused on argument.

Ecklund described his attitude toward standardization before the pilot program as "a little bit skeptical, a little bit cynical, but at the same time, open to it." He was particularly discomfited by the suggestion that instructors needed careful oversight, and he initially saw the mandate to standardize as a demeaning commentary on instructors' knowledge and abilities. Although he was "open in theory to standardization," it "made me in practice a little nervous, and I also, sort of as a first reaction, found it a bit insulting to suggest that teachers don't know what they're doing and that they need someone to come in and tell them what to do."

Carson, Skoda, Wagler, and Ecklund voiced important concerns, and their experiences provide two crucial lessons. First, these instructors generally saw the idea of standardization as "insulting," and a way to "undercut" teachers' authority and expertise. They saw the process of standardization in any form as something that would affect the strength of their autonomy, and all the instructors agreed that autonomy was a unique strength of the department. Second, standardization does in fact have the capacity to constrain instructors' creativity. As Wagler noted, he no longer felt comfortable designing content that offered a more creative exploration of composition. Importantly, standardization has the potential to thwart curricular innovation. Even though we believe that our standardization process allowed for curricular flexibility, we have serious concerns that it has also inhibited instructors, making them less willing and able to take risks with course design, classroom activities, teaching methods, and writing assignments.

Despite these initial doubts and reservations, every instructor after a semester of teaching one of the pilot courses reacted positively to the standardization undertaken by the composition program. Some became more comfortable with the standardization process in general; others were pleased more specifically about the way that the composition program had implemented standardization, even though they continued to resist the trend toward standardization. For example, Carson remained the most skeptical about standardization, but remarked: "I felt good about how it's been handled within the department. I wasn't happy that we were getting this pressure from the administration to implement standardization, but if we have to do it, then I was comfortable that we would come up with a way that was the best thing that we could do. I guess that if our program continues to grow and we continue to have more high-school participation, then probably some of this is a regrettable necessity regardless of whether we got pressure from the administration on it."

Making Standardization Accommodating

Ecklund overcame his initial conflicted feelings about standardization and became "more positive" during the semester because the composition program had constructed standardization criteria that were "roomy and accommodating." An individual instructor "still could have some sense of autonomy and some sense of identity within the framework and guidelines." Ecklund thought that his "attitudinal shift" during the semester was far more significant than the "nuts-and-bolts" changes to his course: "[B]efore, I thought, 'I am the instructor here. These are my students. This is my classroom, and everyone else has their own class.' But standardization made me think differently about colleagues, about sort of a common enterprise, and about being part of a writing program as opposed to just discrete entities all over the place. My conceptualization of being a part of something bigger changed."

A composition program that consisted of "something bigger" than individual instructors teaching discrete courses was also seen as important to students' perceptions of their writing instruction. McManus argued that part of the goal of standardization was to help students develop a better understanding of the composition program as a cohesive unit and to "make sure that there was some sense of uniformity so that students wouldn't be getting radically different experiences and wouldn't be held to significantly different standards section to section." Ecklund saw this "lack of consistency across the sections of comp" as a problem at Washburn, and he thought that standardization could "change their perceptions in a positive way." Consistency across sections, he posed, can help students to "gain confidence that we know what we are doing. Of course, I hope we always know what we're doing, or think about what we're doing, anyway, but I don't know that students always know that or give us credit for it. This kind of standardization or commonality across sections, I think, can help with their perceptions and confidence, which is good."

One particular way that instructors found themselves creating more consistency across sections was through the adoption of more uniform vocabulary—much of it derived from the rubric for scoring portfolios—for describing the elements of composition and for evaluating student writing. Indeed, Carson remarked that the most significant change in his teaching involved terminology, "trying to line up the language that [he] was using in classroom with the language on the rubric as much as possible." He offered this example: "I'd rarely talked in class about synthesis using that word. That wasn't how I usually approached thinking about integrating sources and joining in the conversation, so I did find that I had to think about my terminology and approach it in some new ways so that students had a better sense of what they were being asked to do and how they'd be evaluated on the portfolio." McManus commented that the process of adjusting vocabulary was useful for her teaching practices, because it forced her to reevaluate the details of her teaching strategies: "If anything comes along that makes me more productively self-conscious as a teacher, then I'm for it. I guess I got a little nervously self-conscious, too, but in any case it did make me aware of things that I perhaps had described in different ways. It ratcheted up my consciousness of how a particular day's work fit into what we're collectively trying to accomplish. And it was nice to know that other people were trying to accomplish these kinds of things as well."

A Collective Enterprise

This sense of making composition a more collective enterprise while maintaining instructors' pedagogical autonomy was perhaps the most important benefit of standardization. The fact that the documents and tools for evaluation were developed by faculty members in the program also helped the process to seem more like a participatory, democratic effort than an autocratic one. The high school teachers were the most keenly aware of the benefits of an assessment model that, as Huber noted, "keeps everybody on the same page" and promotes consistency in terms of assignments and paper evaluations, but that also allows for individuals to contribute to the process.

Zimmerman's experiences as a public schoolteacher with measures and procedure dictated by outside forces made her "wince" when she heard the word "standardization." She described her reaction to the standardization process in the Washburn University composition program as "better" because there was "definite instructor input. We created it ourselves. It wasn't imposed upon us, and if it isn't successful, then it has to be something that teachers and professors are personally invested in." Having meetings among the faculty to discuss their teaching methods and the process of standardization, and developing a philosophy for the composition program was "a lot different than someone handing you a sheet of paper and saying, 'You haven't had any input on this whatsoever, but here's what you are going to teach.'" If standardization is indeed a "regrettable necessity," then the most productive way to manage its implementation appears to involve ensuring that it becomes a community enterprise with tangible community benefits.

The unexpected benefit of the assessment process, which hinged upon the care in which the task was approached, was this community building that occurred among faculty. Directly or indirectly, the participants overwhelmingly regarded involvement in the process as key to creating a comfort level for acceptance of assessment. The importance of the sense of ownership created through the collaborative effort cannot be understated. However, some of this community feeling may be the result of a honeymoon effect. When assessment was first mentioned, everyone's attention, for better or worse, was turned to the event. The heightened sense of awareness driven by the newness of the process will obviously wane in subsequent semesters. The primary issue for Washburn and other universities that also want an inclusive approach to meeting university standards, then, involves discovering ways to keep faculty and administrators interested and involved.

Of course, the community is also not static: new faculty members arriving in the program will be presented with materials and requirements developed by their predecessors, and they will be expected to conform. Their responses will be noteworthy. Will they be amenable to implementing standardization procedures that they had no part in developing, or will they resist the intrusion into their classroom practices? If implementing standardization procedures was effective because it was "roomy and accommodating," then its future success likely depends on maintaining a similar kind of flexibility. As composition theory and the needs of the faculty evolve, standardization procedures also need to be revisited continually to ensure that they reflect current practices. Adapting an inclusive reevaluation strategy in which the entire process is again revisited, researched, and re-piloted, may recreate that sense of freshness involved in the initial standardization process. For the larger institution, creating community may be a much more daunting task than it was for Washburn

English; however, given the value of community-building that our study and others like it show, we believe that attempting to engage faculty, giving the individual and collective voices in standardization processes, would benefit any institution and department.

In fact, Banta (2002) espoused most clearly a view that is consistent with our findings: "Effective assessment programs become embedded in the institutional culture. They are acknowledged, discussed, deliberated, reviewed, and refined. Effective assessment is perceived as an integral part of the overall educational mission. And it focuses, very simply, on learning" (45). Overwhelmingly, our participants implicated involvement in the process as a key factor in creating a comfort level for accepting assessment.

Of course, the issue of negotiating curricular standardization that we have discussed here has evolved out of an institutional history that has generally encouraged university faculty to see themselves as independent agents responsible for their own curricular choices and teaching methods. This tradition conflicts directly with emerging institutional needs for data and evidence that allow colleges and universities to demonstrate tangible benefits of the education that they purport to provide. In this study, however, we have found that instructors can and do adapt to common program goals and that the most significant hurdle involves helping instructors to adjust their professional identities. For example, several instructors (some in passing and others in more elaborate narratives) commented on the trepidation that they felt about having their colleagues review their students' work in the portfolio review. Zimmerman joked that she thought the portfolio review was helpful, "and I like that it was just random because I would have loved to have picked, but, of course, it wasn't like that." For Huber, making student portfolios available for review at random became a more complex matter. When he submitted his roster for the portfolio review process, he "marked five students who had stumbled toward the end," and four of the five were randomly selected for review. Huber noted that part of the process of productive self-consciousness also involves these kinds of moments of "nervous self-consciousness." Making a successful transition into an era of increased oversight, standardization, and accountability, then, in part means fostering a somewhat different perspective among faculty members, not only in terms of assessment but also in terms of the ways that they conceptualize their relationship to departments, universities, and the teaching profession.

Although the composition instructors in our study expressed initial trepidation about standardization and its impact on their autonomy and classroom practice, they also revealed areas in which community could assist them if the practice of survey and review were in place each semester. For instance, Wagler indicated that he had difficulty including an assignment for persuasive writing in his course, and his initial questionnaire indicated that his "challenge is to figure out how [he] can continue to include different texts while matching the assessment standards." This concern was realized during the semester as he struggled to adapt, and eventually dropped, a text from his curriculum that he had selected specifically for its ability to engage students. Ecklund's challenges included "students being reluctant to engage the stages of the writing process, students mistaking editing for revision, students not understanding the concept of audience in a way that compels them to write differently for different audiences, and students not being detailed in their writing. Some students do not seem to like the idea of revising and resubmitting earlier work for a new grade as part of the final portfolio." These hurdles and others are difficult for any instructor to manage, but in a group, instructors can share ideas and troubleshoot specific concerns, which can help their colleagues to develop new methods and approaches Within the department, future survey information such as this could be used by program administration to prompt professional development workshops in which specific issues could be addressed throughout a semester to aid instructors with adapting material, selecting texts, and creating assignments that will not only meet standards but intrigue and inspire students to engage more fully in reading and writing as processes. When departmental-wide assessment is handled as an ongoing community project, the implementation of standardization does not have to be a barrier; instead, it can become a ladder to more creative teaching.

APPENDIX 6.A

Contents:

EN 101 Faculty Survey Results
Of the 27 surveys submitted . . .
24 items were selected by over half (14 or more) of respondents:

Effectively proofread one's own writing (27)
Revise one's own writing (27)
Understand how to focus an essay around one unified idea (26)

Present effective and logical details and examples to support a central idea (26)

Portray correct usage of an academic citation system (MLA, APA, Chicago, etc.) (25)

Effectively integrate outside sources into one's writing (25)

Comprehend writing as a process (24)

Understand how to structure a basic paragraph (24)

Read critically and question the content of a text (22)

Effectively write for a variety of purposes (22)

Reflect upon one's own strengths and weaknesses as a writer (22)

Self-analyze one's writing process (21)

Synthesize ideas presented in varied texts (20)

Render experience and opinion through writing (19)

Create a valid argumentative essay which persuades through a clear position and adequate support (19)

Adapt one's writing processes to varying writing tasks (19)

Write varied sentence structures (19)

Summarize a text (19)

Effectively analyze a rhetorical context including but not limited to: audience, purpose, and authorial stance (17)

Effectively write for a variety of audiences (17)

Portray a strong and consistent voice through word choice, stylistic techniques, and structural choices (16)

Read analytically to examine the effects of how a text is written (16)

Connect reading experiences to one's own lived experiences and opinions (16)

Comprehend and master basic grammar and usage rules (14)

Ten items that were marked as "most important" most often:

Understand how to focus an essay around one unified idea (17)

Present effective and logical details and examples to support a central idea (12)

Comprehend and master basic grammar and usage rules (10)

Comprehend writing as a process (10)

Read critically and question the content of a text (8)

Create a valid argumentative essay which persuades through a clear position and adequate support (8)

Effectively integrate outside sources into one's writing (8)

Understand how to structure a basic paragraph (7)

Revise one's own writing (6)

Portray correct usage of an academic citation system (MLA, APA, Chicago, etc.) (6)

Teaching Framework for English 101

English 101 is a requirement for graduation for all Washburn students and introduces incoming students to college-level writing. The course focuses on deepening the connection between thinking and writing, developing ideas appropriately, and editing writing for standard written English.

Strong writers respond flexibly to different writing tasks for various audiences. To teach students to become flexible writers, English 101 provides an array of writing experiences. The course includes assignments that vary from process writing to polished essays. Polished essays result from multiple drafts, and students receive feedback from their instructor and classmates. These assignments allow students to do the following: describe, narrate, reflect, argue, analyze, and synthesize. Process writing gives students the opportunity to practice, invent, reflect upon, and develop writing habits and skills in a low-stakes learning situation. The curriculum includes assigned readings representing a variety of genres and styles to serve as sites of analysis for student writers. Readings should include models of academic writing.

The following English 101 teaching framework articulates the goals and objectives valued by Washburn composition faculty. We believe that writing instruction is best taught through a constructivist position where the instructor brings individual expertise to the classroom and creates curriculum that meets each student's individual needs. We hope our faculty will feel guided by these principles of instruction while still enjoying the professional freedom to construct the assignments and activities necessary for their particular classes. Both formative and summative assessments should take place throughout the semester, and it is recommended that portfolio or some other form of holistic assessment is performed.

I. Process

Students in English 101 will understand writing as a recursive process of inquiry and be able to write in various ways in different situations. They will learn to reflect on their processes and adapt them to short- and long-term goals in writing for a variety of purposes. Students will engage in:

- Discovering ideas
- Developing ideas
- Identifying the goals and purposes of their writing

- Reflecting critically on writing (giving themselves and others substantive feedback)
- Editing
- Proofreading

II. Substance

English 101 teaches students to think critically and creatively so they are able to convey valuable information and experiences to readers. A number of principles connect writing and thinking. These include the ability to:

- Analyze textual information and evaluate sources
- Present evidence and support for arguments
- Synthesize information from multiple sources
- Create a reasoned discussion
- Render novel ideas in lively, thoughtful prose

III. Form

Because writing takes place in a variety of contexts, for different audiences, students in English 101 will learn how to understand and adapt form to reach these audiences and achieve intended goals. Form includes attention to:

- Rhetorical situation—audience, genre, style, tone, and language
- Structure—organization, clarity, unity, coherence, and integration of sources
- Conventions—grammar, mechanics, and documentation

Notes

1. Many sources refer to the need to assess processes and habits of mind alongside skills. Most notably are the *Framework for Success in Post-secondary Writing*; the *Council of Writing Program Administrator's White Paper on Writing Assessment*; the Conference of College Composition and Communication's *Position Statement on Writing Assessment*; and Edward M. White's book, *Teaching and Assessing Writing*.

2. This quotation is often referred to "Edward White's Law of Assessment" and is attributed to a post made by Edward M. White on the Council of Writing Program Administrator's Listserv.

References

Banta, Trudy W. 1996. "Editor's Notes: The Power of a Matrix." *Assessment Update* 8 (4): 3–13. http://dx.doi.org/10.1002/au.3650080403.

Banta, Trudy W. 2002. *Building a Scholarship of Assessment.* San Francisco, CA: Jossey-Bass.

Broad, Bob, Linda Adler-Kassner, Barry Alford, and Jane Detweiler. 2009. "Organic Writing Assessment: Dynamic Criteria Mapping in Action." *All USU Press Publications.* Book 165. http://digitalcommons.usu.edu/usupress_pubs/165.

Callahan, Raymond E. 1962. *Education and the Cult of Efficiency: A Study of the Social Forces that Have Shaped the Administration of the Public Schools.* Chicago: University of Chicago Press.

Carter-Tod, Sheila. 2007. "Standardizing a First-Year Writing Program: Contested Sites of Influence." *WPA: Writing Program Administration* 30 (3): 75–92.

Fontana, Andrea, and James H. Frey. 2005. "The Interview: From Neutral Stance to Political Involvement." In *The SAGE Handbook of Qualitative Research*, ed. Norman K. Denzin and Yvonna S. Lincoln, 695–728. Thousand Oaks, CA: Sage.

Hyslop-Margison, Emery J., and Alan M. Sears. 2010. "Enhancing Teacher Performance: The Role of Professional Autonomy." *Interchange* 41 (1): 1–15. http://dx.doi.org/10.1007/s10780-010-9106-3.

Ingersoll, Richard M., and Nabeel Alsalam. 1997. *Teacher Professionalization and Teacher Commitment: A Multilevel Analysis. NCES 97-069.* Washington, DC: US Department of Education.

Ketter, Jean, and Jonelle Pool. 2001. "Exploring the Impact of a High-Stakes Writing Assessment in Two High School Classrooms." *Research in the Teaching of English* 35 (3): 344–93.

Mabry, Linda. 1999. "Writing to the Rubric." *Phi Delta Kappan* 80:673–9.

Marshall, Catherine, and Gretchen B. Rossman. 2006. *Designing Qualitative Research.* 4th ed. London: Sage.

Pearson, L. Carolyn, and William Moomaw. 2005. "The Relationship between Teacher Autonomy and Stress, Work Satisfaction, Empowerment, and Professionalism." *Educational Research Quarterly* 29 (1): 38–54.

Ramirez, Al. 1999. "Assessment-Driven Reform: The Emperor Still Has No Clothes." *Phi Delta Kappan* 81 (3): 204–8.

Tyler, Ralph. 1949. *Basic Principles of Curriculum and Instruction.* Chicago: University of Chicago Press.

7

A TOOL FOR PROGRAM BUILDING
*Programmatic Assessment and the English
Department at Onondaga Community College*

Malkiel Choseed

INTRODUCTION

A few years ago, I caught up with a friend from high school. After graduation I had gone to college; he had joined the Army. Our conversation came around to the rising cost of a college education and whether or not it was worth it. My friend said that when he was working on trucks for the Army, either the truck was fixed or it wasn't. Either the engine turned over and the thing moved or it didn't. That was his measure of success. What was ours?

One way that this question has been and continues to be answered is through large-scale assessment programs, often referred to as programmatic assessment of student learning outcomes. This chapter presents a critical case study of the ongoing assessment efforts in the English department at an open-admissions, two-year college, Onondaga Community College, in Syracuse, NY, and the potential that assessment has for program building. From my position as a participant observer, I use this case study to present a context for our assessment program, a detailed overview of our current status (we are in the "implementation" stage), intra- and inter-campus collaborations, and possible directions for the future. Readers will see the evolution of our campus and departmental assessment process along with our innovations in ensuring participation and program efficiency, both of which create opportunities within a program and across the college, as well as areas for continued improvement and further implementation. The popular media and our own professional associations abound with discussions of the negative impact of assessment and standards on secondary and now higher education. Through the details of one program's experiences with large-scale assessment, this chapter aims to illustrate that such assessment can

DOI: 10.7330/9781607324355.c007

be, if done thoughtfully, one tool for making institutions a better place for students and faculty by increasing real student learning.

CONTEXTS FOR ASSESSMENT

Assessment is never done in a vacuum. Any practical discussion of assessment has to address the various contexts—local, state, and national—which influence the implementation and resulting analysis of any programmatic assessment efforts. Since the state and national contexts have been ably covered by other chapters in this book, the following section will focus on understanding a local context through a disciplinary lens. Before beginning any sort of assessment project, it is imperative that writing program administrators (WPAs), administrators, or other involved faculty members first understand their local institutional context as well as the evolving disciplinary context. What follows is one potential model for starting this work.

From a disciplinary standpoint, the assessment or "accountability" movement has pushed us to think about student success differently. In the past we thought of the success or failure of individuals. Now we are focused on larger groups of students, looking for patterns, seeking to understand how and in what ways we are systematically setting up our students for success or failure. In terms of the larger field of composition, I would characterize the conversation as being focused on the authenticity of assessment, especially in light of the growing use of automated essay scoring software by for-profit companies like ETS, as well as the myriad competitors being developed by textbook publishing companies like Pearson. Higher education has always been focused on assessing student learning. The ways in which we understand this assessment and the desire or need to make judgments about large groups of students, however, has changed over time. A result of a shift in our economy and culture, large-scale assessment is about working conditions as well as about the value of our profession to the larger culture and our role in the colleges and universities of the twenty-first century. No one, I think, could credibly make the claim that programmatic assessment is not a necessity and, as Gerald Graff (2008, 3–4) has argued, it can even be a seen as a democratizing tool.

An argument has been made, however, about the validity of these assessments as tools to measure actual student learning, which is evident in the comprehensive but growing body of work produced in rhetoric and writing studies (White 2005; Haswell and Ericsson 2006; Peckham 2006; Perelman 2008; Anson 2009). This work informs the numerous position statements and white papers published by the Council of Writing Program Administrators and NCTE as well as CCC and TYCA. These scholars and organizations seek to understand what constitutes an authentic assessment of student learning in terms of assumptions, experimental design, data manipulation, statistical methodology, and so forth.

The push toward a sustained theory and practice of program development, on the other hand, is linked to this growth and change in the field as well. Scholars who think deeply about program development see the difficulties with it as a problem both of working conditions and of professionalizing the faculty who teach first-year composition (FYC) across the nation (Adler-Kassner and Estrem, 2009; Adler-Kassner 2010a, 2010b; Janangelo and Adler-Kassner 2009; Janangelo and Klausman 2012; Klausman 2013). Even as Rhetoric and Composition has gained recognition as a distinct discipline in the last few decades, the majority of faculty actually teaching writing classes lack knowledge of or access to much of these resources. These two defining themes are being played out in microcosm at Onondaga Community College.

From a local perspective, accreditation had been the driving force for all assessment efforts at Onondaga Community College, a member of the State University of New York (SUNY) system. It did not evolve organically or from a faculty desire to measure student learning in this way. Programmatic assessment had been a response to a deadline imposed by SUNY or the Middle States Commission on Higher Education. Assessment was simply not done in the years without an accreditation visit (Gabriel 2013; Tarby 2013).

In 2002, SUNY began to require that all programs have a written mission and measurable outcomes. Programs were now required semiannually to report on outcomes, measures, graduation rates, transfers, and so forth. The Middle States process resulted in recommendations to improve the overall assessment process, concentrating on the notion of "closing the loop" or using results to plan and implement change. Accreditation still drives it, but there has been a growing recognition that, in order to best serve our students and make progress toward the future, we need assessment to understand where we have been and where we are now.

The new emphasis on institution-wide assessment of learning outcomes has meant both practical and theoretical changes on the departmental level as well. In order to be successful, we had to change the way we thought about and performed assessment. The first Writing Program Coordinator (WPC) position was created in 2003. According to Professor Nance Hahn (2013), the first coordinator, the majority of faculty had backgrounds in literary studies and taught FYC without reference to a larger field or with an explicit theoretical framework rooted in rhetoric and writing studies. Whereas the teaching of composition has a long history at Onondaga, it was often done using "lore," trial and error, and intuition, rather than theory or research in rhetoric.

The first time Professor Hahn organized an assessment of General Education outcomes in spring of 2005, she was met with distrust and anxiety on the part of both full- and part-time faculty, which she attributes to two interconnected issues. The first is that assessment, when done correctly, ought to lead to curricular and programmatic change, and real change means engaging in real (e.g., time consuming) work. The material conditions required to successfully "close the loop" present a severe challenge both to WPAs and faculty members, especially at two-year colleges where so many writing faculty hold part-time or adjunct status and where teaching loads are significant. Real change means potentially having to rewrite syllabi, revise assignments, change grading or commenting practices, review and select new textbooks and the like, representing weeks of additional work.[1]

The second challenge involves a very legitimate fear of surveillance, a complex and multi-leveled fear that involves the practical (the concern an individual instructor might have over contract renewal) and the abstract (a fear that his or her approach might be seen as outmoded or the perception of being judged). Realistically, the collection process and scoring sessions cannot be completely anonymous: faculty recognize each other's favorite assignments or topics, the WPA has a list of who did and did not turn in papers, and so forth. Trust and collegiality are vital for the process to work.

In this environment it is no wonder that adjunct and full-time faculty alike were (and to some extent still are) hesitant or even distrustful of the assessment process and the WPA representing it. One of the challenges a WPA faces is that it is hard to communicate to faculty that assessment is primarily about gaining an understanding of the whole that does not rely on anecdotal evidence.[2] Despite these difficulties, Professor Hahn was able to get near 100 percent of the full-time and adjunct faculty teaching Comp I or Comp II to participate in the 2005 assessment, mostly through repeatedly "bugging" faculty members with, visits, notes, emails, and so on.

OVERVIEW AND OUR CURRENT STATUS: IMPLEMENTATION

When I became Writing Program Coordinator in 2008, I realized that the needs and goals of the campus-wide assessment effort could be made to reinforce assessment-driven, rather than lore-driven, program building efforts in my own department. As a WPA, I faced two primary challenges. The first was to get people to participate in good faith in the assessment process. In order to do that, they needed to trust that the results would be used only for their intended purpose: to make the program more conducive to student success. The second (which would help with the first) was to simplify and make the assessment collection, scoring, and reporting as efficient as possible. This was important from a cost and materials standpoint as well as in terms of time and energy. While it may have been possible to meet individually with every adjunct and full-time member of the department in 2005, by 2008, the explosive growth of our department made this no longer feasible.[3]

Ensuring adequate participation in the process quickly became a problem. The collection procedure for papers to be used in assessments remained the same between 2005 and 2011, with each faculty member asked to turn in a more or less complete set of papers for a given assignment, ideally representing all sections of a given course offered that semester. The papers would be randomized and scored against a rubric. Lacking the authority to mandate participation, I had to rely on departmental goodwill, but we were only getting papers representing 40%–60% of the overall sections of a given class. Essentially, people self-selected to participate in the study. With the same folks choosing to participate or not every time, we were generating data, but the picture that formed was incomplete.

Generating this incomplete picture, though, was remarkably resource intensive. It would not be unusual for our department to run between 75 and 80 sections of Comp I, capped at 22 students; Onondaga has a two-course required sequence. If every faculty member turned in one full assignment set (an early draft and a submission draft of a 3–5 page paper from an average of 18 students per section, as we had asked), we would collect over 8,000 pages of text. Even if only 60 percent of the faculty elected to participate, this comes to more than 4,800 pages of text. Add in the sections of Comp II, and we are talking about another 2,000–4,000 pages. With that process, we'd be spending nearly our entire duplicating and printer budget on assessment rather than instruction.

According to our Vice President of Institutional Effectiveness and Planning (IPAR), Wendy Tarby, we could collect fewer papers and still get a valid sample if the selection of sections were truly random. We developed a new protocol in 2010 that randomly samples 20 percent of the students from 20 percent of the sections of a given class. Here is the protocol that we developed and approved:

- IPAR will randomly select 20 percent of sections of a given class, including those taught by full- and part-time faculty.
- IPAR will generate randomized course lists for instructors teaching the selected sections.
- Those individuals whose sections are selected will be required to supply 20 percent of one full set of papers for one assignment that meets the requirements of the assessment (e.g., papers from the first 4–6 students on the randomized course list of an early draft and the submission draft of a paper for Comp I and a paper dealing with literary analysis in Comp II) by a date determined by the Writing Program Coordinator.
- If a faculty member decides for any reason that he or she cannot or will not participate in the assessment, it is up to that individual to communicate this to the WPC, the chair, and to the Provost. In this instance, the Provost's office will have to be made aware of the situation.
- Because this is not about surveillance but rather an authentic assessment of what is going on in terms of student learning, we will maintain as much anonymity as possible. Only IPAR, the WPC, the department chair, and the selected faculty members need know who was selected. Papers will be made anonymous when the actual reading and scoring is done.

In addition, we developed a reading and scoring procedure in which every paper is read twice (double blind), and we ensure inter-rater reliability through norming sessions and a common, SUNY-approved set of rubrics.

The new random sample model reduces costs significantly. Assuming we have the same 75 sections of Comp I running, we would select only 15 sections. Assuming these sections had an average of 18 students, we would then collect papers from 4 to 5 students per selected section. If the student named on the list had effectively dropped out or did not turn in that assignment, the teacher would select the next student on the list. Now we are talking about 500 pages of text. The selection of Comp II papers would be done the same way. In total, we are now talking about less than 1,000 pages of text. This is significantly smaller and more manageable than what we are getting with only 40%–60% participation.

In order for any process to work and be valid, faculty need to take part. Participation cannot be voluntary. The Provost's public support for the process was essential in ensuring compliance. Explicitly lending her authority to the process and making faculty theoretically accountable to a senior administrator helped motivate participants.[4] By doing so, she helped to concretize the idea that this is a college-wide initiative with stakes that go beyond an individual or a department. The Provost has said publicly (and I have strategically repeated it in a variety of reports and memos) that participation in assessment activities is not optional. She considers it, and a union representative confirmed it, to be an expectation of working here for both full-time and part-time faculty members. When the stakes are high, as with accreditation, senior administration will not hesitate to get involved to support assessment efforts.

Regardless of what senior administrators think, any assessment plan will not generate good data without the participation of staff and faculty. Faculty need to understand the process and goals and believe that it is more than just "busy work." While it may not always be possible to come to a consensus, alienating parts of a department by (seemingly) arbitrarily selecting one set of criteria over another is not a good way to generate goodwill or trust. For us, using the SUNY generated rubric for our Basic Communication outcome (measured in the Comp I course) allowed us to elide this debate in our department and rely instead on the authority of the SUNY General Education Assessment Review (GEAR) Group.[5] Because SUNY did not have a readily available rubric for measuring the Humanities outcome (used for our Comp II classes), we generated one internally.

Funding for reading and scoring has been provided by the administration as well, currently paying both adjunct and full-time participants $30.00 per hour and providing lunch. The sessions quickly and efficiently generate data used for the assessment report; expose the readers (often for the first time) to the work of the department as a whole; engage them in productive conversations around teaching, student writing, and assignment generation; help build community; and generate both increased understanding and goodwill on the part of the participating faculty.

The results are shared with the department and also deposited into WEAVEonline, a database licensed by the college to track and manage assessment activities. From there, data can be viewed and reports can be generated by faculty and administrators. For the department, the results provide us with benchmarks and targets for improvement. Assuming the assessments are designed and executed well, they should be a good, objective indicator of student learning.

Innovations related to assessment efficiency on the departmental level took two primary forms. The first had to do with the design of the assessment process detailed above. The second had to do with continuing the college-wide work of aligning learning outcomes across the institution. There are actually several layers of alignment to contend with here. The department has its own course level outcomes and program level outcomes, modeled on the WPA Outcomes Statement for First-Year Composition. In addition, we also needed to take into account the outcomes for our unit (Humanities and Social Science), Onondaga's own general education outcomes and, finally, the system- wide SUNY General Education outcomes.

Currently, the college uses its two-part FYC requirement to satisfy the SUNY General Education requirement in Basic Communication and the Humanities.[6] When possible, we try to replicate the exact language used in the course outcomes as in the General Education materials. When that is not possible, we make sure that, at the very least, the goals can be mapped vertically and horizontally with clear links between a course outcome and a program outcome. Our course level assessment also works as our SUNY mandated Gen Ed assessment and as our Humanities degree program assessment. Instead of doing two or three different assessments on a specific course or in a specific program, now we are able to do one and use the data in different ways.

RESULTS AND ANALYSIS

As of this writing, we have been able to complete two full academic years' worth of statistically rigorous data (Fall 2011/ Spring 2012 and Fall 2012/Spring 2013). The numbers generated allow us to form certain conclusions about our current program and to begin the long, arduous process of change. It has been difficult, but we are finally in a position to measure in some reliable way what it is we are doing as a program. In this light, assessment is the key to program development. Finally, we can talk about what we are doing programmatically as opposed to what individuals are doing at a given moment. In order to best serve students, we must move beyond anecdote, hearsay, and what Stephen North (1987) and others call "lore." We need shared goals and a shared understanding of what those goals mean. All of this will take time and effort, but it *is* possible and worthwhile. Assessment helps us set the stage for this work, but that is all it does. Generating valid data only prepares us for the next step.

It is important, however, to stress both to my colleagues and our administration that the ultimate goal is not a better numerical score; rather, the ultimate goal is improved student success. Without assessment, we cannot really know how well our students are learning. Grades and graduation rates are important metrics, but they do not measure the primary issues that we have control over, namely pedagogical theory and practice. There are innumerable personal issues affecting our students over which we have little or no control. As any faculty member knows, students fail to complete an assignment, a class, a degree, for any number of reasons. Facility with revision or mastery of sentence mechanics are only one set of contributing factors. At the very least, however, faculty need to know what students are getting from the course to make changes accordingly.

The assessment process in our (open admissions) community college is often understood by faculty in one of the following ways:

1. A nuisance imposed from afar, to be done as quickly as possible and forgotten just as quickly, so we can get on with the real work of teaching;

2. A problem which will reveal our weaknesses and ultimately lead to ruin given the challenges inherent in our student body;

3. Necessary and even intellectually stimulating work which helps us to establish a baseline from which we can work to improve student learning.

Under the surface, though, programmatic assessment is complex and multi-layered. I suspect that the first two attitudes are more prevalent than the third at the average institution. They are at mine. In this economic and legislative climate, however, we don't have the luxury of ignoring it. As Ed White (2005) famously said, "*Assess thyself or assessment will be done unto thee*" (33). Since we have the sensitivity, knowledge, and practical experience, since we know what to value and what to discount, we ought to be the ones to design and implement the programmatic assessments. All faculty—whether they are WPAs or not—need to take control of the assessment process to whatever extent is possible in order to make it reflect the values of the faculty and institution.

The second (negative) view is that if we measure something, then we will be responsible for changing it, and, given our student population, we will not be able to change it. Hence we are setting ourselves up for failure, censure, and perhaps punishment if we do not/cannot enact meaningful change based on the assessment. Some fear that by measuring student outcomes we are setting ourselves up for either a dilution of rigor, a change in our mission, or, at its worst, we'll be seen to be ineffective or unnecessary. If we measure, and we get low numbers, and the numbers can't be raised, then we risk negative attention from administrators, Boards of Trustees, accreditors, and even state legislatures, hence the defensive posture toward assessment on the part of some faculty.

The third, more positive view understands assessment as providing a baseline that will enable us to make real and substantive changes to our curriculum in order to increase student success. This view posits that we do not or cannot simply accept the fact that some percentage of our students are just incapable of "getting it." There has to be some approach or set of approaches, some practices and theoretical grounding, that can help these students succeed in an academically rigorous way. We may never be able to help students deal directly with their myriad personal, social, and economic problems, and we certainly cannot guarantee that all students in all situations will achieve success at the top level, but we ought to be able to help them write better, and we need to assume that it is possible for all of them to learn to write better than they did when they started college. That is the real value of assessment.

For example, the SUNY General Education assessment for Basic Communication measures students' ability "to produce coherent texts within common college level forms" and "the ability to revise and improve such texts" ("Report of the Writing-Discipline Committee" 2013). At Onondaga, we use our Comp I class, required by all programs, to fulfill this requirement. The assessment results (from the new 20% + 20% model) for the academic year 2011–2012 showed that while nearly 60 percent of students were "approaching" the specified goal of producing "coherent texts within common college level forms," only about 30 percent were "meeting" or "exceeding" the goal. Approximately 45 percent of those same students were "approaching" and only around 20 percent were "meeting" or "exceeding" the standards for revising such texts.

What are we going to do at OCC as a result of this finding? We have a number of choices to make, none of which, if we want to do it right, are going to be simple or quick. My interpretation of this data is that we need to do a better job of teaching revision. Revision is a fundamental college-level skill that we must teach in our FYC classes. Students must be able to improve a piece of writing by using various revision strategies, and those revision strategies, to be effective, must transfer beyond Comp I and Comp II. Everything we know as a discipline, from anecdotal, experiential evidence to quantitative studies, indicates that if we teach "revision" as a dynamic and complex process, we should see an improvement in both sets of scores and, more important, their corresponding skills. Significantly, a change in students' ability to revise is rooted in the issue of professional development for faculty. Part of the issue is how we do or do not define the term "revision." Most of us use the term "revision," but we do not always mean the same thing by it. We need consistency in understanding, if not in the specific content of our classes, in order to improve the teaching of revision and to improve transfer.

The final step in any assessment cycle is closing the loop. This is, of course, the most difficult part of the process and the one with which, historically, we have the most trouble. With our new collection procedures and baseline data, we are poised to begin the next step, making significant changes to our curriculum based on our assessment results. We struggle, though, to make any sort of meaningful change. For example, while our early assessment results demonstrated that our students consistently struggle with the revision process, and we formed a committee to revise our course in response to this knowledge, the committee was bogged down in seemingly endless debate over minutia. Even when we were able to bring drafts to the department for discussion, we would spend countless hours wordsmithing and compromising on language to allow faculty to maintain whatever practices and approaches they wanted. The reader must remember that in a community college, every faculty member has a stake in FYC. We have (as of the time of this writing) *finally* finished a revision of the first part of our FYC sequence that recasts the course description, topics covered, and so on to focus explicitly on revision, and we hope to get it approved through the larger college next semester. Assuming there are no unexpected complications, we will be able to change course outlines for the start of the next academic year.

It is frustrating, but necessary, to point out that once we have implemented these changes, there are no guarantees that they will have any impact on the way that courses are actually taught, at least for established full-time and adjunct faculty. The realities of a large community college dependent on adjunct labor may be different from those at other types of institutions, but, for us at least, it is very hard for us to navigate college policy, contractual issues, and academic freedom while mandating any kind of change. In addition, our department is so big that effective oversight outside of individual class observations is very hard to do. We have ongoing professional development on various topics, reading groups, discussion groups, workshops, and the like, but our audiences are small. We have tried electronic discussion groups, even a Facebook page, but participation in those is also low. This is not to say that people are not interested or engaged; most are committed to good pedagogical practice and want to do a good job, but few have knowledge of our field. The reality is that the material conditions of our labor make it hard for us to innovate or grow. We know the changes we need to make, we are just unsure how to efficiently and effectively make those changes across an entire program like ours.[7] While we are still working on this, we have also begun to focus more of our efforts on new hires, establishing a formalized mentor program for new full-time and adjunct hires.

POTENTIAL FOR THE FUTURE

Authentic programmatic assessment, as difficult and time consuming as it can be, allows a department or program to put itself in a position to innovate and to create connections across the campus and in the larger community. The potential is there even if we are struggling with the execution. For example, Onondaga has had an ongoing flirtation with a Writing Across the Curriculum/Writing in the Disciplines (WAC/WID) program for several years. In the last few years, however, small segments of the campus community have begun to coalesce around this idea. Our departmental assessment efforts and the larger culture of assessment on our campus connect to WAC/WID in two ways: the tools it gives us to talk about it and the data it gives us to help us argue for its necessity. The culture of assessment on our campus has given us tools to explore WAC/WID as a possible solution for an identified problem, namely, our students are not writing like we want or need them to be. In terms of the writing program specifically, our assessment results are helping us to demonstrate that students need more and sustained practice writing and revising. As many in the field of composition and rhetoric already know, our FYC courses cannot, by themselves, inoculate against "bad" writing. Even though we must and will improve our FYC classes, it is clear that students need more practice. WAC/WID has the potential to give them this in a more rigorous manner. Our challenge, then, is not to convince our colleagues in other departments that this is a worthy endeavor. We need only point to our assessment data and their own experiences reading student writing for that. Our challenge is, rather, to get them to agree on some systematic way of actually implementing it. We have had college-wide meetings where almost everyone in the room agreed that WAC/WID was important but could not agree on how to make it happen.

The larger culture of assessment and our departmental efforts have, however, allowed us to make connections in other, more successful ways. In spring of 2012, a group of faculty at Onondaga were asked to take the lead on the design of a developmental curriculum and academic support program which could be submitted as a part of a Department of Labor's Trade Adjustment Assistance Community College and Career Training (TAACCCT) Grant Program (United States Department of Labor 2012). The grant is designed to create "stackable" credentials (certificates, degrees, etc.) that would facilitate job training and retraining for high tech manufacturing across the state of New York. Onondaga was to be one of the lead institutions in terms of planning for what turned out to be a 23-member SUNY consortium. A group of us in

English, Reading, and Mathematics were tasked with developing innovative, accelerated programs designed to support the needs of adult learners, with an emphasis on developmental education. The total amount of the grant awarded in September of 2012 was $14.6 million, with Onondaga Community College receiving $1.2 million (Weiner 2012).

For purposes of this grant, we recommend a combination of the Washington State Board for Community and Technical Colleges' (SBCTC) IBEST program, the Accelerated Learning Project (ALP) from the Community College of Baltimore County, and the RISE program from Erie Community College. ALP is a highly effective program which co-enrolls developmental students in both their credit and non-credit bearing writing classes. The program gives students the extra support they need while not delaying their access into credit-bearing FYC classes. IBEST pairs the content of the developmental reading, writing, and mathematics courses with that of a student's major, thus giving an engineering student, for example, sustained and intensive practice doing work that directly relates to his or her core curriculum. RISE allows borderline students to take a refresher workshop and re-test on the placement instrument, potentially avoiding a non-credit placement altogether.

These models were chosen in large part because they are demonstrably successful. The Community College Research Center housed at Teachers College, Columbia University, the "leading independent authority on the nation's" community colleges, published numerous qualitative and quantitative studies showing that the IBEST and ALP models increase success. Erie Community College maintains its own records and has shown RISE to work well, a success that we have duplicated and surpassed at Onondaga in our Spring/Summer 2013 pilot. These models give us the best working start to create something which is data-driven, experimentally sound, truly developmental, and collaborative among the instructors of the content courses and the developmental instructors.

In a very real sense, the work we were doing for the TAACCT grant was informed by our ongoing assessment of our writing program and our desire to "close the loop." The connections formed were both abstract—that is, we were already thinking about this sort of material, and there was a lot of theoretical overlap between these projects—and very concrete. We wanted to use the DOL project as a laboratory where we could test out these types of classes, formats, and so forth to see what worked, and how and why it did or did not work. Assessment helped set the stage for the success of the grant in that we were already collecting pass rates, completion rates, assessment results, and the like, which allowed us to take the lead on the developmental education side of things because we were already in the middle of it. The TAACCT grant was not something that we in English sought out, but we were able to take the lead on it because of our culture of assessment. As we near the end of our first semester teaching these innovative, accelerated courses, we are excited about the possibilities for the future.

CONCLUSION

OCC is both unique and representative of many growing community colleges. All colleges, but especially community colleges with a liberal arts mission, must be responsive to changes in the economic and technological environment, as well as aware of the current legislative climate. The world is changing around us, and if we want to stay relevant, we need to change with it. Learning outcomes assessment on the course and program level is becoming part of our mission. As these dynamic changes happen, it is our responsibility as interested and involved faculty members to influence it for the better to the extent that we are able. As anyone who has tried to do it well knows, however, this is not easy work, and the payoff can seem very distant.

Assessment is hard. Even with my graduate coursework in composition and rhetoric and my attempts to stay current, it has been a struggle to learn about assessment, its ideas, principles, best practices, the administrative structures of SUNY, and so on, in the midst of the process itself. We cannot, however, let these barriers stand in the way of our producing authentic assessment of student learning outcomes. The learning curve was and continues to be a steep one, but the work is necessary. Readily available case studies, models, and theoretical explorations of the *how's* and *why's* of outcomes assessment contained in resources like this collection can help provide support to those immersed in this activity. When it is done well, assessment by itself does nothing but set the stage for more work, but this work is necessary if we wish to serve our students to the best of our ability.

There is an interesting parallel, however, between assessment and our work in the classroom, one that we ought not to forget. It takes time for us as faculty to gain our footing and feel comfortable teaching or responding to student writing. As confident as we may be, we are always learning, adapting, responding, and changing in ways both large and small. We are continually knocked off center in the classroom but find ways to regroup and move forward toward real student learning. With assessment, we must learn to be more comfortable with being uncomfortable, of learning as we go.

Notes

1. While it is true that many adjuncts would be hesitant to undertake this, teaching multiple sections at multiple campuses, our full-time faculty are under similar pressures. The standard load at Onondaga Community College is 15 credits per semester with many faculty choosing to do an overload in order to fill last minute schedule additions or to get the opportunity to teach a specialized class, like Women's Studies or Shakespeare. It is not uncommon for tenure-track faculty to teach three sections of Comp I, two sections of Comp II, and one section of a specialty or literature course. As anyone who has taught under similar circumstances knows, it is hard to innovate in this structure. In fact, the material conditions engendered by the system actually dis-incentivize change.

2. See the Council of Writing Program Administrators' *Communication Strategies* document for an interesting discussion of relevant strategies, at http://wpacouncil.org /files/CommunicationStrategies.pdf.

3. Onondaga Community College was "one of the fastest-growing community colleges in the nation and the second-largest undergraduate college in Central New York" (*A Framework 2011–16*). The department now employs as many as 100 adjunct and full-time faculty every term.

4. I should note that I am a tenured, full-time faculty member and took on the role of WPA at my institution with little trepidation. Although it may not be necessary to be tenured in order to be an effective WPA, it certainly helps. I can ask questions or make observations that might make others uncomfortable. For example, the Provost had called a meeting to discuss the results of our Middle States Accreditation annual review. When the discussion turned to assessment, I pressed her for a response to the question of what would happen if a faculty member failed, for whatever reason, to participate in the paper collection for assessment. It was there, in front of all the other chairs and program heads, that she publicly committed to her policy that anyone impeding our assessment efforts would "have to sit down and explain it" to her personally. After that, I was able to include the fourth bullet point (above).

5. It helped that I generally agreed with the rubric and found it to be a good representation of the field of composition. See http://system.suny.edu/media/suny/content -assets/documents/academic-affairs/assessment/SUNY-Writing-Rubric.pdf.

6. Please refer to the "SUNY General Education Requirement Student Learning Outcomes" at http://system.suny.edu/media/suny/content-assets/documents /academic-affairs/general-education/GenedCourseGuidelines_20120530.pdf for more information.

7. I am reminded of an incident told to me by a faculty member at another university. He had spearheaded a massive change to their FYC program, changing a 6-credit, two semester requirement to a 4-credit, one semester requirement with a WID course taken later on. The process took two years and endless, heated debate across the entire college. At a department function after the change had been approved, an adjunct instructor innocently asked him, "So whatever happened to the course change you guys were talking about?" Despite the changes in the credit hours, learning outcomes, etc., he had been teaching it the same way as he had before the curricular changes.

References

Adler-Kassner, Linda. 2010a. "The Activist Academic: Teaching Writing (and Communication) as Public Work." In *Beyond the Ivory Tower: Essays in Honor of Professor Hazel Dicken-Garcia*, ed. School of Journalism and Mass Communication, 73–82. Spokane: Marquette Books.

Adler-Kassner, Linda. 2010b. "The WPA as Activist: Systematic Strategies for Framing, Action, and Representation." In *Going Public: The WPA as Advocate for Engagement*, ed. Shirley Rose and Irwin Weiser, 216–36. Logan: Utah State University Press.

Adler-Kassner, Linda, and Heidi Estrem. 2009. "Building Community through Writing Program Assessment." In *Organic Writing Assessment: Theory Into Practice*, ed. Bob Broad, 14–35. Logan: Utah State University Press.

Anson, Chris M. 2009. "Assessment in Action: A Mobius Tale." In *Assessment in Technical and Professional Communication*, ed. Margaret Hundleby and Jo Allen, 3–15. Amityville, NY: Baywood.

Gabriel, Nancy. 2013. Chair of Learning Outcomes Assessment Committee, Onondaga Community College, personal communication with author, February 12.

Graff, Gerald. 2008. "President's Column: Assessment Changes Everything." *MLA Newsletter* 40 (1): 3–4.

Hahn, Nance. 2013. Professor of English, Onondaga Community College, personal communication with author, February 2.

Haswell, Richard, and Patricia Freitag Ericsson, eds. 2006. *Machine Scoring of Student Essays: Truth and Consequences*. Logan: Utah State University Press.

Janangelo, Joseph, and Linda Adler-Kassner. 2009. "Common Denominators and the Ongoing Culture of Assessment." In *Assessment of Writing*, ed. Marie C. Paretti and Katrina M. Powell, 11–33. Assessment in the Disciplines Series, vol. 4. Tallahassee: Association for Institutional Research.

Janangelo, Joseph, and Jeffrey Klausman. 2012. "Rendering the Idea of a Writing Program: A Look at Six Two-Year Colleges." *Teaching English in the Two-Year College* 40 (2): 131–44.

Klausman, Jeffrey. 2013. "Toward a Definition of a Writing Program at a Two-Year College: You Say You Want a Revolution?" *Teaching English in the Two-Year College* 40 (3): 257–73.

North, Stephen. 1987. *The Making of Knowledge in Composition: Portrait of an Emerging Field*. Portsmouth, NH: Heinemann.

Peckham, Irvin. 2006. "Turning Placement into Practice." *WPA: Writing Program Administration* 29:65–84.

Perelman, Les. 2008. "Information Illiteracy and Mass Market Writing Assessments." *College Composition and Communication* 60 (1): 128–41.

"Report of the Writing-Discipline Committee." 2013. April 15. The State University of New York.

Tarby, Wendy. 2013. Vice President, Office of Institutional Effectiveness and Planning, Onondaga Community College, personal communication with author, February 12.

United States Department of Labor. 2012. "Trade Adjustment Assistance Community College and Career Training (TAACCCT) Program Summary." doleta.gov. Accessed April 15, 2013.

Weiner, Mark. 2012. "Schumer Says Feds Take Leap to Fill 50,000 jobs in New York with $14.6 Million for Job Training at OCC, SUNY Colleges." *The Post-Standard* (Syracuse), Sep 19. Accessed April 15, 2013.

White, Edward M. 2005. "The Misuse of Writing Assessment for Political Purposes." *Journal of Writing Assessment* 2 (1): 21–35.

8
CENTERING AND DE-CENTERING ASSESSMENT
Accountability, Accreditation, and Expertise

Karen Nulton and Rebecca Ingalls

ACCREDITATION AS A WAY IN

Accreditation—in particular, the changes to assessment requirements over the last decade—has driven powerful changes in higher education. As a result of a recent accreditation review, our urban, comprehensive, co-operative educational institution has been intensively engaged in creating pragmatic assessment models to foster faculty dialogue and support. Through this complex process, we have come to understand that participating in accreditation-driven assessment can actually foster relationships and help colleagues uncover shared values and goals. We have used large-scale writing assessment to structure and define a conversation about the reflective and analytical skills that we value for our students. Through this conversation we have certainly begun to understand whether we help to add value to our students' writing over time, but we have also begun to move faculty across the university from focusing exclusively on issues of correctness to asking questions about more holistic writing goals. This university-wide inquiry has allowed us to uncover how we share writing in new, dynamic, and useful ways. While this uncovering has revealed new complexities, it has also helped us to affirm the fundamental role we—the First-Year Writing Program (FWP) and its faculty—play at the university.

The FWP at Drexel is fundamentally based on a two-pronged approach to writing and rhetoric pedagogy: writing-about-writing[1] and rhetorical awareness. What we really want to help our students develop— and what we articulate to them in our university-wide learning goal of "Communication" —are fundamental skills with evidence-based writing and meta-awareness of communication practices. As we do that teaching, we want them to hover over the development of their writing and

DOI: 10.7330/9781607324355.c008

make sense of it, to be actively engaged in an analytical relationship with defined learning goals. Attending a co-op school on a quarter system plays into our students' need for this reflective practice. In our 10-week quarters at Drexel, we (students and faculty alike) start out at a jog and break into sprints as the term progresses. Both faculty and students feel the pressure of the quarter; too often, the pace means that we focus on short-term goals and greet distant vistas with suspicion. Those of us who have shaped the message of writing at Drexel argue that intentional analysis is one of the most profound skills we can offer students who are not otherwise encouraged to pause and reflect. Because of this, we integrate an ethic of awareness into our three-course sequence in the FWP. Woven throughout the curriculum is ongoing inquiry-driven writing, a study of classical and cultural rhetoric, and a final portfolio project in each course that asks them to do evidence-based reflective analysis of their relationship to one of the FWP Outcomes for learning.

***

Where our story begins is hard to pinpoint, for we would argue that how we can be accountable for what we promise to teach our students is probably always a nagging question in the backs of our minds—the reaccreditation process that loomed not far ahead was a catalyst to formally consider the question. To begin our process, we had to address both the local and the global at once. We worked with a skilled team of composition experts to create clear university-wide learning outcomes for communication, guided by the overarching goal that students will "employ an understanding of audience, purpose and context to communicate effectively in a range of situations using appropriate media" ("Drexel Student Learning Priorities" 2012). These outcomes were vetted against writing program administrators (WPA) and other national standards, reviewed by a writing task force composed of faculty across the disciplines, and accepted by the Provost and Faculty Senate; with these endorsements, we had clear goals to guide our work. Over the three years it took to prepare for accreditation review—prompted by necessity and our own genuine curiosity about how much value Drexel was/is adding to student writing—we asked some fundamental questions:

1. Do we add value to students' writing and thinking skills over the course of their FWP experience?

2. If we augment skills, do they transfer past the first year?

3. Are skills of meta-analysis of interest to our extra-departmental colleagues when they consider writing?

4. Could we use meta-analytical writing to help students to synthesize learning in academic and experiential (Co-op) situations?

We have learned that in asking these questions about learning within our program, we were also shedding light on how to make change at our own university: how to understand our colleagues' perspectives on curriculum, how to collaborate with them to channel their expertise in the assessment, how to unify our voices internally as we—the FWP—became more and more externally visible to the university beyond the service we provided to each of its students.

INSIDE OUT: MODELING ASSESSMENT

The audience of this collection will not be surprised to know that in seeking to use writing as a tool for cross-campus conversation, we tapped into a much larger and vexed conversation. In the introduction to their 2009 *CCC* article, "Creating a Culture of Assessment," Moore, O'Neill, and Huot (2009) open with a snippet of a letter written by a dean to the WPA: "Can we have not simply writing-across-the-curriculum but also writing-assessment-across-the-curriculum? If the Department of Writing could model this for the rest of us, that would be great" (107). At our institution, we found ourselves facing a strikingly similar request. But how does a writing program prove success? Indeed, one desperately wants to know the answer to the age-old, mind-boggling question of whether skills transfer beyond the first year. But even if we start local and ask whether skills transfer within the program itself, we're looking at a fraught history of flawed assessment.

Huot argued nearly 20 years ago that writing assessment was at a "stalemate" because of a disconnect between writing pedagogy, students' learning, and assessment practices (Huot 1996, 552); and because of a positivist tendency to "base assessment decisions on the abstract and inaccurate notion of writing quality as a fixed entity" (559). Huot argued instead for an assessment approach that "honors local standards, includes a specific context for both the composing and reading of student writing, and allows for the communal interpretation of written communication" (561). In this claim, he articulated five factors that are critical to writing assessment: "site-based," "locally-controlled," "context-sensitive," "rhetorically-based," and "accessible" (562). This emphasis on "localized, 'bottom-up' assessment practices" is also the focus of more recent work by Anson and others, who argue that in order for writing assessments to authentically reflect the standards and expectations of specific disciplines within the university, assessors should avoid the temptation of "generic rubrics" and instead shape their assessment strategies around the context-specific characteristics of writing in those disciplines (Anson et al. 2012). Anson's work builds closely on earlier discussion of writing assessment; as Faigley and others reminded us 30 years ago, "efforts to assess writing abilities that do not grow out of clearly articulated theoretical assumptions are inevitably *ad hoc* responses to the need for evaluation" (Faigley et al. 1985, 209). As we thought critically in our assessment about the relationship between our specific university outcomes and the approach to writing pedagogy that we fostered in our program, we found that, while our "generic criteria provide[d] a starting point" (Anson et al. 2012) for our colleagues across the disciplines to begin to think about writing assessment, a rubric alone would not meet our ultimate goal of creating a sustainable culture of assessment that encouraged our colleagues to develop their own discipline-specific standards for writing. We will frame our assessments and their rubrics, then, not as concluding evidence but as the opening gambit in an ongoing and ever-evolving conversation.

Luckily for us, we work with an administration that was particularly invested in our developing a local assessment foundation. To avoid the dangers of structurally decontextualized large-scale writing assessments that are unsupported by internal knowledge about how to conduct productive, sustainable assessment (highlighted by Moore, O'Neill, and Huot 2009), we knew that a successful program had to be equipped not only with experts in writing pedagogy but also with expertise in writing assessment. At many institutions, the rarity of finding people who have expertise in both fields is what can prevent large-scale assessment projects from moving forward. Luckily, our institution invested in both skill sets and, despite the challenges presented by our compartmentalized university structure, the WPA, the Director of University Writing Assessment, and many others would try to work together in some of the ways that Huot imagined.

Here at Drexel, the FWP has become a platform upon which to build an argument: in addition to the continued sustainability of our program, we seek, with the support of our administrations at the department, college, and university levels, to scaffold students' learning with writing pedagogy that is anchored in the first year and is taken up by faculty across the disciplines as students make their way through the more challenging academic and pre-professional work that they will do beyond the first year. Critical to providing evidence for this argument has been the assessment of our program and links between this assessment and assessment of the writing students do across the curriculum in later years.

MAKING WRITING MATTER ACROSS THE UNIVERSITY: MEASURING WRITING, CREATING COMMUNITY

As our faculty began to participate in larger conversations about writing, our research led us outside of the cohesiveness of the FWP, then circled back to shine light on our program's practices and goals, and then back outward to consider the program's status in the larger school community. We reminded ourselves that this would not be a linear progression and that this recursive movement outward from and back inward toward the "center" of writing—in this case, the FWP—was fundamental to our vision of sustaining a culture of writing assessment through data gathering and many, many conversations.

STARTING LOCAL: ASSESSING THE FWP

As we considered writing assessment as a tool to drive accessible, context-specific conversations about writing across the curriculum, we saw two logical entries into uncovering and creating shared discourse. The first was in the FWP. For several years, some teachers in the program had been using rubric-building software in some classes to grade student writing. This software also acted as a storehouse of data that could be used by program administrators to make an argument for students' performance in their first-year writing classes over the course of the sequence, and thus for more resources like faculty hires and faculty development. But how would these numbers demonstrate potential transfer of skills from the sequence into later courses? How could we establish and assess a baseline of rhetorical skills that we wanted students to cultivate that they could take with them into other communication writing contexts? Turning back to our fundamental research questions, we created two major assessment studies in the FWP. The provost's office was very supportive of these efforts, seeing them as foundational for our accreditation self-study. First, in consultation with one of our colleagues, a scholar of composition pedagogy and writing across the curriculum, we created an initial study that would measure where students were on their first and last days of first-year writing. This first day/last day meta-analysis assessment asked students to do a writing-about-writing activity on the first day of class in ENGL 101 and during the last week of class in ENGL 103: they were given a writing task, and we asked them to talk about what strategies they would use to create a response. We were very specific: we did not want them to write the task, but rather to talk *about* the task of composition, from brainstorming, to potential research strategies, through revision to pointing to ways of shaping the final presentation for a particular audience. A sample student topic follows:

> This task is intended to give your instructor information about how you would go about completing a researched writing task. You will not be penalized for "wrong" answers; as long as you respond as fully as possible, you will receive credit for the assignment.
>
> What follows is a hypothetical situation in which you are asked to do research and compose a recommendation. Please do **NOT** write the actual assignment; your job is to **DESCRIBE HOW** you would complete the project, not to write an actual researched recommendation. Please describe in paragraph format and in as much detail as possible the steps you would take to complete this assignment successfully.
>
> **TASK:** Assume that you have been asked to present a researched student perspective to the US Senate budget committee about whether to fund a project from National Aeronautics Space Agency (NASA). The Senate is attempting to create a balanced budget for 2012, and if they fund NASA's request to build a rocket that could carry astronauts to Mars, they will have to cut funding to social programs and schools. NASA argues that funding their project will generate interest in space and increase the number of students who pursue careers in engineering and science. Critics argue that rather than sending tax money to space we should spend it right here at home to create better schools and jobs. Your job is to make a researched recommendation to the budget committee about whether they should fund NASA's request. Explain how you would compose your project and how you would know if you had completed your project successfully.
>
> **Reminder:** Please do **NOT** write the actual assignment; your job is to **DESCRIBE HOW** you would complete the project, not to write an actual researched recommendation.

As the task makes clear, we inserted a context, purpose, and audience into the task so that we could see how well our students addressed these features. While we struggled with the fact that these features were contrived for our students, we decided that the artificial boundaries resembled the constraints of other, more genuine, writing situations. In creating this task, we considered both the success of the program and future assessments of transfer: we hoped that measuring students' abilities to articulate composition strategies might offer us a way into discovering whether the rhetorical and meta-analytical strategies we cultivated in the program might transfer out of the FWP and into their writing lives across the disciplines.

As we scored this assessment, we wanted to mask any statistical "noise" coming from unanticipated local practices, goals, or predilections. Using the WPA-list as a networking tool, we invited other teacher-scholars nationally to participate in a training and score our pilot assessment of students' first-day/last-day meta-writing, choosing candidates who offered gender, geographical, ethnic, and positional (from adjunct to full professors) diversity. Our (trait) scoring revealed that (a) we added statistically significant value to students' learning of the FWP Outcomes, (b) students came into our program with the same writing skills no matter what their college or major, and (c) students left our program with equal gains. For us, that students across campus left the FWP with equal growth and at an equivalent level of writing skill was an important talking point for conversations outside the department. The data undercut the arguments that "engineers/business majors/nurses/etc. just can't write," and, further, allowed us to claim that longitudinal changes in writing skill by program were likely due to programmatic reinforcement. Inside our department, having quantitative data that showed that the FWP adds value to students' writing skills has helped us to make arguments for resources like the hiring of new faculty, funding for faculty participation in professional development workshops, and funding for continued internal assessment.

Second, we implemented a portfolio and reflective analysis final project. While our first day/last day assessment addressed questions about students' rhetorical habits of mind, regardless of the writing context, we knew we also had to look at the writing itself. Did it demonstrate meta-analysis and reflection? Could students make an evidence-based argument? Were they able to document their sources? Could they shape their writing for a particular audience? And finally—how sturdy were the sentence-level building blocks of their language? To answer these questions—and to highlight for students the importance of reflection and self-assessment—we created a final portfolio-based project that students composed at the end of each of the FWP courses and that we scored at the end of the final course. In this project, students compose a "reflective analysis" in which they use artifacts of their own writing as evidence for an argument about working with one of the FWP Outcomes for learning. Here are the instructions for the English 103 portfolio reflective analysis, their last one of the course sequence:

Your Reflective Analysis should accomplish four tasks:

1. It should make **an argument** about your writing development. Read the FWP Outcomes and choose *one* of the Outcomes as the focus for your argument. You have lots of options here.

2. It should use pieces of your own writing as evidence for your argument. Specifically, you should integrate the following compositions as sources in your analysis:

  a. 1 major project from 101
  b. 1 major project from 102
  c. 1 major project from 103
  d. 2 informal compositions from 101, 102, or 103
  e. Any other supporting compositions you would like to use

3. It should do "meta-analysis" of those compositions as it makes its argument. "Meta-analysis" is your examination of your own work, your writing-about-your-writing.

4. It should be directed to a specific audience: Professional employer, friend, teacher, parent or guardian, future child, yourself . . . you choose.

In this assignment we attempted to support student agency by asking them to choose the outcome, the audience, and the argument they want to make about their learning. In each subsequent portfolio beyond English 101, the repertoire of texts from which to choose grows so that by the end of English 103, as is described above, students are looking back at a whole year of writing and learning. Our use of an ePortfolio system became both the tool to collect artifacts of writing in the FWP and a system that we could offer to departments to augment with later artifacts of disciplinary student writing. Our portfolio assessment plan married experiential with academic research: portfolio-based national writing assessment overseen by the Director of Writing Assessment through ETS merged with portfolio assessment theory encapsulated in Ed White's 2005 *CCC* article "The Scoring of Writing Portfolios: Phase 2" (rearticulated in his updated *Assigning, Responding and Evaluating* [White 2007]). This pragmatic synthesis shaped an assessment that focused on meta-analytical, evidence-based reflection that did not require primary evidential artifacts to be assessed. We claim with White to have connected "the power of the reflective letter to the actual scoring of portfolios" and, in so doing, connected "the power of the portfolios to reliable scoring" (168). Our data and a subsequent standard setting revealed that the majority of our students met our baseline proficiency level at the end of the third quarter. The data revealed as well some unsettling information about the proficiency of our non-English-Medium-of-Instruction (EMI) international students at the end of the first year; this data (triangulated with TOEFL scores and first day/last day data) helped to drive necessary programmatic augmentation for this group.

FACULTY, STANDARDIZATION, AND ASSESSMENT

The conversations about what we value in writing stimulated a small group of our FWP faculty to see themselves as part of larger conversations about writing at Drexel. As the vision of this developing group grew, so did its stature; with the enthusiastic agreement of our core faculty participants and our department head, the Writing Assessment Advisory Committee (WAAC)—composed of the Directors of Writing Assessment and the FWP, and 5–7 FWP teaching faculty—began bi-weekly conversations. Though this group was small, each of the members who were teaching faculty brought to the table conversations they had with other faculty members. In these meetings, teaching that had seemed both invisible and under-appreciated was repositioned as the foundation for university-wide writing development. By seeing themselves as empowered to assess FWP goals—and seeing these goals as foundational for students' continuing writing development—our faculty situated themselves naturally inside of an expanded discourse. One WAAC member reflects,

> I accepted the invitation [to join a group discussing writing assessment] out of curiosity and a desire to understand how writing seemed to be changing at the university—or at least how and why the "talk" about writing had ramped-up . . . What I immediately realized was that the Writing Assessment Advisory Committee was part of this change. The "talk" I had been hearing was coming, in part, from the director of the committee, and the director had projects in motion. By joining, I would come to understand the changes in writing at the University, and I would help shape that change. Frankly, that was exciting. (Marshall Warfield, email message to author, April 19, 2013)

Another WAAC participant shares how doing the work of the committee was one of the rewards keeping her at Drexel; she confesses that—much as she valued teaching the FWP courses—she felt intellectually isolated at times in her work. Regularly meeting with colleagues in a space where her expertise was clearly valued helped her to remember that she was—in addition to a teacher—a researcher, a composition expert, and a vital, collegial member of a program that linked and defined the classes she taught (Mariana Mendez, email message to author, April 30, 2013).

Of course, as all good utopian literature underscores, dissension is part of most group experiences. In making assessment matter locally in the program, we experienced a range of buy-in from our FWP colleagues. Indeed, the WAAC itself represents this range of support. Another WAAC member reflects, "I think the reflective analysis part of this assignment is wonderful and useful, but using reflective analysis for the purpose of assessment takes the joy out of it. (And yes, some students do beautiful and funny and joyful texts as responses to this assignment. This does not mean that some other assignment wouldn't inspire more beautiful, funny, and joyful texts than these.)" (Fred Siegel, email message to author, April 23, 2013). Today, the ePortfolio project is required of all FWP sections, but in getting it off the ground the project went through a phase that was "almost mandatory." The "almost mandatory" component of this project shapes our narrative, as does Siegel's yearning for the "joy" of unfettered assignments.

Let us digress for a moment. Partnered dance (think salsa or waltz, swing or tango as you prefer) requires a certain level of energy that is expressed as tension, or elasticity, between the bodies of the dancers. As long as the energy is equal, the tension results in fluidity and dynamic movement; if one partner expresses this energy and the other does not, the dance sinks from a continuous creation to a ritual movement of co-remembered steps. The living dance ossifies into artifact. Assessment requires the same dynamic reading of movements to build, grow, and captivate. In any good assessment project the tension between reliability (How accurately could we recreate these results?) and validity (Are we assessing the "thing itself" that we want to assess or just what's easy to measure? Are we using the results to further sound pedagogical goals?) should energize and shape the continuous movements of the program. Once an educational program has identified goals, the program itself becomes a *defacto* assessment project where reliability (expressed as providing an equal learning experience to all students who should meet the same outcomes) pushes and validity (how much instructors can shape learning based on the vagaries of particular classes, students, and interests) pulls. When we shaped the FWP to help students reach clear learning goals to ensure the validity of the FWP experience, we needed to standardize parts of the experience (via shared assignments) to be able to claim reliably that students encounter the same learning opportunities to meet their goals. A challenging dance.

Having instituted our 103 final portfolio project, the WAAC sat around a table, read and exchanged samples, and discussed what we valued in those texts. Since most FWP faculty were in the process of grading the portfolio project, the group focused first on the authentic task of responding as graders. This participatory task uncovered an internal consistency in faculty expectations for the portfolio project that many participants described as "a relief." This description of relief was not unexpected; informal conversations had suggested that some faculty felt conflicted about what to value in the project: in response we offered several segments of faculty meetings, as well as two more formal "grading conversations" (one online, one in person) intended to uncover (not mandate) what our community of instructors valued in student projects. When we asked FWP faculty to participate in a paid scoring exercise of the 103 portfolios projects, then, our grading rubric was not a top-down directive but coded shorthand for identifying elements that we had agreed we valued.

In asking our FWP faculty to integrate this project in their classes, we consciously shaped a tool that encouraged students (and faculty) to see reflection as a valid and valued endeavor while allowing us a snapshot of who was and was not meeting our standards at the end of the FWP sequence. As we looked inward to answer these questions, we kept our eyes outward as well. In creating this assignment, we were simultaneously designing a baseline measure we could offer to our colleagues across the university: that reflective analysis could be a shared and measurable tool to assess how well students use writing to examine and document their learning in any discipline.

BRIDGING LOCAL AND GLOBAL UNIVERSITY ASSESSMENT: "UNCOVERING" THROUGH DATA

As we examined our assessment data, the need for expertise outside of the FWP became clear, and our assessment community that started on a micro-level came to embrace a diversity of faculty in the FWP community, colleagues in other disciplines, and those at the provost level hoping to understand writing development across the university. We had much that required thoughtful advising: first, we needed to know what questions about writing departments wanted answered; as we designed studies and prompts to gather data to answer these questions, we needed colleagues both in the FWP and across the curriculum to decide with us what "good" responses looked like for these tasks. In standard writing assessment, rubric skeletons are fleshed out by the writing artifacts that define and clarify each score point; these artifacts— called "samples," "anchors," "rangefinders," "discussion papers," and so forth, depending on the context—are intended to exemplify the values depicted in the rubric or scoring guide. While we agreed with Broad's argument that rubrics can be dangerous when they "fail as a process of inquiry" (Broad 2003, 47), we argue that well-constructed rubrics can serve as a useful shorthand for describing shared values and, as such, can facilitate rather than stifle conversation. One of Broad's primary arguments against rubrics (more accurately, against an assessment system that employs decontextualized rubrics) is how infrequently they "emerge from an open and systematic inquiry into a writing program's values" (12). Articulating a vision of writing assessment for the university has engaged faculty from across the disciplines in both revising and test-driving our rubric and prompts. In this way our work touches on the values of Broad's "Dynamic Criteria Mapping" while creating a streamlined, manageable process for a pragmatic university.

Simultaneous with our desire to understand writing in the FWP, we had engaged in two years of intensive conversation with an interdisciplinary writing task force. This group—responsible for guiding a decade-old writing intensive (WI) program initiative—had languished for a number of years prior to this major assessment project. Our desire to uncover preconceptions and resentments about writing and teaching writing meant we had to create an open space to allow frustrations to sit at the table with our optimism. We (those of us who were invested in the teaching and research of writing) started by asking the basic questions of what everyone at the table valued about writing; in doing so, we uncovered the shared language that had been hidden within various disciplines. We needed to unpack and define basic words—like grammar, correctness, revision, process, audience, purpose, style, tone, format, organization and cogency—to engage in real discussion. Two years later, we felt that we had learned much more about how to reshape conversations about university-wide writing and were ready to try to understand what—if any—value Drexel added to writing past the first year.

A COOPERATIVE EDUCATION

Our findings from our two FWP assessments and work with the Writing Intensive Task Force led us out of our program and into students' learning about writing across the disciplines. To measure composition skills beyond the FWP, we looked to another significant, shared experience among most Drexel students—the cooperative education program (Co-op). At Drexel, many students choose a five-year option that comes with four Co-op cycles; these six-month Co-ops (in which students find employment in their discipline or field) generally occur the second, third, and fourth year; many of our students, then, encounter three six-months stints in the workforce prior to graduation. While Drexel's 11 colleges, law school, and medical school are bound by a commitment to the Co-op program, they also tend to function as independent silos of learning; conversations about teaching and learning among colleges is often limited by the time, accessibility, and resources that would allow communication and collaboration to happen more easily. In addition, while our school is proud of the Co-op program (85% of our students engage in at least one six-month Co-op), conversations between academic departments and the Co-op program have been intermittent. When upcoming reaccreditation forced Drexel to confront its fragmented identity, it allowed us to posit writing and writing assessment as tools for integration.

Thinking about writing as a campus-wide conversation made clear the glaring omission of writing in the Co-op experience, and we turned to a fundamental tool we were currently using in the FWP: the reflective analysis. We argued that if we asked students to reflect on their work experiences and use experiential evidence to make an argument about their learning, they would naturally begin to synthesize Co-op with academics, and Co-op would become relevant to departments interested in understanding writing. In addition, we stressed the value of augmenting a writing skill already scaffolded in the FWP; such reinforcement, we claimed, could allow departments to build on writing data from the FWP and Co-op assessments in their own programmatic assessments of communication skills. Our Co-op central office agreed to the experiment and required students to complete a reflective analysis that we created when they finished Co-op. The prompt itself was essentially a reduction of the FWP portfolio assignment:

> Please write a 400-word reflective analysis that explores how one aspect of this co-op experience relates to a personal, academic, or professional goal that you are pursuing at Drexel.

We didn't know when we instituted this reflective analysis whether students would take the task seriously. After all, students were required to write their reflective analyses as part of a standard post-Co-op survey, but the survey only needed to be submitted for credit, so students could have given any level of effort to the task. However, instead of major resistance, we found that many students took our request seriously. When asked to reflect on their Co-op goals and experience, they wrote with a candor and directness that was both informative and touching. What's more, many of them showed in this writing that they could make a claim about their learning and support it with evidence.

Since we had raw data in the form of over 1,000 student samples per bi-annual Co-op cycle, we moved to determine whether the writing could be used to identify differences in writing skills aggregately and by varied cohorts. We chose to clone the portfolio reflective analysis rubric, seeking a direct measure of how well the skill of reflective analysis transferred and flourished past the first year. In addition to the larger holistic score for evidence-based argumentative writing, once again a second, three-point rubric was designed to focus on how well Drexel students could compose sentences, the building blocks of writing. This was of interest for two reasons. First, we assessed students' sentence-level writing skills in the FWP assessments, and this was an opportunity to see whether those writing skills changed over time. Second, our earlier conversations with the multi-disciplinary writing task force had made it clear that faculty across departments *started* conversations about writing by talking about students' skills at the sentence level and their ability to use correct formatting conventions. Because of this, we knew we needed a way to examine with faculty whether sentence-level grammar and syntax were the largest issue in unsuccessful compositions. Our Co-op assessment findings showed that, overall, students' sentence-level language skills were clear—and that sentence-level skills did not change over time while other elements did; this data helped us ask faculty to see that often our shared issues are less about students' abilities to use punctuation or a formatting style than they were about larger rhetorical strategies like understanding audience and purpose, and using appropriate proofs for claims.[2] At the same time, we were reminded about the importance of grammar and style pedagogy and about how we might focus more on the rhetorical, contextualized teaching of these important skills. As a result of these cross-disciplinary conversations, the FWP outcomes now articulate more clearly the expectations for grammar, style, formatting, and usage. Thus, while we collected authentic and necessary samples of our students' writing and created a link between academic and Co-op learning, our writing rubrics were designed to support an articulated and carefully constructed pedagogical argument that could only be made after we had scoring analysis.

What's more, the Co-op reflective analysis assessment was instructive for issues of curriculum beyond students' mastery of argument and correctness. In our early view of the arguments about Co-op that students would make—a narrow notion of classroom learning informing later life experience—we failed to account for Co-op as a stage in a learning cycle continuously moving between academic and experiential venues. When we asked departments to examine writing samples from their students, we discovered together that the samples were a window not just into students' writing development but also into their view of the relationship between experiential and academic learning. This revelation was another point of stasis and potential exploration with departments outside of our own, and another place where the questions of accreditation helped make our interests relevant.

Once more, we cycled between macro and micro views and between reliability and validity. After our second scoring of the Co-op samples, which was completed by colleagues from across the disciplines, we met with a provost-level university committee on assessment (including representatives from nursing, education, biomedical engineering, cooperative education, business, media arts, informatics, among others) to discuss our work. We broke the larger group into tables of five and had individual members of this interdisciplinary group rank the samples from our Co-op scoring anchor set without using a rubric. Our WAAC members sat at the tables and recorded the conversations, paying close attention to the discipline-specific values inherent in the discussions, and noting where values converged and diverged across disciplines. After table discussions, we moved to a whole-group discussion and identified the values that informed decisions about the relative merit of papers. At this point we offered the tables our rubric and asked them to consider (1) if the rubric supported their ranking of the papers, and (2) if the rubric left out any important considerations from their conversations. Again, the WAAC members served as scribes for the conversations—which turned, naturally, to the prompt itself as the group checked to see if the prompt elicited the skills that they valued. The tables—independently—asked for minor revisions to the Co-op prompt. As this chapter is written, we are meeting with the provost's office and the Co-op central office about ways we would like to scaffold the learning in Co-op and the reflective analyses that assess this learning. Once more, as we expand the conversation about writing, we find the push for reliability that relies on longitudinal inertia is countered by the pull of validity that asks assessments to move in directions that will foster pedagogical growth.

NEXT STEPS: A MODEL OF PROCESS

Though we created new opportunities to examine student writing, we are mindful of Graff's warning that bad writing assessment can lead to students who devote "years of education to learn to speak with no context to no one" (Graff 2003, 63). However much we have attempted to scaffold our assessments, large-scale assessments in general, like huge caverns, can produce voices that bounce and echo. For example, when we read a sample in which the student is clearly "performing" for us, we recognize that our attempts to do authentic assessment produce some inauthentic results, and our questions about the tensions between reliability, authenticity, and student agency still resonate. And those beautiful moments of convergence with our colleagues? The reality is this: however inspiring those moments are, inspirations fade quickly in the daily repetition and politics of program administration. Part of the process of using accreditation to create a sustained culture of assessment is negotiating feelings of expectation and fatigue, especially in meetings where we struggle to rebuild what we thought was stable; plans that seem logical can be blocked by hierarchies, egos (including our own), and turf wars.

But even as we work through these challenges, we honor their value. As in a Burkean Parlor, our assessments center a particular discourse long enough for a group of people to find stasis, traction, and community. In simultaneously centering and decentering writing assessment, we have begun to create a shared vocabulary to drive pedagogical and structural change that we hope will resonate throughout the university. Further, by leveraging expertise to drive an accreditation assessment conversation, we have empowered some of our FWP faculty to develop assessment expertise and to locate themselves in a larger writing schema. Indeed, this inside-out process of making writing matter through assessment has created a foundation for a sustainable conversation about writing at this university. The continued renewal of funding to repeat our programmatic assessments year after year has sent a strong rhetorical message that the administration, too, is committed to our work. In the past year our dean and provost have funded us to invite faculty from across the university to participate in the compensated scoring-training conversations and in the scoring itself; these sessions have allowed Drexel faculty (nurses, chemists, philosophers, business people, biomedical engineers, education theorists) to engage in focused conversations about how we seek to understand our students' communication skills in the service of teaching and learning. As one anonymous participant commented, "Having the chance to talk out our thoughts gave all of us the ability to see how our thinking was the same or did not match—this was an important step." In addition, the mapping of our local rubric onto the rubric for assessing students' evidence-based Co-op reflections makes sense to the larger questions of transfer. And, most certainly, we will want to map our writing standards in the FWP onto other discipline-specific assessments so that we can continue to ask questions about transfer and get some real, evidence-based answers.

But our efforts in reporting our findings to the university community go beyond claims about how strong the FWP is and how well our students can carry over their skills from their first year into creating evidence-based arguments when they come back from Co-op. The next steps of this de-centering involve exactly the kind of discipline-specific work that Anson and others discuss in their 2012 critique of broadly constructed assessment rubrics that are expected to apply to all disciplines across the university. While we expect to have provided a tangible starting point for programs to start thinking about how they, too, "own" students' writing development, we hope to provide most importantly a model of process. Anson and others acknowledge the heft of work that is required for members of a department or program to decide what they really want students to learn, and how their assignments aim to accomplish that learning. We cannot—should not—tell them how to do it, but perhaps our years of developing assessment strategies in our own program can offer them some shortcuts into developing questions to which they do not yet have answers, organizing internal conversations, making arguments for resources that will help them to streamline their processes, and sparking an awareness of the common ground that they share about their standards for writing. As we have found, one of the biggest obstacles in programmatic assessment is getting started, and one of the greatest revelations in getting started is that there are already shared perspectives upon which to build.

Notes

1. We are indebted to Downs and Wardle's (2007) distillation of the pedagogical, rhetorical, and administrative importance of students' writing about their own writing in first-year writing curricula.

2. As did our FWP data, our Co-op data also show clear differences between the skills of domestic and international students and have facilitated necessary conversations.

References

Anson, Chris M., Deanna P. Dannels, Pamela Flash, and Amy L. Housley Gaffney. 2012. "Big Rubrics and Weird Genres: The Futility of Using Generic Assessment Tools across Diverse Instructional Contexts." *Journal of Writing Assessment* 5 (2012). http://journalofwritingassessment.org/article.php?article=57.

Broad, Bob. 2003. *What We Really Value: Beyond Rubrics in Teaching and Assessing Writing.* Logan: Utah State University Press.

Downs, Doug, and Elizabeth Wardle. 2007. "Teaching about Writing, Righting Misconceptions." *College Composition and Communication* 58 (4): 552–84.

"Drexel Student Learning Priorities." 2012. *Office of the Provost: Drexel University.* http://www.drexel.edu/provost/learningpriorities/.

Faigley, Lester, Roger P. Cherry, David A. Jolliffe, and Anna M. Skinner. 1985. *Assessing Writers' Knowledge and Processes of Composing.* Norwood, NJ: Ablex Publishing.

Graff, Gerald. 2003. *Clueless in Academe.* New Haven: Yale University Press.

Huot, Brian. 1996. "Toward a New Theory of Writing Assessment." *College Composition and Communication* 47 (4): 549–66. http://dx.doi.org/10.2307/358601.

Moore, Cindy, Peggy O'Neill, and Brian Huot. 2009. "Creating a Culture of Assessment in Writing Programs and Beyond." *College Composition and Communication* 61 (1): W107–32. http://www.ncte.org/library/NCTEFiles/Resources/Journals/CCC /0611sep09/CCC0611Creating.pdf.

White, Edward. 2005. "The Scoring of Writing Portfolios: Phase 2." *College Composition and Communication* 56 (4): 581–600.

White, Edward. 2007. *Assigning, Responding, Evaluating: A Writing Teacher's Guide.* Boston: Bedford/St.Martin's Press.

9

USING ACCOUNTABILITY TO GARNER WRITING PROGRAM RESOURCES, SUPPORT EMERGING WRITING RESEARCHERS, AND ENHANCE PROGRAM VISIBILITY

Implementing the UH Writing Mentors during WASC Reaccreditation

Jim Henry

The term "reaccreditation" carries enormous weight among upper-level college and university administrators: without accreditation, whatever cultural capital administrators believe that students gain while at their institution flies out the window, because the degrees granted lose validity. This weighty re-accrediting process is also lengthy—in the case of the Western Association of Schools and Colleges (WASC), spanning at least three years—yet it affords the institution an opportunity to reconsider its missions and effectiveness in attaining them. Although most campuses likely have an institutional research office, an assessment office, and a center supporting effective teaching and learning practices, such offices are at least one step removed from the nuts and bolts of educational effectiveness as writing programs envision and shape them. And while many university departments might see reaccreditation as intrusive or imposing hoops through which to jump, writing programs whose faculty conduct research on their practices as a matter of course can seize the occasion of reaccreditation to advance financial resources for the program, advance research agendas for faculty and graduate students, and advance the program's institutional reputation and visibility. In this chapter I recount how we achieved these three goals while conceptualizing, implementing, documenting, analyzing, and publishing about the UH Writing Mentors program.

In the fall of 2006, I responded to a call to faculty at the University of Hawai'i at Mānoa from the Vice Chancellor's office to join the steering

DOI: 10.7330/9781607324355.c009

committee for reaccreditation review by WASC. Having been hired just one year earlier and also beginning a three-year appointment as Director of Composition and Rhetoric in the department of English, I strategized that reaccreditation would be an opportunity to meet and collaborate with colleagues from across campus and hopefully to lobby for resources. First-year composition (FYC) was taught regularly by all tenure and tenure-line faculty in our department—a fact worth championing to upper administration and accreditors alike as the institution began its review of educational practices. First-year R1 university students rarely find themselves in a classroom capped at 20 with tenured or tenure-line faculty leading the course, and affording these students direct access to faculty also tasked with maintaining a vigorous research agenda can offer students invaluable perspectives on research and writing. Yet the practice was not without its drawbacks, given that many faculty had been trained outside of composition and rhetoric and that certain among them were several decades older than most of the students in a first-year class, reducing shared cultural references and rendering philosophical meeting points sometimes challenging. On a campus in which Caucasian students are in a minority, the English department is dominated by Caucasian instructors, adding another layer of complexity in course design and classroom dynamics. Most salient in this scenario was the fact that because all instructors in the department regularly taught FYC, we had a common interest in improving the course.

Our first-year composition program included classroom-based tutors (CBTs) for five students per course (pre-determined by placement exam), and the recently published *On Location: Theory and Practice in Classroom-Based Writing Tutoring* (Spigelman and Grobman 2005), offered a number of practical and theoretical touchstones that suggested ways in which our program might revise and improve to support learning success across a broader number of students. The editors observed, moreover, that classroom-based tutors change classroom cultures, resulting in "new links, forged among disparate populations of students, tutors, and teachers [to] create supportive, heterogeneous college communities" (Spigelman and Grobman 2005, 8), a laudable goal for our program in light of its cultural complexities. As the director of Composition and Rhetoric and also the inheritor of this first-year composition course, I wanted to build upon its strong points and attenuate the weaker ones. To do this I would need resources, and WASC reaccreditation held promise.

When I began my collaboration with reaccreditation steering committee members, I had scant knowledge of reaccrediting processes and standards; the account that follows benefits from my retrospective analysis, using the UH Writing Mentors as a case study to suggest ways in which WPAs at other institutions can anticipate the work that transpires during reaccreditation and strategize effectively to achieve some program goals.

INSPECTING AND LEVERAGING REACCREDITATION PROCESSES AND STANDARDS

An invaluable initial strategy in yoking writing program goals to re-accrediting processes and standards is to study the accrediting organization's handbook. The WASC handbook explains that reaccreditation involves three separate and sequential reports: the Institutional Proposal (IP), the Capacity and Preparatory Review (CPR), and the Educational Effectiveness Review (EER). The first of these three entails inspecting the institution's missions and formulating a proposal that furthers them while meeting accrediting standards. This IP writing process requires input from many members of the institution and coordination of the input by able report writers; WPAs who serve on reaccrediting committees will quite likely find themselves asked to serve as report writers and, as demanding as such work can be, it also offers opportunity. Reports must implement specific WASC standards that can be inspected to perceive parallels with writing program goals and standards. And report writers (and editors) are afforded the opportunity to perceive parallels between accrediting expectations and program goals and to convey in face-to-face meetings with colleagues just how clearly their programs do in fact further the institution's mission of providing quality education. For the WPA rhetor, discussions of evolving drafts frequently offer moments of kairos to be seized.

In the case of IPs submitted to WASC, they must show evidence of implementing three standards: Defining Institutional Purposes and Ensuring Educational Objectives; Achieving Educational Objectives through Core Functions; and Developing and Applying Resources and Organizational Structures to Ensure Sustainability (WASC Handbook of Accreditation 2008, 11–18.) In the case of UH Mānoa, a public R1 university, a key purpose is that of producing graduate researchers who will obtain the terminal degree, gain research jobs (most often in the Academy), and conduct further research. Very early on in the conceptualization and implementation of our UH Writing Mentors program, we decided to position our graduate mentors to undergraduates not only as tutors but also as researchers in their own rights. Such a positioning, as will be seen, aligned with both the institutional purpose of producing future researchers and with the second WASC standard of achieving educational objectives.

This second standard includes Teaching and Learning, Scholarship and Creative Activity, and Support for Student Learning and Success (WASC Handbook of Accreditation 2008, 14). Because WPAs regularly focus their energies on these three activities—whether by tapping the burgeoning scholarship in Composition and Rhetoric and its related fields to implement process pedagogy, conducting research on teaching and learning, and/or supplying support for student learning and success while leveraging teacher research, assessment, or support services such as writing centers or tutoring—such a standard aligns perfectly with our work. In the case of the UH Writing Mentors, we hoped to institute a support service that would require substantial funding to succeed.

The CPR to be submitted to WASC requires the institution to respond to reviews of the IP by the evaluating team. Its publication follows the IP by a year (or more) and must, as its name suggests, focus on the institution's capacity to meet the standards identified in the IP. As described in the WASC Handbook, "the framework of institutional capacity allows an institution to explore cross-cutting issues such as whether resources, structures and processes are aligned with the institution's mission and priorities, and whether the institution has the capacity to measure, interpret, and use evidence about its effectiveness. An important dimension of institutional capacity is the institution's readiness to define and sustain educational effectiveness" (WASC Handbook of Accreditation 2008, 8). As educational effectiveness lies at the heart of much writing pedagogy, the WASC CPR offers a WPA the opportunity to set up accountability measures to determine if the writing program initiative actually has adequate resources to measure and interpret evidence to be used to determine effectiveness. This phase in reaccreditation enables a WPA to set in place research vectors and/or assessment practices that will contribute to a strong showing in the CPR and stoke program visibility among other report writers—and ultimately with CPR readers. Because the process often involves getting feedback on drafts from campus stakeholders, it furthers the visibility of initiatives included in it. In the case of the WASC review of the CPR for UH Mānoa, the campus visit was also the occasion for a poster session, thus publicizing our initiative in another medium and venue while also gaining insights on other campus initiatives, a point further developed below.

The EER requires the institution to respond to the CPR evaluation by the campus visit team and concludes the cycle of self-assessments submitted by the institution for reaccreditation. As such, it constitutes a summative evaluation of improvement efforts to date that in turn forecast the creation or sustaining of an organization "committed to learning and improvement" (WASC Handbook of Accreditation 2008, 21). The Handbook stresses that the EER should "examine institutional practices for evaluating student learning . . . to develop and share good practices for using educational results to improve the process of teaching and learning" (WASC Handbook of Accreditation 2008, 34), an occasion to refine, further develop, and share results of research with the campus community (and beyond, through scholarly publication).

In the case of the EER at UH Mānoa, it came a full four years after we had begun drafting the IP. Those four years witnessed three different Vice Chancellors overseeing the reaccrediting process, numerous changes in steering committee personnel and report writers and editors, and the institutionalization of some of the initiatives proposed in the IP. Happily, the UH Writing Mentors was one of the initiatives so institutionalized, and in the sections that follow, specific steps taken to meet the twin missions of producing research and enhancing teaching and learning are reviewed to offer strategies for other WPAs to garner resources, advance research agendas, and enhance the initiative's reputation and visibility.

REACCREDITATION AND DEVELOPMENT OF THE UH WRITING MENTORS PROGRAM

While serving as co-editor to draft the IP, I was also teaching a section of English 100: Composition 1. It was my second time teaching the course, and I knew from experience that placement into the course was problematic: an entrance exam identified certain students as needing extra tutoring, and those students were mainstreamed in groups of five into sections of 20. Thus the CBT component existed under an umbrella of remediation. Students were required to meet twice a week with their CBT undergraduate tutor or with a first-semester PhD student apprenticing with tenure-line faculty in the course and attending classes alongside students. However, placement was uneven: some students identified as somewhat "remedial" in fact were not, once in the classroom, and other students who could clearly benefit from extra tutoring, for one reason or another, were denied access to the tutor under the system in place.

Assisting me in this fall 2006 section was PhD apprentice Holly Huff Bruland, who also regretted that she would be restricted to working with just five students. We approached the chair to seek permission to deploy her services across all students, and we were given the go-ahead, along with an undergraduate tutor in one other section being led by a long-time adjunct instructor who was keen on expanding the CBT possibilities.

Bruland was also participating in a graduate seminar I was leading on the topic of analyzing workplace writing cultures, and she focused her term project on her own workplace—and more specifically the version of CBT that she and her counterpart undergraduate student were a part of. The two of them documented all their conferences with students and also kept extensive field notes on classroom practices and dynamics. Bruland had become increasingly excited about the initiative as she drafted and revised her seminar paper, eventually building on the scholarship of Patricia Bizzell (1999) to analyze this novel configuration of CBT as a "hybrid genre" that accomplished intellectual work that could not be accomplished, she maintained, through classroom discourse or tutoring discourse alone. She pursued publication of the seminar paper and was successful: in spring 2007, her article "Accomplishing Intellectual Work: An Investigation of the Re-Locations Enacted through On-Location Tutoring" appeared in *Praxis: A Writing Center Journal* (Bruland 2007). This publication constituted the first research on the initiative by a graduate student, thus signaling its contribution to the university's mission of preparing researchers. As the content of the article conveyed, the initiative was also contributing to the university's mission of effective education. This publication and the track record it established set the scene for seeking more resources for the initiative.

GARNERING FINANCIAL RESOURCES FOR THE PROGRAM

The goal of garnering financial resources while working on reaccreditation was achieved rather quickly, even before the IP had been completed and sent to WASC. Thus this section is the shortest of the three. However, meeting the goal of *securing* financial support also required putting into place mechanisms for *assuring* future support, a key strategy that will be developed in the sections on research and visibility.

While Bruland and I were teaching our section in fall 2006, I petitioned the department chair to offer more pilot sections in which all students would be tutored in the spring semester. The chair, too, regularly taught FYC, so she was aware of the drawbacks of the current configuration; she was also no doubt encouraged by Bruland's budding research. She agreed, this time funding four sections rather than just two. In addition, she joined me in submitting a proposal for a grant from the National Education Association (NEA) to fund five more such sections the following fall. At the time, UH Mānoa was a member of the NEA, and their Learning and Leadership grants offered modest support (up to $5,000) for certain initiatives in public schools. Our proposal included a project summary, a statement of what we believed we would learn from collecting data on the initiative, a list of data we would be collecting (including student evaluations of the mentoring, mentors' logs from conferences, and sample faculty lesson plans incorporating a mentor into writing activities), how we intended to share what we would learn, and a budget. We were awarded the grant, which had noteworthy consequences: we were building a formal writing initiative with increasing dimension (nine sections scheduled as compared with the current two), we were putting into place a system of data collection that aligned with the kind of data required by WASC reaccreditation, and we were affirming the validity of our initiative through this outside funding. The chair and I decided to approach the vice chancellor (VC) to see if we could secure support for additional sections.

The VC was chairing the WASC reaccreditation steering committee, and I had gotten to know him well at that point in my capacity as co-editor of the IP. WASC invites institutions seeking reaccreditation to structure their IPs around themes and objectives commensurate with their Standards, and one of our themes was "Building a Mānoa Community in Support of Student Success" with an objective "to enable and ensure student learning success" (University of Hawai'i at Mānoa 2006, 10). In our face-to-face meetings of the steering committee, occasional moments of kairos had enabled me to mention the English department's pilot sections of FYC with full CBT coverage, and for this meeting with the VC I now had the approved grant from the NEA to assure five sections for the fall semester, my chair's commitment of department funds for four additional sections, and a copy of Bruland's *Praxis* article to demonstrate the efficacy of the initiative, along with one graduate student's research that was linked to it.

The chair and I had planned to ask for funding for an additional six sections for the fall, to bring our total to 15. Although that would be a big leap from the four we were currently running and require a lot more time to manage, I agreed to take on the extra work in my capacity as director of Composition and Rhetoric because I had seen the great potential demonstrated in our pilot sections. Our meeting with the vice chancellor went swimmingly; after about a half hour's discussion, he offered to support not six but *14* sections of FYC with full CBT coverage in the form of one-quarter time TA-ships for MA students. Clearly, he recognized the alignment with the Institutional Proposal. The chair and I, though delighted, were caught a bit off guard and mentioned that as happy as we were to accept his offer, we were a bit daunted by the administrative weight this would add to my duties. The vice chancellor added support for one-course release time for me and a modest stipend for Bruland as administrative and research assistant, bringing the total of his commitment to this three-year pilot to just under $100,000 per year. We left the meeting with yet another reason to establish robust documentation and accounting for the initiative, as we would have to re-apply for support from his office at the end of the three-year pilot. In the following section are details on how the setting up of documentation also resulted in supporting a number of graduate students in their own research on CBT in FYC.

SUPPORTING EMERGING RESEARCHERS

Establishing a context in which graduate students could emerge and flourish as researchers of first-year student writing was one of the most important outcomes of institutionalizing the UH Writing Mentors during reaccreditation. As this goal was met rather convincingly during the cycle from IP to CPR to EER, this section is the most detailed of the case study. Below is a mostly chronological report on the *experience* of conducting research as graduate students lived it, setting the scene for reporting one of the *results* of conducting research: enhancing program visibility and reputation. That result will be treated in the next section.

Buoyed by the success of her first scholarly publication and increasingly intrigued by the version of CBT with which she was involved, Bruland decided in late spring of 2007 to make this initiative the focus of her dissertation. This fact, plus the need for the English department to set up assessment protocol for the initiative to submit to the VC, led us to design a standardized conference log instrument for each tutor to collect data on one key component of the initiative: the regular out-of-class writing conferences. We also met regularly with instructors and tutors in the pilot sessions that spring and soon recognized that the range of roles enacted by the tutors went far beyond those normally played by classroom-based tutors as the scholarship on them suggested. Spigelman and Grobman listed five such roles ("classroom presenters, discussion leaders, workshop troubleshooters, conference consultants, and peer group facilitators" [Spigelman and Grobman 2005, 12]), yet our discussions revealed many more. These roles indicated that the tutors in our case were treading into territory that perhaps surpassed the purview of a "tutor," so we wondered about the appropriateness of the term (e.g., tutors had found themselves coaching students on choosing a major, using campus health services when ill, and mustering the nerve to request an extension from the instructor.). During one review of data, Bruland mentioned that she had served as a "mentor" to student athletes while at her undergraduate institution, and the multiplicity of roles she saw tutors playing reminded her of that job. She and I decided formally to dub this new agent in writing instruction a *mentor* as we implemented the initiative.

In addition, we had become intrigued by the different perspectives on the initiative as lived by program administrators, instructors, and mentors. Drawing on data from the spring 2007 pilot, we collaborated with one of the pilot mentors, Ryan Omizo (who was in the process of enrolling in the PhD program in Rhetoric, Composition, and Literacy at Ohio State), to publish "Mentoring First-Year Students in Composition: Tapping Role Construction to Teach" (Henry, Bruland, and Omizo 2008). In this article we identified a dozen roles that emerged for mentors across the four sections during the semester (the standardized conference log as used that semester is included in this article), and we reflected on how certain of these roles sparked ideas for augmenting teaching practices.

We began to see the potential for more research production on the part of mentors, so we consciously structured their training with respect to composition and rhetoric practices. We knew that many of these incoming MA students had experience as tutors in various capacities while undergraduates, yet we also knew that only a few of them would be concentrating in composition and rhetoric while the others would be concentrating in creative writing, cultural studies in Asia and the Pacific, or literary studies. My own graduate training had focused specifically on the teaching of writing and on using ethnographic methods to analyze such teaching in specific cultural contexts. Mina Shaughnessy's work and the orientation in Composition Studies it had engendered to read student writing not as defective but as data to be interpreted in charting teaching and learning practices joined my graduate training and Bruland's emerging expertise to prompt us to configure our mentors' duties not only as supplemental instructors but also as composition *researchers*. Thus the degree to which our initiative answered the university's mission to shape graduate researchers as expressed in the IP began expanding beyond the cases of Bruland and Omizo.

The roles of our mentors paralleled those of the tutors who contributed to Spigelman and Grobman's volume (e.g., Corroy 2005; Giger 2005; You 2005). Several of the logs of the spring pilot included musings by mentors about students' performances that began with "I wonder if ...," and we decided to include in mentors' job description the requirement to *wonder* about composition students' performances rather than jumping to hasty conclusions. We introduced this job description at a two-day August 2007 orientation for faculty and mentors; we also assigned readings to mentors on fieldwork methods, composition theory, and composition research methods to be used in bi-weekly roundtable meetings with mentors throughout the semester as they attended classes with their mentees, met with them for regular out-of-class conferences, and documented their work through conference logs and weekly reflective memos.

The fall 2007 semester laid the groundwork for mentors to grow into their identities as composition researchers. They had read some key scholarship on mentoring and on fieldwork methodology for qualitative research, and they were taking copious field notes during class, both to model note-taking for first-year students and to garner data that could supplement their conference logs to render their "wondering" about student performances more evidence-based. Their data collections and analyses proved so promising that we urged them to submit proposals to the College's spring peer-reviewed graduate colloquium, and a remarkable eight of them were accepted and delivered. Mentors presented research in subsequent years as well, affording most of them with their first-ever formal presentation of research findings to a scholarly audience. Because the titles of their presentations convey the array of approaches to researching student learning in FYC that the UH Writing Mentors initiative enabled, Table 9.1 lists them for each year. As can be seen, this research often melded research vectors in composition and rhetoric with mentors' other interests and approaches to knowledge production from other fields.

While working on the Institutional Proposal, I had become aware of the University's emphasis on retention, and I reasoned that an initiative that seemed from assessment to produce positive outcomes and that was so overwhelmingly embraced by students (88 percent of them indicated that they were either "very satisfied" or "satisfied" with the mentoring on the fall 2007 anonymous end-of-term evaluations, a fact that Jennifer Sano had explored in her college colloquium presentation listed below) was likely to support retention efforts. Discussions on the reaccreditation steering committee frequently addressed the need

Table 9.1. Graduate students' research presentations at the peer-reviewed college colloquium

Student and Year	Presentation Title
Holly Huff Bruland, 2008	"Trans/Per Forming First-Year Composition: Casting the Role of the Mentor-Researcher"
Chelsey Kojima, 2008	"Individualized Learning Outcomes in Higher Education"
Phillip Drake, 2008	"Working Towards a Better (Essay about the) Environment"
Annette Priesmann, 2008	"Punctuation as a Two-Way Street"
Tracey Williams, 2008	"The Mentor as Transitional Ally"
Alicia Maedo, 2008	"Mentors as Mobile Writing Centers for Collaboration"
Tanya Torres, 2008	"Mentoring and Universal Design"
Jennifer Sano, 2008	"Student Evaluations of Mentor and Program Performance"
Rubsamen, 2010	"Casting Mentors as Self-Efficacy Builders in the FYC Classroom"
Steven Holmes, 2010	"Mentoring Argumentation: Pedagogies in Combining the Toulmin and Rogerian Models"
Melinda Smith, 2011	"The Role of Motivation in Performing as a Writer in Liminal Spaces"

to supply data-driven conclusions about teaching and learning, and the growing wealth of data we were collecting on the UH Writing Mentors—to reference in the CPR and EER, to use ultimately in the report to the VC on initiative performance, and to guide Bruland's dissertation—suggested that we conceptualize our research at least partly with respect to the scholarship of teaching and learning (SoTL). We had located a valuable 2007 SoTL publication on mentoring by Amaury Nora and Gloria Crisp entitled "Mentoring Students: Conceptualizing and Validating the Multi-Dimensions of a Support System" in which they had identified key dimensions of mentoring: "psychological/emotional support; support for setting goals and choosing a career path; academic subject knowledge support aimed at advancing a student's knowledge relevant to their chosen field; and specification of a role model" (Nora and Crisp 2007, 337).

We hypothesized that the student evaluations of mentoring analyzed quantitatively by Sano would affirm the presence of these dimensions, which in turn would make the case that mentoring was supporting retention. So during the summer we coded the sum of students' written evaluations to discover that students did indeed affirm the presence of these dimensions in varying degrees. We yoked these findings with Tinto's (1993) research on student persistence and submitted a manuscript to the *Journal of College Student Retention (JCSR)*. I also composed a poster for a poster session sponsored by the Assessment Office on the occasion of a campus visit by a WASC team to receive the IP. The poster included our methodology, summarized the results of 400 end-of-term anonymous student evaluations, showed a sample of coding, and presented the findings that affirmed Nora and Crisp's constructs as identified by student mentees in varying degrees (University of Hawai'i at Mānoa Assessment Office 2009)

Our manuscript was ultimately rejected by *JCSR* (though we had made the case rhetorically, we lacked the longitudinal data to confirm a direct correlation between mentoring and persistence), which prompted us to regroup. Even though we could not substantiate a direct link to retention, we had nonetheless confirmed empirically that the term that Bruland and I had chosen spontaneously when renaming our CBTs, *mentors*, was a proper use of the term. In addition, our analysis had identified a dimension not identified by Nora and Crisp: mentee willingness. Bruland, Sano (now Sano-Franchini and collaborating long distance from Michigan State where she was a PhD student in the Rhetoric and Writing Program), and I revised our manuscript and submitted it to the *International Journal for the Scholarship of Teaching and Learning*, where it was ultimately published (Henry, Bruland, and Sano-Franchini 2011).

While work on the WASC CPR report got underway, data on the mentoring had reached an *n* that enabled Bruland to propose and have accepted a presentation at the annual convention of College Composition and Communication, entitled "On Location: Adding Writing Mentors to the First-Year Composition Curriculum." This was her first trip to CCCC and thus a valuable step for her as an emerging scholar. (She subsequently presented at CCCC in 2009 and 2010, establishing her position as a national authority on CBT and mentoring in FYC.) The article published in *IJSoTL* made good use of data collected from students on the mentoring initiative, thus providing the kinds of evidence of outcomes expected by WASC in its CPR and EER. However, an analysis of mentors' anonymous semesterly evaluations had yet to be undertaken. These evaluations asked a number of questions of mentors on their work, as can be seen in Table 9.2, Mentors' end-of-term program evaluations.

During the summer and fall of 2009, Bruland and I devoted extensive work to analyzing these evaluations. Increasingly intrigued by the complexities of the institutional position of "mentor" as these classroom agents sought to achieve the initiative's motto, helping *every* student excel in English 100, Bruland and I sought research on institutional positioning of social actors. We eventually made our way back to Bourdieu

Table 9.2. Mentors' end-of-term program evaluations

End-of-term Program Evaluations by Mentors

1. How would you rate your overall level of satisfaction with the mentoring program?

2. What have been the best and/or most fulfilling aspects of your job as a mentor? Please explain why.

3. What have been the most frustrating and/or problematic aspects of your job as a mentor? Please explain why.

4. How would you most accurately describe your role within your English 100 classroom?

5. This past semester, what did your English 100 students teach you?

6. Please give Jim and Holly some feedback on our performance as program administrators. What have we been doing well that you'd like to see us continue? How can we better support your work as a mentor?

7. In what ways have the bi-weekly round-tables been useful? How could they be improved? What are some additional ways that can we enhance the value of the mentoring program in terms of your own professional development?

8. The job description calls for 10 hours per week of work for mentors. Over the course of the semester, how many hours of work did you average per week? (These responses are completely anonymous, so please give us as accurate a response as possible.)

9. What can we as administrators do to make the actual number of hours spent on the job come closer to the job description?

10. Approximately what percentage of your overall time as a mentor did you allot to the following activities:

    - attending your English 100 class

    - preparing for your English 100 class

    - conferencing face-to-face with students

    - emailing students

    - completing conference logs

    - writing in your composition notebook

    - communicating with your instructor

    - attending mentor round-tables

    - other

11. Approximately how many emails did you send to your students per week?

12. Please describe the nature of your emails with students and explain the roles that email communications played in your overall work as mentor.

13. Is there anything else we should know? Please use this box to give us any additional feedback on this past semester or suggestions for the future.

14. We foresee that your responses to these questions could potentially serve as a way to represent the program. Would you be willing for your responses to be used in future reports and/or publications?

and Wacquant's work on reflexive sociology (Bourdieu and Wacquant 1992) in which they underscore the degree to which researchers and their research owe elements to how the researchers are positioned institutionally. Coding mentors' end-of-term evaluations for those comments that indicated a perspective in this pedagogical undertaking as a *student* and those comments that indicated perspective as a *teacher*, we teamed Bourdieu and Wacquant's observations on positional reflexivity with Donald Schön's (1987) work on educating reflective practitioners. (Our findings aligned with Soliday's analysis of classroom-based tutors assigned from her Writing Center [Soliday 1995], yet, unlike her, we did not focus on the tension between CBT and the oft-cited identity of writing centers as offering students an autonomous space. Rather, we were interested in the *kinds* of reflexivity engendered in mentor-researchers through this novel positioning of part-instructor, part-student.) We submitted and subsequently published "Educating Reflexive Practitioners: Casting Graduate Teaching Assistants as Mentors in First-Year Classrooms" in the *International Journal of Teaching and Learning in Higher Education* (*IJTLHE*) (Henry and Bruland 2010). One local outcome of this publication was that it enabled discussions with colleagues in English across all concentrations on the benefits of using TAs not to *grade* but rather to *coach* from their unique institutional positions. These discussions were further enabled by the questions we were asking of our colleagues who had worked with mentors at the end of each semester, as shown in Table 9.3, Instructors' end-of-term evaluations.

In the fall of 2009, I had the opportunity to work with a mentor in my own English 100 classroom for the first time since the initiative's inception. Eager to exploit the pedagogical possibilities offered by the initiative, I focused in particular on how my mentor, Lehua Ledbetter, and I could enhance peer review. We staged a carefully-sequenced series of events in which we each responded to one another's drafts and cover memos composed for the first assignment. We heightened the performative dimension of our mutual reviews by revealing them to students in class on an overhead to point out our varieties of response, then entreating students to attempt similar supportive response as intellectual teammates. Students were then required to upload their responses to peers to our course web space on the campus server, compare their responses with one other classmate and either mine or Lehua's, and compose a memo charting plans for better performance in future reviews. The peer review performances that ensued were the best I had ever witnessed in my first-year writing course, and in the spring of 2010 I teamed with Lehua to compose "Teaching Intellectual Teamwork

Table 9.3. Instructors' end-of-term evaluations

End-of-term Program Evaluations by Instructors
1. How would you rate your overall level of satisfaction with the mentoring program?
2. Please comment on your assigned mentor's overall performance this semester.
3. Please list the various roles your mentor played during class. (i.e., asked clarifying questions, passed out assignments, led discussions ...)
4. In what ways do you believe the mentor's presence influenced the classroom environment? (Please feel free to share any specific examples or anecdotes that come to mind.)
5. In what ways do you believe the mentor's work influenced your students' writing? (Please feel free to share any specific examples or anecdotes that come to mind.)
6. If given the opportunity, would you want to work with an English 100 mentor in the future?
7. What suggestions do you have for how we can improve the mentoring program?
8. We foresee that your responses to these questions could potentially serve as a way to represent the program. Would you be willing for your responses to be used in future reports and/or publications?
9. We also foresee that your responses could provide valuable feedback to your assigned mentor. Please designate the ways you would be willing for us to share your survey responses with your assigned mentor.
10. Would you be willing to provide us with additional feedback and ideas for the mentoring program by participating in a 1-hour focus group interview in the Spring?

in WAC Courses through Peer Review." We submitted it to *Currents in Teaching and Learning* and, after Lehua had gone on to PhD studies in the Rhetoric and Writing Program at Michigan State, the article was published (Henry and Ledbetter 2011).

The EER Report was submitted to WASC in December 2010, with a response scheduled for spring 2011. The theme of "Supporting Student Success" had endured to the end, and the UH Writing Mentors was one of six campus entities singled out and discussed as helping students succeed. The report provided even more data on the UH Writing Mentors than previously featured in the CPR Report, including (1) the fact that more than 1,800 students had been mentored since the initiative's inception, (2) scores from the fall 2009 Assessment Office's (AO) poster session, and (3) the statistic that 90 percent of the students mentored to date had rated their experiences as either "satisfied" or "wholly satisfied" (see University of Hawai'i at Mānoa 2010).

Bruland's third successive presentation at the annual Convention of College Composition and Communication was titled "A New Turn in Teacher-Research: Contesting the Student-Teacher Binary through Trinary Classroom Configurations." This presentation was in some sense a watershed moment in her research, both because it introduced a new term into composition parlance to account for mentors' presences in classrooms as they shifted scenarios for writing performance, and because it marked the emergence of a strong emphasis on place-based writing theory in her research, driven inductively by the recurrent emphasis on place in the first-year composition classrooms in which mentors had performed and deductively by place-based Composition scholarship.

In October 2012 Bruland successfully defended her dissertation, "Trinary Collaborations in First-Year Composition: A Mixed Methods Study of the University of Hawai'i Writing Mentors Program." The four-year study offered a remarkably robust form of accountability as it drew upon

> (a) auto-ethnographic field notes conducted across four years of program workshops and bi-weekly mentor round-tables that I attended as a graduate student writing program administrator (WPA) and researcher; (b) 6,602 conference logs; (c) 653 weekly memos; (d) 89 anonymous end-of-semester program evaluations by mentors; (e) 1,452 anonymous end-of-semester evaluations by students; (f) 133 end-of-semester evaluations by instructors; (g) five participant check round-table discussions conducted with mentors who read chapter drafts; (h) a large-scale writing assessment comparing scores from binary and trinary FYC sections; (i) demographic surveys completed by mentors and instructors across the hundred sections; and (j) institutional records. (Bruland 2012b)

In the discussion following her presentation of findings,[1] the director of Graduate Studies in English, who had also served as a reader, said "It strikes me as significant that the writing mentors program was able to leverage the advent of reaccreditation in order to actually offer a better teaching and learning environment to students, mentors, and faculty." The scholarship undertaken by Bruland and other graduate students had also contributed significantly to the initiative's reputation and visibility in the English Department, the campus, and beyond, as the following section explains.

ENHANCING INSTITUTIONAL REPUTATION AND VISIBILITY

Just as data collection and analysis associated with the mentoring initiative that figured in the WASC IP, CPR, and EER enabled a number of graduate students to emerge as researchers, so did it stoke the visibility and reputation of the UH Writing Mentors. Below I retrace some key steps that contributed to both.

One of the steps I took as director of the initiative was to establish a website that would serve as permanent virtual home for the mentors, to provide links to helpful resources in teaching composition and to document the research efforts that were taking form (http://www.english.hawaii.edu/mentors). The website I established helped us disseminate "exemplary practice through workshops, articles, and a [virtual] resource library" (Moran and Herrington 1997, 138n), a positive outcome of program review already identified in WAC assessment. Maintaining this website enabled us to include ample resource materials for mentors, instructors, and students, and it also served to archive landmark developments. Thus the site enhances visibility of the program both locally and nationally.

Among local audiences is the English department where the initiative took form. In spring 2008, Bruland and I drew upon mentors' logs collected during fall 2007 to deliver our first formal presentation on campus of the mentoring initiative, at a department colloquium. The department had never witnessed empirical research of this kind on FYC, and we sought through the presentation both to inform colleagues who were or might be working with a mentor of our findings and to represent an area of composition and rhetoric with which few were familiar. These logs asked mentors a number of questions about their individual conferences in both multiple-choice and short-answer forms, as Table 9.4 shows.

Across a set of 985 conferences conducted the previous term, the most frequent topic of conversation had been understanding the expectations of the assignment, a finding that seemed significant given that many in the audience either were or would be soon teaching a section of English 100. Time and again, mentors who had been in the classroom when an assignment was made, participated in the discussion of it, and possibly even played a hand in its conceptualization were further quizzed by mentees during out-of-class conferences, revealing not a lack of understanding on students' parts but rather the complexities of *any* transactional writing in an institutional setting. This presentation made the quality of research we were conducting very clear to our colleagues outside of composition and rhetoric, further legitimizing this writing program initiative.

During the discussion that followed, an instructor of an Honors section lamented that he had not had a mentor, because several of his continental students had had a hard time adjusting to life in Hawai'i and the ways in which the history of the state inflected teaching and learning. It was decided then and there to assign mentors to Honors sections when so solicited, thus bolstering the initiative's understanding of mentoring as non-remedial and aligning it with much scholarship on composition and tutoring (Rose 1983; Cooper 1994; Harris 1995;).

Table 9.4. Mentor conference log for each individual conference with mentees

Student's Name:	Mentor's Name:
Date:	Location of Conference:
Length of conference (in minutes):	Conference # (eg 1st, 2nd, 3rd):

When did this session come about, with respect to the writing assignment?

☐ At the Beginning ☐ In the Middle ☐ Near the End ☐ After initial grade

Did you refer the student to any other campus resources: ☐ Yes ☐ No

If yes, please specify the resource(s):

Did the student follow up on your referral: ☐ Yes ☐ No ☐ Not Sure

What elements of the student's performance did your session address:

☐ Preparing for writing conferences

☐ Understanding the assignment's requirements

☐ Choosing (or modifying) a topic

☐ Generating ideas for the paper's content

☐ Finding outside sources

☐ Incorporating outside sources into a piece of writing

☐ Clarifying the paper's purpose

☐ Organizing the paper more effectively

☐ Honing grammar, usage, and style

☐ Collaborating with classmates

☐ Approaching the instructor with concerns, questions, requests

☐ Applying the instructor's comments for revision

☐ Developing confidence as a writer and college student

☐ Upholding class and/or university policies and expectations

☐ Understanding material that was covered in class

☐ Utilizing technology and university resources

☐ Acquiring skills in time management and personal organization

☐ Handling issues of college and personal life not directly related to the course

☐ Other(s): please specify

How did you go about addressing these elements of the student's performance: (please elaborate in a few sentences)

Our mentors' research presentations at the college's annual peer-reviewed graduate conference alerted another campus constituency to the initiative's value. The interim dean of the college (also an English professor) chose this panel among all the concurrent panels to attend in

2008, garnering us another institutional ally and instilling new ideas for his own teaching of FYC upon return to the rotation, he mentioned to me after the panel. Two years later, when a new dean (who hailed from Second Language Studies) was in place, he, too, chose to attend the panel on mentoring. Our visibility was spreading successfully through the college by virtue of our mentors' research presentations.

We also strategized to improve visibility by teaming with another campus entity, the Assessment Office. This office was undertaking assessment of General Education instruction as part of its work on reaccreditation, and AO members approached English to undertake assessment on one of the outcomes for FYC: writing for a specific purpose and audience. The assessment was conducted across sections with and without mentors, and it revealed that mentored students scored more highly than their counterparts. Because those students in mentored sections had not self-selected (mentored sections had not been designated on the course availability website in this inaugural version of the initiative due to timing of course assignments), this result was deemed an encouraging finding. Equally encouraging was the finding that mentored students scored higher than their counterparts in the category assessing students' capacity to reflect critically on the writing they had self-selected as representative of their performance on this outcome. That mentored students might be developing meta-cognitive capacities superior to non-mentored students had seemed likely to us, given the number of conversations about writing held with their mentors during the semester. To see this hypothesis corroborated through outcomes assessment affirmed the initiative's value from yet another important angle, given that students' capacities for meta-cognition have been identified as one of the most important predictors of longitudinal writing growth (Carroll 2002).

The assessment of students' FYC writing performances by the AO added a credible outside voice that substantiated our initiative's value both to department colleagues and to the VC, rendering this stage in implementation a particularly strong part of our strategy to institutionalize the initiative. The assessment was timely, too, as it enabled Bruland to team with Assistant Professor Erica Reynolds Clayton to present a poster at the poster session sponsored by the AO for the WASC IP review team (University of Hawai'i at Mānoa Assessment Office 2009). With my own poster mentioned earlier on display, the UH Writing Mentor initiative was achieving visibility in yet another venue. Our collaboration with the AO continued through the WASC CPR visit. With Bruland now as first author, we presented the poster "The UH Writing Mentors Program: A Multi-Perspectival Assessment," highlighting the extensive data collected to date on the initiative, including 3,000+ mentor logs, 600 end-of-semester surveys by students, 50+ end-of-semester surveys by mentors and faculty, and focus group interviews and field notes (University of Hawai'i at Mānoa 2009).

O'Neill, Moore, and Huot (2009) have observed that assessment is frequently perceived as "a way to satisfy demands that originate outside of a program" rather than as a way to learn more about that program (109). Our poster sessions made it clear to any campus constituency that attended the poster session that our assessment of the UH Writing Mentors was firmly aimed at learning about the program. In fact, the chancellor spent quite a bit of time speaking with Bruland on the contents of the poster and quizzing her on specifics, in the company of two WASC review team members. When the WASC EER team came to campus a year later, I was invited along with two mentors to meet with a reviewer in a meeting that included only a dozen other campus actors.

Probably the broadest campus visibility emerged from our bi-weekly meetings with mentors during the semester to discuss readings, noteworthy events, or to troubleshoot problems. We sought to leverage these meetings pro-actively, and Bruland and I would regularly debrief and strategize to determine how we might use the issues that mentors brought to light to improve orientation and training for them. Over the course of the period from the IP to the EER, we networked with nearly a dozen campus entities to establish and strengthen ties, and in many cases to incorporate their work into our workshops and orientations for mentors. These efforts were deemed noteworthy by the EER writing team and were included in its report (see University of Hawai'i at Mānoa 2009, 12). Table 9.5 lists the campus entities with which we teamed to strengthen student success.

INSTITUTIONALIZING EDUCATIONAL EFFECTIVENESS AS WRITING PROGRAMS SHAPE IT

In March 2011, WASC delivered its response to our EER report and bestowed a record 10-year accreditation on UHM. The report lauded the efforts of the UH Writing Mentors for having served 1800 students during its existence with "careful monitoring of program impact" (WASC Visiting Team 2011, 30). Partly because this careful monitoring was conducted not only by program administrators but also by the mentors themselves through their reflexive engagement, the initiative remained robust. When the three-year trial period funded by the Vice Chancellor's office came to an end, the initiative was immediately institutionalized

Table 9.5. Campus entities supporting student success with which the UH Writing Mentors established connections

- Student Success Center (Mentors were afforded spaces for meeting with students and provided with computers to support mentoring.)

- Campus Librarians (Librarians offered workshops on information literacy for FYC students, and mentors were given an orientation to these workshops in our own pre-semester orientations.)

- Access to College Excellence Program (We met with the director to organize sections of learning communities with mentored sections of FYC.)

- College Opportunities Program (We met with the director to alert him to our initiative and to encourage students to seek out mentored sections.)

- Manawa Kupono Program (supporting Native Hawaiian students from at-risk communities) (We met with the Director to alert him to our initiative and to encourage students to seek out mentored sections.)

- Sustainability Council (Several sections of mentored FYC focused on sustainability, and we listed our initiative with the council to give students yet another reason to choose the section.)

- English Honors (We regularly provided mentors for Honors sections of FYC.)

- Women's Studies (We invited a faculty member whose colloquia Bruland and I attended on positioning students as active learners and stewards of their own destiny to meet with mentors in a round-table.)

- KOKUA (the campus office assisting students with disabilities)(We took mentors to an orientation to their services as part of our pre-semester mentoring orientations.)

- Counseling Center. (We took mentors to an orientation to their services as part of our pre-semester mentoring orientations.)

(and this during a period of budget cuts). The English department had witnessed two changes in chairs since the inception of the initiative, and when I asked the current chair if he had had any feedback on the mentoring initiative from the college dean—who also participated in resource allocation—he told me that the dean not only endorsed the mentoring, he had suggested that other departments emulate it.

So that WPAs elsewhere can leverage reaccreditation to bring resources to their programs, nurture emerging scholars, and achieve visibility, the table below summarizes key actions taken in our case study that can, with hope, be adapted to other contexts and other campus cultures.

Table 9.6 also enables brief commentary on a lingering issue, after reaccreditation and after institutionalization of the UH Writing Mentors. One of the key elements of the initiative was designating the writing mentors as both teachers *and* researchers. This designation not only introduced graduate students from other concentrations to composition research, it enabled them to *live* the value of such research

Table 9.6. Advancing writing initiative goals in tandem with WASC reaccreditation

Goals	Steps Taken by the WPA During WASC Reaccreditation
Garnering Program Resources	• Submitting a proposal to the National Education Association to support more sections of FYC in which all students would receive tutoring from a CBT • Submitting a proposal to the chair of English to expand mentored sections • Submitting a proposal to the vice chancellor to request funding for one-quarter TA-ships for English MA students who would serve as CBTs to FYC students, release time for the WPA, and administrative and research assistants • Initiating and sustaining documentation to present to the chair, dean, and vice chancellor at the end of the 3-year pilot to renew support
Supporting Emerging Writing Researchers	• Designating writing mentors as both teachers and researchers • Supporting a PhD student in publishing research on the initiative • Supporting writing mentors in proposals to a peer-reviewed college-wide graduate student research conference • Collaborating with three mentors and former mentors in publishing on the initiative • Directing a PhD student's doctoral dissertation on the mentoring initiative • Supporting this PhD student's post-doctoral publication efforts
Enhancing Program Visibility	• Establishing a public website that serves both as resource to mentors and as ongoing documentation of mentoring work • Networking with reaccreditation steering committee colleagues to tout the initiative • Delivering formal colloquia to colleagues in English • Developing and presenting posters for poster sessions sponsored by the Assessment Office (AO) during campus visits by the reaccreditation team • Establishing formal relationships with nearly a dozen campus offices and organizations related to student support • Presenting findings on the initiative at local and national colloquia and conferences

when they conceptualized, conducted, and presented their own composition research in a peer-reviewed college conference. When I accepted another writing program administrative position in the University and when Holly Huff Bruland completed her PhD and departed, the department was left with nobody with expertise in composition research of this kind. A colleague filled the gap temporarily until a new hire could take over, but in the interim, three cohorts of mentors were left with little or no instruction as composition researchers, thus neither living its value nor benefitting professionally from it. Campus visibility suffered, as did perceptions of the initiative within the department. Though it may seem obvious in hindsight, successful writing program implementations of this kind require more than one faculty person and one graduate student capable of leadership roles. WPAs who similarly find themselves in departments with a greater research presence in rhetoric than in composition will do well to stress among departmental colleagues the importance of having multiple colleagues with expertise in composition research and assessment to assure that initiatives that have garnered college and university support during periods of accreditation can sustain themselves when administrators move on, as many administrators do.

Note

1. These findings underscore in particular the value of positioning CBTs as researchers, offering some insights not likely to emerge without their perspectives: "Drawing upon theories of performance and spatial composition, I argue that while trinary configurations present a number of challenges to WPAs and classroom participants, they also help first-year students write more effectively; introduce new performative possibilities to FYC; reveal the classroom mise-en-scène to be a paradoxical rather than a transparent space; extend the teaching and learning that occurs in FYC beyond the classroom and across campus; support students' transitions to college by orienting them to academic and cultural facets of the university; offer rich avenues for preparing future composition teachers; provide the profession with researchers who are privy to both student and instructor performances available to few other composition researchers; and present a counter-model to the short-term 'efficiency' approaches that increasingly characterize the national scene of FYC" (Bruland 2012a).

References

Bizzell, Patricia. 1999. "Hybrid Academic Discourses: What, Why, How." *Composition Studies* 27:7–21.

Bourdieu, Pierre, and Loic Wacquant. 1992. *An Invitation to Reflexive Sociology*. Chicago: University of Chicago Press.

Bruland, Holly. 2007. "'Accomplishing Intellectual Work': An Investigation of the Re-Locations Enacted Through On-Location Tutoring." *Praxis. Writing Center Journal* 4. http://www.praxisuwc.com/bruland-42.

Bruland, Holly. 2012a. "Defense Handout." PhD diss., University of Hawai'i at Mānoa.

Bruland, Holly. 2012b. "Trinary Collaborations in First-Year Composition: A Mixed Methods Study of the University of Hawai'i Writing Mentors Program." PhD diss., University of Hawai'i at Mānoa.

Carroll, Lee Ann. 2002. *Rehearsing New Roles: How College Students Develop as Writers*. Carbondale: Southern Illinois University Press.

Cooper, Marilyn. 1994. "Really Useful Knowledge: A Cultural Studies Agenda for Writing Centers." *Writing Center Journal* 14:97–111.

Corroy, Jennifer. 2005. "Institutional Change and the University of Wisconsin-Madison Writing Fellows Program." In *On Location: Theory and Practice in Classroom-Based Writing Tutoring*, ed. Candace Spigelman and Laurie Grobman, 205–18. Logan: Utah State University Press.

Giger, Kelly. 2005. "Active Revision in a Peer Group: The Role of the Peer Group Leader." In *On Location: Theory and Practice in Classroom-Based Writing Tutoring*, ed. Candace Spigelman and Laurie Grobman, 126–36. Logan: Utah State University Press.

Harris, Muriel. 1995. "Talking in the Middle: Why Writers Need Writing Tutors." *College English* 57 (1): 27–42. http://dx.doi.org/10.2307/378348.

Henry, Jim, and Holly Bruland. 2010. "Educating Reflexive Practitioners: Casting Teaching Assistants as Mentors in First-Year Composition." *International Journal on Teaching and Learning in Higher Education* 22:308–19.

Henry, Jim, Holly Bruland, and Ryan Omizo. 2008. "Mentoring First-Year Students in Composition: Tapping Role Construction to Teach." *Currents in Teaching and Learning* 1:17–28.

Henry, Jim, Holly Huff Bruland, and Jennifer Sano-Franchini. 2011. "Course-Embedded Mentoring for First-Year Students: Melding Academic Subject Support with Role Modeling, Psycho-Social Support, and Goal Setting." *International Journal for the Scholarship of Teaching and Learning* 5:1–22.

Henry, Jim, and Lehua Ledbetter. 2011. "Teaching Intellectual Teamwork in WAC Courses through Peer Review." *Currents in Teaching and Learning* 3:4–21.

Moran, Charles, and Anne Herrington. 1997. "Program Review, Program Renewal." In *Assessing Writing across the Curriculum: Diverse Approaches and Practices*, ed. Kathleen Blake Yancey and Brian Huot, 123–40. Greenwich, CN: Ablex Publishing Corporation.

Nora, Amaury, and Gloria Crisp. 2007. "Mentoring Students: Conceptualizing and Validating the Multi-Dimensions of a Support System." *Journal of College Student Retention* 9 (3): 337–56. http://dx.doi.org/10.2190/CS.9.3.e.

O'Neill, Peggy, Cindy Moore, and Brian Huot. 2009. *A Guide to College Writing Assessment*. Logan: Utah State University Press.

Rose, Mike. 1983. "Remedial Writing Courses: A Critique and a Proposal." *College English* 45 (2): 109–28. http://dx.doi.org/10.2307/377219.

Schön, Donald A. 1987. *Educating the Reflective Practitioner*. San Francisco: Jossey-Bass.

Soliday, Mary. 1995. "Shifting Roles in Classroom Tutoring: Cultivating the Art of Boundary Crossing." *Writing Center Journal* 16:59–73.

Spigelman, Candace, and Laurie Grobman. 2005. "Introduction: On Location in Classroom-Based Writing Instruction." In *On Location: Theory and Practice in Classroom-Based Writing Tutoring*, ed. Candace Spigelman and Laurie Grobman, 1–13. Logan: Utah State University Press.

Tinto, Vincent. 1993. *Leaving College: Rethinking the Causes and Cures of Student Attrition*. 2nd ed. Chicago: University of Chicago Press.

University of Hawai'i at Mānoa. 2006. "Institutional Proposal." Accessed March 30, 2013. http://www.manoa.hawaii.edu/wasc/2005-2011/accreditation_process/pdf/Full_Proposal.pdf.

University of Hawai'i at Mānoa. 2009. "Capacity and Preparatory Review Report." http://www.manoa.hawaii.edu/wasc/2005-2011/accreditation_process/pdf/UHM_CPR_Report.pdf.

University of Hawai'i at Mānoa. 2010. "Educational Effectiveness Review Report." http://www.manoa.hawaii.edu/wasc/2005-2011/accreditation_process/pdf/eer/eer_report_2010.pdf.

University of Hawai'i at Mānoa Assessment Office. 2009. "Strengthening Student Success: Assessment in Action Poster Session." http://manoa.hawaii.edu/assessment/workshops/pdf/Posters_Presenters_Abstracts_2009_02_11.pdf.

WASC Handbook of Accreditation. 2008. http://www.manoa.hawaii.edu/wasc/2005-2011/accreditation_process/pdf/handbook_of_Accreditation_2008_with_hyperlinks.pdf.

WASC Visiting Team, Educational Effectiveness Review. 2011. "Report of the WASC Visiting Team, Educational Effectiveness Review." http://www.manoa.hawaii.edu/wasc/2005-2011/accreditation_process/pdf/UHM_Team_Report.pdf.

You, Casey. 2005. "Building Trust and Community in Peer Writing Group Classrooms." In *On Location: Theory and Practice in Classroom-Based Writing Tutoring*, ed. Candace Spigelman and Laurie Grobman, 72–84. Logan: Utah State University Press.

10
SEUFOLIOS

A Tool for Using ePortfolios as Both Departmental
Assessment and Multimodal Pedagogy

Ryan S. Hoover and Mary Rist

Assessment is rarely a pleasant task. It seems to question our professionalism by asking us to justify our work with students and our curriculum design to disciplinary outsiders. Like many of our colleagues, the faculty in the English Writing and Rhetoric program at St. Edward's University in Austin, TX, assessed our program to satisfy outside accreditors. We assessed our undergraduate writing major by evaluating senior portfolios, using a rubric and two independent scorers, and we dutifully reported the results. But this assessment had little meaningful impact. We were convinced that the best innovations we could incorporate would come from scholarship in the discipline, not from the assessment we conducted. At its best, we assumed, assessment could help us to improve what we were already doing but we doubted that it could show us what to do differently. However, a recent move to electronic portfolios for program assessment has stimulated a number of innovative curricular changes and has raised the visibility of the Writing and Rhetoric program across campus.

When we began to move from paper to electronic portfolios in 2011, we thought at first that we were designing a portfolio to solve simple logistical problems of providing a space for archiving texts and a medium for presenting multimodal work. As expected, ePortfolios have improved the process of assessment: ePortfolios are making assessment reporting easier by tracking evaluation scores and calculating historical trends; and ePortfolios are facilitating broad adoption of multimodal composition across our curriculum. More surprisingly, we have found that the ePortfolios have allowed us to reflect on and improve our program in a number of unexpected ways and may allow us to help our colleagues across campus better assign and assess writing projects in the

DOI: 10.7330/9781607324355.c010

disciplines. The surprising benefits that have accrued from this effort are broad in scope:

- ePortfolios are increasing student investment and reflection in the portfolio process;
- ePortfolios are being adopted across campus as a means of facilitating career planning and job searches, with students presenting potential employers with access to a portion of the texts on their sites;
- ePortfolios are being adopted by other majors, giving us opportunities to talk about writing, multimodal composition, and assessment with faculty across the disciplines.

This chapter will sketch out briefly the history of portfolio assessment at St. Edward's and the design of our internally developed ePortfolio platform. We will then review the ways in which the ePortfolio, which we adopted primarily to make the onerous task of assessment a little easier, has provided opportunities for curricular change and cross-campus dialogue about writing, and we will conclude with some reflections on the legacy of the project. While the new assessment design did not solve all our problems with student buy-in, and while many faculty remain uncomfortable evaluating the effectiveness of the visual design and navigation, the project has prompted cross-campus conversations about the nature of composing and the skills and knowledge we want our BA graduates to be able to demonstrate.

ST. EDWARD'S HISTORY WITH PORTFOLIOS

Our writing program is different from most: it incorporates a four-year undergraduate major in Writing and Rhetoric (offered since 1987 and currently the sixth largest major on campus), as well as a two-semester sequence of first-year writing courses and the university's Writing Center. Currently, the writing faculty conduct separate assessments for each of these entities as each has its own goals and expected student learning outcomes. While these assessments did not usually reveal anything new about the program, they have proven useful over the years as a means of documenting department needs and supporting our arguments for funding or for curricular change. For instance, the writing program administrators (WPAs) and the faculty in the writing program used the results of such assessments to add a required course in Revising and Editing to the major and to advocate for funding for workshops to bring new and experienced faculty together to discuss assignment design and sequencing in Rhetoric and Composition II.

Our first-year writing program had long practiced an end-of-semester holistic scoring of student essays written in class. As the university doubled in size, that process was replaced by an assessment of a representative sample of essays, usually a research assignment, in which readers assess the sample papers for a single learning outcome each year. The major had no such well-defined assessment procedure. At one point, the fourth-year majors wrote in-class arguments that were assessed along with those written by first-year writers. The current assessment process for the major, a review of a portfolio of work, was spurred on by a SACS accreditation review in the early 2000s. Our majors were already putting together portfolios; the Writing and Rhetoric major required fourth-year students to take Advanced Writing, which required students to prepare a portfolio of their work "presentable to prospective employers or graduate schools" (St. Edward's University 1994, 85). In the early 2000s, in preparation for our SACS assessment, we introduced a reflective component to the portfolio process. Then, in 2008, we renamed the course "Career Preparation," seeing it as one of the final courses in the major, one which would provide an opportunity for students to reflect on what they had learned and how they had changed as an individual and as a writer. Career Preparation also asked students to consider what they would do in the future, after graduating with a degree in Writing and Rhetoric. The portfolio project, a graded course requirement, encourages students to take a wider perspective on their writing. And we have noticed that students of all skill levels take a vested interest in marketing their skills to the faculty and potential employers through the portfolio. We hoped this new assessment would have all the benefits that Ostheimer and White (2005) claim for portfolio assessment in general:

> This portfolio assessment demonstrates several advantages frequently called for in theory but rarely made operational. In the first place, the assessment draws on existing material prepared by the students over a long span of time and for a variety of purposes, rather than generating new assessment documents, with important economies in time and money for students and faculty as well as enhanced validity of measurement. Second, the evaluator in the first instance is the student preparing the portfolio, who must assess the degree to which the contents document achievement of program goals. (72)

The department's scoring of the portfolios for program assessment is done separately from the course instructor's grading of the student portfolios. For the program assessment, each portfolio is read twice, and the scores for each learning outcome are averaged in our annual assessment report.

In the early 2000s, we began to review these portfolios guided by a rubric based on seven student learning outcomes, a rubric then shared with students as they began building their portfolios in Career Preparation. For the most part, the assessment confirmed what we already sensed about the strengths and weaknesses of the program, but it did provide solid evidence to support changes that we wanted to make, such as requiring Revising and Editing, a course that had been an elective in the past. When we asked for internal funding to provide workshops for new or returning faculty, we used evidence from the assessment to bolster our case. Of course, assessment can only answer the questions that we ask; our evaluation of the program was only as good as the rubric we used and the portfolios that we assessed with it. Therefore, we updated the learning outcomes over time, in particular adding a learning outcome associated with the visual design of texts as it became clear that our students were reading and writing many texts that were "made not only in words" (Yancey 2004). Yet, despite the new emphasis on visual design and online writing, our portfolios remained in large three-ring binders whose contents consisted of traditional academic texts.

Our accrediting agencies and the university assessment coordinator approved of and supported this process. The department, however, has struggled through some of the significant limitations of a paper-based portfolio. Most prominent is the selection of assignments that students have available to include. Since students did not begin work on the portfolio until their final semester, they often struggled to locate past assignments from previous courses. And since the portfolio was paper-based, students were limited to assignments that can be printed—basically, traditional essays. Many of the multimodal assignments that we were introducing in our curriculum could not be effectively included as evidence for student growth. As the core and professional writing specialization in the major began to emphasize design of print and online documents, we started, in 2008, to require all students to take Document Design. As a result, students became more interested in submitting online material that would better showcase their multimodal work. Therefore, we decided to explore the possibilities for converting our paper-based portfolio to an ePortfolio.

Because they often had trouble locating papers and projects from previous courses, the students often had to create new documents for the assessment portfolio, negating some of the advantages which Ostheimer and White cite for portfolio assessment (2005). An online portfolio, created early in each student's career as a writing major, would allow students to archive papers and projects and return to them later to reflect on their progress. It would also mean that the portfolios we assessed were more likely to showcase a wider variety of texts and projects, something we were looking for. In summer 2011, we applied for and received internal grant funding to design an ePortfolio for our majors. In fall 2011, freshman and sophomore students in Document Design began creating portfolios, and in December 2012, we assessed the first ePortfolios to be submitted.

SEUFOLIOS: ST. EDWARD'S EPORTFOLIO SYSTEM

We are currently using SEUFolios, an ePortfolio system that we developed internally (http://seufolios.org/) based on the WordPress blogging platform; through local customization, we were able to provide the key portfolio features needed by our students and for our assessment process. Our current curriculum asks students to create both a job portfolio for external audiences and an assessment portfolio for internal audiences. These portfolios include student work from a range of classes and media types, ranging from traditional word-based essays to print-based designs and websites.

Supporting Multiple Audiences

Historically, our paper portfolios served only as an internal assessment tool. But with the move to SEUFolios, we now encourage students to use the ePortfolio for their job search. Students' websites are public, allowing them to include the link in job or graduate school application materials. And because WordPress produces high-quality contemporary websites, students can use the ePortfolio itself as an example of their professional writing skills.

We recognized quickly that while these multiple audiences sounded like a good idea, the reality was that content students created early in their college career would often not be appropriate for a potential employer. A document from their freshman or sophomore year can effectively show their growth as a writer to faculty, but an employer will be interested only in their current skill level. And conversely, some documents students wished to include in their job portfolio were not appropriate for internal assessment. As an example, one student was applying for positions as a Spanish translator. Her job portfolio needed to have several samples of her translation skills. For our English Writing assessment, though, these documents were irrelevant and posed a distraction for faculty. In short, our students need two ePortfolios: one designed for internal assessment of learning and another as an external showcase of their best skills.

Rather than asking students to manage two websites with overlapping content, we developed a feature allowing students to hide content from certain audiences. They can control the visibility of each page for faculty, fellow students, and the general public. A savvy student can assemble a single website that presents multiple views of the same content for an array of audiences. Having students maintain only one website has proven critical for us. Early in the adoption phase we had students maintain two different sites, one for their job search and another for their assessment portfolio, and given the priorities of graduating seniors, they spent a great deal of time curating the content and design of the job portfolio while the assessment portfolio was treated as an afterthought. One site encourages students to give equal time to both facets.

Supporting All Digital Document Types

One great advantage of using WordPress as the core of our system is its native handling of multimedia documents. WordPress easily integrates videos, images, and html/php text into its posts, and a large degree of web-based content can be embedded using iframes, especially YouTube videos and other websites. While WordPress allows for the inclusion of multimedia documents, it does not handle print-based documents well. Word and PDF formats do not show natively in the website; readers must download the file to their computer and then open it in another program. This was a distraction inside of WordPress that hindered the quality of students' ePortfolios. In response, we authored an addition to the SEUFolios plugin that embeds a document directly into the website. Students can upload Word, PDF, and PowerPoint documents to the ePortfolio and display them directly in the browser. Typical essays can be shown in a scrolling single-page format while magazine and brochure-styled documents can be shown in a two-page booklet format.

Supporting Student Adoption

Our choice of an ePortfolio platform included consideration of students' ability to learn and embrace the tool. Despite misconceptions about "digital natives," undergraduates do not inherently adopt new digital technologies presented to them (Selwyn 2009). Rather, the rate of adoption is directly related to two factors: the ease with which students can learn how to use the tool (the intuitiveness of the tool) and the perceived usefulness of that tool in their lives (Lai, Wang, and Lei 2012). If we are asking students to construct an ePortfolio using a tool provided by us, that tool needs to be easily learned by individuals from a full range of technology skill levels, including those with little online experience. In our experience, students who struggle to learn a software program, especially those who struggle early in the "learning curve," will quickly give up. While those students may still finish the assignment, their work will be below their full potential and not accurately represent what they are capable of or what they have learned. While ePortfolios need to be intuitive, students also need to perceive their value readily. Several studies have shown that students who fail to see how the new software program will make their lives more productive or more successful will not put forth the needed effort to learn how to use it (Davis 1989; Edmunds, Thorpe, and Conole 2012; Lai, Wang, and Lei 2012). Students often adopt a pragmatic cost-benefit analysis to their education. This is especially true for elements not directly tied to their major; ePortfolios are a tool that may or may not provide a benefit exceeding what the students perceive as the cost of learning it. This presents a conflict for administrators: administrators want students to create portfolios for internal assessment; students (especially seniors) want to create a portfolio to support their upcoming job or graduate school applications.

When we reviewed the available commercial and open-source ePortfolio systems, we found that many systems are designed to meet the administrators' needs. They are "instructor-centric" in that the features strongly favor the needs of assessors: grading rubrics are fully integrated, content is restricted to a finite set of options, and appearance is limited to one consistent theme. This makes the assessor's job easy as a number of grading tasks can be automated. However, these systems risk alienating students. The lack of control and customization hamstrings students' abilities to express themselves through the ePortfolio and lessens the benefit of the ePortfolio to the students during their job and graduate school searches. That lack of value, according to the *Technology Acceptance Model,* can lead to students' refusing to engage with the assignment and producing only the minimum required (see, for instance, Bagozzi 2007).

Rather than settle for a commercial system that would discourage students from embracing the portfolio as a personal website, we decided to create a system that is "student-centric." That is, we decided to create a system designed to give students the simplicity and agency they need to develop an online identity that represents who they are (Suler

2002). We chose WordPress because the open source platform allowed us to add in whatever features were needed to support the students and the faculty. This has been a wise choice, as students have easily learned how to construct their sites in just a couple hands-on class sessions. Several students who are self-described "non-techies" have praised WordPress's simple design and easy control of visual themes. Its ease of use stands in contrast to other ePortfolio tools, a situation that Bacabac (2013) encountered with her ePortfolio assignment where her students "found that using the technology to create the professional ePortfolio itself (Assignment 4) could be cumbersome. One student shared that he struggled with the actual designing of the site . . . even though the class was using basic (i.e., simple) programs" (105). With a comparatively small cost in time and energy, our students are currently creating websites with a professional-quality design aesthetic. This has led to many more of our students embracing SEUFolios as their online identity than we would have gotten with a commercial instructor-centric system. Likewise, common learning management systems, like Blackboard, are costly, proprietary systems that students will not use outside the context of school; WordPress is an open source project available free to the public, so it has been used as the website tool for a broad number of popular digital brands, including TechCrunch, *The New Yorker*, BBC America, *Variety*, Sony Music, MTV, Xerox, and Best Buy, just to name a few. Students saw learning to use WordPress as having real-world benefits.

Of course, we continue to have students in the program who are resistant to the SEUFolios technology. This minority of students falls into two camps. One camp resists technology on principle. These students declare themselves proudly aligned with the print media and treasure its traditions. The other camp of students actually find themselves frustrated with the WordPress platform and what it affords. Given the security restrictions in place on SEUFolios, the technologically savvy students find our ePortfolio platform too limiting for what they want to accomplish with their personal portfolio. These students often wanted to explore theme development in WordPress but our multisite setup doesn't allow for individual users to directly edit files at this time.

INNOVATIONS ACHIEVED THROUGH EPORTFOLIOS

As a result of this increased student buy-in, we find that we are more likely to assess our students' best work in our year-end program assessments. That, in and of itself, is a benefit that we did not anticipate when we sought to move our assessment from paper to ePortfolio. The ePortfolios also made our assessment chores easier by streamlining the scoring and reporting processes. This was an intended result, as was the opportunity created for students to showcase more of their multimodal work. Instituting SEUfolios, however, has also provided the department with other, potentially more significant, benefits.

ePortfolios Improve Program Assessment

Assessing students' print portfolios was a clumsy and time-consuming process; the evaluations had to be manually entered into a spreadsheet where calculations could be made. Each year it took approximately 40 hours to complete our assessment report. Given the tedium of this process, one of the major drivers in our move to ePortfolios was the chance to streamline our assessment process.

To facilitate the evaluation process, we developed an integrated form for faculty. The main site has a page visible to faculty that lists all portfolios still needing at least one evaluation that semester. Each portfolio is evaluated twice, and the online tracking system removes the portfolio from the list once it has been evaluated twice. Figure 10.1 provides a screenshot of the evaluation system for faculty. To evaluate one of the portfolios, a faculty member simply completes a form linked from each student's site. The form has proven rather easy for our faculty to use. Appendix 10.A includes the full rubric used in the form, and Figure 10.2 is a screenshot of the evaluation form. We now have the opportunity to change our evaluation process from a required end-of-year meeting to an asynchronous process where faculty can evaluate portfolios when it is convenient for them. SEUFolios creates a number of reports based on the evaluations. We currently produce reports designed for the department chair, for our department's faculty, and for university assessment. These contain average ratings and standard deviations for the current semester, historical trends, inter-rater reliability calculations, and averages of student self-assessment of learning. Appendix 10.B offers a partial report from fall 2014 as an example. The reports, generated with the click of a button, are much more thorough than the reports we were willing to produce manually from our print portfolios.

While an electronic assessment tool has made the process easier for faculty, our students' investment in the portfolio process has led to deeper improvements in our assessment. We introduce the portfolio to students in their sophomore year, and at the end of every semester, students are encouraged to upload their best work to their portfolio. This gives them a large number of artifacts to choose from when, in their

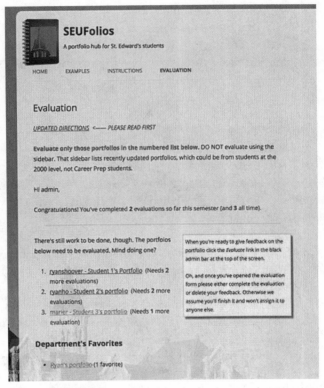

Figure 10.1. *SEUFolios list of portfolios for faculty to evaluate*

senior year, they compile their evidence for the portfolio. Ostheimer and White (2005) note the value of an "assessment [that] draws on existing material prepared by the students over a long span of time and for a variety of purposes, rather than generating new assessment documents, with important economies in time and money for students and faculty as well as enhanced validity of measurement" (72). ePortfolios are now giving us a more representative sample of student performance to assess.

Because students are also using the site as a career portfolio, they are investing more energy in selecting and presenting the included materials. For assessment, this means that we are presented with a more fully developed picture of the student's learning. The students have a stronger sense of ownership of the site (Bacabac 2013), and the students take on a larger role as an evaluator of their own work. As Ostheimer and White (2005) note, "the evaluator in the first instance is the student preparing the portfolio, who must assess the degree to which the contents document achievement of program goals, thus inculcating

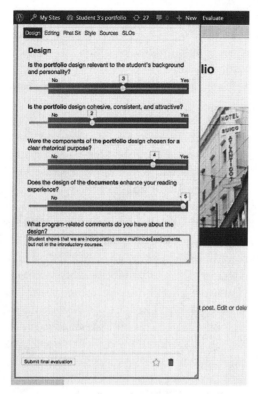

Figure 10.2. SEUFolios evaluation form

metacognitive skills and self-assessment as the essential parts of the process" (72). Because students actively choose from their work created over several years, they can more accurately measure what they have learned and how they have grown as a writer. Those thoughts then get expressed in self reflections that guide us as we assess the success of our program. As such, ePortfolios have led to improvements in our assessment on multiple levels. Yes, the process is simpler and faster, but the move to centralized storage of student work and multiple purposes for the portfolios has also improved the quality of our assessment by providing more representative student texts in the portfolio.

ePortfolios Facilitate Multimodal Composition in the Major

One of the major pedagogical strengths of an ePortfolio is the way it promotes multimodal composition. Scholarship and pedagogy in rhetoric and composition has embraced multimodal composing in the last decade. This is readily seen in the work of the New London group, especially Gunter Kress (2003, in *Literacy for a New Media Age,* among others). The call to broaden our perspective of rhetoric and writing has been changed by the new concepts of literacy, or "multiliteracies," to include multiple modes of communication (Cope and Kalantzis 2000) as well as multiple skill sets for dealing with these modes (Selber 2004). For our department, the call came particularly from Kathleen Yancey's 2004 CCC's chair's address which exhorted compositionists—especially those functioning in undergraduate rhetoric and writing majors who have more curricular space than first-year writing programs—to embrace technological shifts in means and modes of composing so that our students will "compose and create, making use of all the means of persuasion and all the possible resources thereto" (320) rather than following, lemming-like, templates provided by software.

Therefore, in 2005–2006, our major began to increase our elective offerings in visual rhetoric and online writing. Subsequent program reviews revealed that our program, like the ones surveyed by Cynthia Selfe, Cheryl Ball, and their co-authors in 2006 (Anderson et al. 2006), was dealing with multimodal composing on an *ad hoc* basis, as an instructor's choice rather than through a programmatic approach (69). As a result, most of our majors were not engaging with multiple modes, or at least they were not producing evidence of such engagement in their senior portfolios. Therefore, in our 2008 curriculum revision, and following the injunctions of Stuart Selber (2004) and others to help our students develop functional and rhetorical as well as critical literacies, we began to require all majors to become comfortable with several kinds of design software. They began producing multimodal work (in Document Design) in addition to analyzing and critiquing it (especially in another new course, Current Theories of Rhetoric and Composition). With these required core courses in place, faculty began assigning more multimodal compositions throughout the curriculum. Despite these efforts, we found that students still engaged only minimally in multimodal composing; our students were incorporating mostly photos and other still images into printed word documents, ignoring other modes of meaning-making described by Cope and Kalantzis (2000): audio, gestural, and spatial. Anderson et al. (2006) hypothesized that teachers and students engage in this minimal use of multimodality in part because they lack technological and institutional support for creating texts using additional modes (79). In our case, our departmental policy asked for a paper portfolio which limited students' presentation of multimodal work in their portfolios. That limitation kept multimodal texts from playing a defining role in courses, as students needed to be able to produce assignments that were assessment-friendly. The ePortfolio tool allowed us to encourage students to compose in a variety of modes and media formats beyond the written word and, by extension, to more fully and programmatically incorporate additional modes in our required and elective coursework. Now faculty require or encourage students to use video production, advanced document design, website authoring, and interactive media in courses throughout the Writing and Rhetoric curriculum. By encouraging students to submit their best work to their ePortfolio as they take these courses, students gain a deeper, more continuous awareness of how that multimodal work ties in with their larger education (Dubinsky 2003). Once on the job market, students are able to demonstrate their proficiency in a variety of media formats to potential employers.

The multimodal work that students incorporate into their ePortfolios encourages them to develop literacies in a variety of modes and media, developing the layered literacies Cargile Cook (2002) argues are at the core of a full education. Students are forced to choose prose and multimodal elements in their compositions and to draw connections between those contrasting media, as they weave the different formats into a cohesive personal narrative presented through the ePortfolio. Through choosing between the variety of media formats available to them and anticipating how the intended audience will react to those formats, they develop more fully their rhetorical, social, and technological literacies. ePortfolios, and the multimodal documents that they facilitate, have helped our students to "demonstrate a textured literacy different from the literacy of print" (Bacabac 2013, 93). SEUFolios has also helped us to graduate civically savvier students. As Cheryl Ball (Ball and Moeller 2007) argues, if we are to have a shot at producing "students able to critically engage in civic responsibilities, those students need to be able to make meaning from the new media texts with which they are engaged daily" (node D).

Since we introduced SEUFolios, many more graduating seniors include a substantially larger number of visual design elements in their final ePortfolios. When submitting paper portfolios, roughly half the students would include a single sample of their design skills. In our latest collection of ePortfolios, nearly all of our students had at least two (and often three or four) samples, and many of the portfolios displayed a wider range of modes, including interactive web pages, video, and audio links. As a faculty, we now have a better means to evaluate the visual rhetoric skills that our students are developing throughout the curriculum.

With several pieces for each student, we can better judge what students are producing in particular courses and how multimodal composition is integrated into the rest of the student's coursework.

ePortfolios Add Depth to Student Reflection

Deep reflection on layered literacy practices is not an intuitive process for students. Most of our students do not naturally see the connections between their traditional academic prose and multimodal compositions (Powell and Jankovich 1998). Much as Dubinsky noticed with students' awareness of the overlap in the core curriculum, our students need to be guided, to a degree, through the reflective process that leads to Cargile Cook's layered literacies (Cargile Cook 2002; Dubinsky 2003). We have accomplished that, most explicitly, in two courses that bookend the portfolio assignment. Document Design, a sophomore-level course focused on visual rhetoric, introduces the students to ePortfolios and asks them to begin thinking about the relationship between visual and language-based rhetoric. Career Preparation, a senior-level course that asks students to collect and reflect on their best work and to create materials appropriate for a job or graduate school search, has students complete their ePortfolios. Students include complete, polished documents in their ePortfolio and articulate the rhetorical choices they made in choosing the works, in designing the portfolio, and in editing documents that they had written earlier in the program. ePortfolios, as Dubinsky (2003) proposed, allow our students to draw the connections between what are otherwise isolated classes and learning moments.

In synthesizing various documents into a cohesive portfolio, many students realize that the ePortfolio itself is an artifact. Students are required to include a number of reflective pieces, and those reflections, complemented by a writer's autobiography, guide students in drawing the connections between the documents and seeing the portfolio itself as evidence of their education. The multimodal nature of the ePortfolios affords students many different avenues for reflection, a benefit of multimodal assignments noted by Journet et al. (2008). The students aiming for visual design careers in website design or print production routinely put extensive effort into the visual appearance of their websites. They recognize that the site itself is evidence of their design abilities, and that employers focus on "presentation quality" (organization, layout, consistency of design features) and "accessibility quality" (navigation tools and descriptions), as well as on content when evaluating ePortfolios of potential employees (Katerattanakul and Siau 2008).

ePortfolios Help Students with Their Job Search

Both print-based and digital portfolios have, for several years, been seen as a powerful tool for students entering the job market (Elbow and Belanoff 1997; Powell and Jankovich 1998; Kimball 2002; Graves and Epstein 2011; Bacabac 2013). They have an ability to showcase a student's work to potential employers that few other genres can match. Employers, likewise, are increasingly turning to the web to research job applicants, sometimes going so far as to hire outside consulting firms to produce reports on an applicant's social media presence (Hill 2011). Rebecca Worley (2011) notes that one of her web design students at the University of Delaware found ads suggesting students who had no online presence need not apply. Writing students, like students in the arts, have long been asked to submit a sample of their work to prospective employers. Worley (2011) suggests that employers in more areas are asking to see samples of students' work, "spurred in part perhaps by the easy availability of software to facilitate the process" (330).

For all these reasons, administrators from a variety of areas at St. Edward's have been meeting recently with the Writing and Rhetoric faculty to discuss the possibility of instituting SEUFolios campus-wide as a career preparation and job-search tool. This is an exciting possibility. Administrators recognize that if students are to present themselves in the best possible light, they need to take control over as much of their online presence as possible. ePortfolios that show a student's best work alongside a resume, professional statement, and personal statement are a powerful way for students to increase their agency in the job application process. To capitalize on these strengths, St. Edward's is in the process of launching a campus-wide initiative to have every incoming freshman create a job portfolio through SEUFolios that will serve as a four-year guide for preparing to enter the job market. Faculty from the Writing and Rhetoric program are playing a prominent role in determining the structure of this initiative.

We are also advocating for writing education to have an ongoing role in the career portfolio process. Recent studies, particularly in the area of technical and business communication, suggest that ePortfolios with examples of poor writing can do more harm than good in the job search (Katerattanakul and Siau 2008). Complicating the issue is a long-standing recognition that students routinely are unaware of what content to include or how to present it (Powell and Jankovich 1998; Dubinsky 2003; Bacabac 2013). As ePortfolios are adopted across campus, students from all majors need instruction in managing this particular online presence. This broad adoption is giving the writing program yet another opportunity to talk about the importance of clear, professional writing across campus.

We see the discussion as evolving to include considerations of rhetoric as well as writing skills. Because students must organize and describe their best work to complete the portfolio and because they must carefully analyze their prospective audience, students are forced to engage in a deep level of self-reflection and rhetorical analysis. They are forced to make rhetorical choices about modes of communication and navigation, a highly rhetorical process that Shipka (2005) describes well. The benefits of this reflection go beyond the portfolio as product. We have noticed that several Writing and Rhetoric students are thinking through their strengths, their skills, and their weaknesses well before their first interview. While many of our students would work through these issues before their first interview, our ePortfolio assignment guarantees that all our graduates will have done so at some level (Bacabac 2013). Campus administrators have shown interest in having more students across campus engage in a similar process. At this point, we are working with the vice president for Academic Affairs and the staff in the Career Planning Office on ways to make student portfolio development part of each semester's academic advising. As students across campus are given access to SEUFolios, we envision working with students and with faculty advisors on ways to encourage all students to engage in rhetorical self-reflection, deep revision, and careful editing of the texts included in their ePortfolios.

EPORTFOLIOS PROMOTE DISCUSSIONS OF WRITING ACROSS CAMPUS

Although SEUFolios started as an ePortfolio system for English Writing and Rhetoric, administrators and staff in the Career Planning Office quickly saw its utility for students across campus. Also, within months of its launch, several departments and schools expressed interest in using SEUFolios as a pedagogical and assessment tool. Religious and Theological Studies uses it to encourage students to tie classroom and life experiences together for reflection and discussion. Art is using its image gallery features to create portfolios of student work in every course as part of a larger meta-portfolio. Modern Languages is exploring its use for combining written work and audio transcripts of student proficiency. And the School of Education capitalizes on the categorizing features to encourage students to compile a collection of lesson plans and teaching materials for their eventual job search.

All of this interest in ePortfolios is giving the writing program a new opportunity to promote Writing Across the Curriculum and develop cross-campus partnerships (see Elmore and Van Sickle, this collection). As more students across campus begin to use the ePortfolios and as more departments use them for program assessment, we look forward to working with our colleagues across campus to share what our discipline has learned about selecting and revising texts for particular audiences and about composing in multiple modes. Already, as our colleagues in Religious and Theological Studies have begun to implement SEUfolios throughout their curriculum, they have consulted with us on how to assess the writing that is included in the portfolios. One of our Religious Studies colleagues attended the Writing and Rhetoric program assessment workshop in May 2013, as our faculty discussed strategies for assessing the rhetorical effectiveness of multimodal elements in the ePortfolios. We plan to continue discussions with these and other colleagues across campus about how to assess multimodal compositions and how to encourage their students' effective sample selection, peer revision, and careful editing of the texts showcased in the ePortfolios.

IT'S NEVER SIMPLE

The Writing and Rhetoric program at St. Edward's University has benefited immensely from the development of ePortfolio for our students. While the DIY project was initiated to help us solve a very specific problem with the assessment of our undergraduate Writing and Rhetoric major, it has provided a number of significant improvements to our assessment and our curriculum since its implementation in 2011. Yet we are still dealing with some implementation problems within the department. In addition, while the SEUFolios design generated interest among administrators and chairs of other departments, some of the buzz has died down amidst worries about the complexity of the assessment process and a desire to associate our students with a more known quantity (LinkedIn) for career portfolios.

Since 2010, writing majors have created ePortfolios in their second or third semester, giving them a digital storehouse for their projects throughout their academic career. With the ePortfolios, we hoped to evaluate a wide range of texts or to assess the breadth and depth of their skills. When we review portfolios each semester, now, we have found some of this to be true. Some students are now including a larger number of visually complex documents and multimedia in their portfolios, and they are seeing the portfolio itself as a multimodal composition.

That variety has created an opportunity to help these students reflect on and draw connections between their skills with the written word and their skills with visual rhetoric. However, we find that many students ignore the ePortfolio between their sophomore and senior year. These students find themselves scrambling to fill out the ePortfolio during their final semester in the same way that they did the paper portfolios. Clearly just encouraging students to submit in each of the courses in the major was insufficient incentive, but assigning points for submissions was complicated given that not all students in any course were majors. We have recently decided to make ePortfolio submission a prerequisite for academic advising: now students can't register for classes without showing their advisor that they have uploaded a project from each of the major's courses taken the previous semester to their ePortfolios and made that submission visible to the advisor.

We continue to encourage more thorough self-reflection in the ePortfolios and to explore additional opportunities afforded by this assessment tool. For instance, we have historically assessed only how well our students demonstrate final program learning outcomes. This evaluation, however, does not take into account the student's initial skill level. Assessing the students' improvement over the course of the program might provide a more accurate reflection of our own effectiveness as educators. Since students can be encouraged to upload multiple drafts of their work from multiple courses throughout their careers at St. Edward's, they can reflect on their growth as writers, both through the drafts of a single assignment and through the range of the work completed over their years in the program. Again, this is an affordance of SEUFolios that we have not yet taken full advantage of as we are only now implementing the portfolio submission requirement as part of the advising/registration process.

The ePortfolio was intended to stimulate curriculum development in the major, encouraging faculty to assign (and the students to produce) more multimodal and multimedia compositions throughout the Writing and Rhetoric major. We have been somewhat successful on this front. Those courses that already had a seed of multimodal composition in them, such as Technical and Professional Communication and Print Production, have blossomed in their use of SEUFolios. Faculty that have not historically included a technology aspect in their assignments have not yet adopted the multimedia affordances of SEUFolios. These faculty are participating in conversations that may yet lead to changes.

Because our majors create portfolios in their second or third semester, faculty can assume that students have at least rudimentary skills with image manipulation, website design, and WordPress management, and that they can construct assignments that call on these skills. Faculty can have students submit multimodal and multimedia work to their portfolios for instructor and peer evaluation. We hope that, as our faculty become more comfortable with the ePortfolios, our department will expand our multimodal pedagogy. In particular, we can now think of offering creative writing courses that encourage multimodal and multimedia composition. As more and more writing programs—such as the ones profiled in Balzhiser and McLeod 2010; Giberson and Moriarty 2010; or Shamoon et al. 2000—develop into full undergraduate writing majors, these programs will need to facilitate multimodal composing throughout the writing major. They may also want to develop assessment protocols like the ePortfolio that help, rather than hinder, students as they seek to demonstrate their skills and knowledge to their instructors and to potential employers and graduate programs.

On our own campus, as part of our work with other department chairs, we hope to open discussions of multimodal and multimedia composing in the disciplines and to share ideas for assigning and assessing this kind of work. Our faculty have already offered a number of workshops on document design, including a poster presentation that demonstrated why the double-spaced Times New Roman academic essay is hard to read. We hope that as students in more and more majors develop ePortfolios early in their academic careers, more and more departments will find students and faculty prepared to compose in new media and new genres.

Yet other departments across campus have been hesitant to use the ePortfolio for program assessment. Initially, other departments, like Art, Communication, and Religious Studies, expressed interest in using ePortfolios as part of their program assessment. However, they were intimidated by the task of evaluating multiple written pieces in order to assess student learning outcomes. They found that program assessment could be more easily accomplished by assessing a single learning outcome each year and by looking for demonstration of this outcome in a representative sample of a single piece of student work. Portfolio evaluation, in other words, while it provides rich results for programs, is more difficult than most assessment protocols. Furthermore, there is a risk that looking superficially at many documents rather than carefully at one does not improve assessment. Our administrators have expressed concern that our current assessment process provides a broad overview rather than a detailed analysis and doesn't lead to a focused plan for improvement. Learning from our colleagues, we plan to investigate a new process in which we assess a single student learning outcome each semester, using evidence from the full portfolio. A more targeted assessment, especially when coupled with an ePortfolio of documents that better reflects the scope of a student's coursework and development, may allow us to better trace and assess our majors' development of skills and acquisition of knowledge.

At any rate, despite early promise, ePortfolios have not been widely adopted for assessment across campus. Some other programs are using ePortfolios to help students store documents and reflect on their learning—even if the same documents and reflections do not play a role in program assessment. The university, on the other hand, is promoting use of LinkedIn profiles over a WordPress website as a means of encouraging all students to establish a career ePortfolio. After a broad assessment of interdisciplinary needs, the university has decided that many students benefit from the resume-styled presence that LinkedIn provides and that the showcase-focused presentation of SEUFolios does not directly benefit students in majors such as Math, Biology, and Business.

The moral of this tale is not unique: every initiative has to account for local constraints and institutional history and trajectory. Yet assessment, especially for accreditation, often seems to be forced into a one-size-fits-all model. Our DIY ePortfolio process, originally conceived in response to departmental and apparently logistical concerns, is being implemented more slowly than we had hoped, but it promises to have a deeper impact on our major than we had originally envisioned. Across campus, the creation of SEUFolios has led to conversations about portfolio-enhanced learning, even if ePortfolios have not been widely adopted for assessment.

APPENDIX 10.A

ENGW's Current Evaluation Rubric

Design

Is the design relevant to the student's background and career interests?
Is the design cohesive, consistent, and attractive?
Were the components of the design chosen for a clear rhetorical
    purpose?
Does the design of the documents enhance your reading experience?
What program-related comments do you have about the design?

Editing

Do the student's global/big picture edits improve the argument and logical reasoning?

Do the student's line edits enhance the rhetorical power of the text?

Did the student proofread well for errors in spelling, grammar, punctuation, and typos?

What program-related comments do you have about the editing?

Rhetorical Situation

Is the student's portfolio written to create interest in an employer in the student's field?

Do the documents show mastery of the constraints and opportunities of particular genres?

Do the samples reflect a variety of rhetorical situations?

Is there evidence of deliberate rhetorical strategies intended to prompt the appropriate reaction from the audience?

What program-related comments do you have about the understanding of the rhetorical situation?

Style

Does the student use effective, clear transitions and a sound structure?

Does the student use precise, appropriate diction?

Has the student developed a mature and authentic voice?

What program-related comments do you have about the writing style?

Sources

Does the student show awareness of the conversation taking place in the sources (are sources used as more than repositories of information)?

Are sources incorporated thoroughly and effectively?

Does the student handle contradictory opinions with tact, grace, and validity?

What program-related comments do you have about the use of sources?

APPENDIX 10.B

Partial Report of ENGW's Fall 2014 Program Assessment

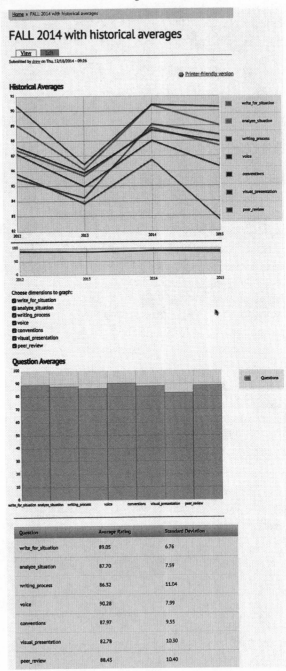

Home » FALL 2014 with historical averages

FALL 2014 with historical averages

View | Edit

Submitted by drew on Thu, 12/18/2014 - 09:26

Printer-friendly version

Historical Averages

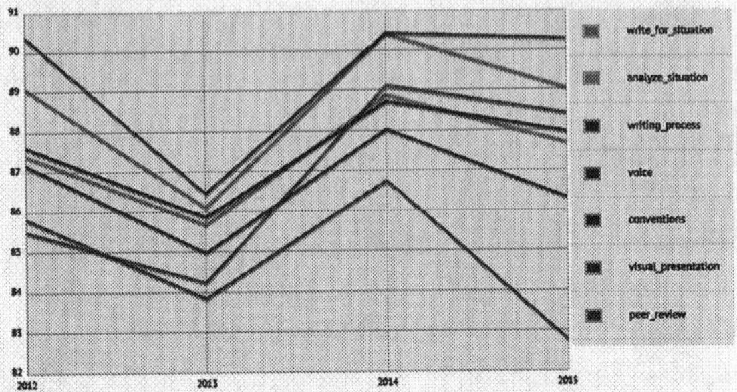

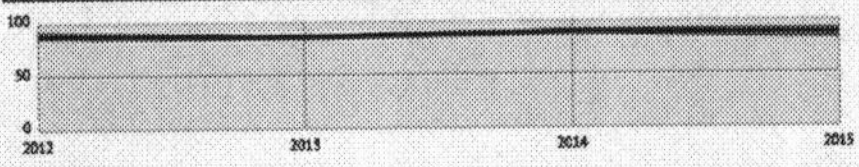

Choose dimensions to graph:
- write_for_situation
- analyze_situation
- writing_process
- voice
- conventions
- visual_presentation
- peer_review

Question Averages

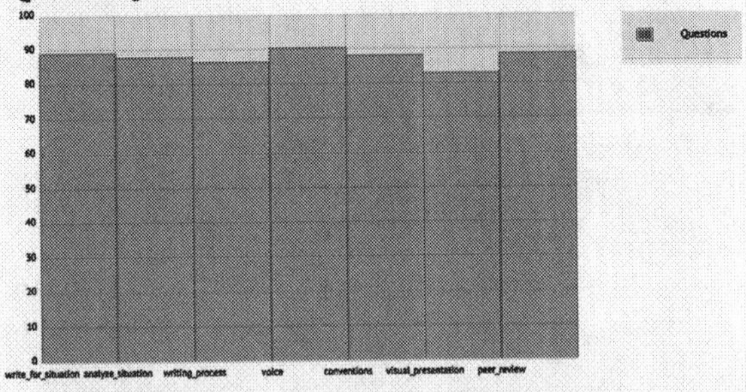

Question	Average Rating	Standard Deviation
write_for_situation	89.05	6.76
analyze_situation	87.70	7.59
writing_process	86.32	11.04
voice	90.28	7.99
conventions	87.97	9.55
visual_presentation	82.78	10.30
peer_review	88.43	10.40

References

Anderson, Daniel, Anthony Atkins, Cheryl Ball, Krista Homicz Millar, Cynthia Selfe, and Richard Selfe. 2006. "Integrating Multimodality into Composition Curricula: Survey Methodology and Results from a CCCC Research Grant." *Composition Studies* 34 (2): 59–84.

Bacabac, Florence. 2013. "Creating Professional ePortfolios in Technical Writing." *Journal of Business and Technical Communication* 27 (1): 91–110. Accessed April 20, 2013. http://dx.doi.org/10.1177/1050651912458921.

Bagozzi, Richard. 2007. "The Legacy of the Technology Acceptance Model and a Proposal for a Paradigm Shift." *Journal of the Association for Information Systems* 8 (4): 243–54. Accessed June 5, 2013.

Ball, Cheryl, and Ryan Moeller. 2007. "FCJ-062 Reinventing the Possibilities: Academic Literacy and New Media." *The Fibreculture Journal* 10. Accessed July 31, 2013. http://ten.fibreculturejournal.org/fcj-062-reinventing-the-possibilities-academic-literacy-and-new-media/.

Balzhiser, Deborah, and Susan McLeod. 2010. "The Undergraduate Writing Major: What Is It? What Should It Be?" *College Composition and Communication* 61 (3): 415–33.

Cook, Kelli Cargile. 2002. "Layered Literacies: A Theoretical Frame for Technical Communication Pedagogy." *Technical Communication Quarterly* 11 (1): 5–29. Accessed April 20, 2013. http://dx.doi.org/10.1207/s15427625tcq1101_1.

Cope, Bill, and Mary Kalantzis. 2000. *Multiliteracies: Literacy Learning and the Design of Social Futures.* London: Routledge.

Davis, Fred. 1989. "Perceived Usefulness, Perceived Ease of Use, and User Acceptance of Information Technology." *Management Information Systems Quarterly* 13 (3): 319–40. Accessed August 12, 2013. http://dx.doi.org/10.2307/249008.

Dubinsky, Jim. 2003. "Creating New Views on Learning: ePortfolios." *Business Communication Quarterly* 66 (4): 96–102. Accessed August 12, 2013. http://dx.doi.org/10.1177/108056990306600410.

Edmunds, Rob, Mary Thorpe, and Grainne Conole. 2012. "Student Attitudes towards and Use of ICT in Course Study, Work and Social Activity: A Technology Acceptance Model Approach." *British Journal of Educational Technology* 43 (1): 71–84. Accessed August 12, 2013. http://dx.doi.org/10.1111/j.1467-8535.2010.01142.x.

Elbow, Peter, and Pat Belanoff. 1997. "Reflections on an Explosion: Portfolios in the '90s and Beyond." In *Situating Portfolios: Four Perspectives*, ed. Kathleen Blake Yancey and Irwin Weiser, 21–33. Logan: Utah State University Press; Accessed April 21, 2013.

Giberson, Greg, and Thomas Moriarty, eds. 2010. *What We Are Becoming: Developments in Undergraduate Writing Majors.* Logan: Utah State University Press.

Graves, Nikki, and Molly Epstein. 2011. "Eportfolio: A Tool for Constructing a Narrative Professional Identity." *Business Communication Quarterly* 74 (3): 342–6. Accessed August 12, 2013. http://dx.doi.org/10.1177/1080569911414555 3.

Hill, Kashmir. 2011. "Social Media Background Check Company Ensures that Job-Threatening Facebook Photos are Part of Your Application." *Forbes*, June 20. Accessed April 21, 2013. http://www.forbes.com/sites/kashmirhill/2011/06/20/now-your-embarrassingjob-threatening-facebook-photos-will-haunt-you-for-seven-years/.

Journet, Debra, Tabetha Adkins, Chris Alexander, Patrick Corbett, and Ryan Trauman. 2008. "Digital Mirrors: Multimodal Reflection in the Composition Classroom." *Computers and Composition Online* (Spring). Accessed June 3, 2013. http://casit.bgsu.edu/cconline/Digital_Mirrors/.

Katerattanakul, Pairin, and Keng Siau. 2008. "Factors Affecting the Information Quality of Personal Web Portfolios." *Journal of the American Society for Information Science and Technology* 59 (1): 63–76. http://dx.doi.org/10.1002/asi.20717.

Kimball, Miles. 2002. *The Web Portfolio Guide: Creating Electronic Portfolios for the Web*. New York: Longman.

Kress, Gunter. 2003. *Literacy in the New Media Age*. London: Routledge. http://dx.doi.org/10.4324/9780203164754.

Lai, Chun, Qiu Wang, and Jing Lei. 2012. "What Factors Predict Undergraduate Students' Use of Technology for Learning? A Case from Hong Kong." *Computers & Education* 59 (2): 569–79. Accessed February 18, 2013. http://dx.doi.org/10.1016/j.compedu.2012.03.006.

Ostheimer, Martha W., and Edward M. White. 2005. "Portfolio Assessment in an American Engineering College." *Assessing Writing* 10 (1): 61–73. Accessed March 19, 2013. http://dx.doi.org/10.1016/j.asw.2005.02.003.

Powell, Karen S., and Jackie L. Jankovich. 1998. "Student Portfolios: A Tool to Enhance the Traditional Job Search." *Business Communication Quarterly* 61 (4): 72–82. Accessed April 21, 2013. http://dx.doi.org/10.1177/108056999806100409.

Selber, Stuart. 2004. *Multiliteracies for a Digital Age*. Carbondale: Southern Illinois University Press.

Selwyn, Neil. 2009. "The Digital Native—Myth and Reality." *Aslib Proceedings* 61 (4): 364–79. Accessed June 5, 2013. http://dx.doi.org/10.1108/00012530910973776.

Shamoon, Linda K, Rebecca Moore Howard, Sandra Jamieson, and Robert A. Schwegler. 2000. *Coming of Age: The Advanced Writing Curriculum*. Portsmouth: Boynton/Cook.

Shipka, Jody. 2005. "A Multimodal Task-Based Framework for Composing." *College Composition and Communication* 57 (2): 277–306.

St. Edward's University. 1994. *Undergraduate Bulletin 1994–1995*. Austin, TX.

Suler, John R. 2002. "Identity Management in Cyberspace." *Journal of Applied Psychoanalytic Studies* 4 (4): 455–9. Accessed May 1, 2013. http://dx.doi.org/10.1023/A:1020392231924.

Worley, Rebecca B. 2011. "EPortfolios Examined: Tools for Exhibit and Evaluation." *Business Communication Quarterly* 74 (3): 330–2. Accessed August 12, 2013. http://dx.doi.org/10.1177/1080569911414558.

Yancey, Kathleen Blake. 2004. "Made Not Only in Words: Composition in a New Key." *College Composition and Communication* 56 (2): 297–328. http://dx.doi.org/10.2307/4140651.

PART THREE

Faculty Development through Assessment and Accreditation

The chapters in this final section provide another set of case study-based tools for writing program administrators (WPAs) and writing specialists: examples of faculty development initiatives designed in response to accreditation processes. Building on a theme introduced in part two, these chapters detail how ongoing accreditation and assessment imperatives have provided valuable opportunities to cultivate campus-wide discussions of writing instruction in ways that have not been possible since the birth of the writing across the curriculum (WAC) movement. Indeed, accreditation and accompanying calls for large-scale assessment can be the impetus for renewed, reinvigorated university-wide conversations among faculty about how they can help students develop as writers throughout the college experience.

Working with faculty is, as most administrators know, often more challenging than working with students. Contributors to this section of the book acknowledge the hurdles they have faced in facilitating campus conversations about writing instruction. These challenges include institutional history and resistance that originated with previous attempts to create a culture of writing; the absence of a shared vocabulary to talk about writing between writing specialists and faculty in the disciplines; a lack of understanding of how writing varies by disciplinary context and an accompanying lack of clearly articulated expectations for writing in different disciplines; the seemingly ubiquitous dearth of financial resources; turnover in faculty and administration; and initially unwieldy and overly ambitious assessment plans. In addition to reflecting on challenges, contributors share strategies they used to clear different hurdles. Through these chapters, readers can learn about professional development workshop themes and structures, faculty incentive programs (fellows programs, grants, etc.), heuristics for talking about writing in different disciplines, processes for collaboratively developing rubrics for writing within and across disciplines, and strategies for ensuring some manner of continuity in the face of personnel turnover.

We believe that, similar to the chapters in the previous sections of the collection, chapters in this section will prove valuable for WPAs and writing specialists who are seeking institutional support to implement parallel programs at their schools. While three of the five schools represented in the section used the Southern Association of Colleges and Schools' (SACS) Quality Enhancement Plan (QEP) requirement to initiate campus-wide conversations and professional development for faculty, the diversity across programs in the section—including two medium-sized, regional state universities, one of which serves an ethnic minority population; two large, urban state universities; and a smaller, private, religiously affiliated urban university—will, we hope, result in useful information for readers in a variety of institutional contexts and locations.

11
WRITE TO THE TOP
How One Regional University Made
Writing Everybody's Business

Polina Chemishanova and Cynthia Miecznikowski

Historically, writing across the curriculum (WAC) has been a bottom-up phenomenon, originating from what has become known as "'the Pilgrim's Progress Model of faculty change'—in which one person with expertise incites a gradual conversion in the minds and practices of faculty outside of composition" (Malenczyk 2012, 98). This cohort of faculty shares a vision of infusing writing in the curriculum and providing students with a multitude of meaningful opportunities to engage with writing in the context of learning. Initiated by faculty committed to fostering an ongoing conversation and increasing emphasis on writing across all disciplines, such initiatives, when successful, ultimately "decentraliz[e] the responsibility for effective writing from the English department alone to virtually every discipline on campus" (Holdstein 2001, 42). A successful WAC entity, then, "involves a comprehensive program of faculty development and curricular change, instituting writing in virtually all university courses in order to improve students' writing and critical thinking skills" (McLeod and Soven 1991, 26). While WAC programs vary from one institution to another (Fulwiler 1988, 62–63), they all share the underpinning premises and core values of the WAC movement: faculty's dedication and commitment to enhancing students' ability to acquire content-area knowledge by teaching them to write within disciplinary contexts.

In recent years many higher education institutions, both public and private, have identified writing as a cross-disciplinary concern and focus for a campus-wide writing initiative driven by the exigency of accreditation. For some, such top-down mandates would seem to threaten academic freedom or compromise what faculty know to be best instructional practices within their own disciplines. At the very

DOI: 10.7330/9781607324355.c011

least, institutionalized programs can become bureaucratic in their implementation and time-consuming, even burdensome, for faculty. Consequently, more often that not, conversations about mandated campus-wide writing programs have largely been framed as cautionary tales of what not to do. What is missing from the discussion, however, is an examination of how, in some cases, the top-down approach to WAC, though less than desirable, may be just what is needed in order for a campus-wide writing program to flourish.

This chapter offers a critical case study of one institution's mandated approach to building a campus-wide writing program in the context of SACS accreditation. We argue that aligning our emphasis on writing with this accreditation mandate afforded an opportunity to build a culture of writing at an institution where local practices and institutional culture did not permit that to happen otherwise. The building of our institution's campus-wide writing program owes much of its success to its high visibility (both lateral and vertical) and its integration with SACS requirements for developing a five-year Quality Enhancement Plan (QEP). Without such integration, administrative and financial support, and the shared commitment from faculty campus-wide that our QEP entailed, a WAC-like program would not have been possible. Writing intensive programs that respond to top-down provisions like accreditation, we argue, must have the resources—from funding to goodwill—to meet the challenges such approaches will likely present. This chapter, therefore, examines the breadth and depth of the University of North Carolina at Pembroke's writing-anchored QEP by providing an overview of its origins and implementation and a discussion of the challenges and successes of this undertaking, including the rhetorical moves that members of the QEP steering committee employed to increase faculty buy-in and institutional commitment. Our story challenges the dominant discourse surrounding WAC and offers one way of reconstructing and refiguring a mandated QEP as the foundational basis on which the WAC-like writing intensive entity can thrive. Our broad-based project illustrates ways in which the professedly insurmountable top-down approach to WAC may be recast less as a hindrance and instead embraced more as an opportunity for meaningful, sustainable change. Like all stories, ours is undoubtedly enmeshed in contexts and agendas both local and institutional; we offer it, however, as one of many approaches to reconciling a mandated campus-wide initiative with best practices in WAC scholarship.

Certainly a mandated approach to WAC that arises from exigencies beyond the classroom is less than ideal and undoubtedly presents myriad of both ideological and pedagogical challenges for supporting and encouraging curricular change on campus, one of the guiding principles of successful WAC programs. By increasingly becoming a top-down phenomenon, as evident in the direction of the WAC movement in the last two decades, it has undergone a radical shift in its fundamental principle and has rightfully drawn criticism from writing scholars, though we might suppose that it is the broad reach of WAC scholarship and the successes it recounts that have inspired outsiders' interest and pressure. WAC pioneers McLeod and Soven (1991), for instance, regard mandated WAC initiatives with skepticism because more often than not such initiatives arise from unrealistic expectations about what the teaching of writing entails and a lack of information about WAC programs among administrators, a perspective that in some sense rightfully describes the origins of our own writing intensive program. Deborah Holdstein, on the other hand, calls for questioning WAC programs—and especially top-down initiated ones—for, as she argues, the discourse surrounding such university-wide curricular endeavors "subverts our best pedagogical intentions and, ultimately, dilutes the literacy education our students receive" (Holdstein 2001, 38), a concern that several of our own composition faculty voiced as well. Similarly, on more than one occasion, Edward White (1990, 1997) has sternly warned us of the dangers of seemingly well-intended writing initiatives that lack institutional, financial, and faculty support because "they appear to solve the problem of insufficient student writing but often make it worse, since writing is no longer every faculty member's responsibility, even in theory" (WPA-L mailing list). Of course, the assumption that writing should be "every faculty member's responsibility" is not always shared institutionally, and it can take more than time to develop a climate in which that assumption becomes a guiding principle. In our case, faculty readily accepted this possibility.

At the same time, however, depending on local context and institutional frame, mandated WAC initiatives could be the very same approach that cultivates one school's culture of writing since, "on most campuses . . . WAC cannot survive as Switzerland; it simply does not have the funding base, the powerful national engines, the 'new' look that will attract funding, or the ability to retain followers to itself alone" (Walvoord 1996, 69–70). When institutional exigency and local constraints preclude a grassroots approach, and when support for faculty leadership and development are sanctioned and promoted, perhaps then alternative routes to WAC design and implementation must be taken seriously, even if that means going against conventional wisdom. Indeed, attending to local context and institutional culture sometimes necessitates going against long-held beliefs and professional values and embracing what has traditionally been considered the indomitable impediment to a successful WAC-like program. As Jay Carson explains, "As schools and their needs differ, so do WAC programs' responses to those needs; understanding local context [then] is key to bringing about change" (Carson 1994, 38) since contexts are the framework within which institutional decisions and programmatic changes make sense. It is precisely these institutional contexts that guide and frame local initiatives, even as they collide with national trends and best practices in the field. And so, rather than resisting and outright denouncing any mandated WAC initiative, we suggest (re)seeing and (re)casting it as an opportunity to develop a writing program that addresses institutional exigency; responds to local priorities, affordances, and constraints; secures faculty buy-in and support; and, ultimately, provides students with meaningful writing experiences—both within and beyond the English department. Our own campus-wide writing initiative is a case in point.

INSTITUTIONAL CONTEXT

The University of North Carolina at Pembroke (UNCP) has been one of the constituent institutions of the University of North Carolina since the system's inception in 1972. The history of the institution, however, dates back to 1887 when the first state-supported college for American Indians in the nation, the Croatan Normal School for Indians, was founded. Its mission was to train American Indian teachers in Robeson County. In 1911, the General Assembly of North Carolina changed the name of the institution to The Indian Normal School of Robeson County, and again in 1913 to the Cherokee Indian Normal School of Robeson County. In 1941, the school became the Pembroke State College for Indians, and three years later, in 1949, the General Assembly shortened the name to Pembroke State College. In 1969, Pembroke State College became Pembroke State University and gained the designation of a regional university. On July 1, 1996, Pembroke State University officially became The University of North Carolina at Pembroke.

A master's level degree-granting and baccalaureate degree-completion university, UNCP currently offers forty-one undergraduate programs and seventeen masters degrees as it serves an eleven-county region in South Central and Southeastern North Carolina. Considered one of the most diverse institutions of higher education in the South, the University's total enrollment for fall 2012 was 6,269 students comprising the following demographic distribution: 16.22 percent American Indian, 31.9 percent African-American, 40.68 percent White, 3.99 percent Hispanic, and 1.52 percent Asian. Gender distribution in 2012 was 62.67 percent female and 37.33 percent male. More than 96 percent of students were in-state residents, and full-time students comprised more than 73 percent of the student body, according to UNCP's *2012 FactBook* (University of North Carolina at Pembroke 2013a). Historically, many students are first generation college students. In addition, consistent with national trends, non-traditional students comprise a significant proportion of the student body. Approximately 30 percent of undergraduate students enrolled in 2012 were twenty-five years of age or older. With an average class size of twenty and a student-faculty ratio of fifteen-to-one, UNCP prides itself on "offering an affordable, highly personalized, student-centered education" that challenges students to "embrace difference and adapt to change, think critically, communicate effectively, and become responsible citizens" (UNCP 2013b).

It is against the background of UNCP's regional location, diverse student body, and long-held institutional traditions and core values that the school focused on strengthening its students' writing proficiency by developing the foundation for a campus-wide writing culture. Perhaps it was the broad reach of WAC scholarship having spread the word convincingly in disciplines other than English and Composition Studies that, in order to stick, the teaching of writing cannot be the sole responsibility of English or even Composition teachers any longer. Emphasis on rhetorical situations, contexts, and reader expectations that inhere in discipline-specific genres, combined with the ever-growing appreciation among disciplinary experts that knowledge and learning are constructed at the point of its articulation in writing—these and other postprocess insights surely have persuaded more and more institutions like ours of the need for more integrated approaches to writing instruction and practice. Or perhaps it was that critical media attention to the literacy skills of newly minted college graduates caught the attention of a critical mass of our own stakeholders—including prospective employers—at the same time our English department decided to commit new faculty lines to composition specialists in order to bolster the first-year writing program. This "perfect storm" of internal and external exigencies would seem to have conspired to make writing instruction a priority on our campus. In the current climate of accountability, more and more public constituencies are asking, in tones of exasperation, a fundamental question of college and university faculty and administration that used to be reserved for English faculty—especially those charged with teaching first-year writing courses: "What are they teaching them over there?" With SACS accreditation requiring that we propose a viable Quality Enhancement Plan that could truly enhance teaching and learning on our campus, we were eventually able to shape what had been a campus-wide problem into an opportunity that would require campus-wide support.

FOUNDATIONAL UNDERPINNINGS

When discussions about what should be the focus of the institution's QEP began in fall 2007, students' writing proficiency quickly emerged as a central concern among faculty as well as other stakeholders. Prior to that time, English department faculty, most of whom were trained in the teaching of literature exclusively, were the primary instructors of academic literacy for the university's two-semester first-year composition sequence. Although results from the 2008 National Survey of Student Engagement (NSSE) showed that UNCP freshmen completed more writing assignments than freshmen at peer institutions as well as at NSSE institutions as a whole, conversely, the NSSE data also indicated that UNCP seniors wrote less than seniors at peer and all NSSE institutions. The data starkly contradicted students' largely positive self-reported perceptions of their experience with writing instruction and their belief that their writing skills improved during their college years. At the same time, the 2008 Faculty Survey of Student Engagement (FSSE) indicated that students' perceptions of how much the college experience improved their writing differ widely from the faculty's perceptions of students' rhetorical performance. Moreover, whereas 79 percent of freshmen and 83 percent of seniors believed that their college experience had contributed significantly to their ability to write clearly and effectively, only 61 percent of lower division faculty and 76 percent of upper division faculty reported that they purposefully structured their courses to help students develop effective writing skills.

Furthermore, the internal 2008 Student Perceptions of Writing Survey reinforced the implications of the NSSE data. The survey gathered data concerning the type and frequency of writing assignments students encountered at UNCP beyond the freshman composition course sequence, as well as students' attitudes toward writing in general. Among other data points, the survey asked students to identify how many of their classes per semester required some type of writing assignments, how many writing assignments, on average, they completed per semester, and how many times per semester they visited the University

Writing Center. In addition, using a seven-point Likert Scale, students rated their level of agreement with statements such as "I enjoy short writing assignments as part of my coursework," "I am able to organize my ideas easily in a short essay," "I prefer short-essay questions over multiple choice exams," "short writing assignments are important for my academic progress," and "I avoid classes that have a lot of writing." Despite the modest response rate (n = 361), the survey supported the conclusions from the 2008 NSSE survey. Forty-two percent of students reported a total of four or fewer writing assignments per semester in all of their classes combined. Over 30 percent of students reported taking only one or two classes per semester requiring any writing assignment at all. The survey also revealed a tendency among students to avoid courses they perceived as requiring a lot of writing. Furthermore, 53 percent of UNCP students reported that they had never visited the University Writing Center during a semester; only 24 percent estimated they used it "rarely."

Similarly, the 2008 UNCP Faculty Perceptions of Writing Survey (appendix 11.A) found that 78 percent of faculty rarely or never required students to use the University Writing Center as part of an assignment. The survey, designed to assess the writing culture on campus, also asked faculty to identify the length of formal and informal writing assignments they assigned on a regular basis and to rate their attitude toward teaching writing-intensive courses and participating in professional development workshops. It included both statements and questions focusing specifically on the writing instruction that faculty incorporated into their courses (e.g., "What kinds of comments do you include on students' essays?" or "When you assign writing, how often do you provide feedback to students' rough drafts?") and faculty's perception of students' writing abilities (e.g., "Students should know how to write before they enroll in my courses" or "Which of the following areas (paragraph organization, paraphrasing, grammar, documentation) do you feel students should have mastered before coming to one of your upper-level classes?"). Forty percent (n = 143) of full-time faculty members responded to the survey. Unfortunately, the internal Faculty Perception of Writing Survey provided mixed results concerning the lack of culture of writing on campus and the perceived need for writing intensive courses beyond the foundational first-year sequence. A very significant 87 percent of faculty respondents believed "students should know how to write" before enrolling in their courses, while 89 percent considered good writing to be independent of the writing style of a particular discipline. At the same time, only 43 percent of the faculty agreed that the first-year writing courses should teach students all they need to know to write successfully throughout their college careers. Finally, survey questions especially relevant to writing intensive courses yielded encouraging results: 69 percent responded favorably to the proposal that more writing intensive courses be taught in their discipline; 57 percent indicated a willingness to teach writing intensive courses in their discipline, if there were smaller enrollments in such courses; and 77 percent expressed interest in attending workshops on teaching writing in their discipline.

Together, the results of the NSSE, the FSSE, the Student Perceptions of Writing Survey, and the Faculty Perception of Writing Survey revealed that once students fulfilled the requirements of the two-semester freshman composition sequence—an ordeal that often took them three or more semesters to complete—they could expect limited writing experiences in college and even more limited exposure to writing instruction thereafter. The data thus indicated the need to institute writing-intensive course requirements in the General Education Program and in the academic majors if students were to reap meaningful benefits from the university's two-course writing requirement and, ultimately, improve their written communication skills. The surveys further reaffirmed what composition faculty knew well, that no matter how strong the final portfolios of students in Composition I and II might be, opportunities for students to practice and develop what they learned about writing beyond freshman composition existed in relatively few courses, most of which were themselves text-heavy (e.g., History, Journalism, Social Work, English, Education). Moreover, it became clear that students were not required to practice and hone their writing skills consistently throughout their academic careers, nor were faculty across the curriculum routinely and systematically providing explicit, discipline-focused writing instruction. If student writing were going to improve on our campus in meaningful ways, the environment for writing—contexts, climate, dispositions, motives—would have to be transformed.

The results of the surveys also revealed two assumptions the QEP would eventually begin to address: (1) that the majority of faculty expected students to have developed above average writing proficiency in freshman composition that they could then seamlessly transfer to any writing assignment in any other discipline beyond the first-year writing sequence, and (2) that all students completed the two-semester freshman composition requirement successfully in their first—or at most—second year. The reality, however, was that until recently, many students repeated one or both of these courses multiple times, sometimes into their junior and senior years, in part perhaps because there appeared to be so little urgency to do otherwise. Without a campus-wide commitment to situate writing in purposeful contexts beyond the composition classroom, students had little reason to believe that writing was a valuable or relevant part of their post-secondary education. Furthermore, outside—and sometimes within—the English department, faculty held unrealistic expectations for students' ability to transfer what they learned about writing in their required composition courses into discipline-specific contexts and genres for applied practice.

Taken together, data from students and faculty alike persuaded QEP steering committee members that writing instruction—to be successful—would have to become everybody's business. Thus, writing emerged as the focus for the QEP, which aimed to build a writing intensive program that would establish and promote a culture of writing across our campus. Grounded in the concept of a vertical approach to writing instruction, the QEP was designed to facilitate students' transfer of rhetorical knowledge from the two-course composition sequence to the more discipline-specific contexts of upper-level writing intensive courses in their major programs. To support this ultimately "pragmatic" goal, beginning Fall 2011, all baccalaureate degree candidates would be required to complete three additional writing courses beyond the composition sequence for a total of at least five writing-intensive courses: Composition I, Composition II, two Writing Enriched (WE) courses, and one Writing in the Discipline (WD) course.

The collective desire to improve student writing on our campus through the writing intensive program is closely aligned with the exigencies of transfer studies. Indeed, research on writing transfer illuminates the design and implementation of our QEP just as transfer theory continues to inform our professional development efforts. Before the QEP, faculty across our campus had long bemoaned the state of student writing in upper-level courses in majors across the disciplines. Lackluster written communication skills among juniors and seniors in virtually every discipline had led faculty across the campus—many of whom subscribed to the time-honored myth that first-year composition courses will produce students who can write anywhere, anytime, on any topic—to question the efficacy and value of the university's first-year writing requirement.

Members of the QEP steering committee, however, knew both intuitively and from experience with student writers that the writing intensive program would have to include a mechanism for repeated, meaningful practice of academic literacy in multiple disciplines and "a pervasive commitment to writing across the curriculum" (Nelms and Dively 2007, 214) if students were to gain any measurable mastery of fundamental skills and proficiencies. The vertical structure of the writing intensive program we devised enacts the foundational premise of the QEP—that writing proficiency is a result of developing over time the ability of students to complete increasingly difficult literacy tasks. Grounded in the concept of vertical transfer, which Donahue defines as "what's learned in one context . . . is (re)used in a next-level-up higher function, acting in fact as a prerequisite for that next level" (Donahue 2012, 150), the program seeks to provide students with logically sequenced writing experiences both across the curriculum and across students' academic careers. To do so, Hall argues, the program "must be concerned not only with the horizontal breadth of writing instruction (the fact that it's happening simultaneously in the social sciences, in the humanities, and in the natural sciences), but also with the vertical integration of writing instruction at various levels and at the various times throughout the whole period of a student's undergraduate career" (Hall 2006, 6). Furthermore, it needs to encompass both WAC and writing in the disciplines (WID) writing intensive courses since, as Jonathan Monroe explains, "while WAC emphasizes the commonality, portability, and communicability of writing practices, WID emphasizes disciplinary differences, diversity, and heterogeneity" (Monroe 2003, 2). The sequence of five writing intensive courses—Composition I, Composition II, two WE courses, and one WD course—responds to Hall's argument for both lateral and vertical integration of writing instruction and incorporates WAC and WID emphases.

The design of our writing intensive program explicitly acknowledges that the contexts and exigencies of discipline-based writing, which define and circumscribe both academic and workplace genres we wanted our students to know, would have to be taught by those who knew them best—the disciplinary experts, many of whom had practiced in the professions for which they now taught and trained our students. Members of the QEP steering committee were convinced that, inasmuch as "genres that arise in the workplace cannot necessarily be lifted out of that context and taught in the utterly different context of the classroom" (Brent 2011, 399) and that "there is no universal educated discourse that students can learn in a writing course and easily apply to courses in history or astronomy" (397) or any other subject for that matter, instructors of first-year writing and of general education or elective writing intensive courses could not reasonably be expected to provide disciplinary knowledge and insights about professions beyond their own. In fact, as Nelms and Dively contend, enhancing the transfer of writing knowledge "implicates not only composition teachers and their students but also writing centers; writing across the curriculum and writing in the disciplines programs; university administrators across colleges, departments, and programs; and employers beyond the academy" (Nelms and Dively 2007, 214).

At the same time, members of the QEP Steering Committee recognized that students needed to appreciate the extent to which writing would be relevant and necessary for their professional success as well as their academic progress. Research on writing transfer (Walvoord and McCarthy 1990; Russell 1997; Carroll 2002; Smit 2004; Beaufort 2007; Bergmann and Zepernick 2007; Wardle 2007; Driscoll 2011; Nowacek 2011; Driscoll and Wells 2012) has convincingly demonstrated the connection between student attitudes and motivation and the potential for transfer of learning. Studying advanced undergraduate students' attitudes toward first-year writing practices, Bergmann and Zepernick, for example, conclude that the primary obstacle to transfer from first-year writing to disciplinary coursework is students' belief that "skills learned in FYC have no value in any other setting" (Bergmann and Zepernick 2007, 139). Wardle echoes their sentiment, reporting that students in her study "did not perceive a need to adopt or adapt most of the writing behaviors they used in FYC for other courses" (2007, 76). More recently, Driscoll's (2011) research illustrates how students' attitudes about future disciplinary writing contexts and limited and narrow definitions of writing relate to their perceived ability to transfer writing knowledge to new contexts. With this in mind, members of the QEP steering committee reshaped the ultimate purpose and goal of the writing intensive program, namely not simply to provide students with more practice toward building their writing skills, but to foster students' rhetorical awareness and knowledge of the choices writers in their disciplines and professions regularly make. Along the way we discovered that more than writing skills, what students needed to learn were what the *Framework for Success in Postsecondary Writing* (2011) terms "habits of mind"—the "ideologies and ways of knowing" (Brent 2011, 402) that distinguish disciplines as communities of discourse and practice. The QEP was therefore designed both to accommodate academic and professional exigencies at "kairotic moments" in students' coursework and to situate their writing practice within broader contexts of motive and utility in an effort to facilitate and foster students' transfer of knowledge about writing.

TO BE AND NOT TO SEEM: ORIGINS OF
A WAC INITIATIVE INCOGNITO

Once the numbers from the surveys of faculty were in, faculty department liaisons were designated as QEP ambassadors and charged with interviewing faculty across the campus for their particular interests and concerns about the state of student writing and the goals for improvement that might be set. By summer 2008, an interdisciplinary steering committee was convened. The group met bi-weekly throughout the remainder of the summer and the next academic year to construct a plan for designing, requiring, teaching, and assessing courses in which students would use writing to demonstrate their content-area learning or their facility with discipline-specific genres. Among the members of the QEP steering committee were tenured or tenure-track faculty in such disciplines as Mass Communications, Social Work, Physics, Political Science, Criminal Justice, Religion, Business, Education, and Literature, as well as two of the three tenure-track English department Rhetoric and Composition faculty, one of whom had been hired the previous year as the University Writing Center director, and another who would serve as the interim director of the Composition Program for the coming academic year. The steering committee was chaired by the director of the Teaching and Learning Center, charged by the provost with coordinating the QEP effort.

Members of the committee worked collaboratively and cooperatively to identify performance goals—the desired competencies and outcomes for students and the methods that would be employed to assess them and to evaluate the efficacy of the QEP itself. The process began with committee members reviewing a number of QEP documents proposed by institutions of similar size and mission. Physics, Religion, and Political Science professors, along with faculty in Literature and Composition Studies, contributed reviews and summaries of scholarship on writing instruction, writing to learn, and writing transfer for the literature review that would have to undergird the proposal for the QEP. As these foundational ideas and goals began to percolate and develop, the group began to articulate the five-year implementation plan. What kinds of instruction would distinguish these new writing-emphasis courses? How would faculty across the university respond to the expectation that they dedicate instructional time toward drafting, peer reviewing, and revising assignments? How many courses would be reasonable or feasible for students to take and faculty to teach? What kinds of institutional support would be required to ensure successful implementation of the program? What kinds of support would be needed to ensure student success? How soon could we reasonably begin designing and offering such courses? And what would they be?

UNCP's QEP proposal eventually laid out four initiatives of which the writing intensive program itself is but one. The four initiatives include:

1. The Writing Intensive Program—a vertical two-tiered program consisting of the foundational two-semester composition sequence supported by a "Plus One" program already in place, i.e., a one-credit writing lab course developed as a scaffold for student-writers (Tier 1); and an additional nine-credit writing requirement to be met by two WE ("writing enriched") courses and one WD ("writing in the disciplines") course (Tier 2). WE are courses at the 2000- and 3000-level, including courses that satisfy General Education requirements, in which writing supplements the coverage of course content. WD are courses at the 3000- and 4000-level within a field of study. Ideally, students will take WE courses in the sophomore and junior year and the WD course in the junior or senior year. Implicit in these designations was the expectation that students would learn and hone fundamental skills of academic literacy, practice them in disciplinary contexts, and ultimately build on this generic expertise as they learned to compose in the specific contexts and genres associated with their major course of study.

2. Faculty Development—a robust plan for faculty development and enrichment to support practices that positively influence student writing. This initiative includes ongoing professional development workshops and other training opportunities intended, over the long run, to produce a cohort of highly skilled writing instructors who will become mentors of their colleagues in departments across the campus.

3. Strengthening the University Writing Center—a three-component plan that entails (1) increasing the number and educational diversity of peer tutors to support the students in the newly established writing intensive program; (2) employing professional, discipline-based peer tutors; and (3) developing an online writing tutoring service.

4. Technology Enhancement—an initiative designed to enhance students' and faculty's information literacy skills and their facility with technologies that enhance writing instruction and promote effective writing.

Currently, at the end of our second year of implementation, there are over 108 WE and WD courses available for students in the full range of disciplines, designed and taught by faculty in the College of Arts and Sciences as well as the Schools of Business and of Education.

THE CHALLENGES OF A MANDATED CAMPUS WRITING INITIATIVE

Campus-wide programs are inextricably woven within other administrative mandates, institutional agendas, and complex local initiatives.
UNCP's writing-intensive program was no exception. Because of a perceived notion that the QEP should not be an "English department project," the interdisciplinary QEP steering committee strategically framed
the initiative as a campus-wide writing intensive program rather than a
Writing Across the Curriculum program. Institutional history and local
perceptions of previous WAC initiatives, led by faculty from the department of English and Theatre, necessitated this rhetorical move. Earlier
attempts at building a WAC program date back to 1993, though they
had not achieved wide popularity or acceptance. With support from a
Title III Strengthening Institutions Program Developmental Grant from
the U. S. Department of Education, UNCP launched a Speaking and
Writing across the Curriculum program from 1993 to 1996. The program grew out of faculty's concerns about students' ability to communicate effectively and aimed to develop "students' abilities to use writing and speaking more effectively and to increase faculty's awareness
of the values of writing and speaking across the curriculum as valuable
means to increase students learning" (Pembroke State University 1993,
73–74). That faculty in all departments should assume responsibility
for writing instruction rather than relegate it to a single department
or course requirement represented the underpinning premise of the
Speaking and Writing across the Curriculum program. To this end, the
initiative included the initial establishment of the University Writing
Center, a series of writing-center professional development seminars
for faculty across disciplines, annual WAC retreats, and the publication
each year of *Works in Progress: Resources for College Courses*, a collection of
writing activities and assignments from various disciplines. In each of
the three years, approximately 12 to 20 faculty members participated in
the multi-session seminars, and 20 to 40 faculty members attended the
individual workshops and presentations by the two guest speakers, WAC
experts Art Young and Barbara Walvoord. Despite the efforts of this core
group of faculty and the school's Communication Proficiency across the
Curriculum Council in incorporating more writing into the curriculum, this bottom-up approach to building a WAC program quickly fiz-
zled once the funding from the three-year grant ended. The University
Writing Center is the primary remaining tangible result of this program.

The second attempt to generate interest in cross-disciplinary writing instruction a few years later began as a sort of grassroots initiative among faculty in disciplines where writing was a professional

expectation—Psychology, Geology, English, Mass Communication, and Journalism among them. A handful of faculty from these disciplines interested in incorporating writing into their courses formed the Writing Across the Curriculum Teaching Circle (2013), "an informal interdisciplinary group of faculty members contemplating the problems our students have with writing, in and out of the classroom, and critical thinking." The WAC Teaching Circle team aspired to organize faculty development workshops and foster discussion to broaden the scope of student writing across disciplines. Unfortunately, no university records exist indicating whether the WAC Teaching Circle succeeded in enacting its vision and bringing together a critical mass of faculty members needed to inculcate any degree of permanence. As a result, the grassroots WAC venture did not achieve the prerequisite buy-in across campus needed for a formalized WAC program to emerge and, similarly to the Speaking and Writing Across the Curriculum program, it lost momentum and withered.

Given this institutional history of short-lived WAC initiatives, the interdisciplinary QEP steering committee purposefully steered away from labeling the writing-anchored QEP a WAC program in an effort to distinguish the new writing initiative from previous unsuccessful attempts at establishing such a program. After all, faculty approbation is crucial to the success of any widespread writing undertaking, yet it could hardly be achieved when recollections of curtailed WAC endeavors lingered in institutional memory. For better or worse, as discussions among steering committee members addressed "scholar skills" and identified genre expectations unique to diverse disciplines, it became clear that the QEP would have to employ a term other than "writing across the curriculum" to garner faculty support and would have to be, if at all possible, directed by faculty in departments other than English if it was to have hope for success. Consequently, in a deliberate rhetorical move, the committee named the new initiative a writing intensive program and made the conscious decision to refrain from any usage of WAC terminology. In fact, the only place the acronym WAC and the phrase "writing across the curriculum" appear in the QEP document is in the Selected Bibliography section. Given that the SACS mandate came with a generous, five-year implementation budget, it seemed likely that, if faculty support could be secured and sustained, the campus-wide writing initiative—whatever its name would turn out to be—might finally succeed.

Furthermore, the two earlier WAC initiatives were directed by English faculty and were largely perceived to be English department projects. The success of the QEP initiative, on the other hand, rested on its strategic position within institutional culture—an accreditation requirement housed in no particular department or educational unit and conceived, developed, and implemented by an interdisciplinary QEP steering committee. It sought to promote the teaching of writing as everybody's business, not just that of the English faculty. To ensure the success of the QEP, faculty across campus needed to engage in practices that positively impacted student writing. That meant having faculty who believed in the significance of writing in their disciplines and who were open to exploring more effective and engaging ways of incorporating writing into their courses and ultimately helping students become better writers. To this end, the English faculty could no longer assume sole expertise in the teaching of writing, nor could they claim leadership of the emerging writing-driven QEP. To do so would have once again positioned the English faculty as *the* experts on writing set on helping faculty across campus incorporate writing into their courses. Many faculty members, however, were already dedicated and effective teachers of writing across the curriculum who saw writing instruction as a university-wide responsibility and who resisted the notion that English faculty alone possessed sole expertise on writing, especially given the fact that under the vertical approach to writing, faculty across campus were considered the writing experts in their disciplines. Consequently, English faculty assumed, albeit some of them reluctantly, the role of consultants rather than experts, an important strategic move to secure faculty buy-in for, as Rebecca Jackson and Deborah Morton remark, "sometimes getting people to listen means not being the expert in the room but being humble. This often means giving up disciplinary or institutional stardom, giving up the dream of being a goddess . . . and instead dreaming of being part of the collective" (Jackson and Morton 2007, 54).

The uneasy tension between experts and non-specialists, leaders and consultants, administrators and faculty presented a number of challenges in the implementation process of the writing intensive initiative. Early on, there were instances of "what [James] Scott calls an 'undeclared ideological guerilla war' that is fought with 'rumor, gossip, disguises, linguistic tricks, metaphors, euphemisms, folktales, ritual gestures, anonymity" (Miller 1998, 205). In some instances a few members of the Faculty Senate objected to what they perceived to be an unreasonable implementation timetable and called for revising the QEP initiative, not taking into consideration that the plan had already been approved, without recommendations for revision, by the SACS' Reaffirmation committee. On other occasions, some departments expressed concern regarding the process of designing WE and WD courses, incorrectly assuming that they needed to add additional brand new courses to their degree pathways to satisfy the writing intensive requirement. On yet another occasion, individual faculty members resented having to submit a formal proposal for a WE or WD course designation, mistakenly believing that any course that included assigned writing tasks was already a writing intensive course. To address these concerns and other anxieties about the writing intensive program, the QEP committee engaged in overt negotiation and consulted with individual departments to help them develop ways of responding to this initiative.

THE PROMISE OF A MANDATED CAMPUS WRITING INITIATIVE

Despite being a mandated initiative, UNCP's QEP exemplifies how this seemingly insurmountable approach to building a writing intensive program, or a "stealth WAC" as Doug Brent (2005, 87) calls it, could lead to promising results. For one, the university's QEP "*Write to the Top*: Enhancing Student Writing through a Writing Intensive Program" was approved without recommendations for revision by the SACS On-Site Reaffirmation committee on March 18, 2010. More important, the lead QEP evaluator, a Composition specialist, praised the plan as a potential national model. She wrote:

> UNCP has developed a broad-based quality enhancement plan that is forward looking in its goal of improving student writing at all levels. The plan is both organic and holistic . . . It establishes a protocol for addressing the issue that is both credible and measureable . . . When implemented, the QEP will establish a culture of writing by impacting students' curricula beginning with first-year composition, moving into writing enriched coursework, and concluding with a professional writing course that introduces them to the conventions of their chosen major. (University of North Carolina at Pembroke, 2010)

While the QEP evaluator considered the plan to be both complex and ambitious, she also characterized it as a potential model for other institutions to follow. Discernibly, if successful WAC programs exemplify certain characteristic features as identified by Townsend (2008) and can be codified based on their location and momentum within institutional structure using Condon and Rutz's (2012) taxonomy, then detailing the present state of UNCP's writing intensive program illustrates how a mandated WAC-like entity can succeed and flourish with sufficient support for faculty leadership and development. The success of the integration of an institution-wide writing intensive requirement, Townsend believes, hinges on several factors such as faculty ownership, institutional support, and sound guidelines for writing intensive courses. Despite its origin as a mandated initiative, the university's writing intensive program builds on best practices in WAC and exemplifies what Martha Townsend identifies as the characteristic features of a successful WAC program.

For one, from the onset faculty ownership constituted a crucial component of the writing intensive endeavor and remains, to this day, one of its integral aspects. The program is faculty conceived, initiated, and reviewed. All writing intensive course proposals are peer-reviewed by the interdisciplinary QEP faculty-composed committee, and, in the spirit of collegiality and collaboration, members of the committee offer detailed feedback and work closely with individual faculty and departments in cases when writing intensive course proposals need to be revised to meet the requirements for WE or WD courses. No proposal is turned down, though some warrant adjustments to ensure feasibility as well as efficacy. At the same time, all curriculum changes, including the writing intensive designations WE and WD, require the final approval of several committee structures, including Faculty Senate, thus ensuring strong faculty ownership of the program.

The second equally important characteristic feature of a successful WAC program is strong institutional support. This means having tangible resources as evidence of commitment at all levels of institutional decision-making. Because the writing intensive program at our institution is a component of a larger, mandated accreditation requirement, we have had strong institutional support, both administrative and fiscal, from the very beginning. The university's commitment to recognizing and valuing the teaching of writing intensive courses is evident in the small class sizes for WE and WD courses, which are limited to 20 students per section. In the past two years, the writing intensive program became integrated into the fabric of the institution, offering more than 108 writing intensive courses. In addition, despite enduring budget cuts every year, we have been able to offer faculty stipends for proposing and developing writing intensive courses; fund professional development workshops led by writing experts such as Chris Anson, Michael Carter, Terry Zawacki, Susan Miller-Cochran, and Kelly Ritter; and provide professional development resources to faculty participating in the workshops, including copies of Terry Zawacki and Paul Roger's *Writing across the Curriculum: A Critical Sourcebook* and John C. Bean's *Engaging Ideas*, dubbed by Condon and Rutz (2012, 368) the "WAC Bible." Additional WAC and discipline-specific writing resources have also been added to the university's library collection.

The professional development program, in particular, proved to be an essential component of the writing intensive program. It included a series of faculty development activities and workshops aimed to help faculty design and implement WE and WD courses. The workshops covered a variety of topics such as "Creating a Writing Intensive Course," "Designing Effective Assignments to Accomplish Course Learning and Writing Goals," "Responding to Students' Writing," "Writing in the Disciplines: How to Teach Disciplinary 'Ways of Knowing' and Writing Conventions," "Improving Student Writing through Peer Response and Revision," "Assigning and Teaching Research Papers and Research Skills," and so forth. At the end of each semester, the QEP committee sought feedback from faculty who participated in the workshops in order to improve the quality of the professional development activities and better serve the needs of faculty interested in teaching writing intensive courses. Workshop participants were asked to complete the "Evaluation of UNCP QEP Writing Workshops" (appendix 11.B), distributed electronically via email, and to evaluate not only individual workshops but the faculty development program overall. Open-ended questions were also included in the evaluation form to give faculty the opportunity to provide additional feedback or elaborate on their rating on statements covered in the Likert-scale portion of the survey.

In addition to offering these professional development workshops, the QEP writing intensive program also developed flexible but sound guidelines for WE and WD courses, based on Farris and Smith's recommendations for writing intensive (WI) courses. Though the specific requirements for writing intensive courses vary across institutions, Farris and Smith (2000, 54–55) identify the following most common criteria for WI courses:

- class size and instructor-to-student ratio
- required number of pages or words to be completed throughout the course
- requirements for direct writing instruction
- guidelines for revision and writing process activities
- criteria for assigning and evaluating written work
- support services for writing instruction

The QEP steering committee adapted Farris and Smith's list of criteria for writing intensive courses in composing the guideline for WE and WD courses. The guidelines were drafted to assist faculty as they develop proposals for writing intensive courses and the QEP advisory committee as they review course proposals and design faculty development activities. These guidelines, available on the school's QEP webpage, cover required or recommended elements such as student learning outcomes related to writing, instruction and evaluation of writing assignments, recommended lengths for formal and informal writing tasks, among other things, for courses to be designated as WE or WD. The guidelines are deliberately crafted to be more descriptive than prescriptive to allow a fair degree of flexibility and applicability to a wide range of disciplines. After all, a writing in the disciplines course in Social Work differs significantly from a writing in the disciplines course in Physical Education, for example. The guidelines, however, were designed to account for these differences and to recognize that there is no one model of a writing intensive course—or a writing intensive program for that matter—that fits every program or every institution.

At the same time, the program's location and momentum position it firmly as a type 2: Established program in Condon and Rutz's 4-stage taxonomy of WAC programs. Drawing on the principles of location and momentum, Condon and Rutz offer a classification system that can be used to describe and evaluate a WAC program and ultimately serve as a rubric for continual program evaluation and planning for growth. They identify four types of WAC programs—foundational, established, integrated, and institutional change agent—based on key characteristics such as primary goals of the program, funding, organizational structure, institutional integration, and indicators for success. The four types represent stages of development of a WAC program and provide benchmarks an institution can use in determining "where the program stands within a national context, according to national norms" (Condon and Rutz 2012, 379).

In regard to Condon and Rutz's taxonomy, the writing intensive program at UNCP has achieved the status of an established program. Such a program is characterized by the presence of institutional funding, curricular improvement, continual faculty development initiatives, and an emerging program identity within the institutional structure. UNCP's writing intensive program has its own, though temporary, funding through the QEP budget, is visible and regularized in the university catalog as part of the graduation requirements, has established its own identity through WE and WD courses, and continues to evolve toward becoming fully integrated into university curriculum and institutional structure. Furthermore, capitalizing on the momentum created by the SACS mandate, members of the QEP steering committee have sought opportunities to interweave the writing intensive program firmly into the institutional fabric, one of the primary goals of a type 3: Integrated

WAC program, by aligning it with larger institutional agendas such as the Quality Matters online teaching initiative. To this end, with support from the Department of Education Native American Serving Non-Tribal Institutions (NASNTI) Title III Grant and the Harnessing Opportunities through Proactive Education and Service (HOPES) program, the QEP steering committee has issued a call for proposals for designing or redesigning writing intensive courses to be offered in an online or hybrid format. The goal of the HOPES program is to improve the quality of online courses through the provision of quality assurance training and course review, using the UNC system's recently adopted Quality Matters Rubric. Similar to the peer-review process for writing intensive courses, the Quality Matters peer-evaluation process for online courses and online course materials aims to ensure they meet or exceed best practices and accreditation standards for online teaching and learning. By linking the two initiatives, the QEP committee reaffirmed the location of the writing intensive program within institutional structure and advanced its momentum toward more comprehensive integration within the institutional framework.

Ultimately, the true success of a WAC-like program could be measured, as Toby Fulwiler suggests, "simply by the strength of the faculty community they succeed in generating" (Fulwiler 1988, 66). If that is the case, then the mandated writing intensive program at UNCP has managed to accomplish what the two earlier grassroots attempts to establish a WAC program could not—a strong and continuously growing community of dedicated, enthusiastic faculty committed to the teaching of writing across the curriculum. While the lasting effect of the writing intensive program is yet to be determined, we have some anecdotal evidence of an emerging campus writing culture. Grounded in institutional culture and local context, our story, nevertheless, offers one possible way of (re)conceptualizing a mandated campus-wide writing initiative and aligning it with best practices in WAC scholarship. Far from following the "the Pilgrim's Progress Model of faculty change," UNCP's *Write to the Top* initiative owes its success to balancing an accreditation mandate with responding to local affordances and constraints and securing faculty buy-in and institutional support, even if that meant not using WAC-related nomenclature. The result is a flourishing writing intensive program, a form of "stealth WAC," since, as Doug Brent explains, "no-one has really complained that what they are doing in practice turns out to look a lot like WAC," even if "WAC roots are spreading rather nicely underground whether [we] call it that or not" (Brent 2005, 87). To us, that is a successful writing intensive program.

APPENDIX 11.A

Faculty Perceptions of Writing Survey (2008)

The purpose of this survey is to assess the current writing culture at UNCP. Please take a few minutes to fill out the survey. This information will be helpful in the design of the Quality Enhancement Plan at UNCP.

1. In which school/college is your teaching appointment?
   - □ Arts & Sciences
   - □ Business
   - □ Education
   - □ Honors College

2. What is the rank of your current appointment?
   - □ Lecturer/Instructor
   - □ Assistant Professor
   - □ Associate Professor
   - □ Full Professor
   - □ Other (please specify)

3. How many years have you been teaching at UNCP?
   - □ 0–3 years
   - □ 4–8 years
   - □ 9–15 years
   - □ 16 or more years

4. Students should know how to write before they enroll in my courses.
   - □ Strongly Disagree   □ Disagree   □ Agree   □ Strongly Agree

5. Good writing is independent of the writing style of a particular discipline.
   - □ Strongly Disagree   □ Disagree   □ Agree   □ Strongly Agree

6. If I take time in my courses to attend to student writing, I will compromise the quality of content instruction.
   - □ Strongly Disagree   □ Disagree   □ Agree   □ Strongly Agree

7. I check students' sources, use Turnitin, or otherwise screen student writing for plagiarism.
   - □ Strongly Disagree   □ Disagree   □ Agree   □ Strongly Agree

8. What kinds of comments do you include on students' essays?
   - □ Comments on content
   - □ Comments on clarity and organization
   - □ Grammatical corrections

9. Which of the following areas do you feel students should have mastered before coming to one of your upper-level classes?
   - □ Paragraph organization
   - □ Paraphrasing
   - □ Grammar
   - □ Documentation

10. How often do you assign short (1–3 pages) formal writing assignments in a course?
    - □ Never
    - □ 1–2 times a semester
    - □ 3–4 times a semester

□ 5–6 times a semester
□ 7–8 times a semester
□ 9–10 times a semester
□ More than 10 times a semester

11. How often do you assign medium length (4–9 pages) formal writing assignments?
    □ Never
    □ 1–2 times a semester
    □ 3–4 times a semester
    □ 5–6 times a semester
    □ 7–8 times a semester
    □ 9–10 times a semester
    □ More than 10 times a semester

12. How often do you assign lengthy (10+ pages) formal writing assignments?
    □ Never
    □ 1–2 times a semester
    □ 3–4 times a semester
    □ 5–6 times a semester
    □ 7–8 times a semester
    □ 9–10 times a semester
    □ More than 10 times a semester

13. When you assign writing, how often do you provide feedback to students' rough drafts?
    □ Frequently
    □ Occasionally
    □ Rarely
    □ Never
    □ Not applicable; I do not assign writing.

14. How often do you make assignments that require the use of the University Writing Center?
    □ Not at all
    □ Rarely
    □ Occasionally
    □ Always

15. The freshman writing courses should teach students all they need to know to write successfully throughout their college careers.
    □ Strongly Disagree   □ Disagree   □ Agree   □ Strongly Agree

16. I would be willing to attend workshops on "Teaching Writing in my Discipline."
    □ Strongly Disagree   □ Disagree   □ Agree   □ Strongly Agree

17. I would like to see more writing-intensive courses taught in my discipline.
    □ Strongly Disagree   □ Disagree   □ Agree   □ Strongly Agree

18. I am willing to teach more writing-intensive courses.
    □ Strongly Disagree   □ Disagree   □ Agree   □ Strongly Agree

19. I would need the following to make it possible for me to teach more writing-intensive courses. (Choose all that apply.)
    □ Workshops on teaching writing
    □ Smaller classes
    □ Other (please explain)

Evaluation of UNCP QEP Writing Workshops (Spring 2011)

Please evaluate each workshop that you attended.

If you did not attend a workshop, please leave it blank.

Please help us improve the quality of these workshops by completing the following evaluation. Thank you.

To what extent do you agree or disagree with the following statements? Please circle the appropriate number for each statement.

Workshop: Creating a Writing Intensive Course Workshop Leader: Chris Anson	*Strongly Agree*				*Strongly Disagree*
1. Included a description of learning objectives to be covered in workshop.	5	4	3	2	1
2. Covered those objectives.	5	4	3	2	1
3. Was appropriate for my level of experience in writing.	5	4	3	2	1
4. Was well organized and followed a logical order.	5	4	3	2	1
5. Incorporated useful examples.	5	4	3	2	1
6. Showed how to apply the content to my discipline.	5	4	3	2	1
7. Created an environment that encouraged learning.	5	4	3	2	1
8. Included helpful exercises that facilitated my learning.	5	4	3	2	1
9. Included useful handouts and other written materials.	5	4	3	2	1
10. Answered questions clearly.	5	4	3	2	1
11. Made effective use of time.	5	4	3	2	1
12. Provided opportunities for me to participate.	5	4	3	2	1

Other Comments:

Workshop: Responding to Student Writing Workshop Leader: Ron Lunsford	*Strongly Agree*				*Strongly Disagree*
1. Included a description of learning objectives to be covered in workshop.	5	4	3	2	1
2. Covered those objectives.	5	4	3	2	1
3. Was appropriate for my level of experience in writing.	5	4	3	2	1
4. Was well organized and followed a logical order.	5	4	3	2	1

Workshop: Responding to Student Writing Workshop Leader: Ron Lunsford	Strongly Agree				Strongly Disagree
5. Incorporated useful examples.	5	4	3	2	1
6. Showed how to apply the content to my discipline.	5	4	3	2	1
7. Created an environment that encouraged learning.	5	4	3	2	1
8. Included helpful exercises that facilitated my learning.	5	4	3	2	1
9. Included useful handouts and other written materials.	5	4	3	2	1
10. Answered questions clearly.	5	4	3	2	1
11. Made effective use of time.	5	4	3	2	1
12. Provided opportunities for me to participate.	5	4	3	2	1

Other Comments:

Workshop: Writing in the Disciplines Workshop Leader: Michael Carter	Strongly Agree				Strongly Disagree
1. Included a description of learning objectives to be covered in workshop.	5	4	3	2	1
2. Covered those objectives.	5	4	3	2	1
3. Was appropriate for my level of experience in writing.	5	4	3	2	1
4. Was well organized and followed a logical order.	5	4	3	2	1
5. Incorporated useful examples.	5	4	3	2	1
6. Showed how to apply the content to my discipline.	5	4	3	2	1
7. Created an environment that encouraged learning.	5	4	3	2	1
8. Included helpful exercises that facilitated my learning.	5	4	3	2	1
9. Included useful handouts and other written materials.	5	4	3	2	1
10. Answered questions clearly.	5	4	3	2	1
11. Made effective use of time.	5	4	3	2	1
12. Provided opportunities for me to participate.	5	4	3	2	1

Other Comments:

Workshop: Academic Research Assignments Workshop Leaders: Michael Alewine and Mark Canada	Strongly Agree				Strongly Disagree
1. Included a description of learning objectives to be covered in workshop.	5	4	3	2	1
2. Covered those objectives.	5	4	3	2	1
3. Was appropriate for my level of experience in writing.	5	4	3	2	1
4. Was well organized and followed a logical order.	5	4	3	2	1
5. Incorporated useful examples.	5	4	3	2	1
6. Showed how to apply the content to my discipline	5	4	3	2	1
7. Created an environment that encouraged learning.	5	4	3	2	1
8. Included helpful exercises that facilitated my learning.	5	4	3	2	1
9. Included useful handouts and other written materials.	5	4	3	2	1
10. Answered questions clearly.	5	4	3	2	1
11. Made effective use of time.	5	4	3	2	1
12. Provided opportunities for me to participate.	5	4	3	2	1

Other Comments:

Workshop: Effective Writing Assignments Workshop Leader: Terry Zawacki	Strongly Agree				Strongly Disagree
1. Included a description of learning objectives to be covered in the workshop.	5	4	3	2	1
2. Covered those objectives.	5	4	3	2	1
3. Was appropriate for my level of experience in writing.	5	4	3	2	1
4. Was well organized and followed a logical order.	5	4	3	2	1
5. Incorporated useful examples.	5	4	3	2	1
6. Showed how to apply the content to my discipline.	5	4	3	2	1
7. Created an environment that encouraged learning.	5	4	3	2	1
8. Included helpful exercises that facilitated my learning.	5	4	3	2	1
9. Included useful handouts and other written materials.	5	4	3	2	1
10. Answered questions clearly.	5	4	3	2	1

Workshop: Effective Writing Assignments Workshop Leader: Terry Zawacki	Strongly Agree				Strongly Disagree
11. Made effective use of time.	5	4	3	2	1
12. Provided opportunities for me to participate.	5	4	3	2	1

Other Comments:

Faculty Development Program Overall	Strongly Agree				Strongly Disagree
13. These workshops increased my knowledge about teaching writing.	5	4	3	2	1
14. These workshops increased my ability to facilitate my WE or WD class.	5	4	3	2	1
15. These workshops encouraged me to re-examine my assessment of student writing.	5	4	3	2	1
16. I expect to use what I learned with my students.	5	4	3	2	1
17. I would recommend these workshops to other faculty.	5	4	3	2	1
18. I have a plan about implementing what I have learned.	5	4	3	2	1

19. What about these workshops was particularly helpful to you?

20. What would you like to see changed or what could be improved (especially regarding any of the above statements you disagreed with)?

21. What follow-up to this workshop would be helpful in order to apply what you have learned to your classes?

22. What other training topics would you like to be offered in the future?

ADDITIONAL COMMENTS:

References

Beaufort, Anne. 2007. *College Writing and Beyond: A New Framework for University Writing Instruction.* Logan: Utah State University Press.

Bergmann, Linda S., and Janet S. Zepernick. 2007. "Disciplinarity and Transfer: Students' Perceptions of Learning to Write." *WPA: Writing Program Administration* 31 (1–2): 124–49.

Brent, Doug. 2005. "Dangerous Partnerships: How Competence Testing Can Sabotage WAC." *WAC Journal* 16:78–88.

Brent, Doug. 2011. "Transfer, Transformation, and Rhetorical Knowledge: Insights from Transfer Theory." *Journal of Business and Technical Communication* 25 (4): 396–420. http://dx.doi.org/10.1177/1050651911410951.

Carroll, Lee Ann. 2002. *Rehearsing New Roles: How College Students Develop as Writers.* Carbondale: Southern Illinois University Press.

Carson, Jay. 1994. "Recognizing and Using Context as a Survival Tool for WAC." *WPA: Writing Program Administration* 17 (3): 35–47.

Condon, William, and Carol Rutz. 2012. "A Taxonomy of Writing Across the Curriculum Programs: Evolving to Serve Broader Agendas." *College Composition and Communication* 64 (2): 357–82.

Council of Writing Program Administrators, National Council of Teachers of English, and National Writing Project. 2011. *Framework for Success in Postsecondary Writing.* http://wpacouncil.org/files/framework-for-success-postsecondary-writing.pdf.

Donahue, Christiane. 2012. "Transfer, Portability, Generalization: (How) Does Composition Expertise 'Carry.'" In *Exploring Composition Studies: Sites, Issues, and Perspectives,* ed. Kelly Ritter and Paul Kei Matsuda, 145–66. Logan: Utah State University Press.

Driscoll, Dana. 2011. "Connected, Disconnected, or Uncertain: Student Attitudes about Future Writing Contexts and Perceptions of Transfer from First Year Writing to the Disciplines." *Across the Disciplines* 8 (2). http://wac.colostate.edu/atd/articles /driscoll2011/index.cfm.

Driscoll, Dana, and Jennifer Wells. 2012. "Beyond Knowledge and Skills: Writing Transfer and the Role of Student Dispositions." *Composition Forum* 26. http://composition forum.com/issue/26/beyond-knowledge-skills.php.

Farris, Christine, and Raymond Smith. 2000. "Writing-Intensive Courses: Tools for Curricular Change." In *Writing Across the Curriculum: A Guide to Developing Programs,* ed. Susan H. McLeod and Margot Soven, 52–62. Newbury Park: Sage Publications; http://wac.colostate.edu/books/mcleod_soven/.

Fulwiler, Toby. 1988. "Evaluating Writing Across the Curriculum Programs." In *Strengthening Programs for Writing Across the Curriculum,* ed. Susan H. McLeod, 61–75. San Francisco: Jossey-Bass.

Hall, Jonathan. 2006. "Towards a Unified Writing Curriculum: Integrating WAC/WID with Freshman Composition." *WAC Journal* 17:5–22.

Holdstein, Deborah H. 2001. "'Writing Across the Curriculum' and the Paradoxes of Institutional Initiatives." *Pedagogy* 1 (1): 37–52. http://dx.doi.org/10.1215/1531420 0-1-1-37.

Jackson, Rebecca, and Deborah Morton. 2007. "Becoming Landscape Architects: A Postmodern Approach to WAC Sustainability." *WAC Journal* 18:43–58.

Malenczyk, Rita. 2012. "WAC's Disappearing Act." In *Exploring Composition Studies: Sites, Issues, and Perspectives,* ed. Kelly Ritter and Paul Kei Matsuda, 89–104. Logan: Utah State University Press.

McLeod, Susan H., and Margot Soven. 1991. "What Do You Need to Start—and Sustain—a Writing-Across-the-Curriculum Program?" *WPA: Writing Program Administration* 15 (1–2): 25–33.

Miller, Richard E. 1998. *As If Learning Mattered: Reforming Higher Education.* Ithaca: Cornell University Press.

Monroe, Jonathan. 2003. "Writing in the Disciplines." *Peer Review: Emerging Trends and Key Debates in Undergraduate Education* 6 (1): 4–7.

Nelms, Gerald, and Ronda L. Dively. 2007. "Perceived Roadblocks to Transferring Knowledge from First-Year Composition to Writing Intensive Major Courses: A Pilot Study." *WPA: Writing Program Administration* 31 (1): 214–40.

Nowacek, Rebecca S. 2011. *Agents of Integration: Understanding Transfer as a Rhetorical Act.* Carbondale: Southern Illinois University Press.

Pembroke State University. 1993. Title III Strengthening Institutions Program Development Grant Proposal.

Russell, David. 1997. "Rethinking Genre in School and Society: An Activity Theory Analysis." *Written Communication* 14 (4): 504–54. http://dx.doi.org/10.1177/0741088 397014004004.

Smit, David W. 2004. *The End of Composition Studies.* Carbondale: Southern Illinois University Press.

Townsend, Martha. 2008. "WAC Program Vulnerability and What to Do about It: An Update and Brief Bibliographic Essay." *WAC Journal* 19:45–61.

University of North Carolina at Pembroke. 2010. *Assessment of Quality Enhancement Plan On-Site Review Committee Report.*

University of North Carolina at Pembroke. 2013a. *The 2012–2013 FactBook.* Accessed April 2. http://uncp.edu/ie/fact_book/12-13/index.htm.

University of North Carolina at Pembroke. 2013b. *UNCP Mission Statement.* Accessed March 20. http://uncp.edu/uncp/about/mission.htm.

Walvoord, Barbara. 1996. "The Future of WAC." *College English* 58 (1): 58–79. http://dx.doi.org/10.2307/378534.

Walvoord, Barbara, and Lucille P. McCarthy. 1990. *Thinking and Writing in College: A Naturalistic Study of Students in Four Disciplines.* Urbana, IL: National Council of Teachers of English.

Wardle, Elizabeth. 2007. "Understanding 'Transfer' from FYC: Preliminary Results of a Longitudinal Study." *WPA: Writing Program Administration* 31 (1–2): 65–85.

White, Edward M. 1990. "The Damage of Innovations Set Adrift." *AAHE Bulletin* 3:3–5.

White, Edward M. 1997. Edward White to WPA-L mailing list, August 20. http://lists.asu.edu/archives/wpa-l.html.

Writing Across the Curriculum Teaching Circle. 2013. *About WAC.* Accessed March 2. http://uncp.edu/wac/about/.

12
"EVERYBODY WRITES"
Accreditation-Based Assessment as Professional
Development at a Research Intensive University

Linda Adler-Kassner and Lorna Gonzalez

Beginning in 2011–2012, as part of our institution's reaccreditation efforts for the Western Association of Schools and Colleges (WASC), Linda was asked by our institution's Academic Senate to chair an ad hoc committee charged with articulating outcomes for the general education (GE) program and developing and undertaking an assessment of that program. She was joined in this process by Lorna, a graduate student pursuing a Ph.D. in Language, Literacy, and Composition at the University of California, Santa Barbara (2012) (UCSB). While GE has long been a subject of considerable interest among faculty on our campus—previous assessment efforts include one in 1985, a second in 1993–94, a third that went, in essence, from 2000 to 2004—the focus of this effort would be not on attempting to change the program, but on clarifying its goals and assessing one element of the program to learn to what extent its learning outcomes were being realized.

In this chapter we describe the ways in which our process has contributed to an ongoing conversation about writing and learning development on our campus, based in and extending from particular principles about writing, learning, and general education. We begin by describing the learning framework and principles that served as the foundation for our efforts, both of which extend from research that Linda has been conducting with another faculty member in history for the last three years (see Adler-Kassner, Majewski, and Koshnick 2012). We then describe the process that we used for our campus's assessment and discuss its connections to this framework. Finally, we draw on interviews with three faculty members to discuss how and whether participation in this process seems to have played a part in their thinking about teaching, and especially the teaching of writing.

OI: 10.7330/9781607324355.c012

PRINCIPLE-BASED ASSESSMENT AT UC SANTA BARBARA

As with any assessment, the first step for our project was to articulate how we believe that learning takes place. Whether explicit or not, all assessments proceed within such beliefs, which then form the boundaries for questions asked in a project. A relatively simple illustration would be an assessment that asks how knowledge delivered in a lecture is repeated by students via responses on a multiple choice test might be said to reflect the belief that learning takes place when information is deposited by a teacher and retrieved in specific ways by students. An assessment like the Collegiate Learning Assessment, a test most often administered separate from the context of particular classes that asks students to analyze and create multiple documents (essays, etc.) related to scenarios presented in the test, could (in part) be said to conceptualize learning as a process whereby somewhat "universal" strategies are developed (e.g., "critical thinking") and demonstrated when applied out of context, i.e., in the entirely fictitious (for students, anyway) scenarios included in the assessment (see O'Neill, Moore, and Huot 2009, for an excellent explanation of assessment theory and method).

For this assessment, we drew on Jean Lave and Etienne Wenger's notion of "communities of practice" to conceptualize learning in our institution's context (Lave and Wenger 1991; see Adler-Kassner and Estrem 2009; Adler-Kassner, Majewski, and Koshnick 2012). Communities of practice are sites that are bound together (and delineated from other communities) by shared rituals, practices, and commitments. To participate in a community of practice, novices must learn what the rituals and practices are that contribute to the creation and perpetuation of the community and learn *how* to learn within that community (Wenger 1998). At the same time, Wenger explains that communities of practice are "ubiquitous[;]. . . so informal and pervasive that they rarely come into explicit focus" (7). In addition and importantly, the more expert/experienced participants become within communities of practice, the less visible the distinct practices of those communities become to them.

Academic disciplines are excellent examples of communities of practice. To be sure, members of disciplines engage in multi- or interdisciplinary work; however, this latitude to move *among* disciplines is only available to a member of an academic community of practice after she or he has demonstrated appropriate understanding of *one* discipline, typically by earning the kind of certification that is granted through completion of milestones like qualifying exams or dissertations. Disciplines are delineated by two things: (1) their members' commitments to shared knowledge (i.e., the "content" of a discipline or interdiscipline), and

(2) shared ways of communicating those ideas through the framing and exploration of questions relevant to the field and through shared practices for representing both method and analyses (also known as research and writing within the discipline). Teaching and learning within this context, then, involves *identifying* and *participating in* the boundaries that surround communities of practice—in our case, academic disciplines and interdisciplines—within an institution (see Carter 2007 for more on the role of disciplinarity in writing).[1]

Following this conceptualization of learning, two critical principles served as the foundation for our assessment work at UCSB. First is the idea that qualities of good writing are context specific (Huot 2002; O'Neill and Adler-Kassner 2010). As communities of practice, academic disciplines and interdisciplines have particular ways of asking, investigating, and representing knowledge. This is why writing in biology, say, is quite different from writing in literature, or why writing in literature is different from writing in history. This is a point eloquently made by Chris Anson et al. in their argument for locally-based assessment. They write that "writers don't develop abilities generically and simply apply them seamlessly to whatever new contexts where they may need or want to write. Instead, as Russell (1995) has put it 'one acquires the genres . . . used by some activity field as one interacts with people involved in the activity field and the material objects and signs those people use'" (Anson et al. 2012, 56). Yet this principle, commonsensical to those of us who teach writing, sometimes comes as a surprise to faculty colleagues precisely because they *are* so expert in their communities of practice.

The second, related, principle underscoring our assessment is the idea that assessment must be grounded in the principles, methods, and practices of academic disciplines, and that assessment processes must be developed with input from those who contribute to the sites of assessments (like classes) and might be affected by the results (Huot 2002; Broad 2003; CCCC n.d.). Bob Broad's "dynamic criteria mapping" (DCM) serves as a generative model of this concept. In Broad's conception, DCM involves faculty in a "communal," text-based discussion about what they define as key elements included in writing, how they define those elements, and what attributes they associate with different levels of performance related to those attributes. In the process of making explicit ideas about writing and their relationships to judgments *about* writing, faculty "become more aware of their own evaluative landscapes [and] they learn how others often evaluate and interpret texts very differently" (121). Our colleague, Charles Bazerman's idea of "conceptual words" is also critical here. As Bazerman defines them, these words "mediate the work and meanings of an activity system (i.e., people gathered in an organized set of relations, rules, and practices in pursuit of some object)" (Bazerman 2012, 260). That is, they are words that carry heavily contextualized meanings that evoke discipline-specific theories, concepts, and conventions. "Yet," Bazerman adds, "the externalized words of the writer and the reader's meanings evoked by those words depend on each participant's history of engagement with those words within each person's communicative interactions" (260). That the meanings of conceptual words depend on the individual's history of interaction with them attests to the idea of disciplinary knowledge that faculty bring to discussions about and evaluations of writing in their courses.

PRINCIPLES IN PRACTICE

Describing the Writing Requirement: Year One

To put these principles in action in our assessment, we designed a multi-staged assessment process that involved several steps. To provide context for these, it is first important to explain that UCSB's GE program combines elements of two models of general education: a "scholarly disciplines" model, where students are exposed to disciplinary concepts (Newton 2000, 172–74), and a distribution model, where the presumption is that students will develop habits of mind critical for postsecondary and civic success (e.g., effective communication, quantitative reasoning, expansive thinking, etc.) by taking a variety of courses across disciplines and intellectual foci (Menand 2010, 27–28). This blend is reflected in the overall framework for the program, which consists of seven "subject" areas and five "special subject areas." English Reading and Composition; Languages; Science, Math, and Technology; Social Sciences; Culture and Thought; Arts; and Literature constitute the "Area A-G requirements," which include discrete courses in each "subject" area. The five "special subject areas"—European Traditions, World Cultures, Ethnicity, Quantitative Relationships, and Writing Requirement—are fulfilled by participating in general education courses that can simultaneously fulfill Area A-G requirements (but do not necessarily need to do so).

During the 2011–2012 academic year, we worked with ninety-four faculty members from thirty-seven departments and/or programs to articulate the outcomes for each of the twelve "areas" within UCSB's general education program. To do this, we identified the top ten highest enrolling GE courses for the two previous academic years (2009–2010 and 2010–2011) in each GE area, gathered syllabi and assignments for the courses, analyzed the goals for these courses, and then abstracted across *all* courses in the areas to develop draft outcomes. We then invited all faculty contributing syllabi and assignments, as well as department chairs and directors of undergraduate education in each contributing department, to a session where they provided feedback on the draft outcomes; we then revised the outcomes based on their feedback and re-circulated until all participants were satisfied with the outcomes and felt that they represented the goals of their courses. While this process of articulation was not assessment *per se* in that no questions were asked and no study was undertaken, it reflected a critical principle of dynamic criteria mapping: it is critical to engage faculty involved in assessment in processes to "discover, negotiate, and publicize . . . values they employ" when assessing student work (Broad 2003, 15, also see 129–30; and Adler-Kassner and Estrem 2009. Broad is referring to *rhetorical* values; we extend this idea to values more generally). In other words, we believed and acted on the principle that we must collaboratively engage those who *do* assess in a discussion to describe the end points of any process that will, ultimately, *be* assessed.

This principle also became the starting place for the second year of our process, a large-scale assessment of the Writing Requirement (or WR) included in UCSB's GE program. Students must complete six WR courses in order to fulfill the requirement; these courses are distinct from the courses included in the Area A ("English Reading and Composition") requirement and are taught outside of UCSB's Writing Program. Well over 100 courses carry WR credit. Extending from the idea that qualities of good writing are context-specific, we knew that the outcomes for these courses should position ideas about "good writing" as something grounded in particular communities of practice as they are represented in disciplines or, in Carter's word, metadisciplines (Carter 2007, 403). These outcomes, developed with faculty teaching WR courses, say that:

> *Students who successfully complete the Writing Requirement will be able to:*
>
> > *Produce writing that uses rhetorical conventions appropriate to different disciplines and, if appropriate, languages*
> > *Identify the roles that types of writing play in the production and circulation of knowledge within specific disciplines*
> > *Identify the role of evidence in writing within specific disciplines*
> > *Locate, interpret, and use discipline-specific evidence appropriately*
> > *Use conventions of organization, style, coherence, structure, syntax, and mechanics appropriate to specific disciplines*
> > *Use citational style and form appropriate to specific disciplines*

Assessing the WR: Year Two

In order to create an appropriate assessment for WR courses, we proceeded from three key beliefs that are also reflected in these outcomes: (1) writing serves as a key practice by which students can find their ways into communities of practice and understand their boundaries (writing to learn); (2) writing is a key strategy by which students demonstrate their participation *in* communities of practice (learning to write/using writing); and (3) faculty members, expert in these communities of practice, are intimately familiar with the strategies and learning concepts that comprise the boundaries of these communities.

The first step in our assessment was to work with faculty to define the key concepts and strategies, especially concerning writing, associated with the communities of practice in which they participated. We needed to hear from them to answer questions inherent in the outcomes: What *are* rhetorical conventions appropriate to *their* disciplines? What roles *does* writing play in the production and circulation of knowledge? (and so on). We also needed to learn about characteristics associated with their answers: What do these rhetorical conventions look like? What does it look like when students create writing that reflects ideas about the role writing plays in the circulation of knowledge? And what does it look like when students do this well? Not as well?

To gather answers to our outcomes-driven questions, we gathered a group of twenty-two faculty from eighteen disciplines for a four-hour workshop. There, they worked in small groups facilitated by a faculty member from the UCSB Writing Program, and at least one note taker, a graduate student from the Language, Literacy, and Composition program and/or a staff member from UCSB's Office of Institutional Research and Assessment. It is important to note that on our campus, this was an unprecedented activity; never before had faculty from across disciplines and interdisciplines gathered for such a specific, writing-related effort.

Drawing on a pilot sample of 100 papers collected from students enrolled in WR courses in fall 2012, faculty participants began their discussions in what we termed "like" disciplinary groups—in other words, groups where, based on a preliminary analysis of papers included in the pilot sample, we believed that there might be sufficient overlap in the characteristics associated with each outcome that faculty members might be able to collaboratively generate shared definitions. In the first stage of our workshop, faculty in these tentative "like" disciplinary groups *defined* characteristics associated with each outcome in their disciplines. Thinking back to Bazerman's "conceptual words," where particular words can connote semantic connections to larger disciplinary concepts and conventions, this stage of our workshop became a moment where faculty extrapolated those meanings from words like "rhetorical conventions" and "evidence" as they pertained to their disciplinary groups. In the second stage, they moved to "unlike" disciplinary groups to compare their definitions to those of others; here, our presumption was that it might be easier for faculty to recognize and articulate what they knew when it was contrasted with what they did not know. Finally, faculty moved back to "like" disciplinary groups to begin to describe successful work with the characteristics associated with each outcome. (Heuristics for these stages are included as appendix 12.A.)

Following the conclusion of the four-hour workshop, we conducted an extensive analysis of the written comments included in each heuristic "worksheet" and of the notes provided by group facilitators and note takers. From these we developed drafts of the characteristics associated with each outcome within specific disciplinary or multi-disciplinary groups. Here, we were to some extent looking for patterns that might help us identify what Mike Carter called "disciplinary ways of knowing" (Carter 2007, 408). Examining program-level outcomes developed as part of a campus accreditation effort, Carter was able to identify metagenres ("similar kinds of typified responses to related recurrent situations" [393]) and metadisciplines ("collections of disciplines that share an emphasis on certain metagenres and are constituted by the various genres within each metagenre" [403]). While our process was different from Carter's (we were looking not at program-specific outcomes, but at discipline-specific definitions of common outcomes), his definitions were nonetheless useful for us as we organized our efforts. We focused on locating characteristics associated with faculty members' definitions of the WR outcomes and drafted common instruments based on these characteristics. We found that of our original five "like" groups, only two—History/Classics and Ecology, Evolutionary, and Marine Biology (EEMB)/Earth Science—defined characteristics closely enough that their papers could be assessed using one rubric. On the other hand, we found that some disciplines that had previously *not* been in "like" disciplinary groups shared similar enough definitions of characteristics that we could create new combinations.

In the end, the workshop led to the development of eight sets of draft characteristics and, ultimately, eight assessment instruments that were circulated to participants: History/Classics; EEMB/Earth Science; Communication/Psychology/Engineering (Ethics only); English/Comparative Literature/Languages (French/Spanish/Portuguese, etc.); "Studies" disciplines (Feminist, Chicano/a, Global, Environmental, Film, Asian American, East Asian, and Black Studies); and Music/ Theater and Dance/Art History were assessed using shared instruments, though some included exceptions (e.g., "If Music, omit Z; if Art History, include B). Because they defined characteristics in ways that could not be comfortably combined with other disciplines, separate instruments were developed for Philosophy and Political Science. Each of the eight instruments included between thirteen to nineteen distinct rating items; these, in turn, were grounded in the practices central to the disciplines (or, communities of practice). To illustrate what we mean, outcome one says that students will "use rhetorical conventions appropriate to the discipline or, if appropriate, language." In the rubric developed with input from faculty members in the History and Classics Department, these characteristics include:

- a thesis that describes an assertion about the past or an historical artifact that is designed to persuade a reader;
- an analytical question that is pursued throughout [the writing];
- analysis that acknowledges the contested nature of interpretation; and
- close analysis of primary sources or interpretations of other scholars.

In the rubric developed with input from faculty members from Communication, Psychology, and Engineering, these characteristics include:

- clear organization around explicitly formulated conceptual or practical problems;
- clear use of existing theory to situate present work in a relevant, ongoing social issue;
- a theory- or data-driven argument; and
- use of a third-person voice that is objective, scholarly, and accessible to a college-educated audience.

These characteristics, then, outline the "rhetorical conventions appropriate to the discipline[s]" using these rubrics—while also pointing out the different conventions used in writing in History and Classics and Communication, Psychology, and Engineering.

When it came time to develop the levels of achievement associated with the rating items, we also made an important (and pragmatic) decision. Our four-hour workshop did not include enough time for faculty to effectively describe levels of performance associated with characteristics that they identified. We began to realize the dizzying possibilities that might have emerged if they had—the amount of text required to describe strong and weak performances associated with each specific characteristic. The variables began to become more and more complex as we considered how (and even whether) it would be possible to aggregate findings from an assessment grounded in principles about *discipline specific* characteristics if we extended to levels of performance this specific. In addition, we considered the time it would take to read and assess the writing included in our sample (340 papers of between three and twelve pages each which were to be read, on a Saturday in February, by eighteen volunteer readers who were largely Writing Program faculty and TAs [graduate students from Humanities and Fine Arts departments]; graduate students in the Language, Literacy, and Composition Ph.D. program; and UCSB's Dean of Undergraduate Studies, who was then also the WASC ALO). Readers would have taken more time than they could afford on each paper—and we also suspected that the findings would be, likely, less meaningful. We decided, then, to use a four-point scale (Consistently, Generally, Inconsistently, Not at All) keyed to the "conceptual words" central to the discipline's practice, instead. See Table 12.1 for an illustration of the History/Classics rubric.

FACULTY PERSPECTIVES: ASSESSMENT AS PROFESSIONAL DEVELOPMENT

From our perspective as writing researchers (and teachers), the process through which faculty articulated explicit expectations for writing within their communities of practice and the development of assessment instruments that reflected these expectations represented an important step at UC Santa Barbara. First, as we have described here, it engaged faculty in a process of discussion about writing using strategies not yet attempted on our campus. Second, it used those discussions as the basis for creating instruments grounded in the outcomes as they are enacted in specific disciplines that were used for an authentic, direct assessment of student writing, also an unprecedented activity.

But while it is possible, from our perspective as writing researchers, to identify some of what we have perceived as benefits of this study, we wondered whether the participants found it as useful. If they did, we also wondered, were their perceptions of what was useful (or not) overlapped with ours? To explore these questions, we interviewed three faculty who participated in the 2011–2012 focus groups to articulate the GE outcomes and the faculty workshop (and subsequent correspondence) to define and describe characteristics associated with the WR outcomes. Our interviews with John Latto (EEMB), Penelope (a pseudonym, from a specific ethnic studies department), and Themistogenes (a pseudonym;

Table 12.1. History/Classics Assessment Rubric

Outcome 1: Use rhetorical conventions appropriate to the discipline or, if appropriate, language.

The writing includes:

> A thesis that describes assertion about the past or historical artifact that is designed to persuade a reader.

Key features: thesis with assertion about the past
- (3)   Consistent thesis that describes an assertion about the past or historical artifact
- (2)   General thesis that describes an assertion about the past or historical artifact
- (1)   Inconsistent thesis does not include an assertion about the past or historical artifact
- (0)   No thesis

The writing includes:
> An analytical question that is pursued throughout

Key features: inclusion and exploration of analytical question
Definition of analytical question:

An analytical question is one that focuses on the "why" of an historical event or phenomenon and guides the writing away from *description* of that event or phenomenon.

Analytical question: Did the dominance of domestic ideology contribute to the rise of suffrage in the early twentieth century? What were major causes of the Civil War?

Nonanalytical question: What happened at the Battle of Antietam?
- (3)   Consistent or surprising analytical question is insightfully pursued
- (2)   Insightful analytical question that is generally pursued
- (1)   Analytical question that is inconsistently pursued
- (0)   No analytical question or no pursuit of the question

Item 3:
The writing includes:

> Analysis that acknowledges contested nature of interpretation (i.e., multiple perspectives) about the topic.

Key features: acknowledgment of contested nature of interpretation
- (3)   Contested nature of interpretation is highlighted and consistently enriches analysis
- (2)   Contested nature of interpretation is generally included
- (1)   Contested nature of interpretation is included but inconsistently explored
- (0)   Contested nature of interpretation is not evident

Item 4:
The writing includes:

> Close analysis of primary sources (original or in translation) or interpretations of other scholars

Key feature: analysis of sources

- (3)   Consistent, precise analysis of primary sources
- (2)   General, close analysis of primary sources
- (1)   Inconsistent analysis of sources
- (0)   No analysis of sources

History) attest to the benefits of thinking about writing as it fits into their academic worlds, and talking with other faculty about roles and expectations for writing in their disciplines.

We should say from the outset that all three of these faculty came to this project with a keen interest in writing in their disciplines. Themistogenes noted that he had started to think about differences between his discipline of history and other disciplines in the university as he encountered and worked closely with faculty on university-level committees. Penelope had developed an exceptionally thoughtful writing course for students in her department (ethnic studies) several years before this process began; before coming to UC Santa Barbara, John Latto had held a faculty position explicitly focused on working with biology majors and their writing. All also talked with us about thoughtful and provocative ways that they incorporated writing into their teaching prior to this effort. While these faculty members came with interest in and experience with considering writing in their disciplines, though, they also said that they began to reevaluate their approaches to writing during the process described in this chapter. From their interviews, we can identify three patterns that reflect this reevaluation.

The first pattern associated with writing change that emerged among all three of these faculty concerned greater recognition of variations in writing expectations experienced by students. Penelope, for example, characterized her work with writing prior to the assessment as "a static way of thinking." To illustrate the ways in which she began to rethink her efforts as a more dynamic process, she showed us a teaching document, "Constructing the Literary Critical Analysis Thesis," that she gave to students to help them with their writing in her class. While Penelope said that she revises the document each year, she pointed to specific revisions in this year's document that drew on her experience in the workshop, emphasizing the idea that the writing she expects of students draws on specific conventions—those of literary and cultural analysis— and are *different* from the conventions of analysis in other disciplines. In Penelope's "old" version, she wrote:

> You've been writing sentences called "thesis statements" since at least high school[.] What more is there to talk about?
>
> Plenty. Fact is, many a college student labors under serious misconceptions about what qualifies as a thesis statement—not fully understanding the function these play. Without a viable thesis, you have no analytical essay—just assorted ideas—*and have already failed your task.*
>
> Remember that an analytical essay is a tool for uncovering new knowledge: establishing patterns, making connections that *aren't obvious from a casual reading of the book*—and then deciding what these mean.

The "new" version of the document points explicitly to *differences* in disciplinary practices and the ways in which practices in her course were specific to her discipline of literary studies.

> **NEW:** You've been writing sentences called "thesis statements" since at least high school[.] What more is there to talk about?
>
> Plenty. Thesis statements do more than "argue"; they are research devices for uncovering new knowledge. And because "knowledge" varies by discipline, so do the tools for its discovery. **Thus, we begin by framing a *research question* that is *answerable* given the discipline's data. What we call a working "thesis" is a hypothesis, a provisional "research answer."** Question and answer work as a pair to guide our investigation.
>
> In literary studies, uncovering new knowledge means establishing patterns, making connections that *aren't obvious from a casual reading of the book*, and deciding what these mean. (Penelope; emphases in original)

As she discussed these revisions in her interview, Penelope said that she had thought previously that students were writing theses incorrectly; "[. . .] and then after going through [the accreditation process, she] was appalled that [she] had said that," adding that "[the thesis] is different for every discipline." She attributed this recognition in part to discussions in the workshop with interdisciplinary colleagues. These conversations helped her recognize that there were particular ways of constructing a literary-critical argument in her discipline. Here, Penelope demonstrated an ability to step outside her own community of practice to recognize its distinct boundaries.

John Latto, the biologist from Ecology, Environmental, and Marine Biology also described the ways in which he began to consider the disciplinary variation in students' writing experience as he participated in our writing-related efforts. Prior to and in the workshop, John said, he wanted students to "write clearly" in their papers in his classes. Later, he was able to elaborate on what this meant in greater detail, saying that writing clearly meant using consistent language to communicate science knowledge to public audiences. He used an example from biology to illustrate his point: "If you [. . .] refer to a plant as *Baccharis pilularis* and in the next sentence you say coyote brush, that's just confusing because somebody [. . .], particularly a non-expert, might not always know that that's the same thing."

John also described ideas about the roles that writing plays for undergraduates in biology courses in compelling ways. In stage two of the workshop, where faculty met with others in "unlike" disciplines, John joined a group with colleagues from Classics and Religious Studies. Their discussion, he said, helped him recognize differences not only in the *kind* of writing that students produce in different disciplines, but in *roles of writing* from one course or discipline to another. Talking with these other faculty, he said, he realized that in their WR courses, students were seen as novices in disciplinary communities of practice. Whereas the student experience in these communities often involved practicing writing that "is not all that unlike what they do in the "profession," his GE WR biology classes were different. In John's disciplinary community of practice, writing includes, "[. . .] the production of a scientific paper which describes your research, and for that there are particular rules that you have to sort of follow." But students in John's GE WR courses were not seen as disciplinary novices and thus were not expected to participate in these practices of biology *researchers*. Instead, he said, "These are students who should come to communicate *about* biology. And the worst thing we can do for those students is to teach them to write in what people perceive as very drab, dull, dry, scientific style." Implicitly, then, John's comments point to multiple communities of practice associated with his discipline—ones for researchers, others for communicators *knowledgeable about science*. This distinction was an important realization for him, reinforcing his desire for students to write clearly. "[Students] think they're meant to be writing like scientists," he said, "and so they often write in this almost stodgy form where they over reference everything . . . We'd actually rather they not do that . . ."

As our participants realized that students' writing experiences were different in different disciplines, another pattern that emerged in our interviews concerned a new attention to the ways that writing in their disciplines—and the writing they ask students to do—looks different and serves different purposes than writing in other disciplines, even on the same campus. They said that the workshop helped to validate the writing that they ask students to do in their courses. For example, Themistogenes, the historian, said that his expectations for working with evidence were implicit in his assignments, but that participating in the assessment process, and especially the workshop, made more explicit the particular demands of writing about evidence in the field of ancient history. He considered these demands during the interview:

> It's . . . a very different intellectual activity to have a set of a hundred documents from which you have to pick key quotations than it is to have a fragmentary inscription where the center is missing and you only have a couple of words on each edge and you cannot read some of it and it's written in an ancient foreign language which needs to be translated, all of those things. It does make me more aware of how we [ancient historians] argue with probability—might have, could have, could possibly have—the logical deductions that we have to use which aren't necessarily needed in

fields where you have a lot more evidence, so yeah, [this process] does make me more aware of those.

Here, Themistogenes distinguished the conventions of evidentiary writing in ancient history and used those to articulate similar expectations implicit in assignments he gave his students. While he always knew historical writing was evidence-based, he said, participation in the GE discussions and workshop offered a space for making implicit disciplinary conventions more explicit: "[Prior to the workshop] I assumed that writing about history was evidence-based, that is, you read or observed some piece of something from the past and used that to make a general statement or conclusion about some past society. So those things were all there but I guess I just hadn't thought about them as explicitly in relation to teaching the class."

Each person also shared with us a moment during the workshop that crystallized their thinking about the writing students do in their disciplines. As she spoke with other faculty in the workshop, Penelope found herself making value judgments about what mattered to her when students write for her courses. For Penelope, this was a sharp focus on constructing theses: "I never let students talk about anything but the text. Because I feel that way lies generalizations and that I wanted them to learn rigor." But she found this to be in contrast to her feminist studies colleagues. "The feminist studies scholars were saying that they allowed and even encouraged students to speak from personal experience and to argue from personal experience . . . the empirical basis was very starkly different for me . . ." Themistogenes also identified contrasting conventions between historical and engineering writing: "For [historians], variation and phrasing and innovation in language is a good thing, but an engineer wants the same word used every time [. . .] And some of [the conventions of history writing] . . . never do passive voice [for example]—. . . are very central to technical, to engineers' writing." John Latto contrasted the purpose of writing in classics to the writing he assigns in his biology classes: "[Classics] were asking students in their example student papers, they were asking students to write a fairly extensive paper that was not a million miles away from what my understanding was that they were writing in their professions and the student work was structured like that, whereas most of the classes I teach, student assessment now is not like that."

These comments demonstrate that for John, as for Penelope and Themistogenes, the processes we used for the accreditation assessment allowed the faculty to engage in professional development that validated, and in some cases challenged, their notions of writing in the academy.

Each story—Penelope's thesis, John's clarity, and Themistogenes' evidence—showed how this professional development tapped into their prior knowledge and triggered thinking about writing in their disciplines and in the courses they teach. Each agreed about the benefit of working with other faculty. John Latto said that it was interesting to find that his expectations for student writing were aligned so closely with the other scientist in his workshop group. Likewise, Themistogenes shared satisfaction in learning that colleagues from his department and like disciplines reinforced the group's expectations about writing and "what we wanted people to get out of the writing." He added that a workshop like this was "[. . .] a kind of a thing that brings the university together, right? Everybody writes." For Penelope, her participation in these processes helped her make more explicit decisions about what matters in the writing her students do and how she can bring in cross-disciplinary examples to help define her own discipline to her students. It was evidenced in our interviews that each faculty member was very thoughtful about the writing they asked students to do and that their participation in these processes helped them articulate discipline-specific expectations that were implicit in the work they did all along.

CONCLUSION

Writing and learning development continue to be an ongoing conversation on our campus, but the principled approach to assessing our General Education program (specifically, the extent to which student learning outcomes for writing were realized in General Education Writing Requirement classes) presented an opportunity to involve faculty in this conversation directly and repeatedly (through workshops and involvement in drafting and revising assessment materials) over a two-year period. First, we conceptualized learning as habits of mind developed through guided participation in communities of practice, where faculty are expert members and their disciplines are their communities. Next, we conceptualized the assessment according to two principles: One, that characteristics of good writing are context-specific; and two, that those affected by the assessment results should be involved in the assessment itself. Our faculty participants rose to the occasion, drawing from exemplary professional and student texts (the "context," *principle 1*) to articulate the broad Writing Requirement outcomes as they pertained to the writing they expected of students in their classes (students, who may or may not go on to major in their academic disciplines).

From our vantage point as writing researchers, the real success of this process lay in the collaborative conversations that we describe here and what we observe as numerous sites of uptake that have followed. A few examples: Individual faculty like (and in addition to) John Latto, Penelope, and Themistogenes have continued to request meetings to talk about working on writing already incorporated in their courses and/or developing new writing-focused courses. Faculty have continued to ask for the instruments developed for this assessment and have contacted Linda about next steps and further development. Our campus has a small assessment grant program; among the proposals submitted for funding during the 2013–2014 academic year (and excluding one from the Writing Program, which naturally focused on writing), three included extensive study of writing at the departmental level. The methods proposed for these new projects, in fact, in some ways echo those used for this project. That is, they proposed a ground-up examination of what departments value in writing, how (and/or if) those values are explicitly laid out for students in assignments for written work, and whether students' written work reflects the values as they are expressed by departments. Each of the three proposals also included space and time for the kind of iterative, inquiry-based examination of these practices included in the WR assessment. Without the institutional assessment process that motivated the assessment that we describe here, we are not sure that these projects would have been conceived in quite the same way.

At the same time, we recognize some rather substantial challenges associated with this assessment, most of which stem from the exigencies surrounding the effort—specifically, time and expertise. In terms of time, this assessment had to be completed by March 2013 so that it could be included in our assessment report; it could not be initiated until the GE outcomes were articulated, a process that occupied the entirety of the 2012–2013 academic year. The window for gathering input and analyzing data, then, was short; the window for analyzing papers was similarly quite tight. We also recognized that in deciding to take on an assessment of the WR requirement we wanted to gather as many papers as we could from a range of students, but knew that these would be scored primarily by volunteers from the Writing Program. (To ask faculty from other disciplines, who had already devoted considerable time to the effort of *developing* the assessment instruments, just wasn't realistic.)

Thus, we encountered challenges like one represented by a question raised during the calibration/norming session we conducted on the rating day. Reading a sample student paper, one of the raters who was familiar with a text used in the paper mentioned that the student wasn't interpreting the text correctly. While *content* is certainly included in "rhetorical conventions appropriate to the discipline" (WR Outcome 1), characteristics associated with content were not included in the eight assessment instruments developed for this particular effort. Nor, realistically, could they be. While writing researchers and our allies (i.e., TAs from other disciplines teaching Writing 2 who had some exposure to genre-based analysis and instruction) can reliably assess *some* elements of writing from disciplines other than our own, we cannot reliably do so for *all* elements of writing outside of our own expertise. And while this reflects one of the fundamental principles underscoring our assessment, that qualities of writing are context-specific, it still represents a limit of the findings; the fact remains that while this assessment provided insight into *some* aspects of qualities associated with the WR outcomes, other qualities must be queried (and assessed) by faculty within the disciplines where their expertise, which differs from our own, extends more deeply than ours can.

The second challenge associated with this assessment concerns the nature of the assessment instruments themselves. While these were developed with considerable input from faculty teaching WR courses within disciplines, they were applied to courses from those disciplines whose instructors may or may not have participated in the workshop. While these faculty engaged in a process to define and describe characteristics associated with the WR outcomes, those characteristics (as they were described by the faculty) were used to create what might be considered "semi-generic" assessment instruments—that is, assessment instruments that spoke to broad characterizations associated with these outcomes, rather than specific ones as they were enacted in specific courses. As Anson et al. contend, examining writing work in these smaller contexts leads to the construction of more useful—and, ultimately, more valid—assessment mechanisms. Assessment of smaller contexts also would likely have meant developing more assessment instruments. This would have meant more papers per discipline (and more for the entire sample). The assessment effort, already weighty, would have needed to be much larger in order to make the contexts for assessment smaller.

Were this assessment the end point for writing assessment on our campus, we would be concerned about these challenges. Happily, however, the process that we describe here represents something of an intermediate point. As with all assessment projects, we have learned an enormous amount from this accreditation-spurred process; we look forward to new lessons—and new findings—as our campus continues to engage in the important work of examining teaching and learning.

APPENDIX 12.A WORKSHOP HUERISTICS

Stage 1: Defining Outcomes

Outcome	Key elements
1. Produce writing that uses rhetorical conventions appropriate to different disciplines and, if appropriate, languages	Identifying and using rhetorical conventions in your discipline requires answering the question: What makes it clear that this is a piece of writing from my discipline? (What makes it a piece of writing from English, History, Music, Environmental Studies, etc.?) Rhetorical conventions are strategies and/or traits common or essential to writing in my discipline (e.g., using first or third person; using particular kinds of evidence; drawing from particular kinds of evidence [experience, text, etc.]; using empirical research or textual analysis).
What this means in my discipline	

Outcome	Key elements
2. Identify the roles that types of writing play in the production and circulation of knowledge within specific disciplines	Identifying the roles that types of writing (genres) play requires answering the question: What are the different types of writing in my discipline, and what roles do these types play in my discipline? Roles that types of writing play means the place of writing within my discipline and the kind of writing that is being created (e.g., summarizing knowledge in a literature review; advancing/contesting theories in an analysis; distilling knowledge in an abstract; publicizing knowledge in a piece of writing for the public; contributing to other forms of discourse, etc.).
What this means in my discipline	

Outcome	Key elements
3. Locate, interpret, and use discipline-specific evidence appropriately	Locating and using discipline-specific evidence appropriately requires answering the question: What is seen as credible/important evidence in my discipline, and how is it used appropriately (and inappropriately)? Discipline-specific / evidence in writing can be anything that counts as evidence in the discipline (literary excerpts, scientific data, qualitative data, direct quotes, etc.). Using it appropriately involves more than correct citation or embedding it in text.
What this means in my discipline	

Outcome	Key elements
4. Identify the role of evidence in writing within specific disciplines	Identifying the role of evidence requires answering the question: What kinds of evidence are used in my discipline, and how are they used, and/or why are they used this way? Role of evidence refers to how evidence is used in specific types of writing (genres) within my discipline (e.g., reporting results in an experiment, supporting a claim in a persuasive piece, etc.).

What this means in my discipline

Outcome	Key elements
5. Use conventions of organization, style, coherence, structure, syntax, and mechanics appropriate to specific disciplines	Using appropriate conventions requires answering the question: What are the expectations of organization (form & structure), style (voice, sentence length and variety, stance), coherence (connections between ideas), syntax (word order), and mechanics (punctuation) in my discipline? These conventions involve knowing how people express ideas in writing in specific disciplines. For example, if a paper involves organizing sections by headers and/or certain wording to introduce new topics, this is a convention of organization.

What this means in my discipline

Outcome	Key elements
6. Use citational style and form appropriate to specific disciplines	Using appropriate citational form requires answering the questions: What citational style is most used in my discipline? What are key elements of that style?(e.g., APA/MLA/CMS formatting for citations and reference pages; embedding in one's own words, etc.).

What this means in my discipline

Stage 2: Clarifying Definitions

Outcome	Clarifications of definitions (based on explaining to someone outside of your disciplinary grouping)
1. Produce writing that uses rhetorical conventions appropriate to different disciplines and, if appropriate, languages	
2. Identify the roles that types of writing play in the production and circulation of knowledge within specific disciplines	

APPENDIX 12.A—*continued*

3. Locate, interpret, and use discipline-specific evidence appropriately

4. Identify the role of evidence in writing within specific disciplines

5. Use conventions of organization, style, coherence, structure, syntax, and mechanics appropriate to specific disciplines

6. Use citational style and form appropriate to specific disciplines

Stage 3: Articulating Criteria

Outcome	Exemplary	Proficient	Developing
1. Produce writing that uses rhetorical conventions appropriate to different disciplines and, if appropriate, languages			
2. Identify the roles that types of writing play in the production and circulation of knowledge within specific disciplines			
3. Locate, interpret, and use discipline-specific evidence appropriately			
4. Identify the role of evidence in writing within specific disciplines			
5. Use conventions of organization, style, coherence, structure, syntax, and mechanics appropriate to specific disciplines			
6. Use citational style and form appropriate to specific disciplines			

Note

1. It is important to note that we also recognize this process as not especially linear. From this perspective, learners do not "internalize transmitted knowledge" (Casanave 2002, 23). Instead, learners must encounter and learn core concepts ("content knowledge") and ways of thinking (epistemological practices) within a field which, combined, constitute what Ray Meyer and J. F. Land call "threshold concepts." Threshold concepts researchers (e.g., Meyer and Land 2006; Perkins 2006) all remark on the liminal nature of learning associated with these concepts. This assessment did not incorporate this principle; thus, it constitutes a limitation of the study that we are describing. At the same time, *all* assessments reflect limitations and represent a series of choices about where, at *this* moment, to focus attention.

References

Adler-Kassner, Linda, and Heidi Estrem. 2009. "The Journey is the Destination: The Place of Assessment in an Activist Writing Program." In *Organic Writing Assessment: Dynamic Criteria Mapping in Action*, ed. Bob Broad, 14–36. Logan: Utah State University Press.

Adler-Kassner, Linda, John Majewski, and Damian Koshnick. 2012. "The Value of Troublesome Knowledge: Transfer and Threshold Concepts in Writing and History." *Composition Forum* 26: 1–17.

Anson, Chris M., Deanna P. Dannels, Pamela Flash, and Amy L. Housley Gaffney. 2012. "Big Rubrics and Weird Genres: The Futility of Using Generic Assessment Tools across Diverse Instructional Contexts." *Journal of Writing Assessment* 5 (1). http://www.journalofwritingassessment.org/article.php?article=57.

Bazerman, Charles. 2012. "Writing with Concepts: Communal, Internalized, and Externalized." *Mind, Culture, and Activity* 19 (3): 259–72. http://dx.doi.org/10.1080/10749039.2012.688231.

Broad, Bob. 2003. *What We Really Value: Beyond Rubrics in Teaching and Assessing Writing.* Logan: Utah State University Press.

Carter, Michael. 2007. "Ways of Knowing, Doing, and Writing in the Disciplines." *CCC* 58 (3): 385–418.

Casanave, Christine. 2002. *Writing Games: Multicultural Case Studies of Academic Literacy Practices in Higher Education.* Mahwah, NJ: Lawrence Erlbaum.

CCCC. n.d. *Writing Assessment: A Position Statement.* http://www.ncte.org/cccc/resources/positions/writingassessment.

Huot, Brian. 2002. *(Re)Articulating Writing Assessment for Teaching and Learning.* Logan: Utah State University Press.

Lave, Jean, and Etienne Wenger. 1991. *Situated Learning: Legitimate Peripheral Participation.* Cambridge: Cambridge University Press. http://dx.doi.org/10.1017/CBO9780511815355.

Menand, Louis. 2010. *The Marketplace of Ideas: Reform and Resistance in the American University (Issues of Our Time).* New York: WW Norton.

Meyer, Jan H. F., and Ray Land. 2006. "Threshold Concepts and Troublesome Knowledge: An Introduction." In *Overcoming Barriers to Student Understanding,* ed. Jan H. F. Meyer and Ray Land, 3–18. London: Routledge.

Newton, Ray R. 2000. "Tensions and Models in General Education Planning." *Journal of General Education* 49 (3): 165–81. http://dx.doi.org/10.1353/jge.2000.0023.

O'Neill, Peggy, and Linda Adler-Kassner. 2010. *Reframing Writing Assessment to Improve Teaching and Learning.* Logan: Utah State University Press.

O'Neill, Peggy, Cindy Moore, and Brian Huot. 2009. *A Guide to College Writing Assessment.* Logan: Utah State University Press.

Perkins, David. 2006. "Constructivism and Troublesome Knowledge." In *Overcoming Barriers to Student Understanding,* ed. Jan H. F. Meyer and Ray Land, 33–47. London: Routledge.

Russell, D. 1995. "Activity Theory and Its Implications for Writing Instruction." In *Reconceiving Writing, Rethinking Writing Instruction,* ed. J. Petraglia, 51–78. Mahwah, NJ: Lawrence Erlbaum.

University of California, Santa Barbara. 2012. "Letters and Sciences Academic Requirements (LASAR) 2012–2013."

Wenger, E. 1998. *Communities of Practice: Learning, Meaning, and Identity.* Cambridge: Cambridge University Press. http://dx.doi.org/10.1017/CBO9780511803932.

13
A FUNNY THING HAPPENED ON THE WAY TO ASSESSMENT
Lessons from a Thresholds-Based Approach

Maggie Debelius

James Slevin (2001), founder and former director of the Georgetown University Writing Program, asked in *Introducing English*, "How do prevailing modes of assessment marginalize the perspectives and work of the faculty? How can faculty work be defined and the purposes of assessment deepened in order to incorporate a more significant faculty role? In what ways are writing programs positioned to help make educational assessment generally a more complex, and therefore more accurate and helpful, contribution to the intellectual life of the university?" (212)

Since Slevin asked those questions in 2001, demands for accountability have only increased, as evidenced by the Spellings Report, the Collegiate Learning Assessment (CLA), the growth of the testing industry, state mandates, and other forms of accreditation pressures (see Moore, O'Neil, and Crow, this volume). Slevin died before many of these more recent measures of accountability appeared, but colleagues have continued to critique the way some versions of assessment marginalize the work of faculty (Perelman 2008; Gallagher 2011). Others have echoed Slevin's call for more authentic and complex forms of writing assessment that enliven rather than stultify the intellectual life of the university (Huot 2002; Broad et al. 2009). Jim was my friend and mentor at Georgetown, and I too have puzzled over answers to his questions in the years following his death. What follows is an attempt to answer his questions with thoughts on how a writing program can develop an intellectually robust form of assessment in which faculty play a central role.

Recent critics of assessment suggest network theory as a promising alternative to outcomes-based assessment. Building on the work of Bruno Latour, Rich Rice (2011) argues that networks are a method for "figuring out agency, influence, connectivity and other factors in a given

DOI: 10.7330/9781607324355.c013

moment or situation" (28). Likewise, Gallagher (2011) argues that we need to reject the stakeholder theory of power in which everyone (faculty, administrators, students, accreditation agencies) has an equal seat at the table and "rewrite the assessment scene" with "the logic of the network" (464). Because he values teaching and learning, Gallagher wants to place greater value on the perspectives of teachers and students rather than remote policymakers (see also Jeff Rice 2011). Although Gallagher and Rice define the network model differently, they both realize its potential to make faculty expertise central rather than tangential to the assessment process.

But *how* can a program practice a networked assessment model in which we put faculty at the center of the network, rather than letting external corporate or government interests dictate the terms of the conversation? And how can we make a case for its validity in the face of accountability pressures from external regulators? I argue that writing programs can support robust assessment by focusing on disciplinary expertise, thereby making visible the complex networks in which students and faculty write and operate. To develop a practical model for making pedagogical use of what has been made visible, I will suggest that program administrators use "threshold concepts," which Meyer and Land (2003) articulate as concepts within disciplines that mark a departure from old ways of viewing the world and entrance into new ways that may be counterintuitive for novice learners but must be grasped in order to move forward in the field.

As an example of a networked assessment, I will describe the Georgetown Student Writing Study to assess writing across the university, launched in 2010. This project began with a faculty development seminar focused on threshold concepts and combined it with a rubric creation method developed and employed by Terry Myers Zawacki and the Writing Assessment Group she chaired at George Mason University. Drawing on the work of Ed White and others, Zawacki's rubric creation method encourages disciplinary faculty to articulate what they value in student writing and use those values for assessment criteria. Although Georgetown's Student Writing Study was launched to satisfy requirements for our Middle States Commission on Higher Education reaccreditation, the benefits of the project extended beyond these requirements. Despite initial resistance, the project grew to include faculty participants from all four of Georgetown's undergraduate schools, as well as colleagues from Georgetown's campus in Doha, Qatar. Working closely with faculty to uncover their expectations for student writing and to understand what they considered to be the essential concepts for advanced study in their disciplines turned assessment into an opportunity for faculty to examine their own curricula and articulate their own goals for student writers, and helped transform the way writing was taught at Georgetown. In what follows, I outline how we introduced faculty to threshold theory and then used that theory to develop a flexible and organic assessment approach. This approach proved useful as a method of introducing a networked assessment culture which put faculty at the center, rather than on the periphery, of a complex but intellectually rich process.

THE THRESHOLD CONCEPTS FACULTY COLLOQUIUM

Faculty resistance to assessment is well-known and widespread, in part because "prevailing modes of assessment marginalize the perspectives and work of the faculty," as Slevin (2001) describes. Georgetown departments in particular have long been what one waggish colleague calls "allergic to assessment," perhaps influenced by the legacy of Slevin's scathing critique of "egregiously anti-intellectual forms of assessment" (Slevin 2001, 212). And it's not just Georgetown faculty who reject assessment. Some of the best minds in composition studies show clear disdain for assessment activities. Steven Krause speaks for many when he describes his "bad attitude" toward "an institutional assessment process that is/was complete pointless bullshit" in a June 29, 2011 entry on his blog. Although he begrudgingly admits that formal assessment has a place in the academy, he nonetheless admits, "I generally find this part of my job and this kind of scholarship kind of, well, boring" (Krause 2011). As long as faculty see themselves performing assessment simply to satisfy external regulators and accreditation agencies, assessment will never be true intellectual work and will never be perceived as anything but boring. But building assessment around disciplinary knowledge turns assessment into an activity that is both intellectually meaningful and useful. It also builds buy-in since few faculty members would admit to finding their own disciplinary expertise dull.

At Georgetown we were able to overcome initial hostility and disdain by recruiting faculty for a project that began not as an assessment but rather as an inquiry about disciplinary moves and expectations. The writing program and Professor Randy Bass, then the executive director of the Center for New Designs in Learning and Scholarship (CNDLS), received a grant in 2008 from the Teagle and Spencer Foundations to explore the application of threshold concepts, or ideas that are essential gateways to thinking in a field, to writing in the disciplines. As part of the grant, we convened faculty cohorts for year-long Thresholds Colloquiums (three cohorts over the course of three years) in which we researched, discussed, and identified threshold concepts in our disciplines.

In the seminars we linked threshold concepts with writing in the disciplines because each discipline, as leading educational researchers Meyer and Land (2003) explain, has a set of ideas that one must master to become an expert practitioner. But Meyer and Land (2003) differentiate between concepts that "represent 'seeing things in a new way' and those that do not"; a threshold concept, they explain, is "something distinct from what most . . . would typically describe as core concepts" (Meyer and Land 2003, 1). These transformative ideas are so fundamental that they become a habit of mind to those within the discipline, which often makes them difficult to explain to students and other outsiders. Examples of such concepts include opportunity cost from economics, the concept of the limit in calculus, or the idea of signification in cultural studies. Another example is deconstruction, a counter-intuitive concept in literary studies. Because deconstruction requires students to look for contradictions and absences in literary texts in order to understand how they are structured by a set of values (often unstated), the method requires students accustomed to reading for themes and consistencies to make "un-sense" of a text.

Meyer and Land (2003) identify five characteristics associated with threshold concepts: they are troublesome, integrative, transformative, irreversible, and bounded. Some of these characteristics proved especially relevant to our colloquium discussions. The first is that threshold concepts usually represent troublesome knowledge. As David Perkins (2006) explains, these concepts can be "counter-intuitive, alien . . . or incoherent" (40) because they challenge existing beliefs, past practices or inert knowledge, or can be conceptually difficult (see also Meyer and Land 2003, 9–14). The second trait is that these concepts are irreversible; once students understand them, they can't go back. Threshold concepts may be "akin to passing through a portal" or "conceptual gateway" that opens up "previously inaccessible way(s) of thinking about something" (Meyer and Land 2003, 9). Movement through these liminal portals does not happen in a straight line but instead in recursive stages. Ultimately, however, these concepts prove transformative: once thinkers understand them, their view of the discipline changes. Such a transformation can make it difficult for expert practitioners to be able to explain these concepts to novices.

In the colloquia, faculty were asked to explore the large integrative concepts that require practice and engagement for real understanding in their disciplines. The faculty seminars began with a deliberate analysis of one's teaching in light of the relationship between concepts of disciplinary thought and student understanding (especially the places where students have difficulty or get stuck). We also introduced faculty to Middendorf and Pace's (2004) "Decoding the Disciplines" approach to help faculty look closely at the spots where students get stuck or have trouble. Readings about thresholds and the Decoding project helped us turn the discussion of troublesome knowledge into an area of intellectual inquiry rather than a mere demonstration of student competency (or lack thereof).

Working with colleagues in psychology, history, English, biology, and other fields, we sought to isolate the distinctive moves and concepts that students encounter (and struggle with) in specific disciplines. Our faculty participants didn't necessarily reach consensus on what constituted threshold concepts in their disciplines, but they engaged in lively debates about the topic. A central finding from the threshold colloquium was the usefulness of slowing down and breaking complex disciplinary moves into smaller steps in order to render the work (and writing) of the discipline more visible to students. Faculty responses to the colloquium included the following:

- There has been a gap between my goals and my process in going to those goals.
- I was surprised to learn how much I was assuming students would simply "pick up" about what I now know is a very complicated process I undergo in my own work. Students have always felt very overwhelmed, confused, and frustrated by the writing assignments in the course, and I honestly never understood why until I went through the exercise of explaining the steps to myself.

Precisely because threshold concepts are transformative, many faculty had lost the perspective of a novice practitioner and thus found it useful to examine the ways that crucial intellectual activities involve steps and stages that often remain tacit in instruction and inaccessible to students. We were pleased with these productive conversations but unsure whether they would result in course modifications or changes in writing instruction. One session with a colleague in the business school who was attempting to describe threshold concepts in finance concluded with his saying, "Well, this has been a really fascinating conversation about finance. But I still don't know how to teach 'em to write." His comment illustrates a split vision of assessment. We in the writing program had begun to see rich conversations about student writing in finance as a form of assessment, while he was still looking for a more practical approach and series of guidelines to ensure mastery.

THE GEORGETOWN STUDENT WRITING STUDY

Soon after we began to question the practical impact of the Thresholds Colloquium, the writing program began working to address assessment requirements for our Middle States accreditation. Wanting to take advantage of this opportunity to engage faculty around assessment, we considered Slevin's question: "How can faculty work be defined and the purposes of assessment deepened in order to incorporate a more significant faculty role?" (Slevin 2001, 212). We decided to build on our Thresholds Colloquium work to launch the Georgetown Student Writing Study, an assessment project that adhered to the basic principles outlined by our profession: it was site-based, locally controlled, context-sensitive, rhetorically based, accessible, and theoretically consistent (Huot 2002, 57). A key breakthrough in our project occurred when we paired threshold concept theory with the rubric creation method developed by Terry Myers Zawacki and others at George Mason University (GMU). The GMU Writing Program launched a discipline-based writing assessment in 2003 in which departmental faculty collected sample papers and used them to create a rubric that identified traits valued in writing in that discipline. We invited Zawacki to Georgetown to demonstrate the process with our faculty prior to adopting it. Pairing Zawacki's practical approach with threshold concepts theory rather than the discourse of assessment helped us get Georgetown faculty invested in the project. In addition, threshold concepts became a way for faculty to describe and coordinate the complex systems in which they operate.

Building on the success of the Thresholds Colloquium, we decided to embed our assessment into disciplinary courses with a substantive writing component. We invited departmental teams of three to four faculty to apply for stipend support (provided by Georgetown's Center for New Designs in Learning and Scholarship) by posing specific questions about areas they wanted to investigate in their curriculum. Most of their questions had to do with places where students got stuck or encountered troublesome knowledge as they worked toward disciplinary understanding. These applications helped the writing program connect disciplinary concerns to questions about the kind of writing faculty assign and the ways in which students interpret and complete such assignments. A team from the Walsh School of Foreign Service (SFS) wanted to compare senior research expectations across sections (see appendix 13.A); a group from the McDonough School of Business (MSB) wanted to look at how students incorporated key concepts from operations into a writing assignment in a sophomore level course; and a team from Human Sciences wanted to develop a protocol for giving better feedback on Honors theses.

Rather than assessing student work solely to satisfy the Middle States Commission, teams posed questions about their curriculum and student learning that emerged from their own departmental concerns. Teams drew on threshold concepts to examine their own disciplinary networks and connections. After submitting applications with detailed descriptions of writing in their major and the questions they hoped to answer, these departmental faculty convened to read a small sample of student papers from an upper-level course. Led by a faculty member from the writing program, participants discussed what they valued in these papers and derived the traits to be included in a scoring rubric (drafted by the writing program representative and a graduate student assistant). Readers then scored the sample papers using these discipline-specific rubrics and met again to discuss the results. The small departmental teams were required to share their results with a larger group of colleagues with the hope of spreading the results to entire programs and departments.

While departmental faculty could usually reach agreement about the criteria to be included in the rubric and the weight of each item, they often disagreed about whether and how papers fulfilled these criteria. An interdisciplinary group from the School of Foreign Service, for example, disagreed about the form of a thesis statement, which led to an interesting discussion about making disciplinary values as displayed in expectations for writing assignments more explicit to students. Even among faculty in the same discipline, there was disagreement about their expectations for certain kinds of assignments, such as the white paper in a Business School finance course. This disagreement served as a valuable reminder that standards for good writing come from a complex mix of sources, not just disciplinary backgrounds. Far from being a negative, these contested discussions proved to be fruitful faculty development opportunities, leading faculty to articulate their expectations for students more clearly and discuss whether particular assignments promoted agreed-upon goals. The disagreements made clear the complex networks in which students write, highlighting the way in which standards and even threshold concepts are rarely absolute but rather shifting and context dependent. Some teams rejected the traditional rubric form with categories and numerical rankings altogether and instead created assignment-specific response questions which faculty had to answer in narrative form (see appendix 13.B).

These disagreements led to revising and refining rubrics until team members agreed on the wording and weighting of categories and questions. A small team of readers then evaluated a larger representative sample of papers and gathered information about trends in student learning. While the rubric scoring data served as useful measurements for both curricular examination and our Middle States report, most participants agreed that the real value of the project came from the deep, almost ethnographic conversations about writing in particular programs and majors. These discussions led to course and program changes, discussed in final reports filed by team members. For example, one program chair found as a result of the study that a number of faculty teaching senior seminars didn't provide written instructions for the senior paper. She noted that many of these seminars are taught by adjunct faculty who are esteemed career diplomats or policy experts (a not uncommon situation at Georgetown) whose schedules preclude them from attending full faculty meetings or pedagogy discussions. But using the rubric data and assignment descriptions collected as part of the study, she was able to contact instructors and request a written assignment with a common set of expectations (derived from the rubric discussion) across the seminars (even as the thematic topics of the seminars continued to vary according to faculty expertise). One measure of success is the fact that the program chair scheduled and performed another assessment round for the following year to determine whether the new assignment guidelines had the desired effect of making expectations consistent and explicit. She wasn't driven by external accreditation factors or stipend support, but rather by a departmental desire to understand and improve student learning.

In this way, the Georgetown Student Writing Study came closer to Brian Huot's ideal of moving assessment away from being "primarily concerned with constructing scoring guidelines and achieving high rates of interrater reliability" and more toward a meaningful examination of teaching and learning (Huot 1996, 552). Because faculty had been engaged in a rich discussion of threshold concepts as part of the colloquium, they were better able to articulate what they value in their own disciplines as well as in student work and could thus create thoughtful and flexible rubrics. While the rubrics can be seen as a form of outcomes based assessment (and are indeed useful in conversations with parties seeking such evidence), the greater value came in the descriptions and conversations about creating the rubrics and scoring of the papers.

The Georgetown Student Writing Study worked because it was theoretically informed and practically grounded but also organic and locally controlled. Unlike the Collegiate Learning Assessment, or other off-the-shelf corporate assessment tools, our assessment tools were developed by faculty to evaluate student writing in their own departments.

Although the work was informed by national standards, including the American Association of Colleges and Universities' Valid Assessment of Learning in Undergraduate Education (VALUE) rubrics, which faculty reviewed as part of the Thresholds Colloquiums and rubric creation process, it has been essential for departmental faculty to own the assessment process at Georgetown. The faculty's work in both creating rubrics and using the rubrics to score papers made them invested in the project and more likely to use the results to guide pedagogical and curricular change.

HOW THRESHOLD CONCEPTS CAN SUPPORT NETWORKED ASSESSMENT

While the Georgetown Student Writing Study did produce results that were used for external accreditation, it also invited faculty to participate in deep discussions about pedagogy and values and to consider the complex networks in which we and our students write. Both Gallagher (2011) and Rice (2011) propose forms of networked assessment as alternatives to outcomes based assessment driven by external accreditation pressures. A thorough explication of network theory is beyond the scope of this paper, but it's worth noting that Gallagher and Rice use the term *network* in different ways. Gallagher (2011) uses the term network more or less synonymously with relationships; he's interested in the way various stakeholders claim equal authority in conversations about assessment. Rice (2011) uses network as Latour uses it, stressing dialog between various constituents and tracing the items involved. He sees assessment not as measurement but as a way of figuring out and describing what is actually happening. The value of this approach is that it can "teach us about the relationships circulating in our own program that we have yet to see as being part of a given network" (Rice 2011, 38). Although Gallagher's and Rice's definitions vary, both types of networks can benefit from the support of an active (activist) Writing Program Administrator either to balance the power in assessment relationships (in Gallagher's model) or to invite, develop, and document deep descriptions (in Rice's model). In what follows, I suggest that writing programs are in a position to combine disciplinary expertise from composition studies with thresholds theory to build and support both kinds of networks, "making educational assessment more complex, and therefore more helpful and accurate, and thus contributing to the intellectual life of the university," as Slevin envisioned in 2001 (Slevin 2001, 212).

Gallagher (2011) critiques top-down assessment practices dependent on what he calls neoliberal policies, suggesting the logic of the network as an alternative. He argues that the stakeholder theory of assessment in which faculty, administrators, accrediting bodies, and students all have a seat at the assessment table is flawed. He argues persuasively that faculty should have greater say than others in assessment processes. Following George Orwell's lead, Gallagher claims that all stakeholders are equal, but some should be more equal than others: "I propose a rewriting of the assessment scene that abandons the stakeholder theory and asserts faculty and student agency in the form of leadership for writing assessment" (Gallagher 2011, 461). His theory of networks relies heavily on "proximity" and examining "patterns of relations" as a means of "understanding how actors exercise power by virtue of their locations and relations" (466).

Rice also seeks to make assessment "an understanding of activity relationships as opposed to generic outcomes" in his theory of networked assessment. He is less concerned with top-down, external assessment pressures than Gallagher is and instead would like to see networked assessment as a self-motivated but guided process (Rice 2011, 29). His ideal form of assessment more closely resembles a mapping or deep description activity, assessment as a way of figuring out what is actually being done in a program and describing that network. In his view, a WPA can productively shift the conversation about assessment from causality to connectivity (37).

While both Gallagher and Rice make convincing theoretical arguments about how network logic can remake the assessment scene, neither fully describes what this practice might look like.[1] I propose that writing programs can employ threshold concept theory to create a viable and intellectually rich assessment network. Threshold concept theory can demonstrate the centrality of faculty in the process and help them (to use Gallagher's terms) "confront the neoliberal order" (Gallagher 2011, 462). Writing programs, because they work with students, administrators, and faculty across disciplines, are well positioned to examine the patterns of relationships that Rice wants to trace. Convening meetings of faculty, both disciplinary and interdisciplinary, to examine student writing invites the kind of deep examination of student learning that might otherwise not happen because of busy schedules. The key here is to turn top-down calls for accountability and accreditation, which both Rice and Gallagher denounce, into occasions for robust examinations of student learning. The way to make this turn, to keep accountability from being driven solely by accrediting bodies and vendors like the

Collegiate Learning Assessment (CLA) and Educational Testing Service (ETS), is to highlight inquiry driven by scholarly expertise. Grounding assessment in threshold concept theory is a way of making that expertise visible and making faculty central. As Rice (2011) argues, "Rather than gathering evidence to convince external auditors that you are doing something right, assessment can become a reflective process that helps departments figure out what is actually being done and understand how to do it even better" (35).

It's no coincidence that both threshold concept theory and network theory rely on the language of space and movement. Meyer and Land (2003) describe threshold concepts "akin to passing through a portal" or "conceptual gateway" that opens up "previously inaccessible ways of thinking about something" (9). They stress that moving through these portals is a recursive process rather than something that happens all at once as students develop as thinkers in a field. Similarly, Gallagher (2011) describes networks in terms of space and connections, describing networks as "patterns of relations that shape interactions" and depend on "location" (465). Using both threshold concepts and networks as a basis for assessment reminds us that standards for student writing aren't fixed points in the way that certain forms of outcomes-based assessment may suggest. It is rather by developing a more flexible form of networked assessment grounded in disciplinary concepts and expertise that we can achieve Slevin's goal of intellectually rich work with faculty at the center.

CONCLUSION

Two key findings emerged from the Georgetown Student Writing Study, neither of which relied on the quantitative rubric scores we collected. The first is about *kairos*: the Middle States reaccreditation provided our writing program the timely opportunity to initiate a conversation about assessing writing with colleagues. The second finding concerns engagement: using threshold concept theory to engage faculty meant we were able to shift the assessment conversation from writing as the representation of knowledge—in short, writing as a tool for *testing* student learning—to writing as a way of making visible distinctive intellectual moves that define higher order work in a variety of disciplines. The lively conversations about the kinds of writing students do in their majors and the faculty expectations for these assignments helped faculty discover the complex systems in which they and our students operate. In working to understand activity relationships rather than just generic outcomes, we were able to conduct a form of assessment that was both intellectually robust and programmatically useful.

More important than the rubric scores we gathered was the way in which we have begun to transform the culture of writing at Georgetown by highlighting the complex networks within which our students write. The study also revealed the way in which multiple networks intersect: the complex systems of academic departments overlap to form a larger university network (which in turn is part of an even larger network of institutions that comprise the membership of the Middle States Commission on Higher Education). Examining, building relationships with, and describing Georgetown's departmental writing networks helped facilitate a major curricular change. Our assessment study came at a critical transition moment as Georgetown was shifting the culture of the teaching of writing, when the campus was moving from a context where the English department had primary responsibility for teaching composition to one where the entire campus shares a commitment to (and an investment in) writing instruction. Georgetown's faculty recently approved its first major general education reform in decades, including a policy that students take their second writing requirement in their major rather than in a humanities department as was previously mandated. As part of this new requirement, individual departments now take responsibility for developing a plan to describe, teach, and assess the kind of writing that students must do to succeed in their chosen fields. By initiating conversations with colleagues about their disciplinary expectations as part of the Writing Study, the writing program developed good relationships with faculty across the campus and garnered support for curricular change by making it clear that writers don't develop in isolation from contexts and disciplines. Grounding our writing assessment in a conversation about threshold concepts also helped convince skeptical faculty that they were prepared to teach writing in their fields if supported by the resources of the writing program. Assessment using threshold concepts helped create coordination among networks, leading to curricular and institutional change.

Of course many of our peer universities have long employed such a model in which students fulfill upper-level writing requirements in their major (reminding us of the larger, multi-institutional network of Writing Studies in which we operate). While many of these institutions have long benefitted from a writing-in–the-disciplines (WID) model (indeed, we have relied upon many of these models to build our own), we believe a next generation WID program shaped by threshold concepts theory (which we are calling Integrated Writing) will allow us to deepen and sustain a commitment to disciplinary writing instruction. New research by Linda Adler-Kassner, John Majewski, and Damian Koshnick suggests that attention to threshold concepts can also promote transfer, an essential area of inquiry in Writing Studies. Their preliminary findings indicate that paying attention to troublesome knowledge and liminal stages on the road to disciplinary understanding can promote metacognition, thereby increasing the likelihood that students will develop the kind of rhetorical agility that allows them to move among disciplines and courses (and beyond) with greater control (Adler-Kassner et al. 2012).

Placing faculty at the center of the assessment scene implies responsibilities as well as rights. By incorporating threshold concepts, our writing program hopes to help faculty develop a sense of responsibility not only for teaching writing in their disciplines but for the continuing study and review of its quality. In order for this to succeed, writing programs need to make their work visible, which often happens as part of an accreditation cycle. As Slevin (2001) explained more than a decade ago, "Faculty need to appreciate and strengthen the critical role writing programs could (but often do not) play in resisting the corporatization of the university and the commercialization of knowledge" (229). It may be that the same commercialization of knowledge (in the form external accountability demands) that Slevin decries can provide the moment for writing programs to become agents of change.

I won't pretend that Jim Slevin would agree with all I have to say here, but I'm certain he would understand the need to speak out and the attempt to reframe current conversations about accountability in the current climate of higher education reform. Rather than endorsing my approach, I suspect his response might be something more along the lines of, "What took you so long?"

Acknowledgments

Thanks to Matthew Pavesich, Norma Tilden, Sherry Linkon and Terry Myers Zawacki for their generous feedback on this article. Thanks also to John Ladd for his invaluable research assistance. Finally, I thank the Teagle and Spencer Foundation for supporting the threshold concept work described here.

APPENDIX 13.A

SFS STIA Senior Paper Rubric

The School of Foreign Service (SFS) Science Technology and International Affairs (STIA) major conducted a study to see whether student writing improved from the sophomore to the senior year. This is an example of the rubric they developed to measure success in the sophomore level course.

Category	Criteria	Level (1–4)
STIA Topic and Argument	• Argument is clearly stated and integrates science and technology with social science or other discipline. • Paper meets assignment guidelines with an international scope that is reasonably ambitious but still manageable. • Writer presents science and technology background in his/her own words in a way that is both understandable to a lay reader and demonstrates understanding of the technical material.	
Analysis and Critical Thinking	• Thinking is clear and logical, using concepts from the course and well chosen qualitative and quantitative evidence as appropriate. • Analysis and conclusions combine science and technology with broader issues. • Analysis shows originality and goes beyond a summary of the literature and a recounting of the history of the issue. • Examples illustrate and expand upon the general theme of the paper. • Writer clearly defines major terms early in the paper and uses them consistently. • Conclusions follow from the statement of the problem and the analysis and include action or policy recommendations as appropriate.	
Research	• Incorporates a balanced mix of academic sources and topical sources into a literature review that serves analysis. • Quotations are modest in quantity and used only when paraphrase would be inadequate. • Uses consistent and correct citation formats.	
Structure and Style	• Abstract states topic and summarizes background, approach, analysis and conclusions. • Introduction sets forth the topic, explains why it is important, explains the approach, and anticipates the conclusion in a way that motivates the reader. • General background section clearly explains the overall context and provides all necessary background information. • Science and technology section displays the author's understanding of the material, leaves no obvious question unanswered. • Includes headings and subheadings as needed. • Style is both succinct and analytical (without repetitions or inconsistencies) while meeting assignment guidelines.	
Mechanics	• Prose consistently meets expectations for Standard Edited US English (grammar/punctuation) with evidence of proofreading. • Prose demonstrates sentence-level fluency. • Page numbers, subheadings, margins, and spacing are consistent with assignment guidelines.	

Key: 1 = Not Competent; 2 = Emerging Competence; 3 = Competent; 4 = Highly Competent

APPENDIX 13.B

Response Questions Rubric

The School of Foreign Service Regional and Comparative Studies (RCST) applied to participate in the Georgetown Student Writing Study because they wanted to give more consistent feedback to seniors writing thesis projects. The department also wanted to reach some understanding about what constituted honors-level work in a thesis to make sure it was awarding this distinction fairly and consistently. Because RCST is an interdisciplinary major, its faculty had different sets of expectations about what a good thesis looks like.

The faculty team rejected a traditional rubric with numerical rankings by category because it seemed too formulaic, but developed the set of questions below to give consistent feedback as part of the Georgetown Writing Study. These questions were later adapted and expanded to be used as part of peer review. Additional rubrics were developed for specific sections of the thesis, such as the literature review. As a result of their participation in the study, the team also agreed to enhance the thesis writing seminar in the fall semester, add a proposal writing workshop during the junior year to elevate the "starting point" of the senior year thesis writing, and circulate the rubrics to all departmental faculty.

SCHOOL OF FOREIGN SERVICE REGIONAL AND COMPARATIVE STUDIES HONORS THESIS ASSESSMENT

Faculty Mentors: The following questions are designed to help you give feedback to your advisees during the writing process and to the Honors Committee at the end of the project. These are the minimum expectations for the project; students should be encouraged to go beyond the limits of this formula as they pursue their research.

1. How clearly is the hypothesis articulated? Is it original?

2. How well does the literature review set up the argument? Does the student include seminal texts and experts in the field?

3. How appropriate are the methods, given the student's hypothesis and research goals? *(Students should confer with you early in the process about appropriate research methods in the field).*

4. Is the data analysis clear, appropriate, and accurate?

5. How relevant are the sources used? Are they properly incorporated, synthesized, and cited? *(Please discuss appropriate citation procedures in your field with your advisee).*

6. How appropriate is the prose for readers who are not necessarily topic experts? Is the thesis free of writing/grammatical errors? Is the paper

well organized, with appropriate section headings and clear transitions? Are charts appropriately labeled and incorporated?

7. How does the thesis make a compelling argument for the significance of the student's research within the context of the current literature? Does it frame key issues and address the hypothesis posed? Does it contribute new knowledge to the field?

Note

1. Gallagher devotes little more than a page to praxis, and Rice left his position as WPA at the University of Missouri for his new job at the University of Kentucky before his assessment vision was fully realized.

References

Adler-Kassner, Linda, John Majewski, and Damian Koshnick. 2012. "The Value of Troublesome Knowledge: Threshold Concepts in Writing and History." *Composition Forum* 26. http://compositionforum.com/issue/26/troublesome-knowledge -threshold.php.

Broad, Bob, Linda Adler-Kassner, Barry Alford, Jane Detweiler, Heidi Estrem, Susanmarie Harrington, Maureen McBride, Eric Stalions, and Scott Weeden. 2009. *Organic Writing Assessment: Dynamic Criteria Mapping in Action.* Logan: Utah State University Press.

Gallagher, Chris. 2011. "Being There: (Re)Making the Assessment Scene." *College Composition and Communication* 62 (3): 450–73.

Huot, Brian. 1996. "Toward a New Theory of Writing Assessment." *College Composition and Communication* 47 (4): 549–66. http://dx.doi.org/10.2307/358601.

Huot, Brian. 2002. *(Re)articulating Writing Assessment for Teaching and Learning.* Logan: Utah State University Press.

Krause, Steven. 2011. "On Rice And Gallagher on Assessment Scholarship." *Stevendkrause. Com.* http://stevendkrause.com/2011/06/29/on-rice-and-gallagher-on-assessment -scholarship/.

Meyer, Jan, and Ray Land. 2003. "Threshold Concepts and Troublesome Knowledge: Linkages to Ways of Thinking and Practising within the Disciplines." *Enhancing Teaching-Learning Environments in Undergraduate Courses,* 1–12. Occasional report by the Enhancing Teaching and Learning project. Edinburgh: University of Edinburgh. http://www.etl.tla.ed.ac.uk//docs/ETLreport4.pdf.

Middendorf, Joan, and David Pace. 2004. "Decoding the Disciplines: A Model for Helping Students Learn Disciplinary Ways of Thinking." *New Directions for Teaching and Learning* (98): 1-12.

Perelman, Les. 2008. "Information Illiteracy and Mass Market Writing Assessments." *College Composition and Communication* 60 (1): 128–41.

Perkins, David. 2006. "Constructivism and Troublesome Knowledge." In *Overcoming Barriers to Student Understanding,* ed. Jan H. F. Meyer and Ray Land, 33–47. London: Routledge.

Rice, Jeff. 2011. "Networked Assessment." *Computers and Composition* 28 (1): 28–39. http://dx.doi.org/10.1016/j.compcom.2010.09.007.

Slevin, James. 2001. *Introducing English: Essays in the Intellectual Work of Composition.* Pittsburgh: University of Pittsburgh Press.

14
FACULTY LEARNING OUTCOMES
The Impact of QEP Workshops on Faculty Beliefs and Practices

Joyce Neff and Remica Bingham-Risher

Research shows that successful Writing Across the Curriculum /Writing in the Disciplines (WAC/WID) programs usually develop in faculty-initiated, grassroots fashion (Russell 2012, 15–45). That was not the process at Old Dominion University in 2011 when the administration appointed a committee to design a Quality Enhancement Plan (QEP) that would meet a reaccreditation requirement of the Southern Association of Colleges and Schools Commission on Colleges (SACSCOC).[1] Of course, the ODU administration had a big stake in the reaccreditation game, but the faculty had an equal stake and had been interested in improving student writing for a long time. Fortunately, all the stakeholders realized what an opportunity they had. The planning committee would be designing a program with five years of guaranteed funding at a level that ODU's previous WAC/WID programs never imagined. In addition, the committee's cross-disciplinary membership meant lively meetings and free-wheeling exchanges of ideas. Their first challenge was agreeing on an initiative that satisfied their differing beliefs about teaching and learning. Could administrators and faculty with contradictory paradigms for research, assessment, and instruction find common ground? After many months of work, the committee created a two-part QEP composed of WID workshops for faculty and faculty-proposed Action Project Grants. They named their QEP *Improving Disciplinary Writing* (IDW).

The committee's next challenge was SACSCOC's mandated assessment component, namely Student Learning Outcomes (SLOs). Could the committee agree on a list of SLOs? Could the SLOs be assessed through student writing? Could the SLOs measure the impact of WID workshops and Action Projects? After multiple types of data were collected from the first year of QEP implementation, the committee began to answer those questions. Meanwhile, an additional assessment possibility became

DOI: 10.7330/9781607324355.c014

apparent to the authors of this chapter. We wanted to know what the data could tell us about *faculty* learning. Four questions guided our study:

1. Did faculty perceptions about writing differ as a result of the QEP Workshops?

2. Did the QEP workshops help or hinder faculty as they (re)created writing assignments for their upper-division disciplinary courses?

3. What impact, if any, did the SLO requirement have on faculty revisions to writing assignments and course designs?

4. How might we assess faculty learning?

In the following pages we describe the context for ODU's *Improving Disciplinary Writing* QEP, and we report on the faculty-learning research project we carried out. We conclude by discussing the implications of our findings for other institutions that are designing assessment plans for a WAC/WID QEP.[2]

THE ODU CONTEXT

ODU, which is a state-supported RU/H[3] institution, fielded successful WAC faculty workshops in the 1980s and again in the mid-1990s. Breaks in the program resulted from funding cuts (or funding diversion to programs such as technology across the curriculum) and the loss of program leaders to other initiatives. Since the 1990s, the university has grown dramatically from 15,000 to 25,000 students and has increased its dependence on contingent faculty. General education curricula have been redesigned, but there has not been a coordinated effort to improve upper-division writing-intensive requirements. From the mid-1980s until 2011, students sat for an exit exam of writing proficiency—a high-stakes essay written to a disciplinary-based prompt in a three-hour time frame. Students could not graduate until they passed the exit exam.

ODU's QEP, *Improving Disciplinary Writing*, opened new possibilities beginning with the planning committee's definition of disciplinary writing as "writing that demonstrates a reasoning process supported by research and reflection on a problem, topic, or issue. Writing is a critical skill that goes beyond demonstrating proficiency with the mechanics and structure of writing *per se*. Writing is a means to communicate what has been learned" (Old Dominion University 2012, 1). The committee further explained the learning-writing connection by stating that the "methods by which research, reflection, and presentation are conducted vary by discipline. Students learn how to *do* the discipline in ways that are particular to the discipline . . . they come to *know* the discipline as they write about what they did and learned using the discipline's specific styles of knowledge presentation, whether these are lab reports, monographs, research reports, field notes, patient notes, design plans, technical reports, or performance reviews. Although written artifacts communicating what was learned vary by discipline, they nonetheless provide evidence of learning" (Old Dominion University 2012, 7).

The ODU QEP has three goals:

1. To assist faculty in understanding the connections between learning and writing

2. To encourage the development of meaningful learning through writing activities

3. To support pedagogical efforts that help students produce documents which meet six student learning outcomes (SLOs)

The two funded components of the QEP are WID workshops for faculty who teach upper-division undergraduate courses and grants for program-based, faculty-proposed action projects. The workshops focus on learning through writing and each session promises:

. . . discussion of a variety of topics along with specific strategies for writing to learn in the disciplines . . . Active learning, including actually doing the kinds of writing being taught, comprises a key component of the workshops. In this way, faculty are expected to learn how to use writing as a means of discovery in their classrooms and in terms of formal writing assignments, as well as why and how writing works to promote student learning. (Old Dominion University 2012, 20; see appendix 14.A)

Participants apply for admission to the workshops and receive a $2,000 stipend upon completing all required sessions (five days from 8:30 AM–3:00 PM) and producing deliverables, which include revised assignments and syllabus statements about the importance of writing in their discipline. Action Projects are internal grants (up to $20,000) "designed to encourage academic programs to learn, develop, and implement best practices to improve writing in the upper division undergraduate courses within their programs" (Old Dominion University 2012, 21). The Action Project awards are flexible and open to "ideas and models that schools and departments can adopt, while also providing for an individual program to develop curricula appropriate to its own unique activities and subject matter" (Old Dominion University 2012, 21).

The formal QEP assessment plan requires the rating of student writing samples against the six Student Learning Outcomes (see appendix 14.B). That is, students should be able to:

- Clearly state a focused problem, question, or topic appropriate for the purpose of the task
- Identify relevant knowledge and credible sources
- Synthesize information and multiple viewpoints related to the problem, question, or topic
- Apply appropriate research methods or theoretical framework to the problem, question, or topic
- Formulate conclusions that are logically tied to inquiry findings and consider applications, limitations, and implications, and
- Reflect on or evaluate what was learned

Student writing samples are collected from the Blackboard sites of courses taught by the faculty who complete the workshops and/or participate in Action Projects. Because the ODU QEP officially began in late 2012, the first assessment of student writing did not occur until 2013.

On the other hand, both quantitative and qualitative data on faculty understandings of WID principles and on faculty intentions to apply those principles in upper-division courses were available after every workshop, and we found them compelling. Those data included results from the Consortium for the Study of Writing in Colleges (CSWC) questionnaire administered at the beginning of the workshops, written reflections collected at the end of the workshops, and surveys from the semester following the workshops.

THE CHALLENGE: ASSESSING QEP OUTCOMES

A recent study of WAC programs by William Condon and Carol Rutz describes how WAC programs with certain characteristics can be transformed into programs with different characteristics (Condon and Rutz 2012). For example, the former ODU WAC/WID programs (from the 1980s and 90s) would have been classified as type 1 (Foundational) or type 2 (Established) according to Condon and Rutz's taxonomy. To move to type 3 (Integrated Program) or type 4 (Institutional Change Agent), a program must include rigorous, ongoing assessment with an active feedback loop. The program must welcome "inquiry that can support research and administrative efforts, so that a flow of information about the program's status continues to inform its progress toward its goals" (Condon and Rutz 2012, 380). That is to say, instruction and assessment must speak to one another. ODU's earlier WAC/WID programs clearly did not go far enough. On the other hand, assessment debates proved essential for ODU's QEP planning committee as they confronted conflicting disciplinary definitions of learning, writing, knowing, and assessing. They eventually reached a compromise by adopting SLOs that reflect steps of the scientific method. However, because of SACSCOC requirements, the SLO rubric became the major assessment instrument in a program predicated on faculty workshops and faculty action plans.

Chris Thaiss and Tara Porter (2010, 524–570) contribute to the assessment conversation with their national mapping of WAC programs. They state that "formal program assessment in universities still lacks agreed-on models," (Thaiss and Porter 2010, 557), is not universal by any measure, and is a recent addition to WAC programs. Ongoing formal assessment by institutional committee is a feature in 41 percent of the 568 programs that responded to Thaiss and Porter's survey; assessment targeting student writing proficiency is found in 42 percent; state or regional mandated assessment in 14 percent; and, most important to our ODU study, assessment of faculty development components is reported by only 21 percent of institutions (Thaiss and Porter 2010, 557). That leads us to agree with Hubball, Clarke, and Beach (2004) who argue for multi-layered, authentic evaluation and assessment that includes not only SLOs but also Faculty Learning Outcomes (FLOs) and outcomes for each proposed initiative in a program.

The results of these previous studies and the debates among members of ODU's planning committee form the background to our study, which analyzes empirical data to get a fuller picture of the impact of our QEP on faculty beliefs and practices and then takes a stab at creating faculty learning outcomes.

METHODOLOGY

The research design for this study was an embedded one. We collected three data sets from different phases of the rollout of the QEP project and used them to triangulate findings. The availability of the three data sets enabled us to analyze quantitative and qualitative data separately and then collate/compare the themes and patterns that emerged.[4]

Participants

All faculty who volunteered for the workshops did so knowing that ongoing assessment was part of the QEP design, and they were informed by representatives from the Office of Assessment that the documents they and their students produced would be made available for analysis.

Data collection

Three data sets were collected from faculty who participated in the QEP workshops.

1. The first data set, collected by ODU's Office of Assessment, includes responses to the Faculty Survey of Student Engagement (FSSE) instrument, which has twenty-three questions from the Consortium for the Study of Writing in College (CSWC). The survey was completed anonymously the first day of the spring 2012, summer 2012, and spring 2013 workshops. Sixty-six faculty completed the instrument (see appendix 14.C).

2. Participants' reflections comprised the second set of data and were collected via Blackboard or as Microsoft Word documents for anonymity on the last day of the spring and summer 2012 workshops. Forty-one participants wrote reflective essays in response to the following prompts:

   • What you did and didn't learn about disciplinary writing
   • The value (or not) of the learning
   • What you will do next to improve disciplinary writing in the major
   • What support or help you might want as you go forward

3. The third data set was collected by the QEP director at a lunch meeting of faculty participants in the semester after they had completed the workshops (October 2012). Participation was voluntary and anonymous. Twenty-seven participants completed the survey (see appendix 14.D).

Data analysis

The authors of this chapter individually analyzed the qualitative data by reading and coding the reflection essays and the answers to the open-ended survey questions. We coded these data sets at least twice, writing memos capturing the categories that emerged from the separate readings. For the next round of analysis, we compared codes, eventually organizing them into themes and patterns that we could confirm with examples from the data set. We used descriptive statistics to analyze numerical responses to the closed-ended survey questions and to the CSWC instrument.

FSSE Findings

The National Survey of Student Engagement (NSSE) has been administered at ODU five times since 2001. Its faculty counterpart, the Faculty Survey of Student Engagement (FSSE) was administered for the first time to a random sampling of all faculty in 2012. Also in 2012, an additional twenty-three questions from the Consortium for the Study of Writing in College (CSWC) were administered as part of the FSSE and NSSE (see appendix 14.C). These twenty-three supplemental questions are ordered into three categories: interactive writing tasks, meaning-constructing writing tasks, and clear instructor expectations.

As part of ODU's QEP, the twenty-three CSWC questions are given to faculty workshop participants on the morning of their first workshop. By spring 2013, that added up to sixty-six faculty. We used the CSWC survey to gather pre-workshop information from faculty because many questions have a direct correlation to the ideas that are taught in the QEP workshops. For example, respondents are asked whether they include writing assignments in their courses and, if so, how they facilitate and use writing in the classroom. Some questions address interactive writing activities done by students prior to completing a formal writing task. For instance, one question asks: *For how many writing assignments was it encouraged or required to: Brainstorm (list ideas, map concepts, prepare an outline, etc.) to develop ideas before they* [students] *started drafting the assignment.* Of the sixty-six respondents who answered this question, 21 percent (14 faculty members) said they did this on *all* or *most assignments*. A large majority, 79 percent (52), said they did this on *some, few,* or *none* of the assignments given.

In the CSWC subsection on meaning-constructing writing tasks, respondents were asked about employing disciplinary writing in their courses: *How many writing assignments asked students to: Write in the style and format of a specific field (engineering, history, psychology, etc.).* Of the sixty-five respondents who answered this question, 63 percent (41) stated that they asked students to do so on *most* or *all* assignments. The remaining 37 percent (24 respondents) said they did this on *some, few,* or *none* of the writing assignments.

Several questions in the instructor expectations subgroup were especially pertinent to our study. First, respondents were asked: *For how many writing assignments did you: Provide clear instructions describing what you wanted your students to do.* Of the sixty-five respondents who answered, an overwhelming 94 percent (61 respondents) said they did this on *all* or *most* assignments and only 6 percent (4 respondents) said they did this on just *some* or *few* assignments.

Another question related to clear instructor expectations: *For how many writing assignments did you: Explain in advance what you wanted your students to learn.* Again, the majority of the sixty-five respondents, 74 percent (49), reported doing this on *most* or *all* assignments. A quarter of respondents, 26 percent (17) said they did this on *some, few,* or *none* of the assignments given.

A corresponding question raised in the *clear expectations* section of the survey was the following: *For how many writing assignments did you: Explain in advance the criteria you would use to grade the assignment.* Of the sixty-six respondents who answered this question, 85 percent (56) said they explained the criteria in advance on *most* or *all* assignments, while only 15 percent (10) said they did this on *some, few,* or *none* of the writing assignments.

We found some interesting patterns when we reviewed the CSWC responses. While 63 percent of faculty felt that they were already engaged in assigning disciplinary writing, 52 percent admitted that low-stakes' writing or preliminary assignment scaffolding (i.e., brainstorming, concept mapping, outlining) was only required on some, a few, or none of their writing assignments.

On the whole, prior to taking the workshops, the faculty firmly believed that they were giving clear instructions with each writing assignment and were explaining in advance the criteria they would use to grade writing assignments. Interestingly enough, we found that after taking the workshops, the majority of faculty cited these very items as what was missing or in greatest need of revision in their assignments. They then named scaffolding, rubrics, and low-stakes writing as the strategies they were most eager to introduce in their courses. The next two sections shed additional light on the transitions from pre- to post-workshop beliefs.

Reflection Findings

After coding the forty-one reflective essays that participants completed on the last day of their workshops, we arrived at three themes related to faculty beliefs and practices. First, participants developed new understandings of writing-learning connections. All of the participants named "tools" they found useful after being exposed to them in the workshops. More important, they wrote about understanding larger principles of learning and writing because of that exposure. One said, "By seeing what other participants are doing in their classes, and how they are doing it, I've gained a new perspective on what I want my own students to take from my classes and become more deliberate about how writing fits into my classes" (R4). Another noted that the workshops "provided a path and plan to improve my writing assignments, improve student writing outcomes, and ultimately, improve learning in my upper level courses" (R5). A third said s/he now understands the power of writing beyond assessment: "Today, thanks to the QEP workshop, I understand writing's potential as a teaching tool, not simply as an assessment mechanism. This has prompted me to re-think the way I teach and the way in which I engage my students" (R13). And a fourth said, "I was expecting to learn how to engage students with challenging writing assignments in my discipline, but I learned much more than this: how to clearly state a focused problem, how to set meaningful evaluation criteria, grading rubrics, and writing assessment" (R15).

The second theme to emerge was that participants appreciated time for engaging with others and getting feedback from peers. Numerous respondents commented on the time and space the workshops provided, using words like "rejuvenation" and "camaraderie." For example, "I am very thankful for learning this new information, for meeting some wonderful people (that I would have not otherwise met), and for re-energizing me in my role as a faculty member!"(R10M12). And another, "We have much more in common than we may sometimes realize. A small group of us who teach leadership courses in different disciplines have made plans to get together on a regular basis to share ideas, successful projects, and frustrations" (R16M12).

The third theme was that participants perceive the lack of a supportive climate for pedagogy in their departments/disciplines, but see QEP workshops as a way to work around that climate. The campus climate regarding teaching is not supportive according to workshop participants. They felt they had to go outside their department/discipline to talk about pedagogy because departmental colleagues didn't value that type of talk. For example, "I will share with my colleagues what I have learned even though MANY may be unwilling to listen" (R7). And another, "At first I felt guilty for attending these workshops because it took away from what I was 'supposed to be doing'—my research and my own writing. However, I know that what I have learned in these workshops will make my work here at ODU more fulfilling and rewarding" (R10). A third example was, "I think the idea of promoting this within the department will be difficult without the level of support that this workshop offered . . . It will be important to keep offering this level of engagement, away from our respective disciplines, to encourage and support writing" (R15). And a fourth, "It was good to exchange ideas and also quite good to get comments-critiques from others, something that I have often asked for of colleagues in the discipline I work in but rarely received" (R30M12).

Survey Findings

In the fall semester following the spring and summer 2012 workshops, we invited participants to a lunch meeting to discuss what was and wasn't working during their implementation of the *Improving Disciplinary Writing* QEP principles. Twenty-seven participants completed a survey with three closed-ended questions and five open-ended questions (see appendix 14.D). The survey, developed by the director of the ODU QEP, addressed concepts and skills that faculty were encouraged to implement during the workshops.

Respondents were asked to "strongly agree, agree, somewhat agree, disagree, or strongly disagree" with three closed-ended statements. For question 1, 94 percent of respondents strongly agreed or agreed with the statement "I am satisfied with the training I received during the QEP Workshops." For question 2, 94 percent of respondents strongly agreed or agreed with the statement "I believe the training I received during the Workshops aptly prepared me to implement new writing practices in my courses." For question 3, 85 percent of respondents strongly agreed or agreed with the statement "I would be interested in attending a follow-up, more advanced workshop on QEP 'write to learn' techniques." The vast majority of respondents felt that the workshops were effective, helped them implement changes, and were interested in learning more about the techniques outlined during the workshops.

These responses were a positive development for our program; not only did so many workshop participants attend this voluntary luncheon/feedback session, but most were eager to share their experiences with us and seemed to have personally benefitted from what they learned about writing in the disciplines, as can be seen in their answers to the five open-ended questions on the survey:

- How have you used the "write-to-learn" techniques highlighted in the QEP Workshops?
- Have you used the QEP Rubric and made it available to students? If so, has holistic scoring been helpful?
- How have you assessed the effectiveness of the new writing techniques you've incorporated (i.e., participation has increased, grades have improved, etc.)?
- What has been the most helpful tool you've received from participating in the QEP Workshops?
- What other kinds of follow-up sessions should be made available to QEP Workshop participants?

Responses were coded separately by each of the authors. We then compared codes and arrived at several findings. We found that participants were engaged in active implementation of many of the strategies and tools presented during the workshops. For instance, participants reported that they had begun using writing to learn (low-stakes writing), rubrics, scaffolding, genre knowledge, and revised methods of feedback (such as peer review) during the fall semester. In addition, the respondents were engaging in improved assignment design by rewriting assignment instructions with students' needs in mind. They were incorporating real-world applications, adding timelines, and using genre knowledge to (re)construct assignments.

Respondents also reported increased student participation in their courses. Although the fall semester was not far enough along (the survey was given in week nine of the term) for faculty to have actual assessment results from formal assignments, ten respondents commented that participation in discussion had improved noticeably. Many attributed this increased participation to the addition of low-stakes writing-to-learn activities. One respondent (LS1) shared data from two observation reports s/he had already graded that semester, noting that the average grade had improved from 13.6/20 to 14.3/20 in one set of reports and from 14.5/20 to 16/20 in the other.

Another interesting finding was that several of the respondents were enjoying a meta-awareness of themselves as teachers. For example, two instructors noted they were focusing on ideas first (before writing mechanics) when responding to students. (LS2; LS17) Others became aware of the value of providing more specific instructions. One participant spoke of "determining *and* communicating the objectives" of an assignment (LS16) as the most helpful tool received from the workshops.

An unexpected finding was that several participants reported reduced student anxiety in their courses. Two faculty attributed it to students' better understanding of the assignments and requirements.

An overarching theme in the survey responses was the appreciation for interaction with other faculty. In line with the category of "heightened awareness of teaching" was the finding that faculty who care about teaching and writing are delighted to find other like-minded faculty across the university. Six respondents specifically asked for more post-workshop interaction along these lines.

DISCUSSION

Before we discuss the results of our study of faculty learning, we would like to summarize the student learning results that have emerged so far from our QEP. In May 2013, an Assessment Summit was held in which 140 written artifacts (papers, reports, essays, etc.) randomly selected from courses taught by faculty who attended the workshops were assessed based on the IDW Writing Rubric (see appendix 14.B). The findings showed that, on four out of the six outcomes, more than half of the student writing artifacts were scored as meeting or exceeding the standard for SLO 1 (Clearly state a focused problem, question, or topic appropriate for the purpose of the task), SLO 2 (Identify relevant knowledge and credible sources), SLO 3 (Synthesize information and multiple viewpoints related to the problem, question, or topic) and SLO 5 (Formulate conclusions that are logically tied to inquiry findings and consider applications, limitations, and implications). Faculty needed clarification on teaching SLO 4 (Apply appropriate research methods or theoretical framework to the problem, question, or topic) and SLO 6 (Reflect on or evaluate what was learned), as more than half of the student artifacts merely approached the standard or needed attention on these outcomes. The material taught in the IDW Faculty Workshops was refined in 2013–14 based on the results of the Assessment Summit and a newly developed curriculum map.

In May 2014, a second annual assessment of the *Improving Disciplinary Writing* program was performed using pre- and post-workshop artifacts from courses that were revised after faculty members participated in the IDW workshops. Six faculty raters scored forty-five pre-workshop artifacts and eight raters scored sixty post-workshop artifacts. The preliminary findings are extremely encouraging, as there was at least a 20 percentage point increase in five out of the six IDW student learning outcomes, with most marked improvement in synthesizing information (SLO 3) and reflection (SLO 6) (see Table 14.1).

We now return to the initial questions of our faculty learning study:

1. Did faculty perceptions about writing differ as a result of the QEP workshops?

2. Did the QEP workshops help or hinder faculty as they (re)created writing assignments for their upper-division disciplinary courses?

3. What impact, if any, did the SLO assessment requirement have on faculty revisions to writing assignments and course designs?

4. How might we assess faculty learning?

One positive conclusion we can draw is that faculty reactions to the workshops, as evidenced in their reflections and survey answers, are the very reactions that we hope faculty will get from their own students in the revised versions of their courses. The reflections provide evidence that faculty are aware that their beliefs and practices have to be (are being) reconfigured and changed. One participant writes, "I learned how to

Table 14.1. Improving disciplinary writing pre- and post-workshop comparisons

	Pre Artifacts (Exceeds and Meets)	Post Artifacts (Exceeds and Meets)
SLO 1: Students will be able to clearly state a focused problem, question, or topic appropriate for the purpose of the task.	67%	70%
SLO 2: Students will be able to identify relevant knowledge and credible sources.	55%	76%
SLO 3: Students will be able to synthesize information and multiple viewpoints related to the problem, question, or topic.	47%	79%
SLO 4: Students will be able to apply appropriate research methods or theoretical framework to the problem, question, or topic.	55%	78%
SLO 5: Students will be able to formulate conclusions that are logically tied to inquiry findings and consider applications, limitations, and implications.	40%	69%
SLO 6: Students will be able to reflect on or evaluate what was learned.	31%	73%

engage students . . . I have also learned about myself" (R10sum12). And it is worth quoting at length from another:

> I had a number of emotions as the week unfolded: On Monday, I can do this it isn't that difficult; on Tuesday, holy crap this is going to take a lot of work, maybe I don't want to do all this (which was really good because it put me in the place of the students) and then Tuesday night getting the aha moment—I really understand how I can implement this and I can do this and I will do it! From there, Wednesday feeling much more optimistic but still feeling overwhelmed by how much I didn't know, trying to understand all of your terminology. At this point, I was still fighting some of this push for low stakes . . . On Thursday, holy crap again, you mean my peers are actually going to critique my work? What if I don't like what they say? Will this mean more work for me? But also thinking to myself, wow, I have learned a lot . . ." (R8M12)

This meta-level of insight into learning leads some participants to regret missed opportunities: "wished you had offered it [the workshops] when I joined ODU six years ago" (R18sp12); "I wished I would have taken these classes 5–7 years ago" (R19sp12). One participant says "[my family] hear me complain all year long about how my students can't write, and how they don't do what I tell them, even though I've been so specific. They are delighted that I'm excited about what I am learning here [in the workshops]. I feel like I can give my courses so much more, and I feel like I've learned so much about new technologies and new strategies . . . So many ways to make a process out of the writing instead of getting yet another disappointing project." (R13M12)

On the negative side, one obstacle to sustained improvement in disciplinary writing seems to be the felt sense among participants that excitement about and attention to pedagogy is undervalued within their departments and colleges. We hope that the Action Projects, the second component of our QEP, will address this obstacle since the projects are aimed at program and department-wide implementation of WID principles.

Another issue that will have to be addressed throughout our QEP's lifespan is the demand from original workshop participants for follow-up opportunities. While past participants do have a chance to help their program apply some of the write-to-learn principles by proposing an Action Project for the department, developing an Action Project is still a rather insular endeavor and most of the participants want other opportunities to interact with faculty outside of their discipline. Moreover, as provisions for these follow-up opportunities were not originally addressed in ODU's QEP plan, funding and resources will have to be acquired or the plan will have to be adjusted to include these activities and, possibly, remove others.

In the future, we would also like to compare the NSSE/FSSE/CSWC data from across the university with the data from our QEP participants. As part of our QEP assessment, participants will be asked to retake the CSWC survey after they have implemented changes to their courses and programs. Comparing pre- and post-results of the CSWC as well as contrasting them with student responses will give a better view of how our QEP may be affecting writing in the disciplines, especially over time.

Because QEP directions from SACSCOC do not implicitly or explicitly address faculty learning, FLOs were not considered for formal assessment by the planning committee during the development of ODU's QEP. However, the findings produced by our study have convinced us it would be advantageous to create faculty learning outcomes (FLOs) for workshop participants. Designing an instrument for this type of assessment could add an important perspective. We recommend that other schools planning or revising their QEPs consider including FLOs during the planning phase, especially if their QEPs involve faculty development. To that end, here is a first draft of FLOs, which we hope to use to assess future workshop deliverables (syllabus statements on writing; low-stakes and formal assignment prompts) and participants' reflective writing.

Faculty should be able to:

1. Connect writing with the learning of disciplinary content

2. Understand and implement write-to-learn practices such as scaffolding, rubrics, low-staking assignments, and so forth

3. Create writing assignments that help teach course content, are educationally sound, and are significant for the professions their students will enter

4. Demonstrate knowledge and understanding of the full QEP/IDW cycle (including SLO assessment)

5. Value pedagogical exchange and be comfortable with it

6. See themselves as writers (i.e., see writing as a part of the practice of teaching)

Now that we have completed our study, we have more questions for the future, especially about faculty motivations for participating and the ethical issues of assessing faculty.[5] As our QEP/WID program came with very different mandates and resources than are attached or afforded to most non-QEP WAC/WID programs, we are interested in finding out if these affordances provided more compelling motivation for faculty to participate.

The final and, we believe, most critical discussion point has to do with the richness of the qualitative data sets that we analyzed. We find power in our colleagues' words just as we hope they will find power in their students' words. The time we have spent listening to them has been rewarded handsomely. This point brings us back to the ongoing debate among members of the ODU QEP planning committee about the best assessment practices for determining the success of our *Improving Disciplinary Writing* initiative. We would argue that multiple types of assessment, including reflective writing from faculty, provide the best approach. Both qualitative and quantitative data should be collected and analyzed. The debates that arise from complex, multi-voiced assessments are themselves an important outcome of a WAC/WID QEP.

APPENDIX 14.A
Faculty Workshop Plan

Faculty Workshop Objectives
Participants in the workshops will:

• Explore connections between writing and learning in upper-division undergraduate courses in their disciplines

- Design assignments that meet course objectives and help students produce documents that meet the student learning outcomes. The QEP student learning outcomes are that students will be able to produce documents that:
  - Clearly state a focused problem, question, or topic appropriate for the purpose of the task
  - Identify relevant knowledge and credible sources
  - Synthesize information and multiple viewpoints related to the problem, question, or topic
  - Apply appropriate research methods or theoretical framework to the problem, question, or topic
  - Formulate conclusions that are logically tied to inquiry findings and consider applications, limitations, and implications, and
  - Reflect on or evaluate what was learned.
- Implement best practices and creative pedagogies that promote upper-division undergraduate disciplinary writing
- Develop strategies for responding to written work which are helpful to students and not overly burdensome for faculty, and
- Strengthen their teaching and learning conversations and collaborations.

Workshop Requirements
Participants will:

- Participate in all workshop sessions
- Complete all workshop assignments:
  - Assignments based on write-to-learn principles
  - Directions for a formal assignment (with full context and evaluative criteria)
  - A syllabus (for a course to be taught in the upcoming academic year) that incorporates material from the workshop
  - A proposal for how they will share what they have learned in the workshop
- Submit student writing samples from the semester prior to their workshop for use in assessment
- Require that students upload artifacts to the learning management system (LMS) for use in assessment
- Participate in at least three of five gatherings of workshop participants over the following year to discuss their experiences using best practices in their courses
- Complete assessments as follows:
  - Pre-treatment at beginning of first workshop: Consortium for the Study of Writing in College (CSWC) questions for faculty

- Post-treatment annually: CSWC questions for faculty
- Pre-treatment at beginning of first workshop: Syllabi with writing assignment instructions
- Post-treatment annually: Syllabi with writing assignment instructions

QEP Workshop Series Structure
Workshop 1: January 20, 2012
Participants are to bring: laptop, syllabus (w/weekly schedule)

- 8:30–9:00am: Breakfast & Chatting
- 9:00–9:20am: Overview of the QEP—focus on why QEP is offering the workshops. What do you get out of it?
- Workshop Objectives
  - 9:20–25am: Assign first Class Notes/Minutes person
  - 9:25–55am: Speed Chat: talk to someone you don't know, take a few notes and then introduce them [directions on HANDOUT]
    - Interview Questions (guided notetaking/cards w/questions):
      - Name, Department, 300/400 level class you teach
      - What you hope to get from workshop
  - 9:55–10:10am: Facilitators Introductions & Overview [all facilitators] (collate goals) (Joyce)
  - 10:10–10:25am: Break
  - 10:25–11:25am: What is Learning? Definitions of Learning
    - 1 minute paper: What is learning?
    - Types of Learning (help put writing components w/in the correct context and relationship w/ other class learning activities)
    - 1 minute revision: What is learning?
  - 11:25am–12:00pm: Learning through Writing
- History & Theory
  - 12:00–1:00pm: Lunch (guest speaker)
  - 1:00–2:45pm: Low-Stakes Writing-to-Learn Workshop
    - Defining Low-Stakes Writing in Terms of QEP SLOs
    - Designing Low-Stakes Writing-to-Learn Exercises
    - Completing participants' exercises
    - Reflecting on learning
  - 2:45pm: Wrap-Up, Homework, Ticket Out
    - Electronic reflection
    - Homework:
      - Reading: TBA

- Doing: try to implement a low-stakes writing activity
- Bring: detailed "major paper" assignment prompt if you have one

Workshop 2: February 10, 2012
- 8:30–9:00am: Breakfast & Chatting
- 9:00–9:20am: Free-write: How did implementation go? (if not, why not?)
- 9:20am: How to Assign Writing When Writing is Hard to Do [Karen]
  - (20–30 minutes) group work/presentation: What are the challenges and how are you already solving the problems?
  - Examples of how to address
  - Include a break . . .

- 11:20am: Guest Speaker
- 12:00–1pm: Lunch (Library Promo)
- 1:00–2:45pm: How to Design/Construct a Formal/Research Assignment in Light of the QEP SLOs
  - Guidelines to help/guide thinking
  - Scaffolding, due dates along the way
  - Objectives as well as how to motivate students to do the assignment
  - Alternative assignments: big paper vs. multiple mini papers
  - Attach to QEP Writing Rubric
- 2:45pm: Wrap-Up, Homework, Ticket Out
  - Wrap up—electronic—(same as day 1)
  - Homework—identify and post to Bb a writing sample specific to your discipline; look for an article on writing in your discipline and bring the abstract

Workshop 3: February 24, 2012
- 8:30–9:00am: Breakfast & Chatting
- 9:00am: Writing/Welcome
- 9:20am: That's Not How WE Do It: Writing in the Disciplines
- 11:20am: Guest Presenters as a panel (writing/research different disciplines) What are the genres in your field? How did you learn them? How do you teach them?
- 12:00–1:00pm: Lunch (CLT Promo)
- 1:00–2:45pm:
  - Workshop Write-to-Learn activities
  - Continue developing your formal writing assignment
- 2:45pm: Wrap-Up, Homework, Ticket Out

Workshop 4: March 16, 2012

- 8:30–9:00am: Breakfast & Chatting
- 9:00am: Case Activity: short project w/different scenarios of what they have to help grade
- 9:20am: Throw Me a Lifeline: Managing and Grading Written Work Using the QEP Writing Rubric
- 11:20am: Guest Presenter (potentially panel sharing how)
- 12:00–1:00pm (Writing Center Promo)
- 1:00–2:45:
  - Workshop formal writing assignment
  - Continue developing rubrics
- 2:45pm: Wrap-Up, Homework, Ticket Out

Workshop 5: March 30, 2012

- 8:30–9:00am: Breakfast & Chatting
- 9:00am: Does It Have to Be a 20-page Paper? Alternatives to traditional term/research papers
- 12:00–1:00pm (QEP Action Project Promo)
- 1:00–2:45: Presentations/digital poster session
- 2:45pm: Wrap-Up, Summative Workshop Assessment

APPENDIX 14.B

ODU QEP Writing Rubric

QEP Writing Rubric*

Student Learning Outcomes	Exceeds Standard 4	Meets Standard 3	Approaches Standard 2	Needs Attention 1
1. Students will be able to clearly state a focused problem, question, or topic appropriate for the purpose of the task.	The topic statement is comprehensive, clearly stated, creative, focused, manageable, and demonstrating of the clear understanding of the purpose of the task.	The topic statement is clearly stated, focused, manageable, and demonstrates adequate consideration of the purpose of the task.	The topic statement is ambiguous and too broadly or narrowly focused, but demonstrates awareness of the purpose of the task.	The topic statement is weak (or missing) and demonstrates minimal knowledge of the purpose of the task.
2. Students will be able to identify relevant knowledge and credible sources.	Identified sources are relevant, credible, and high quality.	Identified sources are mostly relevant and credible.	Identified sources are minimally relevant and credible.	Identified sources are not relevant or credible (or are missing).
3. Students will be able to synthesize information and multiple viewpoints related to the problem, question, or topic.	Evidence is synthesized to reveal insightful patterns, differences, and similarities among multiple viewpoints.	Evidence is synthesized to reveal patterns, differences, and similarities among multiple viewpoints.	Evidence is minimally synthesized and may not reveal patterns, differences, and similarities among multiple viewpoints.	Evidence is not synthesized to reveal patterns, differences, and similarities among multiple viewpoints (or is missing).
4. Students will be able to apply appropriate research methods or theoretical framework to the problem, question, or topic.	The critical elements of the methodology or theoretical framework are skillfully developed or described to address the problem, question, or topic.	The critical elements of the methodology or theoretical framework are satisfactorily developed or described to address the problem, question, or topic.	The critical elements of the methodology or theoretical framework are minimally developed or described to address the problem, question, or topic.	The critical elements of the methodology or theoretical framework are weak (or missing).

Continued

Continued from previous page

Student Learning Outcomes	Exceeds Standard	Meets Standard	Approaches Standard	Needs Attention
	4	3	2	1
5. Students will be able to formulate conclusions that are logically tied to inquiry findings and consider applications, limitations, and implications.	The stated conclusion thoroughly evaluates and organizes all essential information and is the logical outcome of inquiry.	The stated conclusion evaluates and relates logically to all essential information.	The stated conclusion minimally evaluates and relates logically to some essential information.	The stated conclusion is absent or weakly evaluates essential information (or is missing).
6. Students will be able to reflect on or evaluate what was learned.	Reflection of results shows a strong relationship among content, lessons learned, and/or changes in personal perspective.	Reflection of results shows a relationship among content, lessons learned, and/ or changes in personal perspective.	Reflection of results shows a minimal relationship among content, lessons learned, and/or changes in personal perspective.	Reflection of results shows a weak or no relationship among content, lessons learned, and/or changes in personal perspective (or is missing).

Notes:

NA (Not Applicable) means that the artifact cannot be rated on the SLO

NR (Not Required) means that the SLO was not a required part of the assignment or prompt

*Rubric based on Inquiry and Analysis, Written Communication, and Critical Thinking VALUE Rubrics presented in Rhodes, T. L., ed. 2010. *Assessing Outcomes and Improving Achievement: Tips and Tools for Using Rubrics.* Washington, DC: Association of American Colleges and Universities. Also available online at http://www.aacu.org/value/

APPENDIX 14.C. FSSE CONSORTIUM FOR THE STUDY OF WRITING IN COLLEGE QUESTIONS

Supplemental Questions

1. Do you include writing assignments (as described above) in your selected course section?

   [All remaining questions are asked only of respondents who answered "Yes" to this question.]

2. For how many writing assignments was it encouraged or required to:
   [all assignments/most assignments/some assignments/few assignments/ no assignments]

   2A. Brainstorm (list ideas, map concepts, prepare an outline, etc.) to develop ideas before they started drafting the assignment

   2B. Talk with you to develop ideas before they started drafting the assignment

   2C. Visit a campus-based writing or tutoring center to get help with the writing assignment before turning it in

   2D. Use an online tutoring service to get help with a writing assignment before turning it in

   2E. Proofread their final draft for errors before turning it in

3. How many writing assignments asked students to:
   [all assignments/most assignments/some assignments/few assignments/ no assignments]

   3A. Narrate or describe one of their experiences

   3B. Summarize something they read, such as articles, books, or online publications

   3C. Analyze or evaluate something they read, researched, or observed

   3D. Describe their methods or findings related to data they collected in lab or fieldwork, a survey project, etc.

   3E. Argue a position using evidence and reasoning

   3F. Explain in writing the meaning of numerical or statistical data

   3G. Write in the style and format of a specific field (engineering, history, psychology, etc.)

   3H. Include drawings, tables, photos, screenshots, or other visual content in a written assignment

   3I. Create a project with multimedia (web page, poster, slide presentation such as PowerPoint, etc.)

4. For how many writing assignments did you:
   [all assignments/most assignments/some assignments/few assignments/ no assignments]

4A. Provide clear instructions describing what you wanted your students to do

4B. Explain in advance what you wanted your students to learn

4C. Explain in advance the criteria you would use to grade the assignment

4D. Help your students understand your assignment and grading criteria by providing a sample of a completed assignment

4E. Require students to give feedback to one another about drafts or outlines they had written

4F. Provide feedback to students on a draft before they turned in their final assignment

4G. Ask students to complete a group writing project

4H. Ask students to address a real or imagined audience such as their classmates, a politician, non-expert, etc.

APPENDIX 14.D

ODU QEP Workshop Participants' Survey

QEP Workshop Participants' Luncheon Survey—October 23, 2012

I.

Please indicate whether you strongly agree, agree, somewhat agree, disagree, or strongly disagree with each of the following statements:

	Strongly Agree	Agree	Somewhat Agree	Disagree	Strongly Disagree
A. I am satisfied with the training I received during the QEP Workshops.					
B. I believe the training I received during the Workshops aptly prepared me to implement my new writing practices in my courses					
C. I would be interested in attending a follow-up, more advanced workshop on QEP 'write-to-learn' techniques.					

II. How have you used the 'write to learn' techniques highlighted in the QEP Workshops?

III. Have you used the QEP Rubric and made it available to students? If so, has holistic scoring been helpful?

IV. How have you assessed the effectiveness of the new writing techniques you've incorporated (i.e., participation has increased, grades have improved, etc.)?

V. What has been the most helpful tool you've received from participating in the QEP Workshops?

VI. What other kinds of follow-up sessions should be made available to QEP Workshop participants?

Notes

1. The SACSCOC Handbook for Institutions Seeking Affirmation states: "The Quality Enhancement Plan (QEP) is the component of the reaffirmation process that reflects and affirms the commitment of the Commission on Colleges to enhancing the quality of higher education in the region and to focusing attention on student learning. The QEP describes a carefully designed course of action that addresses a well-defined and focused topic or issue related to enhancing student learning and/or the environment supporting student learning and accomplishing the mission of the institution" (SACSCOC 2011, 39).

2. Since 2004, the Southern Association of Colleges and Schools (SACS) has mandated the development of Quality Enhancement Plans (QEPs) at the institutions under its jurisdiction. More than 40 of the SACS schools that have come up for reaccreditation between 2004 and 2012, including Old Dominion University, have designed QEPs that are rooted in writing across the curriculum (WAC) and writing in the disciplines (WID) principles (Neff 2012).

3. RU/H stands for Research University/High research activity according to the Carnegie classifications. www.carnegiefoundation.org 8/12/13.

4. This study received IRB exemption from Old Dominion University.

5. While there isn't room to discuss the matter in-depth here, for a thorough delineation of ethical issues surrounding assessing faculty, see "Identifying Lurking Alligators: An Essay on the Ethical Dimensions of Faculty Development" by Anita Gandolfo, in *Innovative Higher Education*, Winter 97, Vol. 22 Issue 2, 135–150.

References

Condon, William, and Carol Rutz. 2012. "A Taxonomy of Writing Across the Curriculum Programs: Evolving to Serve Broader Agendas." *College Composition and Communication* 64 (2): 357–82.

Hubball, Harry, Anthony Clarke, and Andrea L. Beach. 2004. "Assessing Faculty Learning Communities." *New Directions for Teaching and Learning* 2004 (97): 87–100. http://dx.doi.org/10.1002/tl.136.

Neff, Joyce. 2012. "University Accreditation and Learning through Writing: Can This Marriage Last?" Paper presented at the International Writing Across the Curriculum Conference, Savannah, Georgia, June 8.

Old Dominion University. 2012. *Improving Disciplinary Writing: Quality Enhancement Plan 2012*. Norfolk, VA: Old Dominion University.

Russell, David R. 2012 (2002). "The Writing-Across-the-Curriculum Movement: 1970–1990." *In Writing Across the Curriculum: A Critical Sourcebook*, ed. Terry Myers Zawacki, and Paul M. Rogers, 15–45. New York: Bedford/St. Martin's. Originally published in *Writing in the Academic Disciplines: A Curricular History*, 2nd ed. Carbondale: Southern Illinois University Press.

Southern Association of Colleges and Schools Commission on Colleges (SACSCOC). 2011. "Handbook for Institutions Seeking Affirmation 2011." Accessed August 19, 2013. http://www.sacscoc.org/handbooks.asp.

Thaiss, Chris, and Tara Porter. 2010. "The State of WAC/WID in 2010: Methods and Results of the U.S. Survey of the International WAC/WID Mapping Project." *College Composition and Communication* 61 (3): 524–70.

15

FROM THE OUTSIDE IN

Creating a Culture of Writing through a QEP

Angela Green, Iris Saltiel, and Kyle Christiansen

When the Southern Association of Colleges and Schools (SACS) declared that reaffirmation would require all institutions to implement a Quality Enhancement Plan (QEP), the faculty and administration at Columbus State University (CSU) sought to satisfy the requirement in a manner that would substantially change the academic culture in order to enhance the education of all students. After considering many possible areas for improvements, faculty, staff, students, and administrators devised a QEP that would focus on increasing the use of writing and the teaching of writing across all departments and disciplines. When the QEP was first implemented, it was a voluntary endeavor, with faculty opting to participate or not. Given the nature of the plan, incentives had to be created to engage faculty in a process of reorganizing their instruction not to include more writing assignments per se, but to integrate the use of writing-thinking assignments as a method of learning and as a demonstration of what was learned. Five years later, as part of SACS review process, CSU was reaffirmed, with the five-year QEP Impact Report receiving full approval.

This chapter explores how we built a culture of writing through a QEP program committed to creating an environment of rewards for voluntary faculty involvement. First, the chapter provides an overview of the CSU QEP, including our roles in the QEP administrative structure, the key things that we learned, the background within which the QEP was developed, and an account of some of the goals associated with this plan. Second, a discussion of key programming struggles follows, with emphasis on lessons learned from these struggles and potential implications for other institutions, particularly those institutions implementing changes on a voluntary basis. As part of this discussion on struggles, we briefly consider an especially challenging struggle we faced and that

DOI: 10.7330/9781607324355.c015

others considering making similar changes at their institutions will also face: collecting, analyzing, and assessing data for a voluntary initiative. Third, we overview the effects and outcomes—some unanticipated—of the QEP in the hope that sharing the impact we witnessed might help leaders of other programs foster change at their own institutions.

While it is easy enough to identify the value of writing, improving it, and then measuring and communicating that improvement, are other matters entirely. Choosing to focus on writing in a QEP presents unique challenges given that writing is a skill that develops slowly and must be honed regularly through practice with actual writing that engaged readers respond to. Moreover, what constitutes good writing varies greatly depending upon the discipline, purpose, audience, and genre, meaning that students should be taught writing across the entire curriculum and not just in first-year composition classes. Such teaching requires time, patience, and training, regardless of one's subject area or the skill or experience level of the professor. It is also inherently difficult to measure improvement in writing and to know what "counts" as a measure that is acceptable to others, including accreditors. All of these considerations require a considerable institutional commitment from the administration and faculty, including time, money, faculty buy-in and support, and staff resources. This is especially true when a program is implemented on a voluntary basis, as ours was.

It is difficult to say if our attempt to create a culture of writing would have achieved any traction without the SACS requirement, given the vast changes that occurred in the university's leadership, organizational structure, and budget over the reaffirmation period. It is clear, however, that the QEP held faculty and administrators accountable to the plan we devised together to (1) assess students' learning needs, (2) come up with a workable plan, (3) implement and sustain the plan over five years, and (4) measure and articulate the plan's impact. The SACS requirement made the plan to improve student writing a required shared priority, and having an external mandate fostered real internal change that might not have happened otherwise.

QEP OVERVIEW
Who We Are and What We Learned

The three authors of this chapter supported the QEP in various roles: the writing specialist focused on faculty development to support student writing; the director of the Center for the Enhancement of Teaching and Learning oversaw the QEP and the five-year QEP Impact Report;

and the director of the Social Research Center gathered and analyzed most of the data collected for assessment purposes. In writing this chapter we called upon the five QEP Annual Reports, along with the Impact Report submitted as part of the SACS reaffirmation process, all of which are available on the CSU website.

Although student writing did show improvement, the most promising finding was in the ways that faculty across disciplines approached the teaching of writing. There was a fundamental shift in faculty attitudes about the role that writing can play in classrooms across the university. Some 91 percent of faculty participated in the QEP, many in multiple ways. With more faculty using writing in more classes, writing became more visible to the entire university community and became a featured part of events recognizing student achievements. Writing moved from being the responsibility of the English department to being viewed as the responsibility of all, as well as a significant mode of teaching and learning in any subject. This shift in norms led to a culture of writing at Columbus State University.

Background and Key Initiatives

Columbus State University is a regional state university in the southeast with 8,200 students. It began as a junior college in 1958, became a four-year institution in 1970, and achieved university status in 1996. It offers forty-six undergraduate and forty-two graduate degrees, and serves a highly diverse student body, including many non-traditional students and military members and their families. CSU is similar to many regional colleges and universities across the country in that it serves a diverse constituency and is constantly growing and adapting to meet community needs.

In 2007, SACS approved the writing-focused QEP. The year following the introduction of the QEP, a new university president was appointed, which ushered in a period of significant change in university priorities and caused some uncertainty among faculty and staff. The same year saw a near-collapse of the national economy, which greatly hindered funding in state higher education systems. These factors provided a rather tumultuous environment to implement a QEP, especially one dependent upon voluntary participation.

As was the case with the first QEPs at institutions seeking reaffirmation under the 2002–2006 edition of the *Principles of Accreditation: Foundations for Quality Enhancement,* CSU proposed and was approved to engage in a very ambitious Quality Enhancement Plan. Entitled "Writing the Solution: Steps toward Developing Competent and Professional Student Writers," the plan began fall 2007. From the beginning, the QEP Committee viewed the SACS requirement as a means to profoundly affect the university by enhancing the culture of teaching and learning (Columbus State University 2006). The QEP created the infrastructure for professional development activities for faculty to improve student learning through writing and rewarded faculty for participating in QEP activities. To catalyze a positive transformation of students' academic experiences, faculty were helped through professional development activities and the funding of grants and fellowships to hone their abilities to teach writing in their disciplines. These activities proved especially helpful during a time when faculty were asked to do more with less and pay raises were frozen for the indefinite future. To have required such pedagogical changes, even with compensation, likely would have worsened morale even if it ensured compliance. By offering stipends, honorariums, and other resources for faculty to improve the teaching of writing, we were able to leverage the positive aspects of a voluntary program.

To support faculty with the integration, evaluation, and improvement of student writing, a three-pronged approach was used to encourage participation. Opportunities for involvement—each discussed in more detail below—were plentiful, ranging from attending a workshop or forum, participating on the QEP advisory board, serving as a rater in a Universal Prompt reading session, to receipt of a grant for a yearlong fellowship. In the five-year span of the QEP, 66 percent of faculty attended at least one program, with more than 75 percent of that number attending more than one program. In FY2011, over 50 percent of CSU faculty participated in a QEP-related program, with all colleges represented.

Budget and Oversight at a Glance

Although the QEP was run through the Faculty Center for the Enhancement of Teaching and Learning, administration and supervision over the QEP was provided through an oversight committee and an advisory committee, established in fall 2007. As a university committee, the QEP advisory committee provided the institutional infrastructure necessary to ensure that the QEP would be kept in the forefront at CSU. Careful attention was paid to include faculty from every college on the advisory committee, including the library, along with student representatives, with subcommittees formed to oversee grants, fellowships, faculty and student awards, and other matters. The advisory committee met a minimum of twice per semester, typically over a catered lunch.

Table 15.1. QEP budget overview

	FY08	FY09	FY10	FY11	FY12	Total
Faculty Writing Fellowships	12,000	10,000	10,000	10,000	12,000	54,000
Grants	15,800	17,791	19,850	9,100	11,920	74,461
Outstanding English 1101 and 1102 Essay Awards	1,000	1,000	None awarded	1,000	1,000	4,000
Outstanding Teacher of Writing Award	10,900	11,000	10,000	11,000	11,000	53,900
Other Student Awards				1,500	500	2,000
Dollars Spent	39,700	39,791	39,850	32,600	36,420	188,361

Monies were budgeted and spent on professional development, writing and teaching awards, fellowships, and grants (Table 15.1). Not included in this table are the monies spent on books and other teaching resources, funds for workshop and conference travel, honoraria for assessment raters, or compensation for attendance at intensive workshops over breaks.

Faculty Grants and Programs

Throughout the QEP period, grants were awarded for a variety of purposes, including inviting writing experts to campus, funding travel and materials for writing-related conferences, and supporting faculty research on writing and learning. Grantees were required to submit progress reports showing how their grant funds were used and to what effect. A report from one such project is included in appendix 15.A and provides but one example of the kinds of projects the QEP was used to support. They were also encouraged to share their experiences with other faculty, and many were invited to serve on the QEP advisory committee and/or subcommittees to review future grant applications.

Grant-funded opportunities enabled faculty to learn about teaching and assessing writing; however, a deeper understanding and the capacity to transform all of one's courses came through participation in the Faculty Writing Fellows program. Launched in fall 2007 as a full-year endeavor, the Faculty Writing Fellows program assisted faculty in using writing as a means of improving student learning in their courses. Approximately five Fellows per year were chosen to work with the writing specialist in a series of workshops about writing pedagogy. In seminar-type meetings in the fall term, faculty learned about the connections between writing and thinking, writing and learning, and how writing and thinking differ by discipline. They also learned to incorporate more writing, or to break down complex assignments into a series of "scaffolded" smaller assignments, for at least one spring course. During the spring term, they instituted changes that they designed and worked through how best to respond to student writing, provide strategies for students, and devise rubrics. Workshops throughout the year helped the Fellows to assess the ways that the teaching of writing affects students' learning. These workshops covered topics such as effective assignment design, sequencing of low- and high-stakes assignments, responding to student writing, dealing with academic honesty, working with second-language students, using peer review, and preparing students to give a presentation about what they learned at the Celebration of Student Writing, an event created to honor student writing and effective writing instruction.

Over the first five years, twenty-seven faculty (representing eighteen of twenty-one departments) were selected as Writing Fellows. As a result, 86 percent of university departments currently house faculty who have participated, impacting their course design and daily classroom activities to achieve better writing among students. In addition to preparing their students to present at the Celebration of Student Writing, Fellows during the QEP period submitted a final report indicating how the experience affected their teaching and their students' learning. Many Fellows also went on to serve on the QEP advisory committee and/or its subcommittees to help select future Fellows.

Collectively, the monetary and professional incentives associated with the QEP played a critical role in the success of the CSU QEP. Faculty received strong incentives regarding promotion and tenure for participation in the QEP. Faculty who attended QEP functions or served as Fellows all received notifications regarding attendance and participation to support their promotion and tenure dossiers. Individuals who had previously participated in QEP activities were also eligible to compete for the Outstanding Teacher of Writing Award, given out annually during the Celebration of Student Writing and accompanied by a $1000 prize. This award was established to recognize faculty for substantial contributions to teaching writing in the disciplines. A call for applicants took place annually, and faculty packets were judged by a subcommittee of the QEP advisory committee.

As noted earlier, implementing a program that depends almost entirely on faculty participation likely would not have been possible without the funding made available through the QEP budget. While the economic downturn affected funding, the plan facilitated change by prudent use of resources and maximizing the momentum provided by the early years. We had faculty's goodwill to use to stretch our budget. Equally important, however, the QEP itself made the university accountable to see the plan through. Without that as leverage, it is impossible to say whether our commitment to improving student writing would have survived various rounds of budget cuts.

Initial Goals and Intended Outcomes of the QEP

Since *A Nation At Risk* came out in 1983, educational reform has been discussed in the political arena (United States National Commission on Excellence in Education 1983). Regional and professional accreditation bodies like SACS have been forceful in requiring specific learning and program outcomes in the pursuit of improving the quality of education, specifically higher education (Columbia State University 2006). The QEP might actually be an instance where the changes are designed, implemented, and done right because it is not heavy-handed and gives institutions broad discretion in determining what to improve and how to do it. While the choice of *what* to improve is up to each institution, the outcomes must nonetheless be clear, specific, and measurable, even though institutions may revise their measurement tools and means of achieving their goals as situations merit. To help illustrate how our university attempted to tackle the enormous and often amorphous goal of improving writing, we outline below the main objectives of our QEP. In writing the five-year impact report we discovered that we needed to reprioritize our goals, replacing Goal 3 with Goal 1, since in hindsight we realized that while building an infrastructure for faculty development was indeed essential to our overall success, the most important goal of all was improving student learning. In short, this reordering of goals kept us centered on asking the question, "In what way(s) does faculty development impact and enhance writing pedagogy across the disciplines?"

The three fundamental goals for the CSU QEP, and their accompanying outcomes, are listed below:

OUTCOMES FOR GOAL 1: TO ESTABLISH WRITING AS A MODE FOR ENHANCED STUDENT LEARNING IN UNDERGRADUATE COURSES AND PROGRAMS

- Competent student writing will exhibit critical thinking, style, and fluency appropriate to the audience and task, consistency in focus and reasoning, structural integrity, and mastery of standard edited English.

- Students will demonstrate less apprehension at scholarly writing.
- Students will submit their work to scholarly journals and/or present at scholarly conferences.

OUTCOMES FOR GOAL 2: TO ENHANCE FACULTY AND STAFF KNOWLEDGE, SKILLS, AND ATTITUDES RELATED TO STUDENT WRITING

- Faculty members will identify areas for pedagogical improvement regarding writing and develop appropriate writing standards and assessment methods.
- Communication about writing will increase among faculty, students, and staff.
- Participating faculty will become more competent with integrating writing assignments into the curriculum, evaluating learning through writing assignments, and improving student writing competencies.
- Priority for and emphasis on student writing will increase.

OUTCOMES FOR GOAL 3: TO PROVIDE INFRASTRUCTURE FOR STUDENT AND FACULTY PROFESSIONAL DEVELOPMENT ACTIVITIES

- QEP oversight committee and advisory committee will be established.
- A budget will be established to provide awards, release time, and/ or monetary rewards for excellent teaching and learning through writing.
- Faculty will be provided incentives to enhance student writing in the classroom as well as learning through writing.

Achieving any or all of these goals would require a sea change in attitude about writing and its relation to critical thinking. Simply requiring faculty to assign more writing would not move us any closer to realizing these objectives because a majority of faculty already assigned a substantial amount of writing in their classes. Adding more writing to the curriculum was not likely to effect the realization that writing plays a crucial role in learning itself. For those faculty who did not to assign writing either for personal reasons, because of class size or workload issues, or because they deemed it less applicable to their fields, a requirement to assign writing (or more of it) certainly would have faced even greater hurdles than a voluntary plan did. For these reasons, we decided that changing minds must precede changing the curriculum, and if our university did not value writing as a mode of learning rather than a means of documenting learning, the plan stood little chance of succeeding. Those who did not see the value of writing would have ample opportunities to find out for themselves if and how writing could affect learning.

Prior to the QEP, the teaching of writing occurred primarily in first-year composition classes taught by the English department. In courses in their majors, students most often wrote traditional term papers and essay exams but had little, if any, instruction on the ways of thinking and writing specific to a given discipline. Writing process pedagogy, however, says that students' high-stakes (i.e., formal) writing will improve (1) if faculty assign low-stakes writing (writing-to-learn activities that count for only a small portion of the final grade) and allow it to be revised before demanding high-stakes writing (formal, polished writing to demonstrate learning); and (2) if faculty are involved in the process of helping students produce high-stakes writing by breaking a large, complex writing assignment into manageable stages. Thus, the QEP sought to (1) incorporate a greater variety of high- and low-stakes writing in courses across disciplines, (2) encourage faculty to make explicit the ways of knowing their disciplines, (3) provide students with opportunities and strategies for revision, and (4) have faculty share with colleagues best practices in creating and responding to student writing.

Creating a Culture of Writing

Changing the culture surrounding writing often precedes tangible results and requires considerable time and energy. The QEP development committees believed that the best way to improve student writing proficiency was through faculty development. The key was to increase the number of faculty across disciplines who value student writing, know how to teach writing in their specialty area, and incorporate meaningful writing activities into student learning experiences in courses.

Faculty often understand the writing process with their own scholarship, but guiding the process for students requires a different skill set. Thus, it was necessary to sustain faculty development across the curriculum over the full five years. Creating an infrastructure to carry out these faculty development activities was essential. The QEP oversight committee included faculty from across campus who had expressed an interest in improved writing instruction and had helped establish writing as the QEP's objective. One of the lead writers of the original plan, in fact, was a senior faculty member in business with prior experience teaching writing. Another extremely active participant came from the biology department. It cannot be overstated how valuable it was to have members and leaders of the initiative from outside of the English department who could garner wide support for QEP objectives across the campus. Out of this diverse body, various subcommittees were formed to review grant and fellowship applications. Often, previous grantees and fellows were asked to serve because of their intensive experience with the QEP and their willingness to share their experiences with other faculty. Such members were crucial to our efforts because (1) they gave faculty across every college a voice in planning and oversight, (2) they believed that the teaching of writing "belongs" to everyone and is not the sole province of the English department, and (3) they helped circulate information about the QEP, especially opportunities for funding of writing-related projects during a period of scarce funding. In short, they were excellent ambassadors for the use of writing as a mode of learning and as a way to reinvigorate teaching in general.

In order to achieve the goals of the QEP, faculty also needed to buy into using writing as a mode of instruction, and the university had to make doing so worthwhile for those faculty. The initial QEP budget included monies to hire part-time instructors to take over one class for a term and give a faculty member extra time to spend on the teaching of writing. Even when budget cuts curtailed the availability of immediate financial benefit, the momentum to participate was sustained because faculty had already realized the benefits of using writing and saw the impact on students. The extrinsic rewards initially provided by the QEP were supplemented by the intrinsic rewards of teaching courses enriched by writing, and faculty continued teaching writing-enriched classes even without a reduction in teaching load or credit hours generated.

Continuing faculty involvement in the QEP was reinforced by several efforts. To optimize faculty support for the QEP and reaccreditation effort, faculty forums were held to develop and promote writing pedagogy and listen to concerns about writing. Topics for workshops and seminars were identified through formal surveys taken by faculty as well as informal conversations with faculty. Workshops on writing were held to help faculty develop discipline-appropriate writing standards and best practices in creating writing assignments, ensuring that the QEP and other program standards were addressed. Faculty were educated about the processes involved in writing to learn: that writing to learn is thinking on paper and working through one's ideas; that writing is a nonlinear process of drafting, reviewing, and revising; that everyone's process and rituals are different.

Ongoing faculty forums and lunch-and-learn type meetings provided feedback to faculty about the impact the QEP was having on student performance. These events also showed faculty that the extra effort was worthwhile and that they were not alone in the process. The social nature of the QEP events helped recruit more faculty to engage in QEP activities. With faculty development events happening several times a month, a good deal of energy was injected into the process of program implementation.

Getting faculty to attend these events is notoriously difficult, so it was crucial that the administration from the department level on up articulated the value of the QEP by rewarding participation in QEP programming in tenure and promotion reviews. All faculty received letters for participation, which helped bolster the teaching component of their promotion and tenure dossiers. This component is currently the most important aspect of job performance for promotion and tenure considerations, so materials in this area are highly sought after. QEP participation letters sent a loud and clear message that faculty's time would not be wasted. Moreover, faculty were encouraged to provide feedback on all programming activities both immediately after events and at later dates to follow up on whether and to what extend they had found such programming useful in the classroom.

As faculty required more students to write as part of their learning, more and more students sought assistance through the Writing Center. As a result, the Writing Center expanded access to students on campus and online. In fact, the Writing Center was an integral component of the infrastructure through which the QEP fostered a culture of writing. Although it existed long before the QEP, the Writing Center not only saw increased traffic because of the QEP but also became a valuable partner in programming. The Writing Center director was integrally involved in planning, leading workshops for faculty and students, managing essay contests, and assessing the QEP's impact. It should be noted that the institutional support for the writing specialist and the director of the Writing Center were both critical components in this effort. Combining or consolidating roles would have proved to be too much work for a single individual. In addition, the Writing Center played a significant role in increasing students' confidence in their writing abilities. Eighty-seven percent of students who visited the Writing Center over the five years of the QEP reported they "strongly agree" with the statement, "The Writing Center increases my confidence and overall success at CSU." Ninety-two percent strongly agreed that consulting the Writing Center had improved their current writing assignments, while 84 percent strongly agreed that their overall writing had improved.

Student and faculty engagement with writing has been increased through the QEP in other ways as well. Student writing has been showcased through university events and publishing of a journal featuring undergraduate research, as well as an annual collection of research abstracts for students who present work at conferences. As mentioned earlier, an annual Celebration of Student Writing now highlights the writing-related projects of students taught by the Faculty Fellows, and annual Student Writing Awards recognize outstanding essays by first-year students. Even now, Faculty Writing Fellows are selected and supported annually. Faculty Forums and workshops on writing pedagogy are held annually. Competitive QEP grants have funded various innovations in the teaching of writing, and recipients of the Outstanding Teacher of Writing Awards are recognized for the way they demonstrate the vital role of teaching effective writing.

In short, the importance of reinforcing writing proficiency across the curriculum was given a huge boost because of the QEP and continues to grow as an integral component of CSU's educational mission and campus culture. The QEP gave faculty a means to focus on working with students to develop professional writing appropriate to their disciplines and resulted in various revisions and changes across departments, including adoption of innovative new assignments, development of new instructional materials, and the expansion of writing across the curriculum. The signs of cultural change could also be seen in the number of faculty who assigned writing and the kinds of writing they assigned after participating in QEP programming. In fall 2011, more than half of faculty surveyed about writing assignments in classes reported that the way they taught writing had changed as a result of participation in QEP programming. To quote Barry J. Morris, who spoke of the impact of the QEP at Kennesaw State, a sister university in the USG system, "We've made the Quality Enhancement Plan part of our DNA" (Connell 2011). We believe that is what SACS intended when they required institutions to focus on an area that would impact student learning. Rhodes (2012) described the role of accreditors as a powerhouse in the drive for student learning. That was certainly our experience.

CHALLENGES MET IN CARRYING OUT THE PLAN

Despite the success of the QEP, there were many obstacles to carrying out the plan's objectives and particularly in collecting relevant data. Changes in personnel and revisions of instruments for assessing student writing contributed to greater degrees of difficulty in analyzing and interpreting the available data so as to explain what the university had accomplished. An additional factor was the economic downturn that the state and nation experienced soon after our QEP began, which made it challenging to sustain the university's resource commitment to improve student writing. Fortunately, the QEP already enjoyed widespread support from faculty, which gave it momentum and spared it from deeper budget cuts. However, we found that you "never really know what combination of factors ultimately contribute to the final, desired outcome" (McElroy and Cobb 2010, 18). The buy-in across the university and the excellent administration by all members of the QEP team kept the project moving despite the severe complications provided by budget cuts and leadership transitions.

Many changes to the initial plan resulted from realizing that the scope and reach of the QEP were too ambitious and not dedicated consistently to our primary goal. We streamlined our effort to improve and assess student writing. Other changes were made in response to the realities of implementing the plan during an economic recession along with administrative personnel and leadership changes. Because the goals of the QEP were designed to be completed in a particular order, there were times when we felt like we were building a boat and floating it at the same time (Loughman et al. 2008).

Personnel Turnover

The challenge that personnel turnover presents is simply, "You don't know what you do not know." Each position in our QEP experienced turnover. The founding director of the QEP returned to a full-time faculty position after a little more than 2 years in the position. Nine months later, a new director began. One position created for the QEP, a writing specialist, started in July 2007 and left two years later. Again, a few months later, a replacement was hired. An administrative assistant who was hired at the start of the project left after one year and the position was not replaced. The QEP relied on other offices that also experienced turnover. The director of the Writing Center, the director of the First-Year Composition program, the director of Institutional Research, as well as the SACS liaison all experienced turnover. The impact of starting up again with a new person cannot be underestimated.

While we can only speculate about how these personnel changes might have affected a different QEP, we can say with certainty that it was quite difficult, at times, to keep the momentum going in our program since accountability for the plan's success was so broadly dispersed as not to feel particularly urgent as the clock ticked on reaffirmation. Those of us hired last and tasked with managing as well as carrying out the QEP felt the passage of time more acutely, however, and had to hit the ground running to make up for lost time during the hiring process and first weeks and months on the job. A mandatory program likely would have a more centralized operation, whereas at CSU, different offices handled the various moving parts of the plan. The first order of business for the new team was restructuring and reorganizing both the oversight committee and the advisory board to reflect changes at the university and to regroup our efforts as a collective enterprise. One idea we came up with to ensure continuity was to invite all past members of both groups to come back or to remain on the board.

Assessment Focus and Design

According to Rhodes (2012), requirements of regional accrediting bodies are changing the very way higher education operates. Measurement is required and ensures that programs are linked to the university. Accountability through accreditation focuses the attention on outcomes and how they impact student learning (Jackson et al. 2010). Our focus on faculty development sometimes allowed student learning to take a backseat. In short, faculty development activities proved to be low-hanging fruit, far easier to document than gains in student learning, which take extensive time and sensitive tools to measure.

As might be expected, directly assessing student writing was the most challenging aspect of the QEP. Within the first two years, it was obvious that the original instrument and research design for assessing changes in student writing was impractical to implement on a large scale and on a sustained basis, especially as economic conditions worsened. This section highlights the problems encountered with the initial assessment plan and the subsequent creation and use of a new assessment model that involved a universal, course-embedded writing prompt, the "Universal Prompt."

At the outset of devising the goals and objectives of the QEP, CSU used the Cognitive Level and Quality Writing Assessment (CLAQWA), designed by Flateby and Metzger (2001, 1999), to establish baseline data for the QEP. In the *First Monitoring Report* (CSU, August 30, 2007), CSU outlined the findings of the fall 2006 and spring 2007 baseline sampling and data collection, using the CLAQWA rubric for analyses. The CLAQWA-based assessment plan, however, was hampered by administrative and logistical difficulties. In addition to the complex, sixteen-trait rubric used to assess it, the CLAQWA was administered outside of class and was thus not tied to any given course or its learning objectives.

The difficulties of the CLAQWA led to an experiment, first run in fall 2007, in English 1101 and English 1102, with the Universal Prompt as a course-embedded writing prompt, the responses to which would be assessed on a six-trait, rather than a sixteen-trait, rubric. The Universal Prompt asks students to write a reflective essay on their learning, describe how it relates to a course outcome, how particular coursework helped them achieve that outcome, and how what they learned will be valuable in future endeavors. Students were motivated to participate because they earned a grade/extra credit for their work. In the first year of implementation, CSU piloted the instrument to assess over 60 pieces of student writing, resulting in a revision of the scoring rubric to include cognitive descriptors aligned with Bloom's taxonomy. The prompt was then made available to faculty teaching any course at any level across campus. As the 2008–09 academic year began, the QEP team adopted the Universal Prompt, keeping it voluntary for faculty to distribute in classes and providing feedback to participating instructors such that participation in QEP writing assessment would be attractive to all. By encouraging faculty to use the prompt to help students reflect on their own learning in the course, writing became more visible on campus. In addition, faculty who assigned the Universal Prompt (even those who did not participate in distributed assessment) began to see the usefulness of having a short but telling piece of writing to assign during the latter half of a semester that revealed not only their students' strengths and weaknesses as writers but also what students believed they had learned in their courses.

To better understand how the prompt allowed us to assess writing, it is important to see the six traits of competent and professional writers as defined by the Universal Prompt rubric:

- Trait 1: Assignment Requirements: the degree to which a student attempted to answer all five parts of the prompt.
- Trait 2: Cognitive Development: how well a student carried out the assignment.
- Trait 3: Unity: relationship of the text to the outcome.
- Trait 4: Presentation: observing standard edited English.
- Trait 5: Arrangement: logical organization of material and supporting evidence.
- Trait 6: Audience Awareness: student's ability to meet the needs of an academic audience through appropriate diction, tone, formality, and style.

Writing samples were independently rated two or three times per year on each of six traits using a five-point scale. The five-point scale used to assess each trait ranged from a point value of "1" to a point value of "5." In each trait, "5" equaled an easy to identify positive ranking: excellent, persuasive, consistent focus, observes standard English, or appropriate for an academic audience. Similarly, "1" identified the opposite characteristics. Ratings of "2," "3," and "4" allowed raters to evaluate with more precision.

As a voluntary, ready-made writing assignment, the Universal Prompt provided students and instructors with stronger incentives to complete and assess writing abilities because it was attached to specific courses and learning objectives, meaning that students had concrete examples to reflect on. Students also earned credit for completing the writing assignment. Similarly, faculty received feedback on aspects of course experiences that were most valued for learning, and the university had authentic writing samples to assess across the curriculum. In the words of one consultant, Michael Neal, the result was "a sound writing assessment model that has resulted in impressive outcomes this first year" (quoted in Owens and Cummings 2009, 22).

IMPACT OF THE QEP

Systematically gathered direct (Universal Prompt) and indirect (student and faculty surveys) assessment results documented the positive effects of the QEP's expanded implementation over the five years. Collectively, the results from these instruments reflected the QEP's notable impact on changing the culture of writing at the university. Our results were similar to those found by Rhodes (2012), who reported students that reflected on their learning through "ePortfolios or other media deepened their learning and their understanding of their strengths and weaknesses in practice" (41).

Results of Direct Assessments Involving Student Writing

Data using the Universal Prompt from fall 2008 through fall 2011 revealed statistically significant improvement in three of the six writing traits: Unity, Presentation, and Arrangement.

The scores that students achieved from the years 2008 through 2011 revealed that despite different cohorts of students each year, the ratings along all traits trended in a positive direction as the impact of the QEP expanded throughout the curriculum. This suggests a generalized positive effect on instruction. In looking at the differences between the initial year and the 2011 data, all six traits showed a positive change, with three of six traits showing statistically significant changes. Those

Table 15.2. Universal prompt traits mean scores, 2008–2011

Traits	2008	2009	2010	2011
Assignment Requirements	3.44	3.45	3.30	3.56
Cognitive Development	2.62	2.86	2.59	2.74
Unity	2.72	2.97	2.77	3.21*
Presentation	3.09	3.13	3.07	3.46*
Arrangement	2.64	2.82	2.75	3.09*
Audience Awareness	2.96	2.91	2.71	3.01

* = $p < 0.05$ difference between given year and the 2008 reference group.

traits—Unity, Presentation, and Arrangement—likely improved more than the others because they are more easily affected by instruction and shift of the classroom culture affected by the QEP than are Cognitive Development and Audience Awareness. Reflecting on faculty development efforts, we placed greater emphasis on these three traits of effective writing. It is also easier to develop skill and comfort with rules of grammar, sentence structure, and organization of text than it is to affect dimensions of cognitive development. Attempting to address the assignment requirements of the task in the Universal Prompt was easy to achieve and was consistently assessed at a high level, leaving little room for improvement in such a restricted range for high ratings.

The positive impact that the QEP has had on writing improvement was also demonstrated by student performance on the Board of Regents' Essay Test. Up until 2009, students enrolled in colleges and universities in the University System of Georgia had to take this test upon reaching forty-five semester hours. In the 2005–2006 academic year, CSU had an 80.4 percent passing rate among students taking the writing test, compared to 87.5 percent for the total university system. However, the last time it was administered in AY 2008–2009, CSU had a 97.2 percent passing rate as compared to 89.4 percent for the total university system (University System of Georgia 2016).

Results of Indirect Assessments Involving Student and Faculty Writing Surveys
Increases in faculty using writing as a mode of learning and in students' perceptions of themselves as writers were substantiated by data collected in student and faculty surveys in fall 2011. Survey data collected in 2007 and 2011 compared students' self-assessed ratings of their writing abilities. Results from the 2011 survey indicated a positive

shift in student self-reported ratings of writing skills with fewer students reporting areas in which they felt deficient, even as students described being required to do fewer writing assignments. However, the goal of the program was not for students to produce more finished, polished prose, but rather to use writing more strategically to understand course material and better understand the writing process to include invention, drafting, revising, editing, and proofing. Students recounted spending more time in the revision stage of the writing process, producing multiple drafts on which they received formative feedback. This indicates that faculty were, over time, providing more intensive writing opportunities and experiences for students and suggests that, as students spent more time on somewhat fewer assignments, they benefitted from the opportunity to refine and polish their work. In addition, students responding to a question about time usage on the 2011 National Survey of Student Engagement (NSSE) reported spending more time preparing for class (studying, reading, writing, doing homework or lab work, analyzing data, rehearsing, and other academic activities) than they had in 2004. Part of this change might be accounted for by the increased time required for writing.

To assess students' perceptions of their need for writing instruction and their exposure to writing tasks at CSU, a sample of students drawn from 10 percent of the in-class sections was surveyed in 2011, for a total set of 805 completed surveys. The survey results indicated that on average, across all course levels, 6.7 writing assignments were reported, with a progression in average number of writing assignments per class by level. Freshman, sophomores, juniors, and seniors reported an average of 4, 6.5, 7, and 8.5 writing assignments, respectively. Students reported an increasing level of writing assignments as they made progress toward degree completion. Consistent with the findings from the Universal Prompt data, almost a third of the students reported a need for assistance in developing a writing strategy and almost a quarter expressed a need for assistance with grammar and organization. These data also suggest that the significant improvement found on the Universal Prompt data reflected the impact of the QEP on students.

All full- and part-time faculty were surveyed in 2011 regarding the types of writing they assign, their methods of assessing writing, and the impact their participation in QEP training had on the way they teach writing. A copy of this survey, which we hope will be of use for other writing program administrators seeking information about how faculty on their campuses approach writing instruction, can be found in appendix 15.B. Sixty-nine completed surveys were collected. These surveys were representative of CSU's four colleges. Two-thirds of faculty reported attending at least one QEP programming event during the previous five years, and 23 percent attended six or more QEP programming events. The results of the survey indicated statistically significant differences between faculty who participated in QEP activities and those who did not regarding the application of methods to support and develop writing beyond typical writing assignments such as research and term papers. Over half the faculty attending QEP training indicated that they had changed their style of teaching writing as a direct result of their QEP participation. These faculty members were significantly more likely to utilize pedagogical techniques such as rubrics, in-class peer review, and providing multiple opportunities for correction and resubmission. Similarly, participating faculty were significantly more likely to use reading responses, reflective papers, book reviews, and senior paper assignments that tend to call for more intensive involvement of the student in their writing, as opposed to, or in addition to, assigning the traditional term paper.

UNANTICIPATED EFFECTS OF THE QEP
Assessment as Faculty Development

Perhaps the greatest unexpected outcome of the QEP was the extent to which the challenges of assessment became key opportunities for faculty development. The essay rating sessions proved an invaluable faculty development opportunity in their own right because they served as a venue (an all too rare one for most faculty) for discussing what constitutes good writing and how this varies by discipline. Every semester, faculty were recruited to rate the Universal Prompt essays using the Universal Prompt rubric. Since the start of the Universal Prompt, faculty from all colleges served as raters, including part-time faculty. Each rating session began with an hour-long norming session in which raters worked through sample essays to arrive at a shared understanding of the rubric and discuss what constitutes effective writing. Although the primary purpose of these sessions was to formally assess writing across campus, faculty viewed the exercise as an opportunity to learn more about the evaluation of learning through writing and to discuss with peers in other disciplines what constitutes effective writing. Through serving as raters for the Universal Prompt, faculty became competent with integrating writing assignments and improving student writing. Though not billed as faculty development, it proved to be one of the most valuable such activities CSU offered related to writing. Faculty often reported that they gained tremendous insight into student writing and disciplinary differences in writing through rich discussions during the norming sessions and those conducted within faculty pairs during the actual essay rating. For most faculty, these were the only opportunities they had to discuss what makes a given sample of writing effective or ineffective, and why.

In addition to the professional development value of assessment activities, several unanticipated, positive outcomes from the QEP resulted from the variety of disciplines whose faculty received QEP grants and/or fellowships. Since many faculty members also teach at the graduate level, they made changes to the ways in which writing is used in graduate programs. As a result, curriculum mapping, a widening variety of writing assignments, and the use of rubrics for assessment are more commonplace on campus at the graduate level as well.

Although increasing the amount of research done by undergraduates was not a stated goal of the QEP, student participation in undergraduate research became widespread and was reinforced by the QEP's emphasis on the importance of professional writing, due in large part to the way faculty were encouraged to use writing as a mode of learning about disciplinary knowledge. In place of the traditional term paper, QEP programming allowed faculty to learn about inquiry-guided learning and related approaches to writing as problem solving. Student scholarship and creative endeavors range from the journal that is student run (editors as well as reviewers), to Honors Day (a conference focused on undergraduate research), and numerous students working on research projects with faculty increasing every year. Both in 2011 and 2012, the University System of Georgia Faculty Development Office asked CSU to present its undergraduate research program. The QEP helped further the institution's goal of developing greater faculty-student collaboration on undergraduate research.

THE LASTING EFFECTS OF THE QEP ON CSU

Faculty from all disciplines have embraced developing competent and professional student writers, as well as participating in faculty development opportunities to improve their teaching. Forums, workshops, departmental retreats, and conversations over lunch have resulted in a faculty who are working with students to write more, which has resulted in two-thirds of our students claiming in our 2011 Student Survey that they are confident in their writing abilities based on their coursework. Students have also expressed a strong exposure to traditional types of academic assignments such as research papers, while more discipline-specific forms of writing are also more commonly used. A higher level of writing is more prevalent on campus, as evidenced in the many scholarly journals and outlets produced on campus. Having the QEP focus on writing elevated the scholarly aspects of writing in academe at CSU. It would be wrong, of course, to attribute all gains or changes in the teaching and learning of writing only to the QEP because progress does not happen in a vacuum. But it is undoubtedly true that an external mandate, in the form of the SACS requirement, provided much-needed momentum, significant resources, and a common goal: to change the way writing was taught at our university. We have done this, and it is evident in the way the university recognizes student writing and excellence in the teaching of writing.

APPENDIX 15.A

Sample Final Report for QEP Grant

Developing an Interdisciplinary Course on Undergraduate Editing and Publishing

24 May 2011

In spring 2011, we developed and co-taught the newly approved course, ITDS 2797 Undergraduate Research Journal Editing. This course is a seminar that explores the theoretical and practical concerns of publishing an interdisciplinary undergraduate research journal. Students in the course edited and produced an undergraduate research journal while learning to formally critique research articles, address publishing ethics, and manage a peer review process. Most of the decisions were made by the students in the class, and at the end of the semester we focused on student reflection on these decisions. In retrospect, the students identified several areas for revision next semester, and areas for further guidance. Also, students have identified a few leaders who will be "in charge" of the journal next time, which will allow experience to carry forward.

Our grant supported project focused upon developing assessments for the peer review process and resulted in the production of a peer review rubric. Through a consensus process, the student developed several drafts and revised them after reviewing article submission. The development and employment of the rubrics impacted the students' ability to edit and critique writing since they not only reviewed submission but also received feedback on their critique compared to peers and faculty experts. *Peer evaluation of writing* was the central component and encompassed the other assessment goals that we had originally envisioned for the course, which included:

1. Compliance with *accepted formatting standards* is a part of any professional writing process, and one that faculty and students alike at times find challenging. The students in the class chose to work with MLA and APA standards for formatting and incorporated compliance with these into the peer evaluation rubric.

2. *Writing for a specified audience,* likewise, is a part of any writing process, and students often grappled with balancing the desire to showcase rigorous scholarship and producing a journal that was accessible to a general audience.

3. *Identifying, writing for, and editing for professional standards* were discussed at length, with a specialized focus on the ethics of publishing and ethical standards of research, including the IRB process.

4. *Evaluating writing in related disciplines for content.* The peer evaluation of the writing rubric that was developed this term implemented an approach to this, but the students and faculty reviewers all felt that this was in need of major revision. Students and faculty alike found that guidance here intended to simplify reviewing in the disciplines was unnecessary and at times confusing. Students working on the next edition of this journal will revise this rubric in fall 2011.

APPENDIX 15.B

Survey about Faculty Attitudes toward Writing

CSU needs to report all ongoing writing initiatives. Please complete the following brief survey. Thank you for your assistance.

Your College: _____

Your Department: _____

Please check which of the following writing tasks you assign to your students:

__ in-class essay exams and quizzes
__ journals
__ responses to reading assignments
__ research papers
__ analytical papers (i.e., analyzing an issue of topic)
__ lab reports
__ preparing an article for publication
__ annotated bibliography
__ case-study analysis

__ book reviews emphasizing critical thinking
__ summary and analysis of interviews
__ case law studies
__ writing poofs and theorems
__ online class discussions
__ senior research papers
__ annotated bibliographies
__ summaries of published scientific reports
__ short written assignments

__ reflective papers
__ portfolio exhibits
__ critical incident papers
__ creative papers
__ abstracts
__ fact-based reports
__ student reflections on moments when they
  met the class goals

__ primary source research
__ lesson plans
__ proposals
__ resumes
__ chapter review questions
__ *OTHER (please describe):*

Please identify current assessment practices used with writing assignments:

__ traditional grading practices
__ use of specific rubrics
__ peer review by classmates
__ opportunity for correction and
  resubmission
__ blind review by faculty in discipline

__ data from capstone courses
__ portfolio writing samples
__ *OTHER (please describe)*

Have you attended a Faculty Center sponsored event in the past academic year? For example, have you attended a forum, a workshop, a book group, or a lunch-and-learn?

__ Yes

__ No

References

Columbus State University. 2006. *Writing the Solution: Steps toward Developing Competent and Professional Student Writers: A Quality Enhancement Plan for Columbus State University.* Retrieved from sacs.columbusstate.edu.

Connell, Christopher. 2011. "A Quest to Enhance Quality Spurs Global Learning." *International Educator* 20 (6): 38–44.

Flateby, T. L., and E. Metzger. 1999. "Writing Assessment Instrument for Higher Order Thinking Skills." *Assessment Update* 11 (2): 6–7.

Flateby, T. L., and E. Metzger. 2001. "Instructional Implications of the Cognitive Level and Quality of Writing Assessment." *Assessment Update* 1 (13): 4–5.

Jackson, Rudolph S., Jimmy H. Davis, and Francesina R. Jackson. 2010. "Redesigning Regional Accreditation: The Impact on Institutional Planning." *Planning for Higher Education* 38 (4): 9–19.

Loughman, T. P., J. Hickson, G. L. Sheeks, and J. W. Hortman. 2008. "The Role of the Quality Enhancement Plan in Engendering a Culture of Assessment." *Assessment Update* 20 (3): 3–5.

McElroy, D., and R. Cobb. 2010. "Demonstrating Growth of a Student Engagement Culture: A Multivariate Approach to Assessing Institutional Goals at a Public University." *Planning and Changing* 41 (1/2): 18–41.

Owens, Jim, and Robert Cummings. 2009. "Columbus State University Quality Enhancement Plan Annual Report, 2008–2009." Columbus State University. Accessed January 19, 2015. http://sacs.columbusstate.edu/documents/QEP%202008-2009.pdf.

Rhodes, Terrel L. 2012. "Show Me the Learning: Value, Accreditation, and the Quality of the Degree." *Planning for Higher Education* 40 (3): 36–42.

United States National Commission on Excellence in Education. 1983. *A Nation at Risk: The Imperative for Educational Reform: A Report to the Nation and the Secretary of Education, United States Department of Education.* Washington, DC: The Commission.

University System of Georgia. 2016. 2.8.1. *Regents' Reading and Writing Skills Requirements and Exemptions.* January 30. http://www.usg.edu/academic_affairs_handbook/section2/handbook/C757/#p2.8.1_regents_reading_and_writing_skills_requirements_and_exemptions.

ABOUT THE AUTHORS

WENDY SHARER, Professor of English and Director of the Quality Enhancement Plan at East Carolina University, is co-editor of *Working in the Archives: Practical Research Methods for Rhetoric and Composition* (SIUP 2009), author of *Vote & Voice: Women's Organizations and Political Literacy, 1915–1930* (SIUP 2004), co-author of *1977: A Cultural Moment in Composition* (Parlor 2008), and co-editor of *Rhetorical Education in America* (Alabama 2004).

TRACY ANN MORSE is Director of Composition/Writing Foundations and associate professor of rhetoric and composition in the Department of English at East Carolina University. Her research and writing are in the areas of disability studies, deaf studies, and composition studies. Her work has been published in *Rhetoric Review, Disability Studies Quarterly, inventio,* and the *Journal of Teaching Writing*. Her book, *Signs and Wonders: Religious Rhetoric and the Preservation of Sign Language,* was published by Gallaudet University Press. In addition, she co-edited *Critical Conversations about Plagiarism,* published by Parlor Press.

MICHELLE F. EBLE is Director of Graduate Studies and associate professor of rhetoric and technical communication in the Department of English at East Carolina University. Her research and teaching interests include technical writing theory and practice, especially as it relates to rhetorical intervention, gender studies, and technology in medical and scientific contexts; professional development and mentoring; and research ethics. She has published in *Computers and Composition, Technical Communication,* and *Technical Communication Quarterly,* and several edited collections. She is the co-editor of *Stories on Mentoring: Theory and Praxis* (Parlor Press, 2008) and is working on an edited collection with Angela Hass, *Key Theoretical Frameworks for Teaching Technical Communication in the 21st Century.*

WILLIAM P. BANKS is Director of the University Writing Program and the Tar River Writing Project, and is associate professor of rhetoric and composition at East Carolina University, where he teaches graduate and undergraduate courses in writing, research, and pedagogy. He has published articles on history, rhetoric, pedagogy, writing program administration, technology, and sexuality in several recent books, as well as in *College Composition & Communication, English Journal, College English, Computer & Composition, Dialogue,* and *Teaching English in the Two-Year College.* His current book project, *Queer Literacies,* explores the ways in which gay men and lesbians articulate literacies of queer(ed) identities.

LINDA ADLER-KASSNER is a Professor of Writing Studies and Director of the Writing Program at University of California, Santa Barbara. Her research focuses in examining how literacy is defined and assessed in specific contexts and the implications of those definitions for students and faculty. This chapter comes from research conducted in conjunction with her role as faculty assessment liaison at UC Santa Barbara, where she helps to coordinate general education assessment. Adler-Kassner is author, co-author, or co-editor of nine books, including *Naming What We Know: Threshold Concepts of Writing Studies* (with Elizabeth Wardle) and many articles and book chapters.

REMICA BINGHAM-RISHER is the Director of Writing and Faculty Development and the QEP Director at Old Dominion University (ODU). Currently, she works with faculty to improve student learning through writing by means of faculty workshops as well as oversees the implementation of various Action Projects supported by internal grants that help improve departmental disciplinary writing. In addition, she is an accomplished writer and teaches in the MFA program at ODU. Her first book, *Conversion* (Lotus Press, 2006), won the Naomi Long Madgett Poetry Award, and her second book, *What We Ask of Flesh*, was published by Etruscan Press in 2013.

MELANIE BURDICK is an assistant professor of English and serves as the Director of Composition at Washburn University. She also serves as the English department liaison for the concurrent enrollment program. In 2011 she co-authored and was awarded a research grant from the Council of Writing Program Administrators. She has been published in *English Education*, *The Journal of Teaching Writing*, *The International Journal of Education and the Arts*, and *Teaching English in the Two Year College*. Melanie teaches composition and English education courses and continues to focus her research on the teaching of writing in high school and college, the preparation of high school writing teachers, and writing assessment.

POLINA CHEMISHANOVA is an Assistant Professor and Director of Composition in the Department of English, Theatre, and Foreign Languages at the University of North Carolina at Pembroke where she teaches first-year composition, professional communication, and upper-level rhetoric and composition courses. As a member of the QEP steering committee, she remains active in the implementation of the campus-wide writing initiative, faculty professional development activities, and program assessment. Her current teaching and research interests include WAC/WID, professional communication, writing program assessment, and composition theory and pedagogy.

MALKIEL CHOSEED, Ph.D., is a Professor of English and the Writing Program Coordinator at Onondaga Community College in Syracuse, NY, where he also oversees writing tutoring. His current research and teaching interests are focused on developmental education in its various forms and assessment of programmatic learning outcomes. He is a recipient of the SUNY Chancellor's Award for Scholarship and Creative Activities.

KYLE CHRISTIANSEN is the Director of the Social Research Center at Columbus State University and is an Associate Professor in the Department of Political Science and Public Administration. Dr. Christensen earned his Ph.D. and MA in Political Science from West Virginia University and his BA in Political Science from Mercer University. Dr. Christensen's research interests include comparative public policy, evaluation methodology, and European Union politics.

ANGELA CROW is an Associate Professor at James Madison University in the School of Writing, Rhetoric, and Technical Communication and focuses on research related to social media and data collection.

MAGGIE DEBELIUS is an Associate Teaching Professor of English and the Director of Faculty Initiatives at the Center for New Designs in Learning and Scholarship (CNDLS) at Georgetown University in Washington, DC. She works with departments across the university on curriculum design, writing assessment, and faculty development. She is the co-author (with Susan Basalla) of *So What Are You Going to Do with That?: Finding Careers Outside Academia* (University of Chicago, 2007 and 2015) and a frequent speaker on graduate education. In addition, she publishes on composition pedagogy, writing assessment, and writing centers. She teaches both graduate and undergraduate level courses on writing pedagogy and Victorian literature. She holds a Ph.D. in English from Princeton and an MA from Georgetown.

JONATHAN ELMORE is an Assistant Professor of English and Director of the Writing Center at Savannah State University where he teaches composition, literature, and writing center theory. His research interests include composition theory and pedagogy, British modernism, horror fiction, multimodal literacies, and the future of English departments.

LORNA GONZALEZ is a doctoral candidate in Language, Literacy, and Composition (Education) at University of California, Santa Barbara. Her research interests include multimodal composition, conceptions and consequences of literacy, and instructional design. This research comes from her work as a collaborator in UC Santa Barbara's General Education assessment efforts.

ANGELA GREEN teaches in the Department of Writing and Rhetoric at the University of Mississippi, where she also leads the university's Writing Across the Curriculum/Writing in the Disciplines program. She formerly served as Writing Specialist for the QEP and Assistant Professor of English at Columbus State University. She earned her BA in English from The University of Texas and her PhD in English from the University of Georgia, where she also worked for the Writing Intensive program.

JIM HENRY is Professor of English at the University of Hawai'i at Mānoa, where he founded the UH Writing Mentors. He has published on workplace writing cultures, technical writing, mentoring, writing and sustainability, and writing across the curriculum. Recent scholarship includes "Performing Professionally as a Writer: Research Revival Vlogs," in the second inaugural issue of *College Composition and Communication Online* (2012) and How Can Technical Communicators Fit into Contemporary Organizations?" in Johnson-Eilola and Selber's award-winning *Solving Problems in Technical Communication* (2013). Current research focuses on place-experiential writing across the disciplines and writing intensive instruction in experimental theater. He has won Regents' teaching awards at two universities.

RYAN S. HOOVER is a Senior Software Developer at Marketing Clique in Austin, Texas. Ryan specializes in WordPress development, online learning, and data management. Before his position at Marketing Clique, Ryan was an Assistant Professor of English Writing and Rhetoric at St. Edward's University. He is currently a Member-at-Large for the Council for Programs in Scientific and Technical Communication and was Web Editor for the Association of Teachers of Technical Writing. Ryan is active in the WordPress community, helping to organize regional WordCamps and regularly contributing to WordPress "Core."

REBECCA INGALLS is a former associate professor and former director of the First-Year Writing program at Drexel University. Her work in composition and cultural rhetoric may be found in *inventio, Academe, POROI, Harlot, Journal of Teaching Writing, The Journal of Popular Culture, The Review of Education, Pedagogy, and Cultural Studies,* and *Writing & Pedagogy.* She is also one of the editors of the collection, *Critical Conversations about Plagiarism* (Parlor Press, 2012). After 14 years in the profession, she has retired from her post as professor and administrator, and she is currently studying to be a nurse-midwife.

CYNTHIA MIECZNIKOWSKI is an Associate Professor of English at University of North Carolina at Pembroke, where she teaches courses in first-year and upper-level research-based writing as well as undergraduate and graduate courses in writing and writing pedagogy. Former interim director of UNCP's first-year writing program, she served on the steering committee for the campus-wide writing initiative. She has published articles in *College English* as well as literary journals. Her current teaching and research interests include online writing instruction, the reading process, nonfiction studies, and rhetorical theory and history.

SUSAN MILLER-COCHRAN is Professor of English and Director of the Writing Program at the University of Arizona. Her research focuses on technology, ESL writing, and writing program administration. Her work has appeared in *College Composition and Communication, Composition Studies, Computers and Composition, Enculturation,* and *Teaching English in the Two-Year College,* and she is also an editor of *Rhetorically Rethinking Usability* (Hampton Press, 2009) and *Strategies for Teaching First-Year Composition* (NCTE, 2002). Additionally, she is a co-author of *An Insider's Guide to Academic Writing* (Macmillan, 2016), *The Cengage Guide to*

Research (Cengage, 2017), and *Keys for Writers* (Cengage, 2014). Before joining the faculty at the University of Arizona, she was the Director of First-Year Writing at North Carolina State University (2007–2015) and also a faculty member at Mesa Community College (AZ). She currently serves as President of the Council of Writing Program Administrators.

CINDY MOORE is a Professor of Writing and Associate Dean for the Humanities at Loyola University Maryland. Her publications include articles, chapters, and books on writing pedagogy, professional-development, and assessment.

JOYCE NEFF, Professor Emerita at Old Dominion University, served as Director of Composition, Associate Chair, and Graduate Program Director in the English Department. She was instrumental in developing ODU's Improving Disciplinary Writing QEP and has received ODU's Teaching with Technology Award and University Professor Award. She publishes widely on writing across the curriculum, writing centers, grounded theory, and workplace writing, including *Writing across Distances and Disciplines: Research and Pedagogy in Distributed Learning* (with Carl Whithaus). On the national level, Neff has designed professional writing courses for the US Department of Defense and served as Chair of the Consortium of Doctoral Programs in Rhetoric and Composition.

KAREN NULTON is the Director of Writing Assessment at Drexel University where she teaches writing and works with faculty writing development. Her current research focuses on qualitative assessment of writing as communication. Prior to her role directing Writing Assessment, Dr. Nulton directed Drexel's Writing Center and Writing Program and spent two decades working with large-scale writing assessments at Educational Testing Service.

PEGGY O'NEILL, Professor of Writing, has served as department chair and director of composition at Loyola. She regularly teaches first-year writing as well as advanced writing and rhetoric classes. Her scholarship focuses on writing pedagogy, assessment, program administration and disciplinarity. In addition to many journal articles and book chapters, she has co-authored two books, *A Guide to College Writing Assessment* (with Cindy Moore and Brian Huot) and *Reframing Writing Assessment to Improve Teaching and Learning* (with Linda Adler-Kassner), edited or co-edited four books, and co-edited the *Journal of Writing Assessment*.

JESSICA PARKER is an Assistant Professor of English at Metropolitan State University of Denver, where she directs the First Year Writing program. She is a member of the committee overseeing General Studies assessment for MSU Denver. Her current projects include the expansion of a program that provides an alternative to writing remediation and a research project about why students don't successfully complete First Year Writing classes. She received her BA in English and Biology from Baylor University and her MA and Ph.D. in Literary Studies from University of Denver. She teaches First Year Writing, African American literature, and hip hop studies.

MARY RIST is Professor of English Writing and Rhetoric at St. Edward's University in Austin, Texas, and chair of the Department of Literature, Writing, and Rhetoric. Her areas of specialty include discourse analysis, applied linguistics and, most recently, curriculum development for undergraduate writing majors. A member of the St. Edward's University faculty since 1994, she has also served as Associate Dean of Humanities, director of St. Edward's Freshman Studies program, and director of the Writing Center.

ROCHELLE (SHELLEY) RODRIGO is Visiting Assistant Professor of English at the University of Arizona. She was a full-time faculty member for four years in English at Old Dominion University and for nine years in English and film studies at Mesa Community College in Arizona. Shelley researches how "newer" technologies better facilitate communicative interactions, more specifically teaching and learning. As well as co-authoring two editions of *The Wadsworth Guide to Research*, Shelley also co-edited *Rhetorically Rethinking Usability*. Her work has also appeared in *Computers and Composition, Teaching English in the*

Two-Year College, EDUCAUSE Quarterly, The Journal of Interactive Technology & Pedagogy, as well as various edited collections.

TULORA ROECKERS is currently an instructor of English on both Washburn University and Washburn Institute of Technology campuses in Topeka, Kansas. Her teaching experience ranges from Developmental English, Freshman Composition, and Advanced Composition courses at the university to Technical Writing as well as Basic Writing and Reading Comprehension in the team-taught Bridge Program for at-risk students at "the Tech." Previously, she was an assistant editor to *Eye on Kansas* and the *Online Journal of Rural Research and Policy*, and her poems have appeared in publications such as *Watershed* and *Aethlon*.

SHIRLEY K. ROSE is a Professor and Director of Writing Programs in the Department of English of the College of Liberal Arts and Sciences at Arizona State University. She is a past president of the Council of Writing Program Administrators and she is the Director of the WPA Consultant-Evaluator Service. She has served as a peer reviewer for the Higher Learning Commission of the North Central Association of Schools and Colleges for the past decade. She regularly teaches graduate courses in writing program administration and has published articles on writing pedagogy and on issues in archival research and practice. With Irwin Weiser, she has edited three collections on the intellectual work of writing program administration, including *The WPA as Researcher, The Writing Program Administrator as Theorist,* and *Going Public: What Writing Programs Learn from Engagement.*

IRIS SALTIEL is currently a Professor at Columbus State University (CSU). She served as the Director of the Faculty Center for the Enhancement of Teaching & Learning at CSU from 2010 to 2012. She holds an Ed.D. from Fordham University, an M.Ed. from Rutgers University, and a BS from Trenton State College. Her primary research interests have centered on adult learners and collaboration, partnerships in learning, and cohort based programming. Prior to CSU, she served at Troy University as director of the Quality Enhancement Institute and as a professor. She also worked at Thomas Edison State College.

TERESSA VAN SICKLE has taught, designed English curriculum, and provided professional development for 15 years at the high school, community college, and university levels, while also establishing writing centers and serving on district and state writing curriculum teams. Through her affiliation with the National Writing Project, she has assisted with the start-up of the Red Clay Writing Project at the University of Georgia and has worked as a teacher consultant and associate director of the Tar River Writing Project at East Carolina University. She earned her BA in English and a Certificate in Technical and Professional Writing from East Carolina University, Certificate in Teaching Online Courses from the University of North Carolina at Chapel Hill, and M.Ed. from the University of Georgia.

JANE CHAPMAN VIGIL is a Professor of English at Metropolitan State University of Denver, where she coordinates the Supplemental Academic Instruction and Stretch programs for English. She has served as the Director of the First Year Writing Program in the English Department and as Senior Faculty Associate for Assessment for the university. Her current projects include research on retention and teaching pedagogies for first year writing students. She received her BA in English Secondary Teaching and her MA in American Literature from Brigham Young University and her Ph.D. in Rhetoric and Composition from the University of Nevada, Reno. She teaches First Year Writing, Rhetoric and Composition Studies, and general studies literature courses.

DAVID WEED teaches courses in composition, literature, and literary theory at Washburn University in Topeka, Kansas. His work has appeared in books such as *Miss Grundy Doesn't Teach Here Anymore* and *The Politics of Manhood,* and he has published articles in various journals, including *Eighteenth-Century Studies, Novel,* and *Studies in English Literature 1500–1900.*

INDEX

Paperback, 6" x 9"

344 pages

ISBN: 9781607324348

Utah State University Press

Also available as an ebook. Please check with your preferred ebook vendor.

Media/educator contact:

Beth Svinarich

Sales & Marketing Manager

University Press of Colorado

5589 Arapahoe Ave., Suite 206C

Boulder, CO 80303

720.406.8849 ext. 803

beth@upcolorado.com

initiatives that meet requirements while also helping those agencies to better understand how writing develops and how it can most effectively be assessed. Parts 2 and 3 present case studies of how institutions have used ongoing accreditation and assessment imperatives to meet student learning needs through programmatic changes and faculty development. They provide concrete examples of productive curricular (part 2) and instructional (part 3) changes that can follow from accreditation mandates while providing guidance for navigating challenges and pitfalls that WPAs may encounter within shifting and often volatile local, regional, and national contexts.

In addition to providing examples of how others in the profession might approach such work, *Reclaiming Accountability* addresses assessment requirements beyond those in the writing program itself. It will be of interest to department heads, administrators, writing program directors, and those involved with writing teacher education, among others.

WENDY SHARER, TRACY ANN MORSE, MICHELLE F. EBLE, and **WILLIAM P. BANKS** are writing faculty at East Carolina University. When their program facing reaccreditation in 2013, they chose to address the process as an opportunity to garner institutional support for revisions to their composition and writing across the curriculum programs.

www.upcolorado.com   •   1.800.621.2736

Reclaiming Accountability

Improving Writing Programs through Accreditation and Large-Scale Assessments

Edited by Wendy Sharer,
Tracy Ann Morse,
Michelle F. Eble,
and William P. Banks

Reclaiming Accountability brings together a series of critical case studies of writing programs that have planned, implemented, and/or assessed the impact of large-scale accreditation-supported initiatives. The

utah state
university press

an imprint of the university press of colorado